D1176152

PQ-BIM-818

Gaining Ground

European Critics on Canadian Literature

Gaining Ground
European Critics on Canadian Literature

Edited by
Robert Kroetsch
and
Reingard M. Nischik

Volume VI
Western Canadian Literary Documents Series
General Editor: Shirley Neuman

NeWest Press
Edmonton

Canadian Cataloguing in Publication Data

Main entry under title:

Gaining Ground: European critics on Canadian literature

(Western Canadian literary documents; 6)
Bibliography
ISBN 0-920316-79-4 (bound). — ISBN 0-920316-77-8 (pbk.)

1. Canadian literature - History and criticism - Addresses, essays, lectures.
I. Kroetsch, Robert, 1927-   II. Nischik, Reingard M.   III. Series.
PS8077.G34 1985   C810'.9   C84-091577-2   PR9184.6.G34 1985

50, 737

Credits:

Editor for the Press: Shirley Neuman
Copy Editor: Smaro Kamboureli
Cover Design: Rita Sasges
Book Design: Jorge Frascara
Typesetting: June Charter
Proofreading: Monica Skaken, Debbie Fisher
Book Production: Susan Colberg
Printing: Friesen Printers, Winnipeg
Financial Assistance: Alberta Culture, Canada Council

NeWest Publishers Ltd.
#204, 8631 - 109 Street
Edmonton, Alberta
Canada   T6G 1E8

CONTENTS

A PREFACE

This is a collection of seventeen essays on Canadian literature, written by European critics representing seven countries. It is hardly an exaggeration to say that the essays represent seventeen different critical approaches. What they have in common is their intellectual energy, their curiosity about a new literature, and their stimulating combination of scholarship and insight. I would like simply to add a brief account of how the book came into being.

In January 1983, after participating in the OKanada Festival in West Berlin, I went on a speaking tour of six European universities. The person at the University of Cologne who got me to lunch and then to a classroom and then to the train station was Dr. Reingard M. Nischik.

At lunch in an Italian restaurant within walking distance of her university, and later over Spanish sherry in her office, Dr. Nischik and I discussed the European critical response to Canadian writing. Our conversation was interrupted by a visit to Professor Helmut Bonheim's seminar, where he and a number of his students were doing a fascinating linguistic analysis of the opening of a contemporary Canadian novel.

Dr. Nischik, after the seminar, was on her way to a reading by Margaret Atwood at the Central Library in downtown Cologne. She offered to give me a ride to the *Hauptbahnhof*. We arrived at the station early enough so that we had time for one glass of local beer (*Kölsch*) in the city's oldest beerhouse, in the shadow of the famous *Dom*. It was while drinking that beer that we agreed to correspond about the possibility of putting together a collection of contemporary essays by European critics on Canadian writing. We agreed that we would, if the project went ahead, make no prescriptions of subject to potential contributors. We would ask that they write on what interested them, allowing those interests to shape the book.

Dr. Nischik hurried away to hear Atwood's reading. I spent an hour looking at Roman mosaics in the museum adjacent to the Cathedral, then hurried away myself and caught the night train to Vienna.

It was Dr. Nischik who contacted the numerous critics who have been instrumental in making Canadian literature a subject of lively interest in European universities. It was she who persuaded those critics to write their essays in English and to meet our rather stringent deadlines.

I wish now to thank Dr. Nischik for her enthusiasm, for her exercise of exceptional critical judgment, and for her persistence when the task of soliciting and assembling essays from all over Europe seemed impossible. She compiled the collection of essays in Cologne, did the initial editing, and prepared the invaluable bibliography and the survey of the state of Canadian literary studies in Europe. I hasten to add that any errors in the final editing are my responsibility.

I would also like to thank Smaro Kamboureli who, in Winnipeg, Manitoba, assisted with the copyreading, and Professor Shirley Neuman and Jack Lewis of Edmonton, Alberta, who, on behalf of NeWest Press, saw to the design and production of the book. Professor Neuman was generous enough to include the title in her series, Western Canadian Literary Documents.

The essays speak of and to the international audience that now reads Canadian writing. I wish to thank, finally, the European pioneers who gave (and give) focus and impetus to this interest. This book is their invitation to readers, everywhere, to make new maps of the sprawling and exciting and dangerous ground that is Canadian literature.

Robert Kroetsch, University of Manitoba

I

EUROPEAN CRITICS
ON CANADIAN LITERATURE

Simone Vauthier

THE DUBIOUS BATTLE OF STORY-TELLING: NARRATIVE STRATEGIES IN TIMOTHY FINDLEY'S *THE WARS*

*In memory of Eugène Vauthier and Paul Régnier whose
stories of World War I I did not pay attention to*

In *The Wars* (1977) Timothy Findley boldly sets out to explore the
public dimensions of collective savagery and its secret connections
with individual violence, when he tells the story of 'one man's
initiation' during World War I.[1] If any novelist worth his salt must,
in some way, justify his adding one more piece to the existing body of
fictions, the difficulty is further compounded in the case of the
historical novelist who must write within and against a double
tradition, fictional and historical. As one reviewer puts it, 'in
deciding to write *The Wars* . . . [Timothy Findley] must have been
aware of the potential of failure in dealing freshly with a war about
which so much has been written, including novels and memoirs by
such famous names as Ford, Cummings, Graves, and Remarque.'[2]
The writer's willingness to take risks, however, has produced a
memorable feat of imagination in which the protagonist 'and the
time and the place that made and destroyed him take on a midnight
beauty, the ferocious truth of a work of art.'[3] Negotiating between
repetition, imitation and all the restraints of genre on the one hand,
and imagination, invention and narrative resourcefulness on the
other, *The Wars* asserts the authority of the novelist, even as it
questions the adequacy of narrative to come to grips with the stark
and obscene realities of war. This paper proposes to survey some of
the strategies by which authority is achieved and/or undermined.[4]

The hero and his experience

Invention 'begins' with the protagonist. Literally, if we are to
credit the novelist's account: the 'image of a young man in uniform
walking away from a military encampment' burst into his mind, he
says, in 1974.[5] Textually, at any rate, Robert Ross appears in a
proleptic prologue, on the wait and on the run, poised for what is

going to be his last action. Along with the protagonist, the novelist invents a supporting cast—the Ross family in Canada, the d'Orseys in Britain, fellow officers and soldiers in training camp and on the front, etc. Though their roles may be incidental to the main plot, like that of Levitt, the reader of Clausewitz, their presence not only enriches the thematic harmonies of the novel, it also testifies to the energy with which the novelist has bridged the gap—temporal and psychological—between the past and his creative self. Yet even these fictive autonomous characters partly depend for their credibility on (the fictional use of) the non-fictional—the factuality of setting and topography, the chronology of well-known battles and phases of World War I, the introduction of historical figures. These figures, as is often the case in the historical novel, are kept in the background where they serve purposes of authentication (Sam Hughes taking the farewell salute in the snapshots of 1915) or enhancement (Lady Juliet quoting her poet-brother's friend, Siegfried Sassoon) or both.

As for the hero himself, he can be read against a type. In the contemporary war novel, 'typically the hero brings to his war experience a set of apparently coherent and complete moral precepts which finally prove inadequate.'[6] For Ross, as for many protagonists, 'the war was a call to adventure enveloped in and sanctioned by idealism';[7] but the fields of Flanders and their 'shallow sea of stinking grey' (72) do not turn out to be the testing-ground of courage and manhood which the Pennsylvania countryside still could be to a Henry Fleming. Although he makes a courageous and efficient lieutenant, the sensitive Robert Ross, who enlisted partly out of a desire to make a gesture against his mother and her contradictions,[8] is unable to endure the mindless slaughter, the absurdities of the war machine, and the ensuing brutalization of the human spirit. (Significantly, he breaks down after he has been sexually assaulted by his fellow officers or soldiers.) When he refuses to play a part in the enormities and wanders off, he becomes an anti-hero, or rather, what Stanley Cooperman calls 'a hero of the negative act.'[9] Thus his experience conforms to one of the basic patterns of World War I literature, and to that extent the character is not free from the pressures of the genre. In addition, a few situations—the shuttling back and forth from the idyllic peace of rural England to the hell of Flanders, the affair with Lady Barbara d'Orsey, etc.—echo similar situations in earlier war novels.[10]

But the way in which Robert Ross makes for himself an alternative beyond passive withdrawal is triumphantly his own—and the novel's. His resistance to the war machine is first spurred by his desire to save horses from the useless carnage awaiting them. When he 'break[s] ranks,' disobeying the stupid orders of Captain Leather, he is on his way to 'making a separate peace.' After his attempt fails, he shoots the Captain and tears the lapels from his uniform. The young man who searched for 'model[s] he could emulate' (35), i.e. for patterns of authority, has been transformed by the alchemy of war; and his problem is now to make a new beginning under apocalyptic circumstances. His solution is to secede from the insane world of men and join a new community. Almost providentially, he comes across a mare and a dog: 'It was as if both dog and horse had been waiting for Robert to come to them' (182). And because the mare whinnies to the horses she smells in the cars, as the little company goes to the station yard, Robert Ross takes the decision to release the animals. 'Then we shall all go together' (183). On the one hand, this assuming of new bonds is Robert's undoing. When he is summoned to surrender, his renewed use of the pronoun 'we' ('We shall not be taken') 'dooms' him: to the pursuing officer it signifies that the renegade has one accomplice or more. So, Mickle has his men set fire to the barn where Ross and the horses have sought refuge. On the other hand, the assumption of these new bonds is a redeeming gesture, which manifests Robert's selflessness and his ability, numbed as he is, to care for living things. Indeed, wounded as he is, he still manages to draw his captors' attention to the dog presumably left in the burning barn. 'The dog. The dog.' Those are his last directly quoted words (186). No matter that his self-appointed mission fails, it still affirms life in the midst of death and the possibilities of commitment beyond the self. The pointlessness of his destruction is not denied but at the same time it is paradoxically made valuable.[11] (By another stroke of inventiveness, the author has Robert Ross survive his fire ordeal for six more years. Six years of silence which are almost obliterated from the narrative but which reverberate in the reader's imagination, loudly proclaiming the triumph, however transitory, of the human will to survive.) The authority of such a novelistic alternative derives largely from its cohesive power. While it restores a measure of purposefulness and freedom to the hero, it also maintains the pressure of circumstances on him. The attempt to escape from senseless violence further embroils him in violence. The killing of the inept Leather makes some sort of sense. Not so the shooting of Private Cassles. Beginning in fire, Robert's repudiation of war also ends in fire. In the mirroring flashes of fire and death, there is kindled 'the flame' of which Walter Benjamin spoke. For ultimately fiction derives its authority from its being able to give us that knowledge of

death which is not allowed us in real life, and which we seek.[12] This is
the dark/bright core of Robert Ross's story. In their fascination with
so much death, author, narrators and readers are searching for some
meaning to life. Nor should the reader fail to contemplate the
destruction of the horses. While 'the story of the horses' dramatically
brings in the terrible waste of animal life that accompanied the
slaughter of men during World War I,[13] it also indirectly reminds us
of our own age's drastically increased threat to the natural world.[14]
Human life and animal life cannot be divorced. By involving the
horses, the fiery climax makes a resonance of many scenes of private
and collective violence in the text and a concord of many of the
novel's thematic and symbolic strands.

If all historical fiction strives to supplement history, *The Wars*
goes one step further by thematizing its reason for doing so. The basic
fictional premise is that the story of Robert Ross needs to be rescued
from oblivion, since it has been obscured by the quiet violence of
silence. His brother refuses to speak of him and so do the surviving
veterans: 'Ask what happened, they say: "I don't know." Mention
Robert Ross—they look away. "He's dead," they tell you. This is not
news. "Tell me about the horses," you ask. Sometimes, they weep at
this. Other times they say: "that bastard!" [. . .] In the end, the only
facts you have are public' (10). The last statement, however, is not
quite accurate. First, there are private documents in the archives
(which, incidentally, suggests that someone in the family did want
the young man's memory preserved). Second, two witnesses are
willing, even eager, to tell about Robert Ross, Marian Turner, the
nurse who 'received' his burned and mangled body after his arrest,
and Lady Juliet d'Orsey, the younger sister of Robert's lover. Both are
good sources of information. As women they enjoyed a privileged
observer-outsider status. As friends of Robert Ross, they have the
authority of firsthand, intimate knowledge, and what they tell the
researcher is anything but public. As survivors, they 'have been
through it all . . . the whole of this extraordinary century' (17), and
they look back through the perspective of decades that have seen one
more World War and several major conflicts. Their responses to Ross
and his experience are still vivid and clear, indirectly witnessing to
the impact he had on them and the strength of his personality. Lady
Juliet says that she 'loved and respected' the young man whom she
looked after, as he recovered, then died, from his wounds and burns.
Marian Turner affirms outright that he was a hero. Not after the
accepted pattern: 'Not your everyday Sergeant York or Billy Bishop,
mind you! (LAUGHTER) But a hero nonetheless. You see, he did the

thing that no one else would even dare to think of doing. And that to me's as good a definition of a "hero" as you'll get. Even when the thing that's done is something of which you disapprove' (16). Moreover, she understands why the researcher feels the story must be told. In fact, she is perceptive enough to realize that Ross's brand of heroism would be more easily acknowledged in the context of the present: 'When you think that nowadays so many people—young people especially—might've known what he was all about. But then . . .' (16). History excludes what is extrasystemic in relation to a given system of interpretation, i.e. of values.[15] Just as the military account of the tragedy could not but leave out much that was important, so the dominant narrative concerned with Canadians in World War I naturally tended to suppress the disturbing memory of an aberrant violence which followed neither the approved channels of patriotic murder nor the more customary ways of resistance to 'the wars.'[16] Because the two interviewees never shared in the male code of war and the interviewer belongs to a different generation with different cultural assumptions, they can re-define Robert Ross's gesture and through their combined (re)telling, make available to the present day its positive affirmation within negation.

History also generally excludes the private. Nevertheless some clues to Ross's behavior are to be found in the family environment. His violence, for instance, is to be seen in relation to his mother's attempt to elicit the violence in him: after her daughter's death, she wants him to kill Rowena's rabbits in a blind attempt to retaliate against fate. Or Juliet sees in Robert's affair with Barbara an explanation of what transpired later. Insufficient as this motivation appears to be, the affair certainly is a factor that has to be taken into account. The links between the private and the public sides of Ross's experience are precisely what the reader must puzzle over, what is of significance to the living. In short, when considered as a biography in the making, which it pretends to be, the story draws part of its authority from the recovery of the historically repressed and the discovery of its meaningfulness. When considered as a fiction, it cannot, since the events narrated have no existence apart from the text, recover anything historical but what is already known. *The Wars* indeed recaptures general atmospheres—the mood of Canada in 1915, the routine in the trenches—in such a way as to give the impression of felt life. Yet the real authority of the novel lies elsewhere: in the quiet confidence with which it implicitly claims that it illuminates the past better than history; that, through the textual construction of an imaginary life, it explores the extratextual, filling in gaps that actually did not exist prior to the act of narration; in the assurance with which it proposes an investigation of history and of the ways in which we know history.

At the same time, the very shortcomings of history that made the biography necessary inescapably affect the new referential story. Strive as it may for truth and completeness, it still remains relative, incomplete and subjective, because it proceeds from the same impulse to abolish randomness and obscurity by shaping the chaos of events or data to the order of narrative. Towards the end, the narrator as historian comments on the previous accounts which he has unearthed: 'Here is where the mythology is muddled' (183). In a professional way, he goes on to sort out and evaluate the evidence. Some stories are 'doubtful'; others are 'far more likely.' But if, on some points, he may set the record straight, transforming earlier mythology into history, he is nonetheless impelled by his own different mythological needs. In the **overall** narrative, Robert Ross's journey is structured as a series of confrontations with the four elements, climaxing in the ritual purification of the final holocaust.[18] Such myth-making is more comprehensive and more generous than the 'mythology' recorded in court-martial proceedings and other documents, but it betrays a similar difficulty in facing up to Robert's act and its outcome. Again, therefore, one of the restraints of history as genre is brought to light: the truth of historical narrative is always the limited truth of re-interpretation. But again, the novel which, as it unfolds the pseudo-referential account of events, concurrently invites the reader to see through the pretense, turns any reinterpretation, any mythical or dramatic enhancing of factuality into a triumphant assertion of fiction's peculiar power to build a model that rivals the world.

The narrative stances

Unlike the historian who can consider his right to recount past events as more or less taken for granted, the novelist must in some way establish his own credentials. In *The Wars*, Timothy Findley has adopted the solution of setting up a narrator who is a historian. Certainly the device is not uncommon, but Timothy Findley makes an original and complex use of it.

First the narrator as historian would seem to stand at a double remove from the object of his investigations. For this nameless I-narrator is essentially a mediator.[19] He describes the activities of a no less anonymous researcher—whom he addresses as 'you'—as the latter pores over old photographs and documents or as he interviews the survivors: '- You begin at the archives with photographs' (11); '- Lady Juliet has her back to you. "Just one moment," she says, without turning, and you wait with your briefcase and tape recorder in your hands in the middle of the rug' (99). The historian *persona*, which is usually seen as one, is here split into two—whether two entities or merely two roles is never quite certain. The disjunction creates a double structure of communication since the I-narrator orients his utterances now towards the intradiegetic narratee—the researcher—now towards an extradiegetic one—the 'implied reader'—and on occasion towards both. Such a situation of narration produces effects that have a bearing on the problem of authority and we will return to them.

   The whole question of the narrator, however, is complicated by the fact that the I is not in sole charge of the narrating. Many sections throughout and the whole of Part Three are told by a so-called third person or impersonal narrator.[20] *The Wars* interweaves two narrative strands, in which time and focalization are handled very differently. In the I-narration, story time and discourse time seem to coincide. The I looking over the You's shoulder narrates what the reseacher is doing in the archives, as, from the scanty documents, he reconstructs some of the main events in Robert Ross's life. The 'time of reference,' to use Mendilow's expression, is therefore the ongoing present. In the impersonal narration, story time and discourse time are separated by a temporal gap of several decades, and the 'time of reference' is World War I, more precisely the years 1915-1916, although flashbacks introduce still earlier events and a summary briefly reports the six years of reprieve, before Ross dies of his wounds in 1922.

   In the first-person narration, the narrator can only observe, record and sometimes comment on the **traces** of a life and of an age. To him, Robert Ross is an object of desire always at a distance from him to be constructed out of photographs, manuscript or printed items, and out of his own imagination. Certainly, he can, through empathy, transcribe what the portrait framed in silver is 'striving to say'— which is but the code of Ross's generation and class. But this is an exceptional moment. And when his imagination projects 'the fiery image' of the lieutenant leaping through the flames, he posits himself in the place of the camera. 'Robert Ross comes riding straight towards the camera' (12). The space between the perceiver and the **perceived remains. In the third-person narration, the protagonist** and the age are presented immediately, transparently, as though the past were unfolding itself anew. The narration is **mimesis** 'providing the maximum of information with the minimum of informer.'[21] Such a stance permits more shifts in distance between the narrator and his object. All positions of focalization are available to him, from focalization zero when he takes a bird's eye view of a broad scene (e.g., 174-175, 180-181) to focalization **through** Robert when the narrative reproduces the protagonist's inner motions: 'There were noises he could not identify. Movement. What? What was it? Had the men got up?' (81).

As can be expected, although whole sections may be dominated by one kind of focalization, the narrative often modulates from one to the other. Less frequently, it even modulates from one kind of narration to the other. Section 12 of Part Five begins with a commentary on various testimonies: 'Some versions have it that. . . ,' 'What has never been made clear is why. . . .' But the tense system and the deictics ('this') are the only grammatical marks of the I. The last two paragraphs shift back to third-person narration with no grammatical mark of the speaker and only two semantic ones (the introductory '**At any rate**' and the gloss '**a euphemism for the station yard during the state of emergency**'). Under the circumstances, to generalize about the 'narrator of *The Wars*' is a risky business, whatever one can say of the narrator of a given passage. And when it comes to the problem of authority, it is imperative to discriminate between the two stances. For each narrator exerts a different kind of control and labors under a different set of limitations.

Because of his association with the researcher, the I-narrator needs no outside endorsement. He displays the modest assurance of the historian who has reviewed all the available material and listened to the reminiscences of key-witnesses. He can analyze and comment on old snapshots, telling what songs the soldiers were singing, etc. He can describe with a geographer's lucid chasteness the flats of Flanders (71) and with a touch of lyricism the English countryside (140). He can reproduce **verbatim** long stretches of Marian Turner's and Lady Juliet's taped testimonies. Nor does his effacement on such occasions imply any weakening of control. The narrator is aware of the value of the women's statements. Marian Turner's is 'the only first-hand account of [Robert Ross] we have aside from that of Lady Juliet d'Orsey' (15), and Lady Juliet's memories are 'the most vivid and personal we have' (98). Extensive quotations from these interviews give freshness and impact to the narrative; at the same time the women's firm partisanship allows the I-narrator to make a case for

Robert Ross, without derogating through impartiality. In any case, the narrator has **selected** whatever he wanted to transcribe. Though most of his information on the d'Orseys was obtained from Lady Juliet, he reports a good deal of it in his own speech (140-142). Conversely, he chooses to reject direct quotation from the 'public' accounts—the transcripts of the court-martial, the various versions of the Lieutenant's escape with the horses (183).

Certainly, when analyzing the documents at his disposal, the I-narrator is cautious: 'He appears to be sitting on his left hand. Perhaps it was a chilly day' (190). But he has enough self-confidence to extrapolate. Seeing a snapshot of Robert Ross 'standing on the side lines with pocketed hands' and 'a dubious expression' as he listens to a military band, he first deduces his feelings and then proceeds to animate the still photograph.[22] Or, in the absence of any snapshot of Ross's bursting out of the blazing barn, he describes the imaginary picture that 'leaps through memory without a sound' into the researcher's haunted mind (12-13). Towards the end, he musters and sifts the tangled evidence about Ross's flight and arrest in a masterly way; and his reconstruction of the climactic moment, shuttling between different time-levels, different viewpoints, and between narration and comment, still manages to be vividly compelling. Even the way in which he defines areas of ignorance evinces his knowledgeability and dependability (186). The rare judgments he passes reveal his poise, as for instance this opinion on Mickle: 'Mickle was a brave man. He decided that, plainly, he was dealing with a man gone mad and that he must act in accordance with that interpretation. He must dispense not only with mercy—but with reason. That he did so, puts the state of his own mind in question—for what he did next cannot be interpreted as being any less "mad" than what Robert had done in taking the horses and deserting the battle' (185).

At another level, his meta-comments on his narration, though perhaps a bit heavy-handed, show his intention to shape his narrative to best effect, even when they sound a note of uncertainty: 'This is perhaps a good place to introduce Miss Turner' (15). Of course, one of the earliest and strongest clues to his control, or need of control, is offered by his choice of narratees, and singularly by his decision to address his **alter ego,** the researcher. Insofar as he makes free to tell the researcher his own story, the I institutes a situation of communication which is a power structure. (This remains true even if the I and You are regarded as but two aspects of the same **persona.**) Insofar as the You addressed often conflates the intradiegetic and the extradiegetic narratees, the I-narrator also hustles, and flatters, the implied reader into assuming the researcher's function. The device thus confirms a community of interdependent roles, but it is one in which the speaker wishes to retain his superior position.

If we now consider the obstructions to the I-narrator's freedom, they will appear to be both general and singular. First he is held in check by the resistance of History, the obscuring power of violence against which he struggles: 'Spread over table tops, a whole age lies in fragments underneath the lamps. *The war to end all wars.* All you can hear is the wristwatch on your arm. . . . As the past moves under your fingertips, part of it crumbles. Other parts, you know you'll never find. This is what you have' (11). Then there is the failure of representation to render the unprecedented enormities of World War I. Neither photography nor language can do justice to the horror of gas attacks, mechanized slaughter, or trench life. 'There is no good *picture* of this,' says the narrator at one point, 'except the one you can make in your mind' (71), and he adds soon after: 'The mud. There are no good *similes.* Mud must be a Flemish word' (71, italics mine). Inasmuch as these restraints are simply a magnified version of the difficulties inherent in all narrative, they also naturally affect the impersonal narration. But it is reserved to the I-narrator to express his awareness of these drastic limitations even as he endeavors to overcome them. (His appeal to the imagination as something that can perhaps go beyond pictures and words must needs be clothed in words, thereby signalling that our knowledge and imagination of the past depend on images, verbal and nonverbal).

More peculiar to the I-narrator is his dependence on photographs for the furthering of his narrative. This adherence to photographic documents, which is a guarantee of authenticity, is also a constraint, since it restricts not only the field of vision but also the narrative possibilities. To be sure, the narrator can turn photographs to kinetic use. Out of random snapshots, he creates a brilliant photomontage which conveys the feel and essence of 1915, a year of crucial changes. But, when he comes to the Ross pictures, his narrative drive flags. Although each snapshot is minutely detailed, becoming a network of signs and a focus of comments, the series is haphazardly put together. Whereas the I-narrator could immediately impose a pattern on the collective photographs, he cannot so arrange the private ones, and can only enjoin the researcher to do so: 'Shuffle these cards and lay them out: this is the hand that Robert Ross was born with. Mister and Mrs Ross—Peggy and Stuart—rabbits and Rowena.' (15) The metaphor of the deck of cards in itself suggests the dynamic of restraint and freedom and as such has proved serviceable to various novelists. Its familiarity, however, should not prevent us from looking closely at its function here. Contrary to what might be expected, freedom is reserved for the researcher, the narrator enduring the restraints—which raises an interesting problem of priority. Moreover, the metaphor indirectly points to the narrator's failure. If the photographs are 'the hand that Robert Ross was born with,' that is to say, if they represent the set of limitations put upon him by family and milieu, then an idea of causation, determinism if you will, is brought into play.[23] The narrator, therefore, should explore cause and effect relationships, in other words, resort to kinetic narrative. Instead he is absorbed in the contemplation/ description of discontinuous pictures and leaves it to his narratees to fumble for connections both between the photographs and between what they represent. Either the metaphor or the narrative method is wrong.

In the epilogue, the introduction of two snapshots similarly indicates a certain failing of narrative energy. Since the drama of Ross's existence in time has been played out, the narrator in fact has nothing to add to it. But the fascination with the subject's enigmatic violence lingers. So the I-narrator resorts to the static images that confer upon the dead man a timeless existence. Yet, although he describes the photo of Lethbridge camp with almost manic care for detail—thus recording its signs and symbols of violence and death— the narrator does not attempt to capture its meaning. 'You put this picture aside because it seems important' (190). From a means of exploration of what was outside the frame, the descriptions of photographs have become an end of the narrative discourse. Their discontinuity highlights the I-narrator's failure to maintain the continuity of his control. (Lest I be misunderstood, let me add here that the **narrator's** faltering does not prevent the re-emergence of photographs in the last section and the epilogue from providing a superb **novelistic** coda.)

Also detrimental to the I-narrator's authority are the occasional and minor irregularities in the narrative process. The irruption, for one thing, of the pseudo-photograph of Ross's leap through the flames into the Canadian photomontage. It is as though the narrator, engaged in methodically brushing the Canadian backdrop, were suddenly unable to repress any longer the figure of the victim-hero which has been haunting him. (Again, of course, the narrator's loss of control proves, on another plane of analysis, an increment to the novel.) Or take the puzzling statements which now and then crop up:

'So far, you have read of the deaths of 557,017 people—one of whom was killed by a streetcar, one of whom died of bronchitis and one of whom died in a barn with her rabbits' (158). This summing up is so arresting that it compels us to stop and think. But whatever meaning we finally derive from the comment, we must still wonder at the absurd accurateness of the figure and the no less absurd inappropriateness of the phrasing ('you have **read** of . . .'), which yet do not deprive the statement of its pathos.

Likewise there is something perplexing about the often-quoted warning: 'What you have to accept at the outset is this: many men have died like Robert Ross, obscured by violence. Lawrence was hurled against a wall—Scott entombed in ice and wind—Mallory blasted on the face of Everest. Lost. We're told Euripides was killed by dogs—and this is all we know. The flesh was torn and scattered—eaten. Ross was consumed by fire. These are like statements: *"pay attention!"* People can only be found in what they do' (11). Undoubtedly, the remark hints at some of the novel's major themes and, by introducing the names of people whose violent ends did not occur on the battlefield, is an invitation to extend the metonymy of 'The Wars' into a rich metaphor. But for the reader to develop the implicit meanings of the comments, he must know who Lawrence, Scott and the others were. That is to say that, although these men may have been consumed by their inner fires, they nevertheless are among the few who have not been totally obscured by violence. One can, of course, contend that 'some men's whole lives are overwhelmed by memories of their spectacularly violent ends.'[24] But I find the explanation no more satisfactory than the narrator's statement. Surely, if we can bewail our ignorance of Euripides' death today, it is because his works have not all been lost. Only the survival of the playwright can make us aware of the loss of the man. To be brief, when the narrator issues his warning *'pay attention!'* he, wittingly or unwittingly, suggests that I should also be watching **him.** Narrators, too, can only be found in what they do.[25]

Finally, the I-narrator's power is seriously qualified by the co-existence in the overall narrative of the impersonal narrator. Not that their narratives are antagonistic. On the contrary, supplementing one another, they dovetail and overlap without inconsistency. Of course, the molestation is mutual. But if the I-narration, as we shall later see, curbs to some extent the free play of the other narrative, the third-person narrator, on the whole, has more independence than the first person.

In the case of the impersonal narration, the dynamics of authority and restraint operates more visibly. To begin with, the narrator's access to knowledge about Ross and hence his right to tell the story are not intrinsically justified. Normally, of course, they would not have to be, inasmuch as an impersonal narrator enjoys a freedom denied the personal narrator. But such freedom, though absolute in theory, is, in fact, limited by the context. In this case, since the **overall** narrative, far from opposing 'fact' and 'fiction,' pretends from its first section onwards to trace a real man's career, the presence of the impersonal narration raises the double and related problem of its origins and of its source of information. Does it originate from and depend on the first-person account? But then how can the impersonal narrator know about Robert's spying through the peep-hole on Taffler's homosexual games, or about the gang rape at Désolé, to quote but two examples? His greater knowledge would seem to betray the fictiveness of **his** relation. Such questioning of the narrative instance is, however, counterbalanced in two opposite ways. On the one hand, its reliability in matters that concern Ross is certified from the outside by the general truthfulness of the historical information—which can be checked. A few random verifications easily prove the general accuracy of the military background. Even an incident which might seem invented to today's reader is in fact documented. During a gas attack, Ross, remembering chemistry classes, orders his men to urinate on their handkerchiefs and put them over their faces. Apparently soldiers did resort to such makeshift masks as a protection against chlorine gas.[26] The many brief reports on offensives (e.g., 83-84, 108, 181, etc.), the replacement of military commanders (47), or the introduction of new weapons (132) greatly contribute to the credibility of Ross's experiences. Relying on the reader's knowledge of World War I, the narrator, by the factuality of his account, builds a bridgehead from the known into the unknown. On the other hand, the masterliness with which he marshalls facts, summarizes phases of the war, recounts combat scenes or the relentless shelling, evinces a profound imagination capable of leaping across the gulf of years and lack of personal experience to ignite the narration. After a matter-of-fact description of the first appearance of flame throwers, here is how liquid warfare is evoked: 'Fire storms raged along the front. Men were exploded where they stood—blown apart by the combustion. Winds with the velocity of cyclones tore the guns from their emplacements and flung them about like toys. Horses fell with their bones on fire. Men went blind in the heat. Blood ran out of noses, ears and mouths. Wells and springs of water were plugged and stopped by the bodies of men and mules and dogs who had gone there for safety. The storms might last for hours—until the clay was baked and the earth was seared and sealed with fire' (132). Nowhere of course is the imagination more evident than in the sequences that directly involve Robert Ross. His narrow escape from drowning in a field of mud, where the eerie noises and motions which, on the fog's lifting, turn out to be corpses slapping and crows feeding, his attempt to have guns installed in a crater in which an aberrant ski pole sticks out, the 'muddy circus' of the supply convoys, the traumatic sexual assault in the dark grim cells of the Désolé Asylum—all these scenes with their 'solidity of specification' and their power to evoke something tremulously beyond words, do not smell of the lamp but of a brightly burning imagination.

Nevertheless, at times, the very accurateness of the narrative, which creates the impression that the narrator was an eyewitness to the events, may also hint at the burdens of narrating. Thus, his concern with dates—which contrasts with Lady Juliet's insouciance: *'dates are unimportant. You know when all this happened,'* (144)—is an element of authentication.[27] The relentless dates (17, 22, 47, 61, 71, 84, etc.), which link the hero's fate to historical battles, mark the destructive passing of time or the stretching of hours of anguishing wait. But their recurrence, as it becomes obsessive, finally draws our attention away from what is narrated to the surface of the narration.[28] The excessive clocking in Part Three (4 a.m., 4.25 a.m., 5.30 a.m., and so on) raises once more the question of the narrator's sources of information; and the arbitrariness of some of the times chosen[29] suggests that the narration is 'out of sync,' like some of the chaotic events it relates. The narrator seems to hang on to such indications because they are a grid into which he nervously tries to fit the madness of the war. Breaking the narrative flow, they are a device for distancing, which ultimately betrays the narrator's fear of being too close to the violence which he describes. Here can be apprehended one effect of the major obstruction with which his endeavor to appropriate the bloody past meets.

Another echo of such obstruction is heard in the narrator's speech—in the interrupted syntax, the repetitions, the silences. If Ricou is right in drawing the parallel between 'Robert Ross's stammering thought processes' and the narrator's difficulty with this story,[30] it should nevertheless be noted that in many passages the faltering is an attempt on the narrator's part to render the subject's inarticulateness when under stress. The scene which shows Robert traumatized by the rape is focalized **through** him: the monotony of the syntactical structures, the ellipses, the repetitions, are clearly intended to mimic the stuttering of his mind (168-169), and therefore reveal the narrator's virtuosity and not his own confusion.[31] As an argument *a contrario*, one may adduce the previous section which, narrating the brutal assault itself, is told in internal focalization **on,** and not through, the victim. Therefore, the narrator, while telling us that 'the dark . . . invade[d] his brain' and his 'mind went stumbling over a beach of words,' is not himself at a loss for words. He does not balk at reporting the rape connectedly and in all its revolting details.

However, there are, it is true, occasions, though these may be fewer than may at first appear, when the breaks in the narrative discourse are assignable to the narrator as in the following example:

> In the drawing room, sitting in its silver frame, Robert's picture started to fade.
>
> It got completely dark.
> This was the sixteenth of June (180).

Undoubtedly the narrator's style, albeit varied, often runs to short sentences, ellipses ('Lost,' 'Panic,' 'Movement,' 'Pegasus,' etc.), and the briefest of paragraphs, as though, in order to deal with so many atrocities, it were safer to look at things separately, to isolate actions, to fragment observations, though enormities could only be approached synecdochically in the hopes that 'the corner of . . . the picture will reveal the whole' (10-11). With all its brilliancy, the narrator's discourse has a certain brittleness, suggestive of the fragility of the narration as it attempts to cope with the juggernaut. But devotion to fragility is precisely one of the characteristics of the art lover, as exemplified by Devlin who collects bits of stained glass in his dugout. Significantly these include an image of St. Eloi, 'patron saint of smiths and metalworkers,' recovering a butterfly, an ambivalent symbol of ephemerality and immortality, from the flames of his forge (86-87).[32]

The coexistence of two narrative strands in the same textual space limits to some extent, as I have already remarked, the authority of either. That this hampering is mutual arises from the fact that neither has priority, since the link between the two is never made explicit. The overall narrative is a mosaic of fragments, juxtaposed without narrational hierarchy. (The transcripts are a partial exception: their relationship to the I-narration is clearly emphasized on their first introduction when they appear as stories within stories. Yet later, parts of them are inserted into the impersonal narrative, losing their connection with the I-narration.) Such a mosaic implies an 'arranger of collocations,' to use Frank Kermode's term, hence an authority superior to both narrators. This arranger we may call the **scriptor**. The scriptor is not to be confused with the implied author, however close some of their functions may be. In our novel, whereas the former purportedly organizes the account of a real life, the latter shapes a **fiction**. (His first signature, the title, already indicates as much: *'The Wars'* is both too general or too precise to make a good title for a history book.) Strictly speaking, of course, the scriptor is only the deployment through the text of some of the enunciator's activities, and can only be personified through poetic license.

The scriptor

To the scriptor accrues all the power of the narrative strands— their capacity to bridge the abyss of time and offer truthful and vivid glimpses of how things were—and some of their limitations. But he also displays an energy and constrictions of his own.

No more than the I-narrator could connect the you-researcher's documents scattered on library tables, is the scriptor able to weave a continuous story out of all the fragments of narrative at his disposal. There is no smooth flow to the textual time-space.[33] How to impose continuity on a story of broken bonds, temporary affairs, arbitrary deaths, and the senseless alternation of murderous attacks and counterattacks? In fact, throughout, there can be perceived a double resistance. Of the material—horror on such a mass scale cannot be encompassed—and of the scriptor (and narrators): since fire spreads by continuity, and violence threatens not only the subject but the storyteller, the tactic is to cut off the violent episodes—to the detriment of the traditional form of historical narrative. The scriptor accelerates the process started by the narrators, when for example he strings together, in this order, a summary of events in 1915: a vignette of Kaiser Wilhelm's saluting his troops on August the fourth of 1914, a scene showing twelve-year-old Robert's attempt to run the marathon, and a portrait of Robert Raymond Ross, Second Lieutenant C.F.A.

If fragmentation is largely a response to the dark pressure of 'reality,' and therefore part of the story's burdens (and burden), it also allows room for the scriptor's authority. First he clearly assumes the fragmentation by numbering the sections, labelling the transcripts, the prologue, epilogue, etc. Innocuous as they may seem, such practices are gestures of **appropriation:** the numbering of parts and sections has no relevance for any of the narrators and locutors, and their consecutiveness is only achieved in the scriptural space. Similarly, typographical devices—the large use of blanks and the variations of type—also bring to light the role of the scriptor in the dramatizing or slowing down of the narration. Secondly, the scriptor overcomes fragmentariness by the distribution of his materials into five Parts—a structure which has intrinsic balance and is reminiscent of the drama. After two parts of exposition and rising action, Part Three is the climax when Robert Ross proves his manhood under trying conditions; the reversal begins slowly in Part Four with the affair with Lady Barbara, and the falling action speeds up in Part Five, devoted to the hero's deterioration and tragic fall. In this theatrical patterning—emphasized by the 'prologue' and 'epilogue'—the scriptor seeks for the meaning that goes with structure, as Siegfried Sassoon did in his *Memoirs of an Infantry Officer,* when he divided his experience into three 'Acts.' 'For everyone, the dramaturgic provided a dimension within which the unspeakable could to a degree be familiarized and interpreted.[34]

Some of the scriptor's activities examined so far are but aspects of a larger activity which must now be analyzed in some detail, though full justice cannot be done to it here: the *montage.*[35] The scriptor's *montage,* which doubles the various narrating acts, is not a neutral, but an incremental operation. Like Lévi-Strauss's *bricoleur,* the scriptor, out of a finite set of components, builds a new set, the meaning of which is not simply the sum of its parts, identifiable as these remain. Though the elements gathered are far from being as numerous and heterogeneous as those found in, say, Dos Passos's *1919,* the *montage* is complex enough. Because it interweaves the two stories of Robert Ross's ordeal (story 1) and of the investigation into the past (story 2), it sets the living and the dead side by side in the textual space—instead of confining the former to an opening chapter. And since present and past are continually imbricated, both narratives put each other in perspective. The reader is constantly reminded that he is, like the I-You historian[s], assessing the past through the present, but he is also enabled to gauge the present as the result of that momentous watershed of Western history. 'After the Great War for Civilization,' as Marian Turner remarks, 'sleep was different everywhere' (47). Such constant confrontation is essential to Timothy Findley's purpose. 'A prophet looking backwards,' to use Schlegel's phrase, he writes partly to oblige his readers to 'pay attention' to what is going on around them. 'Wars don't just happen because of politicians and statesmen. Wars happen when the people—that is, "us"—haven't bothered to pay attention in one way or another.'[36] In an age when so many things are in great jeopardy, it is part of the writer's role to help people have a more 'creative response to being alive and to the politics of life.'[37]

The *montage* also cuts back and forth between the main plot of story 1, centered on Robert Ross's soldiering, and the subplot, centered on Mrs. Ross in Canada. The counterpoint between spatially distant events highlights the parallels between the son's and the mother's ordeals. As he is plunged more and more into a world gone mad, she slowly loses her always precarious equilibrium, until both come to a dark nadir on the same day. The syntagmatic discontinuities are an invitation to pick up the recurrences that reticulate the separate units of the two plots—the semantic clusters of light/darkness, water/fire/earth/air, speech/scream/wordlessness/silence—and thus to establish connections, which are nowhere made explicit, between the micro-environment of a Toronto family and the macro-environment of world conflict. The arrangements of parts is one implementation of the metaphor in the title. Soldiers may be tempered in the furnace of war; they are made in the everydayness of the family hearth. After all, in institutionalized, open violence, Robert Ross seeks refuge against the hidden violence of his mother. The crosscutting of the two series does not merely bring out the connectedness of all forms of violence; it also offers us another perspective from which to evaluate Robert's rampage. Whereas, in her madness, Mrs. Ross strikes out at life and finally withdraws from it, Robert, gone berserk, still endeavours to preserve the value of life; and when, purified through fire, he is offered 'grace,' i.e. release from his suffering, by Nurse Turner, he manages to whisper his indomitable will to survive: 'Not yet' (189).

Furthermore, as the scriptor arranges utterances from various sources, he may now achieve contrasts between the narrative modes, now tone down differences, now display the shifts in narrational levels, now efface them. Marian Turner's interview obtained in the course of the narrator/researcher's investigations and first quoted in the I-narration (narration 2) migrates in the text (46, 186) without being introduced by the I-narrator, but stamped with the scriptor's mark, 'Transcript: Marian Turner-2,' 'Transcript: Marian Turner-3.' In the same section are juxtaposed a flashback to Robert's childhood (narrative 1) and a description of a photograph of the young man (narrative 2). Such shading off of the narrative levels constructs a tolerant space of scription where voices converge and commingle. There is no real dissonance among them, even though they do not strike the same notes.[38] (The discordance is between these voices and the public opinion which the narrative corrects.) The locutors and narrators all have the desire to tell the truth as they see it and the belief that 'truth' can be shared. Indeed the textual space becomes the sharing of that (elusive) truth. So, if in the opening sections the sender *(destinateur)* of the story is a well-defined, albeit unidentified, speaker, the I, soon the scriptive assemblage of other voices, blurs that impression until the story seems to emanate from a chorus. In the epilogue, the I does obtrude again but by that time too many people have been drawn in for him to appear as the unique sender. Indeed, the end makes a concordance of those who have participated in the telling, including the intradiegetic and extra-diegetic narratees. When it is time for the text to dismiss the participants in the story and in the storytelling, it reunites them in a final dialogue and a final sentence in which the you has its greatest extension of reference.

Like the ending, the opening is a focus of scriptive effects. Together, they create the impression of a circular pattern, which several critics have already commented on. The circular structure, according to Peter Klovan, parallels the narrator's efforts 'to discover the real Robert Ross out of the circle of events surrounding him: "These are the circles—all drawing inward to the thing that Robert did." '[39] But the narrator's and the critic's image is somewhat misleading because things are not quite so neat. Critics, as a matter of fact, do not even agree on what returns and when.[40] So a closer look may be in order.

If the narrators are to some extent bound to respect something of a chronological development, inasmuch as both are concerned with the implacable progression of the war machine, the increasing dehumanization or mental deterioration of the men, the scriptor breaks further with linearity to create a new time-space of writing/reading, two of the principal rules of which seem to be what, for lack of better words, I shall call de-framing and off-centering. The main story deals with a dead man's life, that is with a stretch of time which has a marked beginning and end. It sets this life against the background of a World War which, no matter how undatable its origins, has apparently definite 'limits.' The French have no hesitation in calling it 'la guerre de 14-18.' Nevertheless, the narrative is rather like the road described on page 71, 'lost at either end in rain.' Even the borders of the textual space are uncertain. Does it begin with the dedication, the epigraph from Euripides, the acknowledgments? Or the last epigraph from Clausewitz? Or with the number 'One,' or with the word 'Prologue'? In a sense, avoidance of beginnings and of centrality is already evident in decisions which are sometimes the implied author's, sometimes the narrators': Robert Ross does not enroll with the first Canadian volunteers nor is his contingent the first to be shipped overseas; the narration eschews his baptism of fire and shows him in charge of a convoy when he 'has been in France for a month and two days' (71). (Notice the two days.) If Ypres, we are told, lies 'at the center of the world' (71), Ross stays close to Bailleul and St. Eloi—off center. But mostly it is the scription which is responsible for those effects of non-linearity which, redoubling beginnings, efface them. There is, for instance, the jumbling of narrative units from section four to section ten of Part One which destroys the time sequence. We start with Robert Ross in Kingston as he is about to join the Field Artillery. Revelation of the traumatic events that have led him to this is postponed, interrupted, repeated. Or, to choose an example that concerns the historical background, the beginning of the war is not mentioned until page 47. As for the biographical dates of Robert Ross, they are only given in the last section, where, together with his epitaph, they serve as closure.

More important still, not only the novel's opening, but its ending too, is redoubled, and both must be studied in relation to each other. The book 'starts' with a prologue which is not a prologue in the strict sense since it does not supply either a framework or explanatory information. Rather it is a scene in the to-be unfolded action, a scene which moreover will be repeated *verbatim* in its proper chronological slot, near, but not at, the end. This frozen moment which, as we first read it, has strong overtones of romance,[41] is a fragment of story 1 (the ordeal of Robert Ross) and a segment of narrative 1 (the impersonal narrative). But for all that it establishes a mood and themes that will be picked up again, it can hardly be considered as a beginning of either. The first section then presents an overview of Robert Ross's military experience from a double perspective, the dominant one which names Ross 'that traitor,' and that of the I-narrator/You-researcher which is based on different premises. Uncharacteristically, the first section is linked anaphorically to the prologue: 'All of this happened a long time ago' (10). It nevertheless makes a new beginning because it initiates both a new action—the investigation—with its own actors, the You-researcher and the I-observer, in other words, story 2, and a new narration under the responsibility of the I-narrator (narration 2): 'It's best to go away and find your information somewhere else. In the end, the only facts you have are public. Out of these you make what you can, knowing that one thing leads to another. Sometime, someone will forget himself and say too much or else the corner of a picture will reveal the whole' (10). A statement of purpose has been made and a warning is issued: 'What you have to accept at the outset is this: many men have died like Robert Ross, obscured by violence' (11). Thus while the prologue aims at transparency, attempting to obliterate the distance between what is narrated and the narrating, the first section foregrounds the act of narration as a transaction between the 'I' and the 'You.'

What it still effaces is the act of **writing,** which is not contemporaneous with the narrating but (as always) deferred. The textual confrontation of the two narrative units startles the reader into an awareness of their different modes of realism and into the realization that both conventions mask their origins. The double opening is then redoubled in sections two and three—two developing story 2, 'You begin at the archives with photographs. . . ,' and three sketching the background of story 1, '1915.' But these are in fact pseudo-beginnings: the 'You' already knew enough to start his research at the archives, and for all its significance, 1915 is an arbitrary starting point. Whether one considers, with Laurie Ricou, that the beginning is delayed and the novel 'begins . . . four times, in four different ways,'[42] or thinks, as I do, that the initial double frame is duplicated, the result is the same. The repetition of the beginning gesture, far from delimiting more neatly the overall story, makes limits hazier and focuses attention on the storytelling and its diffi-culties.

A similar effect is obtained in the last pages. First the final section brings story 1 and narration 1 to an end with a succinct relation of Robert Ross's last six years. Then an epilogue assembles the unintroduced description of a photograph and the narration of the You-researcher's last minutes in the archives—during which he looks at one more picture: 'The archivist closes her book,' as, with the ending of story 2 and narration 2, the book itself closes. But again appearances are slightly misleading. First, section 15 is more in the nature of an epilogue than an ending. The main action has already been brought to a conclusion in section 13; and section 14—a transcript of the Turner tape—has repeated and expanded earlier information, supplied in a unit almost symmetrically located in relation to the frame (section three of Part One). Section 15, for its part, provides elements of after-history and ends on a referential and formal closure, the **inscription** on Ross's grave. Conversely, the epilogue hardly deserves the name, insofar as it offers neither a new perspective nor information on after-history. It is in fact the concluding unit of the sequence 'You begin at the archives.' Moreover the ending is incidental to the researcher's enterprise, imposed on him by the exigencies of an official timetable. His research is not over: 'You begin to arrange your research in bundles— letters—photos—telegrams' (191). The return to the beginning, emphasized by the repetition of 'You begin,' is somewhat ironic: to end is almost as difficult as to begin. Nothing is really ended, not even Robert Ross's life since the sight of photographs brings him back: 'This is the last thing you see before you put on your overcoat: *Robert and Rowena with Meg:* Rowena seated astride the pony—Robert holding her in place. On the back is written: "Look! you can see our breaths!" And you can' (191). A pathetic ghost, unwittingly speaking of death even as he marvels at the traces of his life, also tells us about life-in-death. As we knew from the first, destruction awaited Robert Ross in story 1, but by closing on story 2, the scriptor can resurrect him, can even allow him to make an assertion of survival which, the story and our experience notwithstanding, the text confirms.[43] To that extent it is open-ended. At the same time the meaning of the epilogue sends us back to the pre-text: the epigraph tucked between the dedication and the acknowledgments, the 'Never that which is shall die' ascribed to that Euripides whose flesh was torn and scattered. So, in spite of marked signs of endings, the overall narrative resists closure.

Much as the introductory and concluding units de-emphasize respectively the themes of beginning and ending, they nevertheless form, because of their parallelism, a border, a frame which would seem to enclose the narrative (of which they are a part). On the other hand, because the endings are, in point of technique, symmetrical with the beginnings, the framing is not as confining as it might be.

The series A-B . . . B-A is constrictive in a way in which the series A-B . . . A-B cannot be. Here the order—story 1-story 2 . . . story 1-story 2—suggests a relaying of stories. Closure is less than perfect. Seriality almost triumphs over unity. In view of such meaningful symmetry, Ricou's comment that 'the novel opens stammering' ought to be qualified.[44] The narration—the transaction/s between the narrator/s and the audience/s—opens and ends stammering. But the novel—the transaction between implied author and implied reader—shows the scriptor attempting to make the stutter meaningful. Through his collocation of fragments he orders it in such a way as to turn it into a **silent language.** This sub-language raises questions on the nature of beginnings and endings. Why are they so difficult to achieve? Is it simply because of the deficiencies of narrative? To my mind, *The Wars* strongly intimates that beginnings and endings may be illusory in real life as well, a convenient way, in fact, to obscure violence.[45] From an entirely different perspective, Viviane Forrester makes remarks that are pertinent to the matter at hand: 'Le politique, avec à son service la politique, refuse quelle que soit l'idéologie, d'envisager le corporel, l'inconscient. Il s'invente un monde inorganique, engendré déjà, stable entre deux dates, avec un début, un milieu, une fin. Nécessaire à la consolation des populations qui ne veulent qu'oublier, rassurées, leur étrange aventure, et qui tentent surtout, accablées par l'excès de ce que nous sommes d'ignorer à jamais "ce que nous pourrions être". D'où le succès de tout ce qui nous represente delimites. Les messes, les guerres.'[46] In *The Wars*, which, incidentally, is itself much concerned with the body, the tension between the desire for stasis and symmetry, and the fear of violence and boundaries indicates a willingness to face the paradox of life and to provoke us into thinking about 'what we could be.'

If the scriptor's unobtrusive activity exposes the very strain between the powers and the disabilities of narrative in general, it more specifically draws attention to what the narrative seeks to hide, namely its artificiality. The recurrence of the same fragment in two different places is a case in point. Does the prologue, which is included in Part One but excluded from the numbering of the sections, quote in advance the section to come? Then the narrative already preexists, and the presentness of the I-account is revealed as a fake. Or does Part Five quote the prologue? Then the transparent immediacy of the third-person narrative, the end of which precedes the beginning, is destroyed. Since the questions cannot be exclusive, all is illusion. Or rather, with the reversibility of the movement of the narrative which can go forwards and/or backwards, there occurs a subversion of the notion of beginning and end, a subversion of time itself, which proclaims the literariness of the story. Or take the last scene in the archives. Its placing balances the opening scene in which the researcher was signing out his boxes of materials. Now he is completing a day's work. We are unexpectedly returned to one of the first conventions to be established, the suggestion that the I-narrator is reporting work-in-progress. Such a return to a convention that had been pushed into the background acts as a reminder of the many transgressions against the implicit contract. While the researcher was consulting 'letters—photos—telegrams,' we have been hearing taped interviews which he must have made earlier. (But did he? And when?) By achieving some sort of formal closure for story 2, the epilogue brings home to the reader the fictionality of the situation, however symbolic it may be of ours as we stop reading. The present that collapses the time of narration **and** the time of the researcher's action **and** the time of enunciation appears as a synthetic, timeless present. For when the claim is made again that narrated time and narrating time coincide, we are in a position to understand the trick that has been played upon us. Two incommensurate things, the time-space of story 2, i.e. a few hours in the archives, and the time-space of the I-narration, i.e. the accumulation of words aligned in a textual space, are presented as congruent with one another. When the claim is furthermore supported by the use of the pronoun 'us,' which places the I-narrator on the spot, we are also confronted with an area of undecidability. Does the 'us' invalidate or confirm the hypothesis that the researcher is the narrator's alter ego? Does it refer to 'you' and 'I' and eventually other readers in the archives? Or to I-the-historian (You-researcher and I-narrator combined) and nameless others? We cannot say. Such deliberate confusion, together with the conflation of time-spaces, is something which only language can achieve and only fiction (as distinguished from history) can afford.

In short, the scriptor sabotages the pretense to historicity, fostered by the narrators.[47] With the evidence of the sham we are sent back to the **author,** to the creator of this alternative world which has been presented as part of the real world. But the energy with which he has staged his private fears and fantasies against the background of a collective nightmare of the West still makes the alternative world **appear** as contiguous somehow with ours. The impact of *The Wars* derives from the successful transformation of the author's 'demons,' to use Mario Vargas Llosa's phrase, into 'theme,' and its naturalness from the equilibrium achieved between the personal, historical and cultural 'demons' that have been transmuted.[48] Such impact, however, is gained partly through a downplaying of some aspects of **author**ity. There is the author's renunciation of continuity, his willingness to risk fragmentariness. More importantly, there is the nagging sense of molestation.

Certainly, if molestation—'a consciousness of one's duplicity and one's confinement to a scriptive realm'—is inherent to the fictional process,[49] the author of *The Wars* attempts to make a virtue of necessity by faking and unmasking a historical record. Through the demystification of his pseudo-account, he seeks to ascribe a certain kind of truth to fiction, even as he is reminded, and reminds us, of its limits. Insofar as he largely mimics not real life but **mimesis**, the author, at any rate, can avoid being too closely embroiled in his **father**ing role, while on the other hand, his **scriptive** role is emphasized. Such willingness to relinquish, or at least obfuscate, paternal responsibility, projects a decentered worldview, opens up a non-authoritarian space of scription in which, as we have seen, characters, narrators and narratees are all together and which engages the reader deeply. As co-participants, we must both suspend disbelief and acknowledge the artifice, both see through the layers of illusion to the verbal nature of the events and respond to the novel as if it were life.

For the text strives to illuminate what is beyond it—the world out there. To regard *The Wars* as a narrative about narrative is undoubtedly a necessary move in the strategies of interpretation. And it is good that much of the growing body of criticism on the novel should have focussed on its formal aspects. Certainly too, narrative itself is part of the world. Nevertheless, *The Wars* is also concerned with historical life. True, it is not simply 'about World War I,' even though it represents convincingly one phase of it, in a particular sector of the Flanders front line. But it is very much about wars—of all kinds, past, present and future. In the depiction of a fictional character's involvement in violence, it endeavors to trace constants of the human experience without giving up a sense of man's historicity. The historical vehicle of the symbolic truths embodied in *The Wars* is so well rendered that the critic's mind stammers. I, for one, would have liked to engage the novel as historical fiction and have found myself unable to do so. Both the wish—since the referential approach is not one I usually favor—and the resistance it met with, testify, in different ways, to the vividness of the author's fictional evocation of the unnameable, and the complexity of the responses it calls forth. As secondary and precarious as it may be, the authority of Timothy Findley poignantly informs *The Wars*.*

University of Strasbourg, France

---

[1]Timothy Findley, *The Wars* (Toronto: Clarke, Irwin, 1977). All references (indicated between brackets in the text) are to the Penguin edition, Harmondsworth, 1978.

[2]Eric Thompson, 'Of Wars & Men,' *Canadian Literature*, No. 78 (Autumn 1978), p. 100. On Findley, see the issue of *Canadian Literature*, 91 (Winter 1981), devoted to 'Timothy Findley & the War Novel,' and Virginia Hager-Grindling and Terry Goldie (eds.), *Violence in the Canadian Novel since 1960* (St. John's: Memorial University Press, 1980).

[3]Anonymous review in *The New Yorker*, August 21, 1978, p. 94.

[4]It will easily be seen that my paper owes much to Edward Said's formidable book, *Beginnings* (New York: Johns Hopkins Press, 1975). But since I do not apply his concepts of 'authority' and 'molestation' with the rigor that his theory deserves, I cannot use him as the umbrella that will protect me from critical sins.

[5]As reported by David MacFarlane in 'The Perfect Gesture,' *Books in Canada*, 11, No. 3 (March 1982), 5.

[6]Peter Jones, *War and the Novelist: Appraising the American War Novel* (Columbia: Univ. of Missouri Press, 1976), p. 6.

[7]Stanley Cooperman, *World War I and the American War Novel* (Baltimore: Johns Hopkins Press, 1967), p. 46.

[8]Mrs. Ross is both an inwardly violent person, who insists that Robert kill his dead sister's rabbits, and a pacifist who, giving away chocolate bars to departing soldiers, feels that she is 'mitigating bullets,' and later turns away from support of the war effort and the patriotic platitudes of the Bishop's sermon.

[9]Cooperman, p. 189.

[10]See Eric Thompson, 'Canadian Fiction of the Great War,' *Canadian Literature*, No. 91 (Winter 1981), 81-96, and Paul Fussel, *The Great War and Modern Memory* (Oxford: Oxford Univ. Press, 1981).

[11]'The great deaths of literature are few, but they show us with an exemplary clarity the way in which art invigorates us by a juxtaposition, almost an identification, of pointlessness and value. The death of Patroclus, the death of Cordelia [. . .] All is vanity. The only thing which is of real importance is the ability to see it all clearly and respond to it justly, which is inseparable from virtue.' Iris Murdoch, *The Sovereignty of the Good* (London: Routledge & Kegan Paul, 1970), p. 87, quoted in Martin Price, 'The Fictional Contract,' in Frank Brady (ed.), *Literary Theory and Structure* (New Haven: Yale Univ. Press, 1973), p. 164.

[12]Walter Benjamin, *Illuminations* (New York: Schocken, 1969).

[13]One estimate has 9,586,000 horses killed during World War I. Ernst Johanssen, *Fronterinnerungen eines Pferdes* (Hamburg, 1925), quoted in Léon Riegel, *Guerre et Littérature* (Paris: Klincksieck, 1978), p. 224.

[14]Findley's interest in the protection of nature is evident in all his interviews. The following statement is but one of the early examples of such interest: 'I can't write it, I can't talk it, but I understand it in my bones, what's happening to us. I really think that we have gone beyond the meaning of civilization. We have accomplished all that civilization can accomplish, and all that is left is waste and meaninglessness.' In Donald Cameron, *Conversations with Canadian Novelists* (Toronto: Macmillan of Canada, 1973), p. 51.

[15]Youri Lotman, 'un modèle dynamique du système sémiotique,' in école de tartu, *travaux sur les systèmes de signes* (Paris, 1976), p. 79.

[16]More typical attitudes of rejection are illustrated in the novel: Clifford Purchas deserts and is shot down by the Military Police; Rodwell, unable to stand the brutalization of the men around him, kills himself. The pacifists are represented by Clive's Cambridge friends . . . and by Mrs. Woolf.

[17]I do not intend to examine here the conflicting conventions linked to the double polarity of *The Wars*, as historical fiction. But of course, the problem crops up.

[18]This aspect of the work has been stressed by Peter Klovan, ' "Bright and Good": Findley's *The Wars*,' *Canadian Literature*, No. 91 (Winter 1981), 58-69. And Bruce Pirie's 'The Dragon in the Fog: "Displaced Mythology" in *The Wars*,' *ibid.*, pp. 70-79, is a mythical approach which sees in Ross a solar hero.

[19]There are a few instances (71, 140) in which the I-narrator recounts some of Robert's experiences but the account is mediated, e.g., 'There is no good **picture** of this except **the one you can make in your mind**' (emphasis mine).

[20]'Impersonal narrator' and 'third-person narrator' are only critical commodities since, as Gérard Genette has remarked, 'toute narration est, par définition, virtuellement faite a la premiere personne' (*Figures III*, Paris: Editions du Seuil, 1972, p. 252). In this case the phrase 'impersonal narrator' has a certain appropriateness insofar as it suggests the increasing abstraction in the spectrum of narrational procedures. The You-researcher is a character assigned a number of physical actions: he handles the material fragments of the past. To him falls the task of taping the interviews of Marian Turner and Lady Juliet. The I-narrator is a disembodied voice and eye, yet he remains anchored in the fictional world by reason of his bond with the You, whereas the impersonal narrator is but a narrational agency.

[21]Genette, p. 183. From *Figures III*, I have also borrowed the by now often used concepts of focalization (pp. 206-223) of the diegetic levels (pp. 238-241) and of the narratee (p. 265). On the narratee, Gerald Prince's 'Introduction à l'étude du narrataire' (*Poetique*, 14 (April 1973) 178-96) is extremely useful.

[22]See my article, 'Photo/Roman: *The Wars* of Timothy Findley,' in *Études Canadiennes/Canadian Studies* (June 1983).

[23]Peter Klovan speaks of the 'Darwinized universe' of *The Wars*, *op. cit.*, p. 60.

[24]Laurie Ricou, 'Obscured by Violence: Timothy Findley's *The Wars*,' *Violence in the Canadian Novel, op, cit.*, p. 30. I find Ricou's analysis stimulating, even though I do not accept all the points he makes.

[25]In support of this interpretation, there is the epigraph from *Euripides* 'Never that which is shall die' which qualifies the narrator's statement that Euripides has been obscured by violence. That the narrator bears watching is furthermore proved by his quotation of the 'Irish essayist and critic Nicholas Fagan' (191). As Eva-Marie Kröller

suspected in 'The Exploding Frame: Uses of Photography in Timothy Findley's *The Wars*,' *Journal of Canadian Studies*, 16, Nos. 3/4 (Autumn/Winter 1981), 68-74, there is no such author.

[26]G. R. Stevens on CBC Radio program 'Flanders Fields' gave one example of how 'the first gas mask of the war was used by him under the orders of a lieutenant who had been a chemist in civilian life.' Quoted in William D. Mathieson, *My Grandfather's War: Canadians Remember the First World War, 1914-1918* (Toronto: Macmillan, 1981), p. 106.

[27]An example of enhancement; the main action starts at **Easter** 1915 and finishes on June 17th or 18th, 1916, close that is, to the summer solstice, which opens the declining phase of the sun cycle, its phase of obscuration, and is linked in Christian myth to the symbolism of Christ Chronocrator.

[28]John F. Hulcoop has developed this aspect of the novel in ' "Look! Listen! Mark My Words!": Paying Attention to Timothy Findley's Fictions,' *Canadian Literature*, No. 91 (Winter 1981), pp. 22-47.

[29]For example, the 4.25 a.m. entry, coming after the 4 a.m. entry, does not introduce a change or accentuate the lack of it, but begins with a retrospect: 'The previous evening Robert had taken Levitt down . . .'

[30]Ricou, pp. 132-35. See also Hulcoop's remarks on Findley's style.

[31]The scene is a repetition (though much more nightmarish) and a discursive expansion of an earlier scene in the brothel—when Robert panics at the sight of male lovemaking and breaks things in his room. 'His mind,' we are told, 'began to stammer the way it always did whenever it was challenged by something it could not accept' (45; cf. 13 and 26 for similar statements).

[32]There are other images of the artist in the novel: Rodwell, Clive and Harris the story-teller, and of course St. Eloi himself whose activities constitute a *mise en abyme* of the narration.

[33]It is significant that the longest paragraphs and greatest consecutiveness should be found in Lady Juliet's transcripts, though she reads from her diary—a genre that fosters ellipsis and fragmentation.

[34]Fussell, p. 139. Fussell's is an invaluable study of the ways in which 'literary tradition and real life notably transect,' based on World War I materials. Amateurs of mythological interpretation may also ponder the symbolic significance of the number five.

[35]I prefer the term *montage* to *collage*, used by Ricou. Narrative criticism would be clearer, it seems to me, if collage were reserved for the non-motivated insertion into a narrative of a piece of pre-existing material, whether iconic or verbal. Thus one may consider that the following passage is a micro-collage: 'Spread over table tops, a whole age lies in fragments underneath the lamps. *The War to end all wars.* All you can hear is the wristwatch on your arm' (11, emphasis not mine).

[36]Alison Summers, 'An Interview with Timothy Findley,' *The Malahat Review*, No. 58 (April 1981), p. 107.

[37]'An Interview with Timothy Findley,' *The Ontarian*, Nov. 20, 1979, p. 9. On 'paying attention,' see Hulcoop's article.

[38]For instance, although Marian Turner, Lady Juliet and Ross himself use the word 'ordinary' in ways that might seem contradictory, they are all trying to grasp the same thing, the dialectic relation between war and the common man.

[39]Klovan, p. 59. Cf. Hulcoop and Pirie in the same issue of *Canadian Literature*, and Christopher Scott in 'Hello to All That,' *Books in Canada*, 6, No. 8 (October 1977), p. 8 ff.

[40]For Klovan, for example, it is the prologue which is the starting point and section 11 of Part Five the closing one; thus his cycle is completed before the end. For Hulcoop, on the contrary, it is the 'fiery image' and the photograph in the last section, in which case the return is to a place **'near** the beginning of the book' (emphasis mine).

[41]The mood, themes and motifs of romance were not alien to World War I experience and the recording of it, as Paul Fussell shows in a fascinating chapter, 'Myth, Ritual and Romance' of his *The Great War and Modern Memory*.

[42]Ricou, p. 129.

[43]Ross's drawing attention to his breath is a gesture, which, however ambivalent to us, contrasts with the implications of the Lethbridge snapshot, also described in the epilogue, in which Ross holds the skull of a small beast. It retrospectively enhances his answer to Marian Turner, 'not yet.' And, of course, because of his inscription on the photograph, all the discursive figures of the I-narration can be rounded up in the final paragraph, as the subject himself, breaking through the limits of time and space, addresses his friends, the I-narrator, the you-researcher (the intradiegetic narratee), the extradiegetic narratee, the implied reader, finally reaching out to us.

[44]Ricou, p. 129.

[45]Cf. the excerpt from Findley's story 'Losers, Finders: Strangers at the Door,' quoted by Hulcoop in support of his comparison of Findley and Woolf:

"2 . . . there are no beginnings, not even to stories. There are only places where you make an entrance . . . and either stay or turn and go away."

"18 . . . nor are there endings. Even to stories. There are only places where you exit from another life. Or turn again and stay. Not knowing why" (Hulcoop, p. 39).

[46]Viviane Forrester, *La Violence du Calme* (Paris, 1980), p. 141.

[47]Transgressions of the story's norms, however, can also be found in the I-narrator's discourse, and the built-in signals of fictionality are not restricted to scriptive effects. See my 'Photo/Roman . . .'

[48]Mario Vargas Llosa, *García Márquez: Historia de un Deicidio* (Barcelona, 1973), p. 84.

[49]Said, p. 84.

---

*I am deeply grateful to Monsieur Gilles Desbiens and Mademoiselle Aimée Hermann, then of the Canadian Consulate in Strasbourg, for their courteous and generous assistance.

Rosmarin Heidenreich

ASPECTS OF INDETERMINACY IN HUBERT AQUIN'S *TROU DE MÉMOIRE*

It has always been recognized that the nongiven, or those elements that are withheld or excluded, constitute an important feature in the process of communication. Furthermore, this withholding of information and the resulting 'blank' in the structure of the communication to be achieved has, from Aristotle on, been closely identified with the aesthetic principle determining art as a process of interaction with the subject perceiving it.

What Walter Pater, in affirming that beauty is in the eye of the beholder, formulated as a purely aesthetic concept has since been recognized by phenomenologists such as Sartre[1] and Merleau-Ponty[2] as describing a feature present in any act of perception. The substance of Pater's argument has re-emerged in its aesthetic-theoretical context in studies by Roman Ingarden,[3] Hans Gadamer,[4] and E. H. Gombrich,[5] the latter being heavily influenced by the theories of Gestalt psychology.

The function of indeterminacy as considered in these and other studies serves as a point of departure for identifying the role of this concept in the dyadic interaction between text and reader as described by Wolfgang Iser.[6] Referring to both speech-act and general systems theory, Iser argues that like linguistic action, 'literary texts also require a resolution of indeterminacies, but, by definition, for fiction there can be no such given frames of reference. On the contrary, the reader must first discover for himself the code underlying the text, and this is tantamount to bringing out the meaning. The process of discovery is itself a linguistic action insofar as it constitutes the means by which the reader may communicate with the text.'[7]

It is obvious that all texts contain a certain number of blanks, or a certain degree of indeterminacy, for 'there must always be an element of the nongiven in the given, if the latter is to be grasped at all.'[8] In other words, the nongiven is essential in allowing the reader to determine the significance of the given as perceived against the overall structure of the text.

In contrast to the conventions characterizing the function of blanks up to the late nineteenth century, certain aspects of indeterminacy manifesting themselves in the novel since that time tend to draw attention to themselves by cancelling out any possibility for the reader to resolve them on the basis of his previous literary experience. The modern novel tends to invoke traditional literary conventions only to violate them. This radicalization of the function of indeterminacy has taken a number of different forms such as the spatial and/or temporal disorientation of the reader, and the suggestion of multiple identities of one or more of the characters. Whereas traditionally allusion was responsible for creating extensions of the identities of certain figures, the modern novel juxtaposes and superimposes the historical and the contemporary, the immediate and the remote, often without any narrative mediation.

Since Joyce's *Ulysses* and *Finnegan's Wake,* indeterminacy has taken on a highly radical function with respect to the responses it induces in the reader. In addition to initiating the reader's ideational activity and making him aware of the nature of this activity, indeterminacy tends to thematize the process of the communicatory act itself. Blanks are more and more likely to occur on the metaliterary level, due, for instance, to deliberate confusion as to the identity of the narrator and/or hero, to perspectival ambiguities, or to the consistent deformation of a given reality by the consciousness perceiving it.

Novels thus preoccupied with their own communicatory strategies, variously referred to as post-modern, autoreferential or narcissistic,[9] represent a form of fiction that is playing an increasingly important role in the current avant-garde controversy. The occurrence of this type of fiction in Canadian and *québécois* literature seems to be of particular significance: since for its effects it relies heavily on thematic and formal allusions to previous literature, the post-modern novel in Canada has played an important part in making visible the emancipation of the emerging culture from its European parents. Only a literature that has thoroughly incorporated existing literary traditions can break through these traditions to transcend them in the form of parody, intertextuality and autoreferentiality.[10]

In Québec, the novels of writers like Hubert Aquin, Jacques Godbout and Réjean Ducharme have presented an implicit equation of the artistic avant-garde with generally emancipatory movements. In this sense, recent developments in Québec fiction may be compared with those that have taken place in the flourishing Latin-American literatures, although these relationships remain to be more fully explored.

Hubert Aquin's *Trou de mémoire*[11] may be seen to illustrate radical aspects of the multiple functions of indeterminacy as prestructured blanks. In this it resembles novels such as Graeme Gibson's *Five Legs* or André Langevin's *L'Elan d'Amérique,* in both of which, however, the high degree of indeterminacy is created chiefly by the blanks resulting from the streams of consciousness of various figures and their different ways of experiencing the same events. Leonard Cohen's *Beautiful Losers* is technically even closer to *Trou de mémoire* in that its blanks arise not only out of the segmentation of the plot, perspective and narrative, but also out of the superimposition of disparate realities.

In Aquin's novel, segmentation and superimposition are taken even further. *Trou de mémoire,* as the title suggests, may be seen as a play on the notion of the blank itself. Like anamorphosis in painting, which it describes as a metaphor for itself, the novel creates an omnipresent blank by abolishing the central perspective entirely. Corresponding to the oblique perspective that reveals the hidden object of the anamorphosis, each successive segment of the novel abolishes the perspective that precedes it, actually transforming (rather than merely altering, modifying or expanding) the elements initially presented into entirely different objects in the perception of the reader.

The disorienting effects of *Trou de mémoire* are created by Aquin's isomorphic superimposition of Holbein's *The Ambassadors* (which contains one of the most famous anamorphoses in the history of western art) on a modern narrative. These effects nevertheless cannot be described without referring to the norm underlying both works of art, namely the central perspective, which governs not only the representational technique of the artist but also the viewer's (or reader's) way of perceiving and grasping the represented object, or the text.

The extent to which viewers of painting and readers of fiction have become conditioned to the central perspective as a representational and perceptual norm becomes evident only when it is deliberately broken or self-consciously manipulated. In representational art, the anamorphosis as a form of such manipulation remains a curiosity, as is indicated by the subtitle of one of the two modern studies of anamorphosis in art undertaken so far.[12] In fiction, the concept of perspectivisation has absorbed modern writers and critics alike since Henry James, but it has remained closely bound to the traditional notions of character and point of view.

The central perspective, however, is precisely what *Trou de mémoire* seems to withhold from the reader, blurring and even cancelling the distinction between the experience and the representation of life so dramatically expressed by manipulation of the central perspective in Holbein's painting. For in *Trou de mémoire* the central perspective is not segmented into two mutually exclusive images, as in *The Ambassadors;* perspectival segmentation becomes an ongoing process resulting in a constant transformation of the object perceived. This perpetual segmentation thus constantly invokes and seemingly cancels the central perspective as norm. In the novel as in Holbein's painting, the segmentation of perspective constitutes the central blank.

The most obvious basis for the correlation between the painting and the novel is that the latter describes itself as containing an anamorphosis, or *figure cachée*. To help the reader recognize it, the text provides him with two examples, both of which turn out to be part of the novel's own *figure cachée*. Thus the two illustrations that are reproduced within this study may be seen to constitute central points of reference for *Trou de mémoire*. Père du Breuil's 'Anamorphose du crâne pour un miroir cylindrique' (1649) appears as the graphic on the cover of the novel (extending over front and back). A description of Holbein's *The Ambassadors*, with its anamorphic figure, presented by one narrator, is recognized as a *texte à clé* or *texte codé* (p. 136) by another, and a third narrator explicitly formulates symbolic connections between individual elements of the painting and the novel ('Suite et fin,' pp. 133-45).

In Holbein's famous portrait, the segmentation consists in the fact that the skull as an emblem of death is perceivable as such only from a certain point of vision, namely at a distance and from the left. Viewed from this angle, the skull dominates the picture. From all other points of view, however, the painting represents a highly conventional portrait of two historical figures masterfully executed according to the principles of illusionary art.

In his study entitled *Anamorphoses ou perspectives curieuses*, Jurgis Baltrusaitis describes this striking double effect of *The Ambassadors* as follows:

> Le 'Mystère des deux Ambassadeurs' est en deux actes. . . . Le premier acte se joue lorsque le spectateur entre par la porte principale et se trouve, à une certaine distance, devant deux seigneurs, dressés comme sur une scène. Il est émerveillé par leur allure, par la somptuosité de l'apparat, par la réalité intense de la figuration. Un seul point troublant: l'étrange corps aux pieds des personnages. Le visiteur avance pour voir les choses de près. Le caractère physique et matériel de la vision se trouve encore accru lorsqu'on s'en approche, mais l'objet n'en est que plus indéchiffrable. Déconcerté, le visiteur se retire par la porte gauche, la seule ouverte, et c'est le deuxième acte. En s'engageant dans le salon voisin, il lève la tête pour jeter un dernier regard sur le tableau, et c'est alors qu'il comprend tout: le rétrécissement visuel fait disparaître complètement la scène et apparaître la figure cachée. Au lieu de la splendeur humaine, il voit le crâne. Les personnages et tout leur attirail scientifique s'évanouissent et à leur place surgit le signe de la Fin. La pièce est terminée.[13]

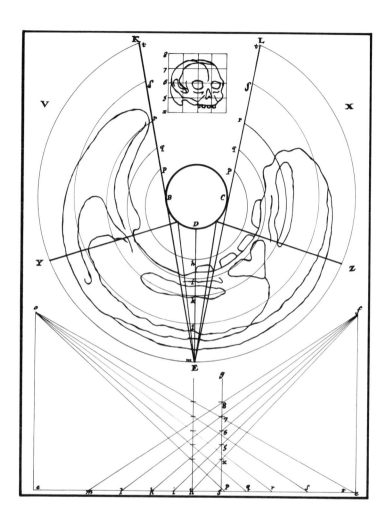

The other illustration, Père Du Breuil's 'Anamorphose du crâne pour un miroir cylindrique,' demonstrates the principle which makes possible the achievement of such a curious effect. The technique involves a deformation of the object by a fixed system of the lengthening of certain features and the foreshortening of others; its effects are determined by the multiplicity of virtual perspectives from which the object can be viewed in the cylindrical mirror.

Considered retrospectively, i.e. after reading the novel, the evocativeness of the lay-out of its cover achieves its full significance.

In a sort of anamorphosis of Du Breuil's 'Anamorphose,' the front cover is dominated by a shaded circle, identified in type by the title *Trou de mémoire* which appears in the widening space indicating the angle at which the object is to be viewed to be recognizable. On the back cover we find a system of diagonal (oblique) lines intersecting at regular intervals to indicate the virtual points of perspective, while a graphic schematization of the object itself—the *crâne*—is to be found underneath this network of intersecting lines of vision.

Without pressing the question of literary correlatives too far, it is possible to recognize in this complex cover graphic certain key features of the novel itself. For what is indicated in this illustration is the multiplicity of perspectives available for viewing a given object, the arbitrariness with which certain of these virtual perspectives are selected and actualized, and the segmentation of perspectives which is necessary to perceive and grasp the object which is presented to view. The image of the cylindrical mirror thus constitutes at once an optical and symbolical model for the phenomenon of perspectivisation, but also designates the reflexiveness of perceiving subject and object perceived. The hollow space, or that which is enclosed within or behind the *miroir cylindrique,* may be seen as a metaphor for the presence of an unnameable absence, and constitutes a symbolic allusion to *Trou de mémoire* as a mnemonic phenomenon, while it also invokes the cranial void implied by the representation of the skull as the object reflected in the mirror. Thus *Trou de mémoir,* in addition to designating a loss characterized by its unnameability, circumscribes the temporal and spatial categories which represent the perceptual norms of conscious experience.

A primary effect of the withholding of the central perspective is to change the very nature of the reader's activity in the reading process. Unlike that in a traditional novel, his involvement is not initiated by the familiar novelistic elements of plot and character, but by his own effort to learn the truth; his activity is bent on constituting, from the multiple options open to him throughout the novel, a superior perspective which will enable him to evaluate the relative validity of the contributions of Olympe, Magnant, the editor and RR in the novel he is reading. In this he is handicapped not only by his ignorance but by the irreconcilable contradictions of the various sections and the apparent arbitrariness of editorial selectivity and annotation.

If this quest of the reader for the truth is initiated by the novel's denying him recourse to the formal norms of traditional narrative discourse, it is complicated by the negation of the familiar social and moral norms that make up the reader's ordinary everyday reality. The equation of sexuality with rape and masturbation, the description of pharmacologically induced self-narcosis as a desirable state, the invocation of violence as self-liberation, all represent to the reader a physical and moral world which is both exotic and taboo.

The effect of this defamiliarization of the reader's social and literary repertoire is heightened by the temporal and spatial disorientation created by the text. Where, for instance, is he to place the 'Cahier noir' or RR's 'Semi-Finale' chronologically? How can Magnant be simultaneously in Montreal carrying out his homicidal intentions with Joan and at the same time stalking RR in Lausanne? As in *Prochain épisode*, the reader's disorientation reaches its climax with the converging of identities of the various personae, while this identicality is seen to allude to its own category of experience as belonging to the fantastic, the unreal.

But due precisely to his own experience of the text, this kind of explanation of its inconsistencies on the basis of a schematization of reality has become unsatisfactory for the reader. At the latest with RR's complete contradiction of the fictional reality created by the text prior to her 'Semi-Finale,' the reader is confronted with the virtuality of the textual reality itself, but also with that of his own interpretation. His habitual separation of the experience of reality and the experience of illusion is cancelled by the way reality and illusion respectively present themselves, and by his increased awareness of the nature of their interaction.

Instead of representing the multiple facets of a complex fictional reality, as in the conventional novel, or at least revealing the complementary nature of that which is felt to be realistic and that which is felt to be fantastic (as is still the case in *Beautiful Losers*, for example), each perspectival segment in *Trou de mémoire* functions to disturb the hermeneutic performance of the reader in the segment which precedes it. Initially this is achieved by the apparent irrelevance of the sequence in which the segments occur, while ultimately the reader's consistency-conditioned imagination is taxed to the utmost by the flat contradiction of one segment by another.

Viewed by externally marked headings, or chapters, there are four separate perspectives presented throughout the novel, namely those of Olympe Ghezzo-Quénum, the African pharmacist and revolutionary; Pierre X. Magnant, his *québécois* counterpart, whose perspective, though not central, dominates the novel; the anonymous editor of Magnant's manuscripts; and RR, whom the reader takes to be Rachel Ruskin, Olympe's lover and the sister of Magnant's lover Joan.

Complicating these alternately foregrounded perspectives are copious footnotes, which constitute a context and a background, and thus a contrasting perspective to whatever perspectival view is foregrounded. Furthermore, since they are appended to the pages of the text to which they refer, and so interrupt and even disrupt the reading of the foregrounded text, the footnotes effect not only a temporal and linear discontinuity but also the simultaneous availability of two and sometimes three contrasting perspectives.

In the traditional novel the elements constituting the individual perspectival views combine to form a sort of code, the deciphering of which takes place as the reader assembles and groups the elements to form constantly enriched or broadened contexts for the particular passage he is reading. In *Trou de mémoire* there is also this tangency between the individual elements of one section and those of another. Indeed, the reader finds a certain symmetry, suggesting a possible code, in the perspectival views presented through Olympe and Magnant, and in the documents presenting them. But this symmetry is cancelled by the capricious revelations of the editor and RR. It is the interventions of the editor and RR that guarantee the reader's perpetual alteration of the code he is using to decipher the meaning of the novel by disallowing any schematization.

Nevertheless, like the individual and apparently heterogenic segments themselves, the elements presented through any given perspectival view are meant to be connected to those presented in other contexts. These connections are formed by the reader not only on the basis of certain differences or similarities in the way given elements appear through the various perspectival views, but are also determined by the reader's recognition that each perspectival view itself represents only a mask of the respective narrator. The self-representation, in many segments overtly narcissistic, of any one given perspectival view *vis-à-vis* the others, involves revelation by strategies of dissimulation which increase the indeterminacies created by the perspectival segmentation itself.

In demonstrating the arbitrary nature of the segmentation of perspective achieved in the novel, RR's 'Note Finale' reveals to the reader how the actualization of any one perspective relegates the other indicated perspectives to their original virtual status. The multiplicity of possible perspectives in their virtuality constitute a *trou de mémoire*, which can only be filled when the previously actualized perspective is abandoned.

This principle of perspectivisation which emerges for the reader as he recognizes the effect of the novel's strategies of segmentation may be invoked with respect to all the thematic elements presented in the novel. Thus it also reveals the significance of the term *trou de mémoire* as applied to the collective amnesia of a people who have been forced to adopt the cultural perspective predetermined by the nation that conquered them. At the same time the numerous references to the role of perspective in art as illusion, and particularly the effect of Holbein's anamorphosis in *The Ambassadors* in the novel, let the reader recognize the nature of his own role in the aesthetic experience constituted by his reading of the novel.

Somewhat in the manner of the double ending in Fowles's *The French Lieutenant's Woman,* the novel reveals the aesthetic object perceived to be a product of the projections the reader himself has formed as he adopts and then abandons perspectives following the 'instructions' of the text. In *The French Lieutenant's Woman* the two endings are mutually irreconcilable. In *Trou de mémoire* the artificiality of the ending is irreconcilable with the illusion of reality created by the rest of the text. In Holbein's *The Ambassadors,* the perspective which allows recognition of the skull as *figure cachée* is irreconcilable with that which presents the realistic portrait of Jean de Dinteville and Georges de Selve.

The isomorphism between Holbein's painting and the novel is explicitly indicated by the novel itself in the correspondences formulated by the editor. In 'Suite et Fin' (pp. 141-45), the two ambassadors correspond to the figures of Pierre X. Magnant and Joan; the Oriental tapestry uniting the two ambassadors has its equivalent in 'la texture des mots . . . dans ce livre' (p. 142); the enigmatic shape, the skull, at the feet of the ambassadors forms the secret center of the painting just as 'le meurtre de Joan est le socle sombre du roman' (p. 143).

The reader, however, recognizes a deeper resemblance between the painting and the novel once he has grasped the function of the novel's perspectival segmentation. Like the double perspective in the painting, in the novel the foregrounding of one perspective results in the blurring, elimination, or loss of that which was previously foregrounded. This phenomenon is expressed in the novel in that their mutual irreconcilability abolishes the figure presenting one of the perspectives, namely the one which is abandoned, nevertheless without destroying it: it remains virtually present in the form of memory, but it loses its function of representing a given reality. The loss of memory, or, in the Holbein painting the loss of sight of the subject of the portrait, results in the elimination of ambiguity, but also in the all-pervasiveness of the one perceived perspective. In *The Ambassadors* it is the representation of the skull, a symbol of death. In *Trou de mémoire* the final perspective ironically vanquishes this spectre by the fact that RR not only survives, but also shapes a future for herself and her child by changing her identity and bestowing one on her child. The ending, as the reader recognizes, is ironic not only in its artificiality, but also in that it is not the figures of RR and her child that will prevail, but rather that both will be superseded by the final perspective of Holbein's painting.

Though repeated allusions to itself as a *roman policier* occur in the novel, this generic allusion does not play the central role in *Trou de mémoire* that it does in Aquin's first novel, *Prochain épisode*, where it represents the governing communicatory strategy. In *Trou de mémoire* it is the narrative and perspectival segmentation, the isomorphism and isochronism between the individual segments and elements, and the isomorphic relationship between the text and Holbein's double portrait that create a high level of indeterminacy and so constitute the main narrative strategies of the novel. The enormous demands made on the reader as a consequence of its indeterminacies place the novel in the modern esoteric tradition of Joyce, Beckett and Nabokov.

With its invocation of the fantastic and the metaliterary, *Trou de mémoire*, like *Beautiful Losers*, also contains the aesthetic playfulness with the reader that characterizes a number of more recent novels of other literatures, such as Gabriel García Márquez's *One Hundred Years of Solitude*, Italo Calvino's *If on a Winter's Night a Traveller*, and John Fowles's *The French Lieutenant's Woman*, which has already been referred to in connection with Aquin's novel. Underlying these common features is a more and more explicitly formulated preoccupation of the authors in question with the kind of relationship created between text and reader as part of the communicatory process of literature. Aquin's description of this relationship as he presents it (from the writer's perspective) in his essay "La disparition élocutoire du poete (Mallarmé)" may be seen to sum up the position characterizing the authors of the autoreferential or metaliterary text:

> . . . je suis préoccupé jusqu'à l'obsession par le lecteur. En écrivant, j'imagine que je me lis par les yeux de cet inconnu et je voudrais que son plaisir de lire mon texte ne soit pas uniforme,

constant, prévisible en quelque sorte, mais avec plusieurs seuils d'intensité, enrichissant, capable de le surprendre, voire de l'ébranler et difficile à prévoir. Quand j'écris, je pense au lecteur comme à la moitié de mon être, et j'éprouve le besoin de le trouver et de l'investir. Une écriture totale est celle qui est tout entière tournée vers la possible lecture qui en sera faite par le destinataire. Les recherches éloculoires de l'écrivain, ses figures, ses truquages, ses stratégies verbales sont autant d'éléments relationnels et non d'abord expressifs, car ces éléments reposent sur un rapport entre l'auteur et le lecteur.[14]

In *Trou de mémoire* we observe the 'obsession with the reader' to be manifested in the degree to which the participation of the reader as 'cocréateur de l'oeuvre'[15] is demanded. As a highly autoreferential novel, *Trou de mémoire* requires a reciprocation on the part of the reader of the author's obsession with him and his responses to the text. In inviting and even forcing the reader to participate in the making of a work whose effect is precisely the recognition of how the work is actualized by the reader, the text demands an obsession with fiction of the same order as the obsession with the reader manifested in them. *Trou de mémoire* stands out in Canadian fiction not only because of its high indeterminacy, but because the **kind** of participation required on the part of the reader actively involves him in the creative process itself.

Collège Universitaire de Saint-Boniface, Canada

---

[1]Jean-Paul Sartre, *L'Imaginaire* (Paris: Gallimard, 1948).

[2]Maurice Merleau-Ponty, *Phénoménologie de la perception* (Paris: Gallimard, 1945).

[3]Roman Ingarden, *Das literarische Kunstwerk* (Tubingen: Niemeyer, 1980 [1931]).

[4]Hans Gadamer, *Wahrheit und Methode: Grundzüge einer philosophischen Hermeneutik* (Tubingen: Mohr, 1960).

[5]E. H. Gombrich, *Art and Illusion: A Study in the Psychology of Pictorial Representation* (London: Phaidon, 1972).

[6]Wolfgang Iser, *The Act of Reading* (Baltimore: The Johns Hopkins Univ. Press, 1978; originally published in Germany under the title *Der Akt des Lesens*, Munich: Fink, 1976).

[7]Iser, p. 60.

[8]*Ibid.*, p. 64.

[9]See Linda Hutcheon, *Narcissistic Narrative: The Metafictional Paradox* (Waterloo: Wilfrid Laurier Univ. Press, 1980).

[10]See Linda Hutcheon, 'Parody Without Ridicule: Observations on Modern Literary Parody,' *Canadian Review of Comparative Literature*, 5, No. 2 (Spring 1978), 201-211.

[11]Hubert Aquin, *Trou de mémoire* (Montréal: Le Cercle du Livre de France, 1968).

[12]Jurgis Baltrušaitis, *Anamorphoses ou perspectives curieuses* (Paris: Olivier Perrin, 1955).

[13]*Ibid.*, p. 65.

[14]Hubert Aquin, 'La Disparition élocutoire du poète (Mallarmé),' in *Blocs erratiques* (Montréal: Les Éditions Quinze, 1977), pp. 263-64.

[15]*Ibid.*, p. 266.

Pierre Spriet

STRUCTURE AND MEANING IN
RUDY WIEBE'S *MY LOVELY ENEMY*

In a recent analysis of Wiebe's novels written a few months before
the publication of *My Lovely Enemy,* I suggested that below the
variety of plots and themes a deep structure could be detected in the
six novels written to date which I called 'structure de l'echec' or
failure structure.[1] All those novels functioned on the radical
opposition between worldly values and those of a lunatic fringe
represented by the main protagonists—dreamers, dissenters, Indians,
outlaws—who are eventually destroyed by the violence of society.

In a more recent study of Wiebe's short stories,[2] I extended my
demonstration to the author's entire fictional production excluding
My Lovely Enemy. The matrix which accounted for the variety of
narrative techniques, themes, and characters appeared to be a refusal
of coherent sense: a gap, a frustrated expectation, some form of
inconsistency constantly prevented easy reading, as if Wiebe's
purpose were more to disturb and confuse than to comfort and
reassure, more to raise doubts about accepted values and ask
questions than to solve problems and provide answers.

Can Wiebe's recent novel be read as another variant of the same
structure? A summary reading of *My Lovely Enemy* cannot fail to
cause a shock to the analyst who dared write that Wiebe avoided the
theme of physical love and emphasized suffering and pain rather
than pleasure and sex. The novel may represent a turning point in
Wiebe's novelistic career: the Mennonite author seems to have turned
into a hedonist celebrating sexual intercourse with elation and
fervour; his new Gospel is free love if not promiscuousness, and *My
Lovely Enemy* is superficially not very different from the novels
which he derided in *The Blue Mountains of China.*[3]

Indeed, the main motif would suggest a comparison with Leonard
Cohen's novels: the hero is easily seduced by the luscious wife of a
university colleague and they have an affair. The betrayed husband
and the hero's wife are soon informed, and the two couples go
through an eerie experience which does not bring the love affair to an
end, but leaves the problem unsolved or solves it in a kind of
dreamland.

Two secondary motifs are integrated into the main one: the hero visits his aging mother in May and she dies in September. The other motif is no surprise in Wiebe's novels: it is the story of Broken Arm, a Cree Indian, which is linked to the main narrative by the profession of the narrator hero who studies Canadian history. The stories of a Mennonite mother and of a defeated Indian are familiar elements in a novel by Wiebe. The main narrative is more unexpected and is not easily reconciled with Wiebe's usual themes: the dénouement of the adultery story does not restore sound morality; indeed, the affair is presented as a healthy, elevating experience. The novel may even be read as a portrayal of the gradual liberation of the male lover from the sense of sexual guilt that his Mennonite education has rooted in his mind.[4] So far, Wiebe's plots have been moral, and the stories could be read as metaphors of Christ's sacrifice, ending as they had to in failure and death. The 'conversion' of the author in *My Lovely Enemy* is apparently as radical and complete as that of his hero.

But this presentation of the novel only accounts for its most sensational features. Wiebe is obviously interested in other themes than sex, even if sex plays a decisive role in the evolution of his characters. With or without irony, they combine love-making and metaphysics; one of the interlocutors of the protagonist happens to be Christ himself, who appears twice and discusses sex and love with him. In the sexual scenes, discovery and communication are the concern rather than physical pleasure, and Wiebe's glorification of love excludes any sadistic or masochist form of violence. His new obsession, if it is one, has nothing to do with Richler's or Cohen's.

On a purely thematic level, *My Lovely Enemy* is perhaps not so different from Wiebe's previous novels, after all. Wiebe continues to blend past and present, Indian stories and modern adventures, and Western Canada provides a basic setting. The same religious concerns haunt the protagonists; the denunciation of a form of Christianity and morality which, to Wiebe, is definitely not Christian remains a constant of the novel as it was in *Peace Shall Destroy Many, The Blue Mountains of China* or *The Temptations of Big Bear*. It seems that, if he now focuses on the relationship between husband and wife to reveal its limitation, this particular theme is not in opposition with the views held in other novels. *My Lovely Enemy* can be read as the exposure of so-called Christian morality which sanctifies the most egoistical forms of possessiveness. Wiebe denounces the ambiguity of earnestness and thrift, work and its material rewards, self-righteousness and purity. These Mennonite values may be those which are praised in the Old Testament but they are in radical opposition to the Gospel doctrine.[5] The novel offers the same kind of destructive comments on the fear of sex and the feeling of guilt which were already present in *Peace Shall Destroy Many*. The anabaptist in Wiebe is far from dead; it is alive and quite articulate.[6] Prophet-like, Wiebe proclaims his message of love and reunion of men and women in God as he never had, at least so openly, in his earlier fiction. The inadequacy of the world has never been so forcefully maintained. *My Lovely Enemy* is Wiebe's most religious novel in spite of, or because of, its sexual concern.

But a purely thematic approach is bound to remain unsatisfactory. It cannot clarify issues that the novel deliberately confuses. Even more than the previous works, this one is a mixed bag. The Christian sense that has just been sketched may indeed be apprehended in the novel, but it cannot exclude other interpretations. The bewildering variety of statements, judgments and utterances of all kinds make the novel a didactic muddle which resists thematic reduction no less bafflingly than does *The Blue Mountains of China*, though quite differently. And, as in my two studies of Wiebe's fiction, I remain convinced that the meaning of this novel should be apprehended through a delineation of its deeper structure rather than an analysis of its surface themes.

My Lovely Enemy can be read as the development of a matrix which I will call fusion of incompatibilities,[7] and which is identical to the refusal of a coherent sense detected in the short stories. The variants of this matrix are diverse—narrative incongruities, thematic contradictions, poetic deviations, and ungrammatical sentences. A new stage seems to be reached with *My Lovely Enemy:* coherence is not just avoided; incoherence is now asserted as the new order; anomaly is established as the norm, and incompatibilities become the actual criterion of truth and value.

Incongruity can first be detected in the surface structure of the narrative. It consists of two parts of unequal length: a 'May' section of four chapters and a 'September' section of two. The first part is written in the present tense; character and narrator coincide, expression and perspective being attributed to the same existent, the 'I' of the narrative voice.[8] In the second part, the narrative is in the past tense and the narrator is no longer the 'I' of the main protagonist whose privileged status of the first part is thus reduced. It seems that a distance is established between narrator and hero. Even though the discourse remains centred on the main protagonist, other figures are seen in the same terms of perception. This distancing is reinforced by the use of the past tense, in contrast to the present tense used in the book's first section. These discrepancies seem to foreground distortions between 'May' and 'September.' The two sequences constitute an obvious chronological continuity underlined by the titles, but the final effect is one of dissonance.

The arrangement of the Broken Arm episodes also produces dissonance: the Indian lived in the nineteenth century; the story of his life is introduced at irregular intervals into the contemporary narrative, without logical transitions. The abrupt change in time and space is both concealed (since no transitions are provided) and accentuated by typographical devices (the intruding scenes are printed in italics).

These dissonances are no obstacle to the reconstruction by the reader of the different temporal planes of the novel: the remote past of the Indians, the past of the Mennonite parents in Russia and of their son in Canada, the present of the main protagonist, and finally a sort of unmarked time which may be read as future and which is not really in time, though it is written in the past tense. These planes constantly merge in the different chapters. What is emphasized is not so much confusion as continuity and simultaneousness of past, present and future.

Between 'May' and 'September,' the novel introduces a short section of two pages (pp. 182-83) whose title, 'The Black Bridge,' points to its function in the narrative: the short section is a bridge linking and separating the two parts. It is built on two isotopies. The first isotopy allows a reading of the pages as a description of a modern bridge, one-half mile long, built in 1913 across an Alberta valley and providing a passage to trains and cars. The second isotopy is made to clash with the first. It places within the description notations which signify another level of perception: the bridge sings 'an incredible, terrifying song'; it is associated with violent death and becomes the mysterious entrance into another world which is reached through a fall; it disappears in 'a white mist' on which human beings are made to cross the wide valley, but its strange song can still be heard.

This page would be termed 'poetic' by traditional criticism because it cannot be read on one coherent isotopy: the whole text cannot be made plausible; it refuses to be 'naturalized' yet it remains linked to a referential world. It breaks the rules of classical description and, by disconcerting the reader, it prepares him to accept a mythic reading of the September section which, even more than the episodes of the May section, requires another consciousness and a different response to the strange fictionality of the last chapters. 'The Black Bridge,' fusing verisimilitude and fantasy, is an obvious variant of the structure of incompatibilities which informs the whole novel.

The spatial organization of the novel is as confusing as its temporal one: the main story is set in Edmonton, Calgary, and the country around; the second part of the narrative is located in a disused mine which, like the black bridge, is turned into another place—a dark, bottomless hole, simultaneously in Alberta and nowhere. At the end of the novel, other fantastic locations are again introduced: a snow beach as hot as fire, a stubble field which becomes the meeting place of the new community.

This constant interplay of narrative incongruities or impossibilities is complemented by a pattern of character construction which simultaneously roots the protagonists in a life-like world and yet rejects the rules of conventional novel writing. Characterization in *My Lovely Enemy* is patently more symbolic than psychological. James and Gillian are made to fall in love without any attempt at plausibility. Logical reasons that might explain their behaviour are explicitly refused; the monologue points to inconsistencies and excludes a verbal resolution: 'I will not speak such contradictories' (p. 103). In opposition to this fundamental inconsistency of the lovers, the novel provides Gillian's husband with all the attributes of logic, common sense and calculation, making him the archetype of rational man rather than a life-like character. The father and mother of the hero, the minister of the Mennonite community, the Alberta politician and his wife, and young Aaron also correspond to types found in genres which Northrop Frye would call mythic and ironic, certainly not mimetic. Actually, they move freely from the mimetic level to the mythic in a bewildering confusion which is another variant of the same structure of incompatibilities. The narrative motifs of the second part are the death of the mother on the one hand and the dénouement of the love affair on the other; the resolution of both motifs is effected in a way that forces the confusion of planes: the mother's death is narrated and then is narratively destroyed; like Lazarus, she rises from the dead (p. 257). And the lovers are transferred from the level of ordinary reality to one which looks like death but is life; indeed, it is neither and both;

like the description of the black bridge, the narrative fuses incompatible elements and it abruptly stops, providing no resolution of the inconsistencies. A similar defiance of the laws of verisimilitude can be detected in the scenes which introduce Christ as a character in the novel: the sentence which opens the dialogue between Jesus and James fuses both mimetic and mythic modes: 'A man stands between the bed and the wall, the wall against which the bed is tight' (p. 78). Christ is physically present and he is not. The novel could not more provocatively impose the fusion of contradictory elements. This fusion affects the other protagonists too, and its formulation at the end of the second visit of Christ is another variant of the fundamental structure: 'It is neither she nor her body, it is both and neither, it is myself and it is not either . . .' (p. 143).

The fusion of narratives and the inconsistencies introduced in time, space and character construction which have been briefly analysed above constitute the 'story' level of the novel. At the purely discursive level, the same variants of the fundamental matrix may also be detected. The fragmentation of the different narratives into separate episodes is maintained but the syntactic organization blurs their limits. Within each chapter, the discourse is conducted as a continuum excluding blanks and logical transitions. It is often within the same sentence that a radical shift in time and space is effected, causing the reader to lose his bearings. Instead of helping him construct a world of separate entities, a solid, sensible structure, the text multiplies the obstacles to coherent reading and uses various techniques of defamiliarization and destabilization. The instances are countless: James's monologue turns Gillian into a Cree woman: 'she is one of them seated there among the poplars . . . to be touched by anyone who dares to find her' (p. 45). Then James follows her into the past, out of time: 'all I have to do is follow her where she is already.' And the discourse turns him into a Cree warrior; he is linguistically converted into a companion of Broken Arm and he speaks of his Indian ancestors, all these transformations occurring in the same sentence. The process of identification of the main protagonist with an Indian becomes the device which introduces the story of Broken Arm. The sentence which marks the beginning of the embedded narrative is not even a new paragraph; the italics which typographically separate the secondary motif from the main one are not even placed at the beginning of the sentence. All this points both to continuity and separation. The embedded narrative remains linked to the main one: it happened 'when **we** had a great chief'—the **we** refers grammatically to the Indians of former times, among whom the **I** of the interior monologue is included. Here again, the form of this strange, confusing narrative appears as the very content of the novel: the confusion of times, places and identities aims at turning what seems to be solidly and reassuringly 'in-dependent' into destabilized, **pendent** elements which may then and only then reveal their mutual 'de-pendence.' The text forces the reader to walk on his hands, and this discovery is both 'sweet and terrifying,' as the narrative phrases it, before attributing to Gillian the words of its formulation: 'If one morning you began walking on your hands, the whole world would be hanging. The trees, these ugly brick and tile buildings wouldn't be fixed here so solid and reassuring, they'd be pendent. The more safe and reliable they seem now the more helpless they'd be then, dependent' (p. 45).

The same pattern recurs in other forms. The discourse may withdraw information necessary to the identification of characters involved in an episode by the use of personal pronouns which indifferently refer to several existents. It may create even more deliberate confusion in the reader's mind as, for instance, when Harold has sexual intercourse with a woman who may be his wife or James's; the text foregrounds the hesitation and does not solve the ambiguity (p. 234).

The refusal of coherence may appear in various forms of poetic deviation: ungrammatical sentences and semantic inconsistencies. Not a few sentences make no sense. There are few pages which present no obscurity by traditional standards, and the novel reads as a long poem. The poeticity of *My Lovely Enemy* is underlined by the frequent use of quotations from poems, making the novel an actual 'collage.' This tends to undermine the referentiality of the story by multiplying the possibilities of symbolic relations of equivalence, opposition or contiguity which do not exist in prose, at least to the same extent.[9] This systematic deconstruction of logical language is not an accident or a superficial obscurity which a firmly conducted analysis might dispel. It amounts to a refusal of rational coherence. If a logical sense cannot be established, it is because the text forbids it. When the writer makes warm sand and cold snow function as doubles (p. 224), he is deliberately making it impossible to read the novel, in its narrative and discursive organization, within the codes of so-called realism.

The text alludes to Donne's predilection for oxymorons (p. 200).

In *My Lovely Enemy* Wiebe transgresses the rules of referential discourse far beyond the limits of this trope. He does not simply combine contraries. He fuses contradictories, thus destroying the very foundations of logical language. One cannot, using logic, simultaneously affirm that something is and is not. Yet this is exactly what the novel does repeatedly. The other novels refused happy, conventional endings; *My Lovely Enemy* is not differently constructed, but the rejection is even more radical. More subtly than the others, it denies itself any resolution in this world (p. 10). If James is to find a means to reconcile his marriage and his love affair—to put it in realistic terminology—it is definitely not in the Edmonton of the 1980's. A resolution is offered but it is openly ironical, since the text points to its non-referentiality and prevents the possibility of reading the novel on the isotopy of the real world. To reach a solution, James will be made to cross the valley upon the mist and not upon the steel bridge of logic. The contradictions are not solved and it is obvious that this is a deliberate choice. The words attributed to the hero at the end are unequivocal in their denunciation of coherent language: 'he felt very close to weeping for all the words he had scattered, those great words his mind gathered and piled within him like rocks to fence in the enormous, o endless field of his longing and ignorance' (p. 223).

A verbal resolution would maintain the narrative within itself, that is within its words. *My Lovely Enemy* signifies the inadequacy of words and points to a reality which cannot be put into words and which is symbolized in the text by 'the perfect white between the words' (p. 58 and also p. 45). Wiebe's quest is condemned to fail in order to succeed. Success does not belong in this world of reason and logic. The paradox is that it cannot be hinted at without a necessary passage through words.

Before he is a philosopher or a mystic, Wiebe is a poet. His material is verbal and, while he is obviously interested in putting forward a vision of the world, what characterizes his writing more than that of more traditional novelists may be the use he makes of words. They are not just the vehicle of his ideas and of his vision;[10] they enact their own destruction and announce their absence—the 'perfect white' or blank which it is their function in the novel to postulate.

My Lovely Enemy is one of the most 'poetic' novels of the Wiebe corpus because it destabilizes language and fuses contraries and contradictories. As Coral Ann Howells recently said, all short stories composed by Wiebe seem to be about the limitations of language,[11] which is another way of saying that they are about the limitations of this world. The novel tends to perturb and to confuse the reader and at the same time to spur him into seeking a higher level of awareness.[12] It signals that it cannot be read as another piece of traditional fiction. The reader must be deprived of his usual landmarks if he is to be led to the discovery of another world no longer governed by the laws of verisimilitude or limited by the norms of logical sense. In order for a new possibility of communication to appear between men and women, the old system has to be wrecked. To use another symbol of the novel, 'the ordered necklaces of our lives' must break and the pearls be scattered on the floor to be gathered again differently (p. 179). Wiebe's verbal art is one of indirection; it excludes open propaganda and preaching.[13] The message is delivered obliquely, negatively one might say: the barriers of logic and reason are broken, self-righteousness and spiritual comfort are undermined: this process of disorientation is the condition for the discovery of a world which lies beyond words and will therefore not be made explicit. More than the other novels, *My Lovely Enemy* is founded on the supreme refusal of the very principle of contradiction and it functions instead on the violent fusion of incompatibilities. The rejection of worldly values had never been so radical.

My Lovely Enemy marks the triumph of the primitive mind.[14] It also expresses the victory of 'love.' In this novel, love is the privileged semantic formulation of a quest for a reality beyond words: it is the great manifestation of this process of fusion of opposite poles which is the dominant verbal device in Wiebe's work. '[T]he most profound unions are between opposites' (p. 151): male and female, spirit and matter, mind and body. Love is not just the metaphor of this fusion but its essential realization: it unites a man and a woman not because of their similarities but because they are opposites. Love **is** fusion of contradictions: James will not have to choose between his wife and his mistress: 'I want to have both rather than either,' he says (p. 167). Morally and logically it is impossible. On another level, it is possible, Wiebe claims.

The intrusion of love in the main protagonist's life operates as language when it is handled by Wiebe: it disturbs and destabilizes, and ultimately it provides an entrance into another world, made of husband and wife, lover and mistress, father and daughter, brother and sister, Indians and white Canadians, man and God—since God is feminine too. And this discovery is founded on inconsistency and contradiction: James discovers the Indians by following Gillian against all logic (p. 45). Love for his mother, his wife, his daughter and his mistress are all one form of communion; indeed it is his mother that he loves in all other women: 'she was the first and she is the last and she will live me into the meaning of all the others' (p. 90). And the final reunion is one of love, as illogical and irrational as love itself: 'So for a time he looked at each of those who were, the people he loved and who loved him, and he prayed to see them all at one and know them all, not distinct and separate, even himself, but all one' (p. 262).

Thus, the rejection of rational sense which informs *My Lovely Enemy* is not different from the failure structure which organized the other novels, and it is identical to the refusal of logical or conventional meaning detected in the short stories. In this novel, it seems possible to say that it appears more clearly as a mere stage in a dialectical process of negation which ultimately aims at transcending confusion and proclaiming the existence of a truth beyond this world of words and logic.

Fortunately for the novel's readers, this transcendence is only asserted indirectly and obliquely; otherwise, the novel would turn into a sermon and Wiebe's remarkable ability to undermine words by using all the resources of words would no longer be needed and enjoyed.

University of Bordeaux III, France

---

[1] 'Formes du recit et vision religieuse du monde dans les romans de Rudy Wiebe,' *Le Facteur religieux en Amerique du Nord*, 1, 4 (Bordeaux: Maison des Sciences de l'Homme d'Aquitaine, 1983), pp. 13-32.

[2] 'Les formes du refus dans les nouvelles de Rudy Wiebe,' *Recherches Anglaises et Americaines*, 16 (1983), pp. 105-19.

[3] New Canadian Library edition (1970), p. 184.

[4] Cf. for instance pp. 21, 63, 100 (Toronto: McClelland & Stewart, 1983); all references to this edition will appear in the text.

[5] Wiebe often denounces the 'cultural trappings' of Mennonitism; cf. his article entitled 'For the Mennonite Churches: A Last Chance,' in *A Voice in the Land: Essays by and about Rudy Wiebe*, ed. W. J. Keith (Edmonton: NeWest Press, 1981), p. 27.

[6]Cf. H. E. Tiessen, 'A Mighty Inner River: "Peace" in the Early Fiction of Rudy Wiebe,' revised ed. of his 1973 article, in *Here and Now*, ed. John Moss (Toronto: NC Press, 1978), p. 169: 'In each novel, the material is Mennonite and the thematic framework in which it is cast is a theological one.'

[7]Cf. Michael Riffaterre, *Semiotics of Poetry* (Bloomington: Indiana Univ. Press, 1978), pp. 47 ff.

[8]Cf. Seymour Chatman, *Story and Discourse: Narrative Structure in Fiction and Film* (Ithaca: Cornell Univ. Press, 1978), p. 153.

[9]Cf. Nicolas Ruwet, 'Parallelism and Deviation in Poetry,' in *French Literary Theory Today: A Reader*, ed. Tzvetan Todorov (Cambridge Univ. Press, 1982), pp. 92-124.

[10]Wiebe's rejection of a Mennonitism of culture and social rites is a particular aspect of its denunciation of worldly values; cf. *A Voice in the Land*, pp. 28 & 30.

[11]' "If I had a Reliable Interpreter Who Would Make a Reliable Interpretation"': Language Screams and Silence in Rudy Wiebe's *Where Is the Voice Coming From*,' *Recherches Anglaises et Americaines*, 16 (1983), 95-104.

[12]Wiebe uses a curious expression: 'prodding people into thinking' in 'The Artist as a Critic and a Witness,' in *A Voice in the Land*, p. 47.

[13]*Ibid.*, pp. 41-43.

[14]Cf. A. Dueck, 'Rudy Wiebe's Approach to Historical Fiction,' *Here and Now*, pp. 187-88, where the rejection of conceptual philosophy and Wiebe's predilection for 'the primitive mind' are linked.

Walter Pache

'THE FICTION MAKES US REAL': ASPECTS OF POSTMODERNISM IN CANADA[1]

I

'Canada is so far away it hardly exists.'[2] José Luis Borges' apochryphal remark today appears to be no longer as true as it might have been a decade ago. Those critics on both sides of the 49th parallel who are anxious to overcome the rigid clichés of American cultural domination on the one hand, and the Canadian inferiority complex on the other, have of late begun to examine Canadian-American literary relations in more detail. The contacts between American postmodernism and contemporary Canadian fiction promise to be a particularly rich field for a comparative study of both literatures.[3]

The obstacles are obvious: all critical judgments on an ongoing process will be provisional, notably if it is a process charged with conflicting emotions of a not exclusively literary kind. With due caution, therefore, I should like to examine a few aspects of this relationship: 1) the Canadian reception of postmodernism as a literary movement that originated in the United States; 2) the Canadian view of postmodernism as a tool against modernism and its implications of literary domination; and 3) the 'invention' of a collective past as a central concept of postmodernism in Canada.

Such an approach, it is hoped, might not only contribute towards an assessment of the affinities and the differences between the two North American literatures, but also shed some light on the question of how new literatures in the process of developing their own literary strategies can adopt and adapt external models without becoming derivative.

II

The term 'postmodern,' which Arnold Toynbee appears to have introduced into critical discourse as a historical category sometime during the fifties, was soon taken over by other disciplines. By 1960, 'postmodern fiction' had established itself primarily in the United

States as a mode of writing, accompanied by a set of critical rules, thanks to the vigorous efforts of a very vocal group of critics and author-critics. This strong theoretical bias of the new movement makes it relatively easy to summarize some of the main features of postmodernism—not just for ths sake of the argument, but because of the situation the Canadian writers found themselves in during the late sixties. They had to respond to a comprehensive body of narrative texts and critical theory that had grown in close symbiosis.

The 'death of modernism' might serve as a starting point; it had been announced by authors like John Barth ('The Literature of Exhaustion') and critics like Ihab Hassan *(The Dismemberment of Orpheus)*.[4] In their view, the end of the psychological and social realism of mimetic fiction was at hand. The disappearance of a unified and hierarchically structured world picture made human experience useless. Fiction as an individual reflection of the real world, the 'postmoderns' argued, had exhausted all its potential. With the advent of new mass media for transmitting facts as well as moral and emotional interpretations, fiction seemed deprived of its primary functions. In a short story which carries the significant title 'The Death of the Novel,' Ronald Sukenick characterizes the writer's new position after the breakdown of the literary conventions of 'modernism': 'The contemporary writer . . . is forced to start from scratch: Reality doesn't exist, time doesn't exist, personality doesn't exit. God was the omniscient author, but he died; now no one knows the plot, and since our reality lacks the sanction of a creator, there's no guarantee as to the authenticity of the received version.'[5] While modernists were seen as vainly struggling to cope with an increasingly fragmented world by using more and more subtle narrative devices, the new experimental writers abandoned any attempt to describe and analyse the 'real world.' They decreed that the communicative function of literature was superseded by the new poetics of a 'literature of silence.' Many of their texts, by deliberately exposing their own artificiality, refuse to provide readers with traditional means of orientation and identification. The reader's role becomes more and more complex as he is asked to reconstruct a new context from disparate fragments or to discover this context by deconstructing the structure of a written text. Consequently, postmodern novels frequently tend to lay open the rules governing the reader's perception of reality.

There is a general tendency for contemporary writing to become openly self-reflexive. New terms like *metafiction* or *surfiction*

(Raymond Federman) indicate that fiction focuses more and more on the creative process itself, whereas its referential function is reduced. As the literary imagination becomes engrossed with explaining its own workings, fiction turns to fantasy or fabulation, experimenting with word games and sound patterns. Older genres like romance and allegory are revived—if only to be subjected to new forms of parody and travesty.[6] This subversive tendency is emphasized by John Hawkes: 'I began to write fiction on the assumption that the true enemies of the novel were plot, character, setting, and theme, and having once abandoned these familiar ways of thinking about fiction, totality of vision or structure was really all that remained.'[7] Historical narrative, in particular, turned out to be a favorite target for this process of deconstruction and transformation, because it represented a type of fiction tied more closely than others to the existence of an objective reality. In the epilogue to his novel *The Sot-Weed Factor* (1960), the elaborate pastiche of an 18th century historical novel, John Barth states: 'be it remembered . . . that we all invent our pasts, more or less, as we go along, at the dictates of Whim and Interest; the happenings of former times are a clay in the present moment that will-we, nill-we, the lot of us must sculpt.'[8] Since then, not only John Barth but also Thomas Pynchon and others have radically questioned the assumptions underlying historical fiction. Their attack is aimed not just at certain inconsistent uses of history but tends to unmask history itself as just another kind of fiction.

III

The Canadian contribution towards the growth of experimental fiction in the United States during the sixties seems obvious, if limited. It was, after all, Marshall McLuhan who suggested that the end of the analytical and mechanical age of Gutenberg coincided with the beginning of a new era of collective or 'tribal' forms of behavior. McLuhan's theories have undoubtedly influenced American writers and theoreticians of the postmodern movement. John Hawkes' formula of the 'totality of vision' confirms this awareness as do collage-like texts like Donald Barthelme's short story 'At the End of the Mechanical Age.'

As far as English-Canadian literature is concerned, the immediate influence of McLuhan's theories of communication is far more difficult to assess. Until the late 1960s, it appears to have been minimal. Even after its 'renaissance,' Canadian fiction remained firmly committed to the theoretical premises and narrative conventions of modernism. Geoffrey Hancock, who has examined this anti-experimental bias,[9] claims that a number of Canadian authors during the late fifties and early sixties went through an innovative phase: many writers then felt they had to catch up with the mainstream of international realism. From 1960 onwards, however, Hancock goes on to argue, literary nationalism and the normative concept of 'identity' once again restricted productive contacts with the new international avant-garde. Non-realist techniques, especially those coming from American sources, seemed suspicious. Even those few writers who like Chris Scott or, for a while, Brian Moore, experimented with breaking away from descriptive realism during the early seventies, did so in a haphazard and undecisive way.

It required a writer of the independent stature of Robert Kroetsch to liberate the postmodern debate in Canada from the national/ international deadlock and turn it into a productive force. If we want to understand Kroetsch's central role in this process, it is essential to recall his close affiliation with postmodern critics at the State University of New York at Binghamton and his stint as editor of *Boundary 2*. But Kroetsch's comprehensive immersion in contemporary American fiction and narrative theory only prepared the ground for the transformation of this influence in his own oeuvre. Although Kroetsch's turn towards narrative fabulation is already evident in his early novel *The Words of My Roaring* (1966), it is only in the two following novels, *The Studhorse Man* (1969) and *Gone Indian* (1973), that he makes full use of the whole repertoire of postmodern narrative techniques. Even in retrospect, these two novels emerge as the climax of narrative experiment in Kroetsch's fiction.[10]

On the surface, *The Studhorse Man* is firmly placed in space and time: its action takes place in the Canadian West towards the end of the Second World War. The novel's plot is modelled on the picaresque quest story: Hazard Lepage, the 'Studhorse Man,' travels in several stages across the province of Alberta. In search of a suitable mare for his 'blue stallion,' Lepage is fighting a losing battle against a new technological age where horses are no longer needed. But Lepage also struggles against the narrator, who claims to tell his story truthfully, but turns out to be unable (or unwilling) to do so. Lepage's stallion is called Poseidon—an obvious allusion to Ebenezer Cooke's ship in John Barth's *The Sot-Weed Factor*, but also indicative of an underlying mythological pattern which the narrative both imitates and parodies. Numerous inaccurate and misleading cross-references to classical mythology are scattered throughout the novel (the narrator, Demeter Proudfoot, is a man with a woman's first name), so that on one level *The Studhorse Man* can be read as a deliberately trivial parody of Homer's *Odyssey*.

The narrative situation is complicated. The novel is told from the point of view of the mentally deranged Proudfoot who, using a bathtub as his vantage point, purports to reconstruct the fortunes of Hazard Lepage, his rival in love, but at the same time seeks to justify his own efforts at bringing about Lepage's failure in order to take over himself as the new Studhorse Man. Proudfoot, a grossly unreliable first-person narrator, thus tells someone else's story which eventually, however, becomes his own. From what he says about his own point of view, it is clear that a parody of Fielding's famous definition of the realistic novel as a 'mirror on the road' is intended: 'By a fortunate combination of light and reflection, I am able to see out of my window without leaving my bathtub. A mirror is so placed above my sink that I have been able to sit for hours, attempting to imagine what in fact did happen (allowing for the reversal of the image) exactly where I imagine it. It is then *time* that I must reconstruct, not space.'[11] *The Studhorse Man* marks the final stage of a narrative convention which dates back to the 18th century. The narrator, who once guaranteed the authenticity of the story, ends up immobilized and incompetent as a lunatic in a bathtub. Proudfoot's biography of Hazard Lepage and the story of his quest is nothing more than the synthetic result of a careless, badly informed, even hostile reconstruction, quite unsuitable to bridge the gap between reality and fiction. In its utter failure, the narrative report reveals the intrinsic absurdity of any fictional representation of reality.

Robert Kroetsch's novels have been praised for putting the Canadian West and, more specifically, Alberta on the map. But their topographical accuracy is deceptive. *The Studhorse Man* centres around the 'creative and innovative process' in a dual sense: as animal instinct and as artistic energy. Both are shown to be foiled in their aspirations. Poseidon, having trampled his master Lepage to death, ends up at a farm where contraceptives are produced from the urine of pregnant mares. Equally, Demeter Proudfoot's creative efforts not only lead to nothing but are doomed from the very start. The narrative, instead of reflecting empirical reality, reflects only itself, i.e., the process through which reality is invented. Thus, *The*

Studhorse Man becomes overtly metafictional: it is a book about writing a book. The repetitive and ultimately sterile nature of the creative act forms one of the focal points of the novel. Hazard Lepage himself reflects on it when he says: 'Men of more experience than I have lamented at the repetitious nature of the ultimate creative act itself. It is only by a mastery of the process of *repetition* . . . that we can learn to endure; yet we can only master the process by a lifetime of repetition. Many, I suspect, are tempted to despair. But I have sought other solutions and, I might add, with no little success. The path that would appear to lead to madness is surely the highroad to art.'[12]

Because the narrator's perspective and the events he refers to openly contradict each other, the reader experiences the narrative as fictitious, as an ingenious experiment of the poetic imagination which cannot (and should not, the author seems to imply) be restrained. It is no accident, by the way, that 'Poesy' is the pet name of the stallion Poseidon.

The novel's claim to originality rests, paradoxically, on its insistence on the inescapable dialectic of creation and reproduction, of innovation and imitation. Critics have pointed out that Kroetsch's fiction shows an increasing tendency 'towards the minimal novel, towards the point where only enough is given to stimulate the reader to maximum involvement, maximum participation in the work.'[13] Kroetsch's following novel, *Gone Indian* (1973), represents the next stage of this process of reduction. Here, the failure to cope with reality both as central theme and as a problem of narrative structure is taken a step further.

Again, the plot seems simple. Jeremy Sadness, an unsuccessful doctoral candidate from Binghamton, New York, is sent to Edmonton by his supervisor, Professor Madham. Instead of going for a job interview at the University of Alberta, Sadness gets involved in a series of chance events, and ends up eventually at a beauty contest held during a winter festival. There, he meets a woman who has been waiting for her vanished husband, and disappears with her on a snowmobile into the subarctic winter.

The novel's motto is taken from Frederick Jackson Turner's famous essay on 'The Significance of the Frontier in American History': 'For a moment, at the frontier, the bonds of custom are broken and unrestraint is triumphant.' The epigraph serves as an ironic comment on the protagonist's confused and confusing flight from American civilization to the Northern wilderness. At the same time, it characterizes an important structural principle of the narrative which takes the reluctant reader to the 'frontier' of fictional experiment. At this extreme point, the conventions governing mimetic fiction lose their importance and the narrator wins back his freedom of inventing stories.

It is in this 'triumph of unrestraint' that *Gone Indian* deviates from Kroetsch's earlier fiction. Although the narrator of *The Studhorse Man* realizes that the order he imposes upon events by trying to fit together different segments of his story may be faulty, he eventually manages to arrange them in a more or less conclusive sequence. In *Gone Indian*, there are two competing narrators claiming equal credibility. The reader is faced with two versions of events: Sadness's story, recorded on tapes, the transcripts of which occupy half of the book's chapters, and Professor Madham's entirely subjective reconstruction of the recordings which frequently amounts to a fabrication against his better judgment. Although Madham is given the last word in the matter, this fundamental ambiguity prevails to the very end.

In *Gone Indian*, there are two narratives contradicting each other like the two halves of a split personality. The very names of **Mad**ham and **Sad**ness, in fact, suggest that they both have to be seen in a *Doppelgänger*-relationship. The reader's conventional quest for 'meaning' is foiled throughout. Both the unresolved duplicity of the novel's plot and the blatantly obvious unreliability of the interpretations offered function as an ironic critique of the traditional activities of the reader of realistic fiction. 'Imposing an order, that's what readers do,' the author himself stated in an interview.

Robert Kroetsch's *The Studhorse Man* and *Gone Indian* may serve as paradigmatic examples of postmodern narrative in Canada because they take a radical stand against the validity of 'realism' as a method of writing and 'imposing an order' on a chaotic world. In a 1972 interview, Kroetsch reduces realism to a historical concept that has had its day: 'I'm fascinated right now by the effects of moving away from realism—the kinds of freedom you get, and the kinds of truth you get at, by departing from the sterner varieties of realism. I'm not so sure anyone has a 'realistic' experience; it's a literary convention to begin with, the notion of realism. We get a false sense of communion out of that convention.'[14] Even though it is certainly true that Kroetsch's attack on the reality principle and on realism in fiction is indebted to contemporary American models, it has obvious Canadian implications. Most noticeable are the topical allusions throughout his texts. *The Studhorse Man,* for instance, repeatedly puns on the dual meaning of 'mare' in the sense of 'female horse' and Latin 'sea.' 'A mari usque ad mare' is Canada's heraldic device, and Lepage's search for the mare, which takes him from coast to coast across a large part of Canada, resembles an ironic reenactment of a national myth.

At a deeper level, Kroetsch's narrative experiment would seem to be in keeping with the Canadian tradition because it rarely goes to extremes: important epic categories—plot, characters, time and space—are upheld even if deprived of their traditional weight. This adherence to familiar elements is further enhanced by Kroetsch's tendency to use factual fragments in his play with reality. In *The Studhorse Man,* such a point of reference is *The General Stud Book,* the book which Demeter Proudfoot is trying to rewrite. Similarly, in *Gone Indian,* the tape recordings establish an 'objective' framework which remains in force, even if it is contradicted by the novel's plot. Kroetsch's texts keep a subtle balance of structural artifact and unstructured fabulation. Kroetsch himself has called this balance a typical element of the Canadian imagination, distinguishing it from that of Canada's southern neighbors: 'We become fascinated with problems of equilibrium. Americans are interested in expansion.'[15]

There is yet another way in which Kroetsch's concept of post-modernism is closely linked with the specific condition of fiction in Canada and its historical development. Through their structure, Kroetsch's novels cast doubt on the conventional notion that descriptive realism is the 'natural' mode of rendering Canadian reality and of interpreting Canadian 'identity.' Thus, his protest against the 'tyranny of narrative'[16] is not only aimed at the stereotypes of what Northrop Frye called 'formula writing,' which for a long time dominated Canadian fiction, but also at the distortion of an authentic experience of reality by superimposed foreign models. In Kroetsch's view, 'identity' cannot be defined in terms of a series of collective qualities but rather emerges as the ability to speak in one's own voice, the ability of collective self-articulation. 'In a sense,' Kroetsch remarks, 'we haven't got an identity until somebody tells our story. The fiction makes us real.'[17] This seemingly paradoxical statement reverses the usual relationship between reality and fiction. At the same time it indicates that the ironic destruction of realistic narrative is more than just an aesthetic exercise: it is an essential step towards an independent national literature.

In the Canadian perspective, the liberation of the creative imagination runs parallel with the emancipation from foreign literary models and from the sterility of the identity discussion. It is no accident that Kroetsch concentrates on the prairie or pioneer novel as a highly stereotyped form of realistic narrative that had proved fairly resistant to formal innovations. By selecting as target of his attack the 'Canadian myth' of lonely man pitted against the vastness of space and fighting a losing battle against inexorable fate, Kroetsch questions the view that literature merely reflects universal truths, firmly rooted in the soil itself.

IV

A second line of experimental narrative in Canada is represented by Kroetsch's contemporary George Bowering. He concentrates on the history of discovery as another area where the collective experience of Canadians seems to be rigidly codified once and for all. The historical novel as the corresponding literary genre has for a long time, and longer than elsewhere, been regarded in Canada as a quasi-objective medium for recording the past and transforming it into a collective myth. It is this documentary and didactic function of fiction that Bowering's texts address.

Bowering's link with contemporary American literature, through the *Tish* group and its affiliation with the Black Mountain poets, is well known. Like Kroetsch, Bowering has openly acknowledged this influence without feeling impelled to resort to the familiar categories of the Canadian struggle for emancipation from American domination. 'Canadian fiction,' he states, 'is as good, though not as plentiful, as U.S. fiction, and does not suffer by being seen in a North American context.'[18] As writer, university teacher, and coeditor of *Open Letter,* Bowering resembles Kroetsch in his theoretical and practical involvement with avant-garde literature. His essay 'The Painted Window: Notes on Post-Realist Fiction'[19] to date remains one of the comparatively few original contributions to the post-modernist debate in Canada. While summing up current American opinion, it does not explicitly refer to Canadian fiction. Bowering's refusal to recognize 'Canadianness' as a critical category is in line with his supra-national approach to narrative technique.

The essence of Bowering's resolute rejection of conventional realism becomes evident from the conclusion he draws at the end of his essay: 'The modernist novel charted this world we found ourselves in; now the new fiction tries to make contact with creatures living here. In other words, the novel is now saying, "Hey, I'm human, too!" '[20] At first glance, this is little more than a summary of what has by now become a commonplace view. Its style, however, throws an interesting light on Bowering's idiosyncratic way of expressing his opinions and defining his own version of postmodern narrative.

Bowering's novel *Burning Water* (1980) offers the most striking example. Drawing on documentary evidence, the novel describes in considerable detail the expedition undertaken in 1791-1794 by George Vancouver to survey the Northwest Coast of the American continent. The narrator's vivid account of Vancouver's eccentric character, of the various incidents during his voyage, and of his eventual failure to come to terms with an alien reality, provides the deceptive surface of the narrative. Just as Vancouver proves unable to subject this unfamiliar environment to a purely rational grid, so Bowering's novel revolves round the impossibility of charting reality. Like Kroetsch's *The Studhorse Man*, Bowering's *Burning Water* rejects and parodies the elaborate time-scheme which modernists thought necessary. In both novels it is replaced by 'spatial form,' a collage-like series of loosely connected episodes. In *Burning Water*, moreover, the illusion of historical time is not allowed to establish itself. It is continually interrupted by the narrator and his anachronistic intrusions.

Burning Water, as the paradox of the title seems to suggest, tries to demonstrate that the pattern of the historical novel which has tended to codify history is obsolete. The problems Vancouver encounters during his mapping expedition are used as metaphors not only for the inevitable conflict between the rational perspective of the European explorers and the magic world view of the Indian tribes they meet, but also for the inevitable clash between fiction and historical 'truth.' Bowering's text—'a real historical fiction,' as he calls it in the prologue with shrewd ambiguity—only pretends to reconstruct historical patterns like the adventurous struggle of the heroic individual agains the unknown. Fiction creates history, rather than representing and interpreting it. Bowering's remark, '[i]n Canada the only history is writing history,' used as leitmotiv in one of his earlier novels, *A Short Sad Book* (1977),[21] does not only ironically refer to the uneventfulness of Canadian history, but also implies that it is only in the mirror of fiction that history becomes history.

Burning Water focuses on this transformation. In a review of the novel, Chris Scott has summed up the essence of Bowering's text.

Posturing as a conservative critic, he says: 'This is a truly ugly book, ugly in spirit as in appearance . . . a book possessing no authentic voice, no authentic sense of time and place, a book adrift in the author's fancy. . . . Historical novel this ain't, real fiction it is, and how . . .'[22] Scott identifies the destruction of the figment of historical authenticity as the central issue of *Burning Water*. Besides, by parodying certain conventional phrases of contemporary literary criticism, the review offers a rare example of an interpretation 'against interpretation' employing a deliberately subjective style.

Bowering's interpretation of history as fictitious construct, of discovery as invention, and Kroetsch's remark that 'the fiction makes us real,' clearly point in the same direction. Both authors also stress the importance of 'telling' a story. They maintain that the rediscovery of the modes of oral communication must not be seen exclusively in terms of rejecting the established modernist traditions of narrative fiction and the hierarchical universe they reflect. In departing from the mimetic concepts of written literature and reinstating the teller of the tale as the focal point, Canadian post-modernists also see a suitable way of casting off identity clichés imposed from outside. To win back an independent authentic voice, Kroetsch argues that '[t]he Canadian writer must uninvent the word. He must destroy the homonymous American and English languages that keep him from hearing his own tongue. But to uninvent the word, he knows, is to uninvent the world.'[23] Here, the rejection of literary conventions, patterns of thought, and old value systems clearly implies more than a new structure for the narrative text. It becomes a means of giving a new 'voice' to Canadian fiction.

V

The more radical implications of this argument have been explored by other contemporary Canadian authors. Dennis Lee's claim, for instance, comes to mind, that only by withdrawing into silence and by refusing to play the game of mimetic realism, which involves the use of alien forms of thought and communication, will Canadian literature eventually be able to free itself from its colonial heritage. Only by listening to the 'cadence' of space, Lee states, can Canadian writers win through to genuine self-expression: 'To speak unreflectingly in a colony . . . is to use words that speak only alien space. To reflect is to fall silent, discovering that your authentic space does not have words.'[24] Even if one hesitates to agree with such vague mythopoetic conclusions, Lee's statement is a reminder that Canadian postmodernism cannot adequately be judged in purely aesthetic terms. As a reaction against modernism, understood both as a literary period and as a set of borrowed fictional techniques, it has a political dimension.

For the literatures of Europe and the United States, modernism marks a period of supreme artistic achievement. In the literary history of Canada, the same time span emerges at best as a phase of transition. Until well into the fifties, Canadian authors were trying to catch up with international movements. At the same time, they became aware of the secondary role of what is sometimes called a 'client literature.' In recent years, this awareness has become more acute. In discarding the formal conventions of realism, postmodern critics also challenge the leading role of the European/American culture which had reserved a passive and receptive role for a 'young' and less sophisticated literature like that of Canada.

Instead of merely registering the traumatic consequences of this backlog—a prime example of which is Margaret Atwood's *Survival* (1972)—experimental writers have begun to interpret the lack of a fully fledged modern movement in Canadian literature as the ideal starting point for an autonomous Canadian literature. Kroetsch remarks that 'Canadian literature evolved directly from Victorian into Postmodern. Morley Callaghan [Hemingway's contemporary and colleague] went to Paris and met the Modern writers; he, for Canada, experienced the real and symbolic encounter; he, heroically and successfully, resisted. The country that invented Marshall McLuhan and Northrop Frye did so by not ever being Modern.'[25] Seen against this backdrop, Canadian postmodernism, rather than being the Trojan horse of a small group of authors paving the way for another wave of American literary domination, assumes a wider significance. Frank Davey has suggested that only the collapse of modernism as a normative and hierarchical model made it possible for regional and peripheral literatures to thrive: 'The modernist collapse is evident throughout contemporary Canadian writing. . . . The modernists sought to control both their world and their art; the post-modernists seek to participate in anarchic cooperation with the elements of an environment in which no one element fully controls any other. . . . Most of the new Canadian writing of the sixties and seventies has taken process, discontinuity, and organic shape as its values rather than the humanistic ideal of the "well-wrought urn." '[26]

Both Kroetsch and Bowering have contributed their share to this post-European and post-realist discontinuity, nor do they provide the only examples. Much of the fiction written by David Godfrey during the late sixties and early seventies seems to fall into the same category. In his short fiction, notably in the collection *Death Goes Better with Coca-Cola* (1968), and in the novel *The New Ancestors* (1970), Godfrey juxtaposes matter-of-fact report and magic realism in an attempt to use experimental techniques as a vehicle for his anti-colonial and anti-American message. Like the modernists, postmodern writers in Canada use myth as a narrative device rather than as a set of universal images to be reflected in fiction. Unlike the modernists, however, who tended to employ mythical patterns as structuring and controlling principles, contemporary authors have emphasized the a-logical, a-realistic, incoherent, and non-hierarchical qualities of mythical narrative and used it to gain access to older, pre-rational areas of human experience.

If we stretch this definition a little, even Northrop Frye's view of literature as 'conscious mythology' comes somewhat unexpectedly into focus. Literature, Frye has said, 'creates an autonomous world that gives us an imaginative perspective on the actual one.'[27] From this point of view, many contemporary novels—Robertson Davies' *Deptford Trilogy* (1970/72/75), Margaret Laurence's *The Diviners* (1974), Rudy Wiebe's historical novels, e.g., *The Temptations of Big Bear* (1974)—can be seen as contributions towards the creation of a collective myth in the sense described here. Even though they might claim to record a common Canadian past, their importance lies rather in its imaginative projection.

On the basis of the assumption that postmodernism in Canada has to be placed and evaluated in the wider context of a gradual emancipation of Canadian literature, we might draw a few more general if tentative conclusions:

1) Rather than regarding itself as a 'literature of exhaustion,' experimental fiction in Canada sees the exhaustion of hitherto dominating literatures, like American literature, as prerequisite for an independent national literature. Canadian postmodernism, beyond being a purely literary movement, emerges as an integral part of the cultural and political changes taking place in contemporary Canada.

2) Postmodernism in Canada tends to become partly synonymous with 'post-colonialism' or 'post-Europeanism,' coinciding as it does with a new phase in the development of Canadian fiction. In

breaking away from descriptive realism, contemporary writers also dissociate themselves from literary modernism as a form of literary domination as well as from a defeatist concept of literature.[28] The postmodern imagination has developed into an important literary force of the post-survival era.

3) Canadian modernists from Frederick Philip Grove to Hugh MacLennan had stressed that literature should anticipate a national identity, mainly through defining and elaborating national themes—a function frequently biased by a tendency to protect a 'Canadian way of writing' from baneful foreign influences. While contemporary writers like George Bowering and Robert Kroetsch have not entirely abandoned this view, they have modified it by seeking national self-expression through new narrative structures rather than national themes. They adopt these themes freely from international sources and adapt them to domestic uses. Thus, fiction as an imaginative 'invention of the world'[29] may contribute to a national identity—not through its referential function, but through the productive force of the creative act itself.

University of Trier, Federal Republic of Germany

---

[1]This essay is a revised and expanded version of a paper read at the Xth Congress of the International Comparative Literature Association, New York University, August 1982.

[2]Borges' remark is quoted in John Robert Colombo, *Concise Canadian Quotations* (Edmonton: Hurtig, 1976), p. 31.

[3]Dick Harrison, ed., *Crossing Frontiers: Papers in American and Canadian Western Literature* (Edmonton: Univ. of Alberta Press, 1979). Cf. also the special issue on 'Canadian-American Literary Relations' of *Essays on Canadian Writing*, 22 (1981).

[4]John Barth, 'The Literature of Exhaustion,' *Atlantic Monthly*, 220 (August 1967), pp. 29-34; Ihab Hassan, *The Dismemberment of Orpheus: Toward a Postmodern Literature* (New York: Oxford Univ. Press, 1971).

[5]Ronald Sukenick, *The Death of the Novel and Other Stories* (New York: Dial, 1969), p. 41.

[6]As Linda Hutcheon (whose study *Narcissistic Narrative: The Metafictional Paradox* [1980] is a prime example of Canadian critical response to the postmodernist debate) has pointed out, parody integrates the parodied text into the new norm; parodic art both deviates from a literary norm and includes that norm without itself as a background ('Parody without Ridicule: Observations on Modern Literature Parody,' *Canadian Review of Comparative Literature*, 5, 2 (1978), 204). I owe this reference (and several other useful suggestions) to Martin Kuester's unpublished thesis 'Narrative Structure in the Contemporary Canadian Novel' (Trier, 1983).

[7]Interview with John Hawkes, *Wisconsin Studies in Contemporary Literature*, 6, 2 (Summer 1965), p. 154.

[8]John Barth, *The Sot-Weed Factor* (New York: Grosset & Dunlap, 1966), p. 793. ('The author apologizes to his readers; the laureate composes his epitaph.')

[9]Geoffrey Hancock, 'Here and Now: Innovation and Change in the Canadian Short Story,' *Canadian Fiction Magazine*, 27 (1977), pp. 4-22.

[10]In his more recent novels, notably in *What the Crow Said* (1978), Kroetsch appears to have turned to magic realism as an alternative form of experimental fiction.

[11]Kroetsch, *The Studhorse Man* (New York: Simon and Schuster, 1969), p. 94.

[12]*Ibid.*, pp. 138-39.

[13]Laurie Ricou, 'Field Notes and Notes in a Field: Forms of the West in Robert Kroetsch and Tom Robbins,' *Journal of Canadian Studies*, 17, 3 (1982), p. 120.

[14]Donald Cameron, 'Robert Kroetsch: The American Experience and the Canadian Voice,' *Journal of Canadian Fiction*, 1, 3 (1972), p. 48.

[15]*Ibid.*, p. 49.

[16]Geoffrey Hancock, 'An Interview with Robert Kroetsch,' *Canadian Fiction Magazine*, 24/25 (1977), p. 43.

[17]Kroetsch et al., *Creation* (Toronto: New Press, 1970), p. 63.

[18]George Bowering, 'True North Home and Fiction,' *The Mask in Place: Essays on Fiction in North America* (Winnipeg: Turnstone, 1982), p. 1.

[19]Bowering, 'The Painted Window: Notes on Post-Realist Fiction,' *University of Windsor Review*, 13, 2 (1978), pp. 24-36.

[20]*Ibid.*, pp. 35 ff.

[21]Bowering, *A Short Sad Book* (Vancouver: Talonbooks, 1977), p. 76.

[22]*Books in Canada* 9, 9 (November 1980), p. 9.

[23]Kroetsch, 'A Canadian Issue,' *Boundary 2*, 3, 1 (1974), p. 1.

[24]Dennis Lee, 'Cadence, Country, Silence: Writing in Colonial Space,' *Boundary 2*, 3, 1 (1974), p. 163.

[25]Kroetsch, 'A Canadian Issue,' p. 1. Cf. *Labyrinths of Voice: Conversations with Robert Kroetsch*, eds. Shirley Neuman and Robert Wilson (Edmonton: NeWest Press, 1982), pp. 111 ff.

[26]Frank Davey, 'Introduction,' *From There to Here* (Erin, Ontario: Press Porcepic, 1974), pp. 20 ff.

[27]Northrop Frye, 'Conclusion to a *Literary History of Canada*,' *The Bush Garden: Essays on the Canadian Imagination* (Toronto: Anansi, 1971), p. 235.

[28]Linda Sandler, 'Interview with Margaret Atwood,' in *Malahat Review*, 41 (1977), p. 22.

[29]Jack Hodgins' *The Invention of the World* (1977) might also have been considered in the postmodern context.

Jürgen Schäfer

A FAREWELL TO EUROPE: RUDY WIEBE'S *THE TEMPTATIONS OF BIG BEAR* AND ROBERT KROETSCH'S *GONE INDIAN*

In his various disguises the Indian of Western literature has remained an alien, vacillating between the conflicting images of hellish fiend and noble savage, between Shakespeare's Caliban and Chateaubriand's Chactas.[1] In the New World these European projections of Christian zeal and enlightened utopianism were occasionally modified and adapted, but increasing contacts during the 18th and 19th centuries, mostly of a hostile nature, did little to change the literary reflection. With regard to Canadian literature Leslie Monkman's comprehensive survey has recently confirmed the continuity of this image.[2] In 1975 Norman Newton could still maintain that Canadian authors had persistently used the concept of 'wilderness' in order to evade what he called 'the intellectual history of our country,' identifying it as preponderantly Indian.[3]

The paradox of Newton's statement lies in postulating a continuity by adopting a radically different stance. His surprising view, sweepingly rejecting the European tradition of Canadian culture and civilization, would have been unthinkable a generation ago and can be understood only as deliberately provocative. It is indicative of a radical break with former values, a new readiness to bridge a chasm of two solitudes next to which MacLennan's proverbial division appears as a shallow ford. This new image of the Indian did not gradually evolve from the noble savage or Indian hero,[4] celebrated perhaps more warmly in Canadian than in American literature because of historical alliances. The figure of Tecumseh may have remained a handy stick with which to belabor the United States for more than a hundred years but even Charles Mair's glowing dramatic tribute indicates more than once that basic differences between white man and red man remain; it is surely one of the ironies of Canadian literary history that the drama castigating the Americans for dispossessing Tecumseh's tribe was published one year after the Northwest Insurrection of 1885. The most recent literary image of the Indian has shed these separate-but-equal provisos and emphasizes not so much positive or even ideal values, but identity in a common humanity and a common Canadianness. This drastic change entails a new national consciousness: Canadian history suddenly begins to extend backwards beyond the first white settlers; there is a continuity of the Indian past no longer preserved in place names only but also cultivated in memory and fictionalized in literature.

The reasons for this intricate and ongoing process are still difficult to assess. On the national level there seems to be a connection with the political crisis of the sixties, the further separation from Britain, and the new emphasis on multiculturalism. On a universal level the change is apparently due to a new ecological awareness viewing the trend towards total urbanization with dismay, to the teachings of structural anthropology devaluating the traditional Western concept of civilization, and to a general emancipation from European concepts, observable also in other parts of the globe. Among the various literary works imaginatively conceiving this radically new image of the Canadian Indian two novels have been selected for exemplification: Rudy Wiebe's *The Temptations of Big Bear* and Robert Kroetsch's *Gone Indian*. They are the works of two major contemporary novelists who develop this new approach to the Indian convincingly, although they pursue very different themes, employ contrasting narrative techniques, and have chosen the diametrically opposed modes of comedy and tragedy. Yet they are also exponents, perhaps unintentionally, of a new ideology assigning the red man a role of paramount significance in Canadian consciousness.

When I first read Rudy Wiebe's *The Temptations of Big Bear* several years ago I was struck with certain similarities in theme and concept between this Canadian novel and *Things Fall Apart* (1958), the first novel of the Nigerian author Chinua Achebe,[5] considered one of the most impressive works in Anglo-African fiction. To be sure, the Nigerian novel is very different. It is a comparatively slender work of less than 200 pages, much simpler in narrative technique than Wiebe's multiperspectival study and, of course, it presents a very different geographical setting. Yet parallels there are and, it seems to me, significant ones.

As in *The Temptations of Big Bear*, the theme of *Things Fall Apart* is the destruction of an indigenous culture through its clash with advancing Western civilization before the historical background of the colonization of the Ibo country in the 1880s. This chronological parallel is a mere coincidence, but adds piquancy to the comparison: the Cree and the Ibo suffer the expansion of the British Empire at the same time. Both novels stress the uniqueness and the wholeness of the doomed societies. Neither Achebe nor Wiebe depict noble savages in an unearthly paradise; both authors point out blemishes and moral failings, superstitious exposure of twins in Iboland, for example, or ruthless raids among Indian tribes. Yet there is the same profound respect towards these aboriginal communities and, at the end of both novels, a feeling of irreplaceable loss, the sense that mankind is all the poorer for the destruction of these traditional ways of life. Both novels give point and focus to this traumatic experience in the figure of a leader alienated from his own people. Big Bear's analogue is the dignified Okonkwo, less wise than his Indian contemporary in his futile resistance against the white invader, but also attaining tragic stature in his fight against the decree of history.

Again, there are conspicuous differences between the Nigerian and the Canadian work of fiction. Wiebe, like Shakespeare in his histories, has filtered historical figures through his personal vision; Okonkwo and his tribe, though based on Achebe's careful ethnographic studies, are fictitious. Wiebe's throng of Indians, Metis, and whites is much reduced in the Nigerian novel; Achebe's whites are restricted to two missionaries, Mr. Brown and Mr. Smith, and a nameless District Commissioner. The narrator's bitter irony, however, stresses mutual incomprehension and is identical in both narratives. The official busybodiness of Big Bear's trial, ludicrous against the monumental death of Indian society, has its poignant counterpart in the District Commissioner's readily transforming Okonkwo's suicide into an interesting paragraph for his work in progress, 'The Pacification of the Primitive Tribes of the Lower Niger.'

These similarities deserve further comment. Achebe is no simple historian, no indifferent archivist of a past dead and forgotten, nor is he a mere ethnographer telling the fascinating tale of an exotic people before the flood of Western colonization. Achebe, himself an Ibo who proved a committed patriot in the Biafran war, is writing about his own people, trying to connect an ambiguous present with the roots of the past. *Things Fall Apart* maintains a delicate balance between the national particular and a philosophic universal: the title, taken from William Butler Yeats' 'The Second Coming,' transforms the Ibo colonization trauma into a symbol of the alienation of modern man. This dual aspect also characterizes Wiebe's novel.

He begins by establishing with great care the temporal dimension of *The Temptations of Big Bear*. On the surface, its calendar limits are precisely delineated: twelve years from the signing of Treaty No. 6 on September 13, 1876, to the death of the hero on January 17, 1888. But the ineluctable progress of these historical events is interspersed with characteristic scenes from traditional Indian life: the initiation raid of the young warriors, the buffalo hunt, the thirst dance. Dialectically, Wiebe has fused this timeless world with the irruption of history: on their return the braves encounter Government surveyors; the buffalo hunt is the last, since the white man has destroyed the herds; the thirst dance is interrupted by the news of an ominous incident. This superimposition of timeless recurrence on historical moment makes Big Bear and his Cree the quintessential symbol of all Indian life since time immemorial. Their destruction is not a negligible episode in Canadian expansion to the West, but a tragic event of national magnitude.

Despite the evocation of these dimensions the Indian figures retain their human proportions; there is no hint of operatic grandeur, of Wagnerian heroics. The traditional alien image can be discarded since Wiebe insists on our common humanity: 'In every way that's important [the Indians] are exactly the same as you and me.'[6] He makes us identify with the Indians and experience their fatal entry into history through their eyes. For this purpose he alienates us, not so much from the Whites and Métis who have traditionally lived in the West, the missionaries and priests, traders and trappers, but from the intruders from the East. There are a few fictitious documents, in particular young Kitty McLean's engaging captivity narrative, whose intimate and sympathetic view of Big Bear is diametrically opposed to the hostile stuffiness of the genuine reports;[7] but on the whole the reader's identification is achieved by other means: the appeal of the Indians' plain and simple speech, their love of nature, and their innate religiousness. Colorful exoticism is eschewed in favor of biblical pithiness and Christian imagery. The cumulative effect, vital in our context, is the integration of the Indian experience into a pan-Canadian consciousness with the Indian as the true preserver of those values professed but not practised by the white man.

On a stylo-linguistic level the speciousness of the white arguments is brought out by a dual strategy. The natural eloquence of Big Bear, his biblical cadences, the simplicity and clarity of his speeches contrast sharply with the aridity and callousness of the white historical documents, so profusely integrated into the narrative. The continuous ironic commentary on official policy is highlighted by the desperate attempts of the translators to bridge the chasm between two sets of values. In view of the ultimate deprivation and degradation of the Indian the repeated reference to the British monarch as the grandmother of her red children appears as a diabolic perversion of the biblical father concept.

Wiebe's second element, his merging of the Indian into the Canadian landscape, has frequently been noted. He has told us how much his belated awareness of being born and growing up in an area once roamed by Big Bear and his Cree has affected him. There is a shared belief in the land as God's legacy to man, even though a farmer's son will look at it differently than a buffalo hunter. One of the most impressive examples of this inseparableness is the unification of Big Bear with the Canadian soil at the end of the novel: 'Slowly, slowly, all changed continually into indistinguishable, as it seemed, and everlasting, unchanging, rock.'[8] Even more surprising is Wiebe's effortless conversion of the CPR, the celebrated symbol of Canadian unity, into a sinister monster, permanently dividing and destroying the natural habitat of man and buffalo.

The most significant means of identifying with the Indian point of view is through the insistence on their religious faith. Wiebe is a religious author in a concrete Christian sense, deeply influenced by his Mennonite roots: 'I would like to think of myself as someone who's trying to live what the original Anabaptists were about.... To be an Anabaptist is to be a radical follower of the person of Jesus Christ.'[9] There may be a general readiness to side with the persecuted, and one may see a particular parallel between the brutal expropriation of the Russian Mennonites depicted in *The Blue Mountains of China* and the dispossession of the Indians at the hands of the white administration; but these elements of natural empathy are far surpassed by the radical, conscious step of depicting the Indians, heathens still and far from conversion despite intense missionary efforts, in terms of Christian imagery. The very title evokes the extreme condition of the Christian hero confronting a triad of temptations—to sign the treaty, to take up arms, and, finally, to despair, the greatest possible sin in Christian theology—and strongly suggests an analogy to the three temptations of Christ in the wilderness. While these christological aspects are reinforced by sun imagery and by suggestions of expiation and resurrection,[10] the natural religiousness of the whole Indian community, their belief in the Only One, is repeatedly stressed, most pointedly in the detailed rendering of the thirst dance. Wiebe's Indians are no saints; the confusion and carnage of the Frog Lake Massacre is faced squarely in one of the most dramatic sections of the novel. They are sinful men, yet capable of redemption. Their readiness to relate their whole existence, each and every act, to the Divinity, impresses itself upon the reader. There is a mystic communion with the land which contrasts stridently with the attitude of the new settlers and entrepreneurs.

A poignant example is to be found at the beginning of the novel when John McDougall, son and successor of a devoted Methodist missionary, reports a conversation with a certain Shaw who is to become a founder of the Alberta ranching industry: 'John your father's gone. You surely won't remain in missionary work any longer. This land's all empty, look at it. I see nothing but progress here from now on, so let's work together in the stock business, you on this side of the mountains and I on the other. I'll give you half my stock right now' (p. 48). Seemingly innocent words hide Wiebe's multitiered irony. Down to its diction, here is the essence of the Victorian success story in Canada: *empty land, stock business, progress.* We feel revulsion, however, because we have already been taught to see the ambiguity of this message. The land is empty because the buffalo, the sustenance of the Indian, has been killed; it is also empty because the Indian, his soul and his prayer, is departing. The unfeeling callousness of Shaw's well-meant offer is surpassed by the irony of several biblical allusions, the most pertinent to Jesus' recruiting Simon and Andrew at the sea of Galilee: 'And he saith unto them, Follow me, and I will make you fishers of men' (Matthew 4.19). Wiebe's fisher of men is to be recruited by the Antichrist to dance round the golden calf. If we feel alienated in this novel, it is from Shaw and his gospel of progress.

At first glance Rudy Wiebe's *The Temptations of Big Bear* and Robert Kroetsch's *Gone Indian* seem to have little in common except the fact that both works were published in 1973. Wiebe has written a long epic on the final defeat of the Cree Indians in the historic Northwest Insurrection; Kroetsch, in a short and clever novel, sets out to relate the mad pranks of a picaresque hero in our times. Wiebe's tone is solemn, Kroetsch's farcical. Big Bear, the leader of a doomed people, is a figure of heroic proportion and develops tragic dimensions; Jeremy Sadness is an irresponsible American graduate student who will never finish his dissertation but will continue instead to gratify his promiscuous tastes, conveniently supported by his long-suffering wife. *The Temptations of Big Bear* is a closely textured historical novel, fairly traditional in its narrative structure despite its many points of view; *Gone Indian* is a postmodern construct, set in a realistic world precariously bordering on the surreal, whose fast-moving plot and characters constantly seem to elude the reader's grasp.

It is, therefore, significant that *Gone Indian* can be seen as another attempt to integrate the Indian dimension into Canadian consciousness. As part of Kroetsch's prairie tryptich 'Out West' the novel has a special temporal dimension. *The Words of My Roaring* (1966) dealt with the period of the Great Depression; the two following novels reached simultaneously further forward in time and backward in history. *The Studhorse Man* (1968), set immediately after World War II, harks back to the twenties, whereas *Gone Indian* relates the urbanized present to the prairies prior to white settlement. The Indian tradition is embraced, albeit in a way different from Wiebe's concentration on the moment if historic clash; there is a structuralist synthesis on the mythic level.

The hero's frantic search for his identity provides the basic structure of *Gone Indian*. Its pervasive irony, expressed in the ambiguous title, lies in the fact that Jeremy, named after the utilitarian philosopher Bentham and born and bred in Manhattan, is inspired by his juvenile enthusiasm for Grey Owl. This historic figure, the Englishman Archibald Belaney (1888-1938), best-selling author of seemingly authentic Indian stories during the thirties, was a fake who disappeared into the Canadian wilderness and reemerged a full-blooded Indian.[11] Questionable identities dominate the Canadian scene of *Gone Indian* from the moment Jeremy arrives at Edmonton International Airport and witnesses a transvestite being stripped by police, but this leitmotif of deceptive appearances does not invalidate the Indian theme nor Jeremy's genuine desire to be transformed into 'the truest Indian of them all.'[12] In contrast to Belaney who merely posed as an Indian and confirmed the child-of-nature cliché in his stories, Kroetsch's hero encounters reality, past and present, in an apocalyptic vision of the return of the Indians with their buffalo to wreak a Wellsian destruction on Edmonton, and in Mr. and Mrs. Beaver, a Cree and Blackfoot couple, with their unruly children, stinking dogs, and battered pick-up truck. What is more, Jeremy begins to discover his Indian identity in the ecstatic experience of his first snowshoe race. Indian and buffalo whom he had seen frozen in time, i.e., carved in ice for the winter festival of fictitious Notikeewin, come alive in this epiphany: 'I swear I could smell the blood of a buffalo jump: right there in those hills the Cree and the Blackfoot drove the unknown herds to a fatal leap' (p. 85). Since he refuses to identify himself as a white after his victory and begins to speak in a strange tongue, he is taken for an Indian, beaten up by envious white competitors and left unconscious. He is restored by the Cree/Blackfoot couple who help him into Indian clothes. He discovers that in discarding his jacket he has also literally thrown away the keys to his past, his various mistresses, his university office, his apartment and his typewriter; his final transformation is completed in a dream vision. After the destruction of Western civilization he is significantly renamed Has-Two-Chances by Poundmaker, and the cause of his embarrassing sexual handicap is finally revealed: he can make love only while standing up because he identifies with the bull of Indian legend uniting with the beautiful buffalo woman. Bit by bit his old identity, clothes, habits, name, have all been stripped away and his Indian core has been laid bare; even the opening sentence of his dissertation, 'Christopher Columbus, not knowing that he had not come to the Indies' (p. 21), gains a new meaning in retrospect. Jeremy is completing the discovery of the Indian, imperfectly understood by the original emissary from the East, in his own person.

Together with his doctoral advisor, Professor Madham, a native Canadian who is editing and commenting on the tapes that Jeremy sent to him before mysteriously disappearing in the Northwest, we could, of course, dismiss Jeremy's new self-awareness as ludicrous self-deception. We realize, however, that Madham, who left the Canadian Northwest for the peace and safety of the ivory tower of the State University at Binghamton, is deeply disturbed by Jeremy's bold and determined crossing of the final frontier: he is an unreliable narrator. More radically, we could dismiss the novel itself as a mere virtuoso display of postmodern structuralist technique, its sense and message ultimately disappearing in a maelstrom of symbols, myths, and crazily intersecting points of view.[13] We know, however, that fragmentation and dissolution of character and plot are characteristic traits of the postmodern novel; as in absurd drama, the grotesque is an essential part of the genre, not a sign of the author's personal frivolousness.

Even though the novel remains open-ended and Jeremy's indianization necessarily lacks structural linearity, there can be no question that *Gone Indian* is about alienation and identity, Western and Indian consciousness. Admittedly, this contrast is occasionally broadened, especially in the emphasis on shamanism, to include the traditional dichotomy between oriental mysticism and occidental rationality. There is also the specifically Canadian image of a 'Northern Utopia,' 'where men and women in flight from . . . the decadent and sterile values of the "South" may seek a heightened self-awareness.'[14] Structurally, too, there are non-Indian elements: the white, but equally mythic double love triangle between Jeremy and the elder Dorck, the Notikeewin winter king, on the one side, and Bea Sunderman, the earth mother, and her daughter Jill on the other side; there is also the ambiguous son-father relationship between Jeremy and Madham. Among the various themes and structural elements, however, the idea of a Canadian fusion of Western and Indian identity and the discovery of the Indian tradition on Canadian soil are clearly predominant. Professor Madham's persistent efforts to cut and censor Jeremy's tale of symbolism and dream vision, his insistence on having successfully lived down his own Indian encounters, ultimately reveal his desperate attempt to repress a truth uncomfortable for Western rationality: the Indian spiritual tradition has to be absorbed by the white settler on Canadian soil.

So that they can detach themselves from experiences British or American, but not authentically Canadian, hidden in language and literary tradition, Robert Kroetsch has suggested to his fellow writers a radical 'uninvention' of the Canadian past.[15] A significant part of this uninvention consists in the incorporation of the Indian past into Canadian consciousness not as an alien graft, but as ur-Canadian, as the quintessence of Canadianness. In the present search for a new identity, for roots and ancestors, this Indian past has suddenly assumed a new grandeur, far removed indeed from what Wiebe has called the drunken Indian bums and thieves of the Depression novel.[16] This approach cannot be seen as a mere effort at local color, nor is it identical with what Leslie Fiedler, in his fascinating study of the image of the Indian in American literature, has called 'the higher sentimentality,' referring to fiction with the premise 'if one is White, he should do his best to go Native.'[17] There is no possibility of return to the simpler ways of the past. Neither Wiebe's nor Kroetsch's novel is a guide to building better campfires. The buffalo are dead and gone and will not return. Accepting this historical reality, both novels present not a celebration of nostalgic primitivism but an imaginative evocation of the Indian past as a new and significant dimension of Canadian history.

Aristotle realized that the advantage of the poet over the historian lies in the poet's freedom to narrate what might have happened.[18] We may be less certain nowadays that a historian, even with the best of intentions and the greatest scholarly endeavor, is able to arrive at an unprejudiced view of any particular period of history,[19] but we certainly subscribe to Aristotle's view of the poet. As Rudy Wiebe put it when working on *The Temptations of Big Bear:* 'The advantage a fiction writer has is that right from the beginning he doesn't pretend that he has *the* authentic account of what happened. He goes in and shows you, This is the way I see it, as it could have happened.'[20] It is indeed irrelevant whether this new role of the Indian in the national myth is reconcilable with historical research. We are dealing with an image, a fictive account of the role of the red man in white imagination. This does not preclude the possibility that this image, if it gains further strength, might influence both Canadian historiography[21] and Canadian society. To meet a national need the effort is directed towards constructing a usable past on foundations hitherto neglected, to sink firm roots into the continent of choice whilst the bridges to Europe are being dismantled.

This complex cultural and emotional process is not without precedent. In the European history of literature and ideas two major movements in establishing and interpreting national identity can be distinguished. The first extended from the Renaissance to the Neoclassic period and is characterized by the desire to imitate and attain the perfection of the authors of classical antiquity, to absorb their literary culture. In England this attitude can be documented from the dominating influence of Senecan revenge tragedy on Elizabethan dramatists to Pope's imitations of Horace's satires. At the very apex of this development there was a revulsion from the classic tradition and a sudden desire to discover one's roots not in distant Mediterranean countries but on native soil in a past once considered uncouth and barbaric. Percy's *Reliques of Ancient English Poetry*, Macpherson's, Gray's and Chatterton's celebrations of Nordic doom, complete with raven, battle-axe and Valkyrie, pointed the way to a radically different understanding of the national past and its cultural heritage.[22] It is not implied that history simply repeats itself—anthropological structuralism is more than romanticism revived—nor that adapted European patterns will forever shape the intellectual development of Canada. But is there not a certain analogy present here? There are innumerable differences between Gray's and Chatterton's Norsemen and Wiebe's and Kroetsch's Indians, but these writers do have in common an unexpected poetic revaluation of the past. Dick Harrison has seen the basic problem of prairie fiction as the dichotomy between the 'new land' and the 'old, i.e., European, culture.'[23] The evocation of the Indian past, however, reverses these patronizing assumptions about virgin soil and superior European civilization. The new land is really the old land, and the European newcomers will not have completed their Canadianization until they have absorbed the traditions of their old/new country.

University of Augsburg, Federal Republic of Germany

---

[1]See the complementary studies by H. N. Fairchild, *The Noble Savage: A Study in Romantic Naturalism* (New York: Columbia Univ. Press, 1928), and E. Dudley and M. E. Novak (eds.), *The Wild Man Within: An Image in Western Thought from the Renaissance to Romanticism* (Pittsburgh: Univ. of Pittsburgh Press, 1972). Historically, Shakespeare's Caliban is to be seen in the classic/medieval concept of the 'wild man,' but modern critics have repeatedly emphasized the Indian image; cf. G. W. Knight, 'Caliban as Red Man,' *Shakespeare's Styles: Essays in Honour of Kenneth Muir*, ed. P. Edwards et al. (Cambridge: Cambridge Univ. Press, 1980), pp. 205-20.

[2]*A Native Heritage: Images of the Indian in English-Canadian Literature* (Toronto: Univ. of Toronto Press, 1981). It is a basic weakness of this otherwise valuable study that little attempt is made to relate the images isolated in Canadian literature to European (and American) forebears and parallels.

[3]'Wilderness No Wilderness,' *Canadian Literature*, 63 (Winter 1975), p. 20; cf. also David Williams, 'The Indian Our Ancestor,' *Dalhousie Review*, 58 (1978), pp. 309-28.

[4]The thematic categories of Monkman's last two chapters tend to obscure this radical break.

[5]On Achebe cf. C. L. Innes and Bernth Lindfors, (eds.), *Critical Perspectives on Chinua Achebe* (London: Heinemann, 1979); David Carroll, *Chinua Achebe* (London: Macmillan, 1980); Robert M. Wren, *Achebe's World: The Historical and Cultural Context of the Novels of Chinua Achebe* (Washington, D. C.: Three Continents Press, 1980).

[6]Donald Cameron, *Conversations with Canadian Novelists, Part Two* (Toronto: Macmillan, 1973), p. 151.

[7]Cf. the historical captivity narratives by Theresa Gowanlock and Theresa Delaney in *The Frog Lake 'Massacre': Personal Perspectives on Ethnic Conflict*, ed. Stuart Hughes (Toronto: Carleton, 1976), pp. 168-242.

[8]*The Temptations of Big Bear* (Toronto: McClelland and Stewart, 1976), p. 415. Subsequent references appear in the essay.

[9]Cameron, *Conversations*, p. 148.

[10]Further christological analogies and allusions are detailed in Glenn Meeter, 'Rudy Wiebe: Spatial Form and Christianity in *The Blue Mountains of China* and *The Temptations of Big Bear*,' *Essays on Canadian Writing*, 22 (Summer 1981), pp. 57-58.

[11]Cf. Lovat Dickson, *Wilderness Man: The Strange Story of Grey Owl* (London: Macmillan, 1974).

[12]Robert Kroetsch, *Gone Indian* (Toronto: New Press, 1973), p. 94. Subsequent references appear in the essay.

[13]For a courageous attempt at an all-embracing analysis cf. Robert Lecker, 'Caught in the Balance: Robert Kroetsch's *Gone Indian*,' *The American Review of Canadian Studies*, 13, 3 (1983), pp. 139-56.

[14]Allison Mitcham, 'Northern Utopia,' *Canadian Literature*, 63 (Winter 1975), p. 35; the concept is illustrated with examples from Roy, Atwood, Horwood, Jasmin, Kreisel and Thériault.

[15]Cf. Kroetsch, 'Unhiding the Hidden: Recent Canadian Fiction,' *Journal of Canadian Fiction*, 3, 3 (1974), pp. 43-45.

[16]George Melnyk, 'The Western Canadian Imagination: An Interview with Rudy Wiebe,' *Canadian Fiction Magazine*, 12 (1974), p. 30.

[17]Leslie Fiedler, *The Return of the Vanishing American* (London: Jonathan Cape, 1968), p. 169. Fiedler's study also makes clear two major components of the Indian image missing in Canada, the threat (both generally and specifically sexual) to the white woman, and the constantly interfering image of the American Black.

[18]*Poetics*, IX, pp. 1-3.

[19]Cf. studies like R. G. Collingwood, *The Idea of History* (Oxford: Clarendon, 1948), or W. B. Gallie, *Philosophy and the Historical Understanding* (New York: Schocken, 1968), as expressions of modern scepticism.

[20]Cameron, *Conversations*, p. 152.

[21]An interesting example of historiography following the lead of literature is John L. Tobias, 'Canada's Subjugation of the Plains Cree, 1879-1885,' *Canadian Historical Review*, 64 (1983), pp. 519-48, who explores the old myth of Canada's just and honorable Indian policy.

[22]Frank E. Farley's magisterial study, *Scandinavian Influences in the English Romantic Movement* (1903), has been recently supplemented by Margaret Omberg, *Scandinavian Themes in English Poetry, 1760-1800* (Stockholm: Almqvist & Wiksell, 1976); cf. also Edward Snyder, *The Celtic Revival in English Literature, 1760-1800* (Cambridge, Mass.: Harvard Univ. Press, 1923).

[23]Dick Harrison, *Unnamed Country: The Struggle for a Canadian Prairie Fiction* (Edmonton: Univ. of Alberta Press, 1977), pp. ix, xiii.

Franz K. Stanzel

TEXTS RECYCLED: 'FOUND' POEMS FOUND IN CANADA

'The world exists to end in a book'
(Mallarmé, quoted by Colombo)

'Out of the garbage, into The Book'
(Andy Warhol)

Until recently the borderline separating nonliterary texts from literary texts—poems, plays, fiction—was strictly maintained. Consequently, there was little traffic between the two realms. Any text wishing to pass from the nonliterary to the literary side of the border was required to show its literary credentials: the fictionality of what it had to communicate or a special use of language, language used with a 'poetic function' in the sense suggested by Roman Jakobson. Since modernist and postmodernist critics have begun to call the validity of these credentials into question, the guards at the border have become quite negligent; as a result, more and more texts now pass daily from the nonliterary side into the realm of literature. One of the most fascinating trespassers over the once so well-guarded line is 'found' poetry, poetry not written by a poet but found, that is to say, taken from a nonliterary context and printed in the traditional format of poetry. Louis Dudek defines found poetry as follows: 'the found poem is really a piece of realistic literature, in which significance appears inherent in the object—either as extravagant absurdity or as unexpected worth. It is like driftwood, or pop art, where natural objects and utilitarian objects are seen as the focus of generative form or meaning.'[1]

What in poetry happened only recently had happened earlier in the arts. The vogue of the 'objet trouvé,' a direct offspring of the Dada movement, inspired Marcel Duchamps to present a urinoir or a bottle dryer as a work of art or caused Pablo Picasso to mount a piece of stove pipe on a wooden block and call it 'La Vénus de Gaz.' Dada, Pop Art, Junk Sculpture and similar movements in modern art have exploited this vogue 'to pillage the culture of the past and the present' as John Robert Colombo says, mainly with the purpose of 'shocking the bourgeois public which idolized Art.'[2] But 'épater le bourgeois' is, as we shall see, only one of the functions of found poetry; there are others, more important perhaps because more germane to poetry itself.

Found poetry, achieving its effect chiefly by typographical, that is to say, visual means, has its opposite in pure sound poetry. Concrete poetry could be considered a combination of the visuality of found poetry and the acoustic patterning as attempted by pure sound poetry. Compared to the radically experimental character of concrete poetry, found poems appear traditional in their sober reaching out for non-esoteric meaning which can also be comprehended by a larger reading audience. Its main orientation is not towards surrealism but rather towards realism. In fact, many if not most of the found poems, certainly most of those produced by Canadian writers, belong to documentary literature, employing historical or social documents as literature.[3]

In order to show how found poetry is embedded in contemporary experimental poetry I shall try to sketch out a typology of the various forms of found poems. Our typological scale begins with works which are more or less photographic reproductions of fragments of a text taken randomly from a historical document, a page of newspaper, a political leaflet, an advertisement, etc. Found poems near this end of our scale have an affinity with Surrealism, Cubism and especially Dada, with its aesthetic glorification of the 'objet trouvé,' a thing deprived of its original functionality and dislocated from its former environment, such as Picasso's stove pipe. The most extravagant example of such a literary 'objet trouvé' is Peter Handke's 'Die Aufstellung des 1. F. C. Nurnberg vom 27.1.1968' which consists of nothing but the formation of one of the top German soccer teams for a match played on a certain day. It is to be found in his collection of found and original poems entitled *Die Innenwelt der Aussenwelt der Innenwelt*.[4] The English translation of this book omits this celebrated piece.[5] Another item in the same volume is called 'Japanese Hit Parade of May 25, 1968.' In this case only the title required translation, the hits and the names of the bands enumerated are part of the international 'lingua franca' of the pop music or jazz scene today:

The Japanese Hit Parade of May 25, 1968

1
HANA NO KUBIZAKARI/GINGA NO ROMANCE
Tigers

2
KOI NO SHIZUKU
Ito Yukari
3
MASSACHUSETTS
Bee Gees
4
YUBE NO HIMITSU
Ogawa Tomoko
5
KAMISAMA ONEGAI
Tempters
6
KANASHIKUTE YARIKERENAI (UNBEARABLE SAD)
Folk Crusade
7
HOSHIKAGE NO WALTZ
Sen Masao
. . .
18
LOVE IS BLUE (L'AMOUR EST BLEU)
Paul Mariat [sic]
19
DAYDREAM BELIEVER
Monkees
20
AMAIRO NO KAMI NO OTOME (ON THE WINDY HILL)
Village Singers
   (*Innerworld,* pp. 95f. and 98)

A Canadian example of this type, characterized by the radical
exploitation of the 'objet trouvé,' is Eli Mandel's 'First Political
Speech,' discussed further on in this article.

The kind of found poem which comes next in our typology is the
found poem proper. Its distinctive characteristic is again the
authentic reproduction of a nonliterary text, but this time with a
rearrangement of the lines according to the typographical format of
traditional poetry, as in the following example from Frank R. Scott:

The Beaver

The beaver
is a most respectable animal
but he is also a type
of unvarying instincts
and Old World traditions.
He does not improve,
and becomes extinct
rather than change his ways.
    (Sir William Dawson, 1863, quoted in *Saturday Night*,
    Jan. 1967)[6]

Scott reprints the text of his prose source literally, adds a title, and breaks the lines as is usual in traditional poetry. Less obvious in this found poem is the use of what Barbara Herrnstein-Smith[7] calls closure. Closure, as used here, means the selection of a certain number of lines from a longer text and the consequent rounding off or encapsulating of the selected section into a new and self-contained unit.

There is finally the form combining documentary or found and composed material. This combination is usually achieved by the technique of montage or collage. Collage originated in Cubist painting and sculpture but was adopted into literature, usually under the name of montage. T. S. Eliot's *The Waste Land*[8] and James Joyce's *Ulysses*[9] make conspicuous use of this technique. Much of the textual material incorporated into *The Waste Land* consists of literary quotations, whereas the found poems considered here rarely quote literary sources; more often they incorporate documentary or nonliterary textual material. The method of montage is employed most conspicuously in the longer found or documentary poems. Robert Kroetsch uses montage in *The Ledger* and *Seed Catalogue*[10] in order to weld together original and found poems, poems and prose, historical documents and literary sources.

I shall concentrate on the found poem proper, the short poem consisting exclusively of found textual matter rearranged according to the typographical format of traditional poetry. This definition of the found poem proper corresponds with Scott's prescription for found poems: 'In a strict manner no words should be added or subtracted; the original should be printed with only a change from the prose to a free verse form.'[11] Further, I shall present a kind of poetics of the found poem, in order to explain how found poems function as poems. Critics dealing with found poetry have been concerned so far with establishing the literary and historical traditions in which the found poem can be placed. They have not yet attempted an explanation of how the found poem functions as a poem, or of where its 'poeticality' is to be located.

Any poetics of the found poem has to start from the question of what gives a text originally produced as a piece of prose the quality of a poem. Such an inquiry will have to begin with the changes to which the original prose text is subjected when it is presented as a poem. It seems that this change begins with the displacement of the text from its original, usually banal, everyday context and its relocation in the context of a volume of poetry. It does not, however, depend on traditional poetic elements such as diction, style, figurative language, rhythm (apart from the rhythmic pattern introduced by the line breaks) because the words as such remain the same. The newly acquired 'poeticalness' must, therefore, reside in those elements which are added to the original text when it is printed as a found poem. They are mainly the following:

—Frame provided by place and format of publication (e.g. volume of poetry). This frame signals to the reader: this is a highly structured text, read it with maximum attention.
—Left-justified printing and typographical spacing of stanzas and lines are characteristics of traditional poetry. Left-justified printing imposes on the 'natural' syntactic structure of a sentence a visual as well as a prosodic pattern which has semantic implications.
—Run-on lines and line breaks as indicators of syntactic ambiguity, forcing the reader very often to restructure the meaning of the original text.
—Closure, selection of a particular segment from a longer context and its presentation as a self-contained, rounded-off unit of meaning.

If the reading of traditional poetry can be understood as a process of naturalizing poetic language, that is to say, attempting to bring back what in poetry has been made to look strange, unacceptable, contradictory, into the order and rules of our empirical world, then the creating of found poetry as poetry could be regarded as a process of denaturalizing, making strange what before was familiar and acceptable in everyday discourse. A contemporary reader sensitized to the increased participatory character of modern art will be well prepared to submit his reading of a found poem to this process of denaturalization or defamiliarization. Parallel to this process, aesthetic significance will be attributed to the text, where originally no such significance was intended. The competence for this aesthetic attribution comes well within the 'reader-power' as described in theories based either on reader-response aesthetics or the linguistics of communication, in particular the speech act theories.[12]

All the constituent elements of a found poem can be identified in a single poem by Eli Mandel:

> News Item
>
> man throws himself onto
> Ottawa's eternal flame
>
> suffers
>
> superficial burns
>
> (Toronto Star, Oct. 23, 1970)

The reader finds this short text in a book which is immediately identified as a collection of poems: Eli Mandel, *Crusoe: Poems Selected and New*.[13] Thus the reader reads 'News Item' with a heightened awareness that the language, the images, and the structure of the text are poetic, charged with more significance than the word sequence of a nonliterary text.

Having discovered in the last line of the poem that he has in fact read a literary 'objet trouvé,' the reader might then consider the effect of the left-justified printing on the broken lines of a newspaper story. Left-justified presentation of words has from the days of medieval manuscript writing been the characteristic of verse as distinct from prose. In our time left-justified print is increasingly used to give visual emphasis to a certain section of the text on a printed page, usually suggesting special semiotic significance. In that function it has become quite common in advertising.

Left-justified printing of lines and its corollary, the typographical spacing of the words on the page, in addition to this general semiotic intensification of meaning, assumes another specific function: the lines are organized not according to their natural syntax but are subjected to a deliberate division into, as it seems, arbitrary visual, prosodic and semantic units. As a consequence the reader's mental processing of the lines (and stanzas) is largely determined by the temporal and spatial structuring of the printed words on the page. A syntactic gap at the end of a line with enjambement suggests spatial distance between the things named before and after the line break. The classical instance, often quoted to illustrate the effect of enjambement, is Milton's description of the fall of Satan in *Paradise Lost*:[14] '. . . and how he fell / From Heaven,' where the break evokes the vastness of the distance traversed by Satan during his fall. The divisions indicated by typographical spacing will also induce the reader to pause at the end of a line or stanza, perhaps only for a split second, yet long enough to make him realize that the line (or the stanza) presents itself to his perception as a, perhaps only provisional, unit. This division into units, if it is repeated several times, can also become the basis for a rhythmical patterning of a text, even of a text which has none of the usual properties marking metrical regularity.[15] In our paradigm, 'News Item,' with the exception of the first line, line breaks coincide with the stanzaic divisions. 'Suffers,' forming a one-word stanza, is isolated from the surrounding words in such a way that the reader cannot but read the typographical isolation of the word as if it were the musical notation for a pause, a pause for thought. This lengthening of the duration of the reading process must be regarded as the imitative form suggesting semantic distance between the act described (attempted suicide in a sensational manner) and its consequences (which are negligible).

Let us now look at the phenomenon of enjambement from a slightly different angle. The breaking of the line interrupts the natural, expected flow of the sentence construction. This interruption suggests semantic distance, as I have shown above; it also causes a moment of syntactic uncertainty or ambiguity as to the intended continuation of the sentence. This moment of suspended meaning will be relieved by surprise or disappointment, or even shock, when the construction of the true sentence is revealed in the words following the line break. This split second of syntactic uncertainty is enough to draw the reader's attention to the linguistic structure of the sentence, making him aware that in the text he is reading certain things are being done with words which are not done with words in a newspaper article, in a recipe, in an instruction for the use of a tool. The simplest example is perhaps the best illustration. Scott arranges the motto of the R.C.M.P. as follows:

Uphold the

Right.

Separating the imperative form of the verb from its direct object, and thus producing a momentary hiatus between them in reading or reciting the motto, creates a moment of uncertainty or doubt. There are so many things which can be upheld by the police force of a country, of any country; and there are many meanings hidden in the word 'Right,' as we suddenly realize. The decision as to where to break the line is a basic and central poetic element in the writing of found poems.

The last and perhaps most significant constituent in our poetics of the found poem is closure. Closure is not so obvious an element in this poetics as is the line break. It is, however, a very effective means of attributing poeticalness to an originally non-poetic text. Jonathan Holden thinks that closure is the most fundamental of modern poetic conventions in general: 'The ruling convention of our verse—more fundamental than rhyme and rhythm—is our assumption that verse asserts closure, that there must be some reason for isolating only *these* words together in the middle of the page.'[16] Closure means first of all selection, as was made clear by Herrnstein-Smith, selection and segregation of lines with a highly organized structure from a textual background of 'relative disorder and randomness.'[17] In a found poem usually only a short section is selected from a longer prose passage. Very often both the edges where the cuts were made remain jagged, sharp, raw. The reader senses that something is missing here, at the beginning and the end, something which supported the original text. It is true that many modern short stories have similarly abrupt beginnings and endings. But in such stories this form of closure or 'anti-closure'[18] does not affect the structure of the whole work so completely as it does in the usually short or very short found poem. Even in the shortest story in *Dubliners,* 'Clay,' there is enough narrative space for establishing the world of Maria, the main character. In the end the reader can fill in for himself the indeterminate areas of Maria's story. This is impossible in the case of the incident presented in 'News Item,' a fact which does not, however, diminish the significance of the poem; on the contrary, it even seems to increase it. The solution of this paradox lies in a special proclivity of the human mind when having to deal with what has been called a semantic vacuum: an insoluble problem, aporias, apparently contradictory or nonsensical situations. Man confronted with such a semantic vacuum in the act of reading will not accept a blank on the page as a blank, the silence of a speaker as nothing but silence, or something that appears to be nonsense as nothing but gibberish, because, as the psycholinguist I. M. Schlesinger has observed: 'Human nature abhors a semantic vacuum.'[19] A linguistically sensitized reader who finds himself confronting such a semantic vacuum will reread the line or stanza or poem and ransack it for any clues which might help him to bridge or fill in this vacuum. Very often a second reading will then uncover new layers of meaning, ironies or counterpoints in the relationship of the parts to the whole and similar complexities which were not noticed at the first reading.

Let us look once again at our paradigmatic found poem, 'News Item,' this time in the light of the effects of closure. The newspaper from which this poem was taken will most probably have gone on to describe why the man got away almost unscathed, whether he was taken to hospital for treatment, what his motives were, etc. Such details are omitted from the found poem by virtue of the kind of poetic closure applied to it. They are omitted because they are irrelevant to the one significant aspect to which the whole poem points: the ironic discrepancy between the limited combustive efficiency and the nation-wide symbolic effect attributed to 'Ottawa's eternal flame.' The 'superficial burns' suffered by the man who tried to destroy himself in the nation's emblematic fire seem to become a comment on the value of emblems of national identity in general. The headline of a relatively uninteresting news item by a kind of mysterious poetic alchemy has been changed into something 'rich and strange,' into something with a complex intensity of meaning which by any standard deserves to be called poetic.

Rearranging the rearranged text of a found poem can be used as a kind of parlor game among friends or in a poetry class. Even if it does not produce improved found poems, it can be used to exercise our awareness of the poetic potentialities of language for foregrounding certain semantic and syntagmatic qualities inherent in its structure. Exploiting these potentialities is synonymous with making that use of language which Jakobson designates as the 'poetic function,' that is, focusing on the message for its own sake. Jakobson's definition is perhaps the most often quoted sentence in the field of linguistic poetics: 'The poetic function projects the principle of equivalence from the axis of selection into the axis of combination.'[20]

In an analysis of the textual structure of found poems a distinction would, therefore, be made between found poems whose structure is dominated by syntagmatic relations, and found poems dominated by paradigmatic (or associative) relations. 'News Item' belongs to the first group because the rearrangement aims at foregrounding chiefly the syntagmatic relations between the parts of the sentence by means of left-justified printing, line breaks and closure, all of them happening on the axis of combination. Handke's 'Japanese Hit Parade of May 25, 1968,' with its catalogue of names all belonging to one and the same paradigm (titles of popular hits and names of jazz bands), would have to be put into the second group. Mandel's 'First Political Speech,' which consists entirely of phrases belonging to the paradigm 'grammatical forms of transition,' also belongs to the second group. Moving up (or down) the paradigmatic scale of transition, repeating the act of transition in all its possible variations, the political speech gets nowhere. The poem is a superb parody of the vacuity of a political debutant's speech:

First Political Speech

first, in the first place, to begin with, secondly
in the second place, lastly

again, also, in the next place, once more, moreover,
furthermore, likewise, besides, similarly, for example,
for instance, another

then, nevertheless, still, however, at the same time,
yet, in spite of that, on the other hand, on the contrary

certainly, surely, doubtless, indeed, perhaps, possibly,
probably, anyway, in all probability, in all likelihood,
at all events, in any case

therefore, consequently, accordingly, thus, as a result,
in consequence of this, as might be expected

the foregoing, the preceding, as previously mentioned

as already stated

Transition Table
from *Learning to Write* by Ernest
H. Winter (Second Revised Edition)
Macmillan (Toronto, 1961), p. 156.

Here the well-prepared (notice the crescendo of the fourth stanza) but meaningless maiden speech of a politician has been stripped bare. What remains is a scary skeleton of conjunctions and adverbs of transition. It is difficult to imagine a more effective dramatization of this kind of political rhetoric, particularly if the found poem is recited aloud.

Since closure cannot be applied as effectively in the long as in the short found poem, the poetic structure of the longer poem is slacker than that of the shorter poem. John Robert Colombo, who has produced many long found poems, suggests the term 'redeemed prose' for his *Mackenzie Poems.* This is certainly a more appropriate term for the longer texts of this kind than 'found poem.' The essential difference between the poetic structure of the short and the longer found poem affects the reader's attitude toward the literary 'objet trouvé.' Colombo, for instance, included the following short section from his long *Mackenzie Poems* in his collection of original and found poems called *Abracadabra:*

Cholera in London
from the English of William Lyon Mackenzie

Be this as it may,
I have no intention of again changing my lodgings.
I am here on what I believe to be a good, honourable, and
    proper errand;
and if it pleases the Creator to cut me or mine off
    while in what we consider the way of duty,
we can bear in mind that he is able to raise up
    other fit and proper persons
to fulfill his wise purposes.
Here then we are,
in the House with the Cholera,
and not dismayed.[22]

Here, in congenial proximity to original poems, these lines make a fine found poem. There can be no doubt that the 'redeemed prose' of the longer poem also has its literary merits. Let us look at one of the best-known examples of the longer found poems, *The Great San Francisco Earthquake and Fire* (1971). Colombo describes it as 'A Cycle of Found Poems Based on Wilson's Memorial Volume *San Francisco's Horror of Earthquake and Fire* (Philadelphia 1906).' It is a sequence of passages selected from J. R. Wilson's chronicle of the San Francisco disaster, the passages varying in length from three to twenty-five lines. It cannot be denied that many parts of this sequence have a powerful effect, but it is the peculiar effect of a chrestomathy, a collection of beautiful, strong passages which, however, lack an elaborate or complex poetic structure. There is relatively little real poetry **found** here. The vestiges of poetic quality which can be detected reside in the original, in Wilson's dignified style, in the rhythmic quality of his prose and, of course, in the pathos of the reported event. The following is the opening passage of *The Great San Francisco Earthquake and Fire*:

> But there was no panic.
> The people were calm, stunned.
> They did not seem to realize
> the extent of the calamity.
> They heard that the city
> was being destroyed;
> they told each other
> in the most natural tone
> that their residences were destroyed
> by the flames, but there
> was no hysteria,
> no outcry,
> no criticism.[23]

Perhaps it was Colombo's intention to interfere as little as possible with his source. This would explain why he has used the art of rearranging so sparingly here.

Things are handled somewhat differently in Colombo's earlier work, *The Great Wall of China*, in which the Great Wall is transformed into a metaphor for the universal paranoia of the rulers of a country trying to keep out whatever appears as new, outlandish or threatening. There are references to the Berlin Wall as well as to René Lévesque's separatist policy for Québec. *The Great Wall of China* differs from the *San Francisco Earthquake* in being composed of heterogeneous material: original poems, other people's poems, original prose, other people's prose, found poetry, found prose. As a result *The Great Wall of China* offers more textual variety and greater diversity of poetic forms than does *The San Francisco Earthquake*. Who, for instance, would recognize the source from which the following exchange of compliments between a British traveller and 'the old pilot,' an official Chinese guide at the Great Wall, is taken?

> I told him
> it was a most excellent thing
> to keep off the Tartars;
> which he happened not to understand
> as I meant it, and so took it
> for a compliment;
> but the old pilot laughed.
> 'O Seignior Inglese,'
> says he,
> 'you speak in colours'
> 'In colours,'
> say I,
> 'what do you mean by that,'
> 'Why, you speak
> what looks white this way,
> and black that way -
> gay one way,
> and dull another way.
> You tell him
> it is a good wall
> to keep out Tartars?
> You tell me by that,
> it is good for nothing
> but to keep out Tartars,
> or it will keep out none
> but Tartars. I understand you,
> Seignior Inglese,
> I understand you,'
> says he . . .[24]

The British tourist is no less illustrious and experienced a traveller than Robinson Crusoe!

Colombo's technique of collage in *The Great Wall*—incorporating documentary text, literary 'objet trouvé,' concrete, found and original poems—is refined upon by Robert Kroetsch in *Seed Catalogue.* The title refers to the catalogue of garden seeds, which in the poet's memory usually arrived at an Alberta farm just in time to brighten some of the darkest days of the Canadian winter:

> Into the dark of January
> the seed catalogue bloomed
>
> a winter proposition, if
> spring should come, then,
>
> with illustrations:

> No. 25—*McKenzie's Improved Golden Wax Bean:* 'THE MOST PRIZED OF ALL BEANS. *Virtue* is its *own reward.* We have had *many expressions* from *keen discriminating gardeners extolling our seed* and this *variety.*'

> > Beans, beans
> > the musical fruit;
> > the more you eat,
> > the more you virtue.[25]

Line breaks, closure, and spacing on the printed page are used here to spin a very subtle and intricate web of significant references, reconnecting the dislocated words and phrases on the page. In this way it seems quite natural when the contingencies of growing garden plants in so severe a climate as Alberta's are related to the contingencies of the 'growth of a poet's mind.'

In this survey of found poems in Canada we have traversed much ground between Eli Mandel's 'News Item' and Robert Kroetsch's *Seed Catalogue.* The distance covered is a measure of the significance and variety of found poetry in contemporary Canadian literature. As in other countries, the vogue of the found poem, which reached its height in the sixties and early seventies, seems to have subsided now. The poetic potentialities of the found poem have, however, as *Seed Catalogue* shows, not yet been exhausted. Its subject matter is by definition inexhaustible. Colombo quotes Zola as an epigraph to *The San Francisco Earthquake:* '[i]f it has been lived or thought it will one day become literature.'[26] I would make this sound a little less ominous (to future students of literature): if it has been lived or thought and well said, it may one day become a found poem.

University of Graz, Austria

---

[1]Louis Dudek, 'Introduction' to Frank R. Scott, *Trouvailles: Poems from Prose* (Montreal: Delta Canada, 1967), p. 2.

[2]John Robert Colombo, 'A Found Introduction,' in *Open Poetry: Four Anthologies of Expanded Poems,* ed. Ronald Gross and George Quasha (New York: Simon & Schuster, 1973), p. 432.

[3]Dorothy Livesay in 'The Documentary Poem: A Canadian Genre' uses the term in a wider sense. She includes poems which **describe** historical events. Cf. *Contexts of Canadian Criticism,* ed. Eli Mandel (Chicago/London: The Univ. of Chicago Press, 1971), pp. 267-81.

[4]Peter Handke, *Die Innenwelt der Aussenwelt der Innenwelt* (10. ed., Frankfurt/M.: Suhrkamp, 1981), p. 59.

[5]Peter Handke, *Innerworld of the Outerworld of the Innerworld,* translated and with a Postscript by Michael Roloff (New York: Continuum, 1974).

[6]Scott, *Trouvailles,* p. 13.

[7]Barbara Herrnstein-Smith, *Poetic Closure: A Study of How Poems End* (Chicago: Chicago Univ. Press, 1968). 'Closure' is more than the way a poem ends; it is the drawing of 'an enclosing line around it, distinctly and continuously separating [the poem] from less highly structured and nonmimetic discourse,' p. 25.

[8]Cf. the incorporation of the 'found' passage with the pub dialogue in Eliot's 'A Game of Chess' *(The Waste Land).*

[9]Cf. James Joyce, *Ulysses,* 'Wandering Rocks' and several of the later episodes in this novel. (Harmondsworth: Penguin, 1969), pp. 218-54 *et passim.*

[10]Robert Kroetsch, *The Ledger* (London, Ont.: Applegarth Follies, 1975); *Seed Catalogue* (2nd ed., Winnipeg: Turnstone Press, 1979).

[11]Scott, *Trouvailles,* 'Foreword,' p. 5.

[12]Cf. Catherine Belsey's chapter on 'Reader-Power' in her book *Critical Practice,* (London: Methuen, 1980), pp. 29-36, and Mary Louise Pratt, *Toward a Speech Act Theory of Literary Discourse* (Bloomington: Indiana Univ. Press, 1977), pp. 152ff.

[13]Eli Mandel, *Crusoe: Poems Selected and New* (Toronto: Anansi, 1973), p. 93.

[14]Book I, lines 740ff.

[15]It is probably with this rhythm-making effect of spacing on the printed page in mind that John Cage has written (and delivered) lectures such as 'Composition as Process' or 'Lecture on Nothing,' in which the lines are left-justified four times between the left and right margins of the page. In the 'Foreword' to *Silence,* the collection of his writings, Cage explains why these lectures appear in such an unusual form: 'I have employed in them means of composing analogous to my composing means in the field of music.' The analogy is, of course, mainly on the level of rhythm. Cage, *Silence: Lectures and Writings* (Cambridge, Mass.: M.I.T. Press, 1967), pp. ix, 18ff. and 109ff.

[16]Jonathan Holden, *The Rhetoric of the Contemporary Lyric* (Bloomington: Indiana Univ. Press, 1980), p. 26.

[17]Herrnstein-Smith, p. 2.

[18]*Ibid.*, pp. 234ff.

[19]I. M. Schlesinger, 'Production of Utterances and Language Acquisition,' in *Ontogenesis of Grammar*, ed. Dan I. Slobin (New York: Academic Press, 1971), p. 86.

[20]Roman Jakobson, 'Closing Statement: Linguistics and Poetics,' in *Style in Language*, ed. Thomas A. Sebeok (Cambridge, Mass.: M.I.T. Press, 1960), p. 358.

[21]Mandel, *Crusoe*, p. 94.

[22]John Robert Colombo, *ABRACADABRA* (Toronto: McClelland and Stewart, 1967), p. 41.

[23]Colombo, *The Great San Francisco Earthquake and Fire* (Fredericton, N.B.: Fiddlehead Poetry Books, 1971), p. 7.

[24]Colombo, *The Great Wall of China: An Entertainment* (Montreal: Delta, 1966), pp. 34f. On p. 50 there is a misprint which has a familiar ring to the ears of an Austrian who receives some of his mail from Canada via Sydney, Australia: 'In European terms, if the Wall were elastic and given the shape of a rectangle, it would enclose large parts of France, Italy, Australia [sic], Switzerland, Hungary, Roumania, Bulgaria, Poland and segments of Russia.'

[25]Kroetsch, *Seed Catalogue*, p. 14.

[26]*The San Francisco Earthquake*, p. 5.

Reingard M. Nischik

NARRATIVE TECHNIQUE IN ARITHA VAN HERK'S NOVELS

It is a symptom of the healthy state of Canadian literature in the 1970s and 1980s that increasingly more new, young writers come to the foreground and demand the literary public's attention. As often as not these writers are female. The female Canadian author of today works within a more pronounced tradition of female authorship than do her colleagues in other countries, a tradition founded by writers like Frances Brooke, Susanna Moodie, Catharine Parr Traill, Sara Jeannette Duncan, Mazo de la Roche, Martha Ostenso, and Ethel Wilson. The female Canadian author of today also works against a background of contemporary achievements by compatriate female writers which seems to be even wider, relatively speaking, in Canada than in other countries. Among the best contemporary Canadian fiction writers, by many a count, would be Margaret Atwood, Margaret Laurence, Alice Munro, and Mavis Gallant. The literary climate in Canada, then, traditionally has not been and is not now hostile to women.

The achievements of women writers lie in opening up new realms to fiction, the female experience, more particularly the consciousness of mostly female protagonists trying to come to terms with people around them, and, just as importantly, with themselves. Yet the fiction of Canadian women has also been technically innovative, original, skillful and demanding. Sheila Watson's novel *The Double Hook*, to pick out one example, remained unpublished for several years after completion, and when it finally appeared in 1959, its experimental narrative technique was still ahead of its time in Canada.

Aritha van Herk, turned thirty in 1984, is a young author now gaining her place in the long row of female Canadian writers of reputation. This study attempts to give a first survey of her fiction writing, especially of her technical achievements to date. A former student of Rudy Wiebe, van Herk became known in 1978 with the publication of her first novel, *Judith*. The novel had been her MA thesis (entitled "When Pigs Fly"), with Wiebe acting as supervisor. *Judith* won van Herk the Seal Books First Novel Award, after the Nobel Prize financially the second highest literary prize existent. The novel has since been translated into German, French, Italian, Dutch,

Finnish, and Serbo-Croatian. In 1981 van Herk's second novel, *The Tent Peg*, appeared (the German translation, *Mackenzies Koch*, came out in 1982). She is currently working on her third novel, *Who Travels Too*.

Van Herk's first two novels are distinguished by an elaborate use of narrative technique, in keeping with the content of the works. Both novels are concerned with complex psychological developments, but their techniques and structures are very different. In *Judith* a by and large single point of view and several time stages combine to draw a well-rounded picture of the development of the title figure, with a special prominence given to the past. In *The Tent Peg* a multiplicity of points of view is used, fifteen altogether. They are mainly applied to the narrative present, without a second time-level gaining the status of a separate structural unity; here the shifts in the relationships within a group of people are minutely followed, the roundedness of the picture lying less in the time-range covered or the number of situations presented, as in *Judith*, but rather in the number of points of view applied, often several times to the same situation. Thus both of van Herk's novels appear as mosaics, the elements of which are to be assembled by the reader: in *Judith* one has to integrate several time-levels, in *The Tent Peg* several points of view to grasp the essential meaning of the works. In both cases van Herk uses a kind of resonance technique supporting this integration: in *Judith* events of the narrative present trigger off events of the narrative past on account of some similarity between the events,[1] in *The Tent Peg* the very same situation may be treated several times from different points of view. The resonance technique thus links the different time-levels in the first novel and the different points of view in the second one.

A closer look at *Judith* shows that three levels of narrative time are maintained throughout. The largest part of the novel is made up of the narrative present, in which we see Judith on the pig farm she owns and runs by herself. Interspersed are two strands of plot of the narrative past, which show Judith with the men who have been important in her life: her father, 'he' (the unnamed employer for whom she worked as a secretary and whose lover she became), and, to a lesser extent, Norman, her boyfriend while she still lived on her parents' farm.

Most of the events in the narrative present are presented from a neutral omniscient point of view.[2] The reader thus views Judith from a certain distance, in keeping with her own distancing evaluation of herself, her past, her present situation, her intentions, and the people important to her. The omniscient point of view becomes most apparent in the passages with the pigs, for example:

> After Judith was gone, they shifted restlessly, eyes gleaming in the straw-smelling darkness. Sniffing along the boards, they inhaled her resentment, snuffled at the mixed smell of her hatred and necessity. Still pondering, they stretched on their sides and extended their laden bellies on the straw to sleep calm and all-knowing. (p. 4)

> Surprised at her own anticipation, Judith did chores early the next night. The sows were puzzled; they edged about their pens rejecting the impermanence of a different time, their schedule destroyed. She worked carefully but too quickly. In her hurry they sensed an eagerness for something they did not have and could not give to her. Instinctively they knew that she would go to other humans tonight, and they felt vaguely disappointed. The best part of her was her aloneness; she did not carry the acrid smell of humans who mingled with each other constantly. But there was a subtle excitement in her quick movements that transmitted itself to them and pleased them. (p. 49)

In these passages the pigs take on human qualities. Their perceptive and interpretative power, being unrealistic, establishes an uncanny atmosphere. Judith and the pigs enter into a mystical relationship—in the treatment of the narrative indeed a two-sided one—and this relationship is the essential vehicle for Judith to come to terms with her past, especially with her deep-rooted connection with her father, the pig farmer. The omniscient point of view, which contravenes the conventions of realism in its treatment of the pigs, confers on the pig passages a symbolic key position in the novel.

At times the treatment of the pigs even comes close to a figural point of view:[3] 'Yes, yes, the pigs knew it was what Judith needed—laughter, laughter echoing around her. If they could have laughed, they would have joined in' (p. 90). The figural point of view, however, is mainly used with respect to Judith on the level of the narrative present, as an occasional variant on the predominant omniscient one: 'She followed Mina into the huge bright kitchen where the table stood set for six. So she was the only woman in the house. She tried with difficulty to picture it. How old was she. Thirty? Forty? Fifty?' (p. 52).

None of the other characters in the novel share this privilege of a figural point of view. Because we are given Judith's thoughts directly, apparently without the intercession of a narrative medium, Judith is closer to us than are any other of the characters. The narrative constantly centres on the title figure, the only character always present in the narration.

The point of view is handled similarly in the passages belonging to the narrative past, though the context makes for more complexity here. The passages vary in length between four lines and 2½ pages. The majority of them, altogether fifty-three, are devoted to Judith's reminiscences of her father, of her childhood and youth which bore the stamp of his overruling influence. At first glance, then, the point of view used in these insertions is the same as that used in the narrative present, that is neutral omniscience occasionally mixed with the figural. The language is mostly that of a narrator, not that of the protagonist. Again, the effect is a certain distancing, a distancing of the protagonist from her past and present, a distancing of the reader from the events and facts presented. This narrative stance is in keeping with the way in which the novel proceeds. For *Judith* is an analytic narrative: it shows the protagonist as a product of her past, the past with which she tries to come to terms throughout the novel.

We see, then, that the point of view technique is handled with a fair degree of consistency. The tone, too, is relatively unvarying: distant and cool, both in presenting events and in evaluating them. One may consider the appropriateness of this homogeneity to the structure of the novel. As mentioned above, Aritha van Herk uses a resonance technique to link the narrative past and present. In spite of the predominance of the neutral omniscient point of view in the narrative past as well as in the present, it is fair to say that the associations triggering off reminiscences of Judith's past are those of the main character. After a description of Judith's feeding of her pigs, for example, an episode follows to show what the child Judy and her father would do after having fed the pigs. Judith's looking out of the kitchen window onto the barn is followed by an episode which begins with Judy as a child looking out of the kitchen window wondering when her Daddy will come back from the barn. When the adult Judith buys liquid iron for the piglets at a drugstore, an episode of the past is added which opens with the information as to where Judy's father bought the same animal tonic. Still, considered formally, most of these associations and reminiscences are mediated by a narrator other than the main character. To be sure, the narrator in *Judith* is not bodily present, as Franz K. Stanzel would have it;[4] the medium stays very much in the background and is hardly felt, with neutral omniscience, indeed, verging on the figural. Occasionally the point of view does turn figural as, for example, in: 'She hated green, such an ugly color. . . . Judy followed her carefully, slowly—Would she see blood?—down some steps . . .' (p. 42). In such instances it is evident that we experience the episodes from Judith's past through her own re-presenting memories. All in all, however, we may see in *Judith* a peculiar example of that point of view which is most frequently used nowadays, namely the hybrid omniscient-figural: the narrative situation—remembering—would call for a character-oriented point of view; the language and narrative stance, however, are that of a disembodied, neutral medium, which confines itself, by and large, to the protagonist's experiences and thoughts. Through this particular handling of the point of view Judith's past—which is obviously very close to her, frequently and readily invoked by almost any situation of the narrative present—is kept at bay a little. The past is re-lived, but from a certain distance. The overall impression engendered by the narrative technique is one of an analytical, critical stance towards the past rather than, say, a nostalgic one. This effect of the technique matches Judith's approach to her past.

The point of view in the passages evoking Judith's relationship with her unnamed lover is handled a little differently. Here it is more obvious that we participate in the memories of a character. The point of view turns more frequently into the figural. The language more often seems to mirror the thinking mechanisms, as evidenced in short or incomplete or run-on sentences, particularly in the frequent lack of a (finite) verb:

> Like his eyes on her naked back, the same insatiable hunger, so masculine, that instant desire, she wanted to clutch his arm, insist that she was different from the lines of the car. (p. 39)

> The comforting bus; everyone unobtrusive with the unwritten rules of morning commuters. Ten minutes to collect herself in its humming calm before the long day, the desk, the typewriter. (p. 36)

> What in God's name was she doing with sows? It had been so easy, every day the electric gray keys singing under her fingers, every day the routine; eight-thirty to pull the cover off the typewriter, ten to take his cup to the sink and wash it, fill it with coffee and bring it to him. Twelve for lunch. Back at one, the

afternoon folding into the morning with the paper and the last
of the day's new letters. Three, his coffee again, and five,
flicking the switch on the machine, slipping the cover over its
face like reassuring a child for the next day. (p. 22)

Such passages approach apparently unmediated, i.e. direct thought,
perception or speech of the main character, and terms like 'narrated
monologue,' 'narrated perception,' or 'substitutionary speech' may
be applied to them.[5] To be sure, Judith, and with her the reader,
recapitulate her job situation and her relationship with her employer
with less distance than is the case with Judy's childhood and her
crucial relationship with her beloved father. This difference in
involvement does not, however, say anything about a possible
difference in their influence on Judith's life, as also becomes clear
from the context of the novel. It may simply be due to the different
gaps in time between the narrative present on the one hand and the
two sequences of the past on the other hand. Some of the events of
Judith's office life are separated by only a few days or weeks from the
narrative present; so they can naturally be rendered more vividly than
are the events of her childhood, which lie ten or more years back.

Judith's relationship with her boyfriend Norman has not left a
mark on her life and stays in the background of her memories. The
constellation, with Norman adoring her and Judith feeling
contempt if not hatred towards him, is straightforward and needs no
elaborating. Six glimpses of their relationship are given, but they do
not form a separate strand of plot as do the other two memory
sequences. Like the other memory sequences, these glimpses are
offered by means of the resonance technique and from the same point
of view.

A look at the handling of the time element may tell us more about
the intricate structure of the novel. The events of the narrative present
are given in chronological sequence. By contrast, the episodes of the
narrative past, i.e. the childhood/father sequence on the one hand
and the job/lover sequence on the other hand, are not always
arranged chronologically—not surprisingly, since they take their
clues from various episodes of the narrative present. Love scenes
between Judith and her lover are, for example, briefly presented
before their first bodily encounter is prepared for and described at
some length. We can more easily determine the temporal relation
between the separate episodes in this sequence than in the childhood/
father sequence, since the job/lover sequence treats a shorter period
of time, and its content lends itself more easily to the abstraction of a

development of the action described: from Judith's taking up her job as a secretary and the first approaches of her employer to their first love scenes, arguments, and Judith's final escape. The occasional displacement of scenes does not hamper our understanding of this development and makes for a more realistic effect of the resonance technique.

With this renouncing of a strict chronology in the presentation of the events of the past van Herk avoids the impression of artificial contrivance, which we cannot help but have occasionally in Margaret Laurence's *The Stone Angel*, a classic example of the resonance technique in the modern Canadian novel. In Laurence's novel the events of the past are almost without exception presented chronologically, and the associative links sometimes seem a little far-fetched and overburdened; there a neatly wrought structure is achieved at the expense of credibility.[6]

Van Herk's shifts between the narrative present and past seem by and large to develop naturally. The different time-levels or the transitions between them are not marked grammatically or typographically as in Margaret Laurence's novels *The Diviners* ('MEMORYBANK MOVIE,' changes in tense), *The Fire-Dwellers* (indenting of the episodes of the past), or *The Stone Angel* (changes in tense).[7] On the contrary, in *Judith* the changes come quite abruptly, just as thoughts jump back and forth. There are no intervening signals other than the usual paragraphing. At the beginning of the novel this abruptness and lack of reader guidance may create some confusion, but fairly soon one becomes used to the pattern of alternations, which take place on almost every page. The use of the pet name 'Judy' in narratorial speech is the most reliable linguistic marker of the childhood/father sequence,[8] 'he,' 'his,' 'him' mark the job/lover sequence.

At the level of form, then, the shifts between narrative past and narrative present are sudden and unprepared for; but this abruptness is counteracted to a certain extent by the associative linkages which, at the content level, do in fact introduce each shift. These links work in accordance with the principle of the free association of ideas: each reminiscence is triggered off because it is in some element similar to the present. Here, too, van Herk manages to avoid the impression of contrivance. The shift seems in every instance psychologically motivated.

Apart from the associative hinges, the narrative present and the two strands of the narrative past are kept independent of each other structurally. The past may intrude upon the events of the present, but once the narration of some past episode has got under way, its rendering takes place without essential reference to or intrusion of the narrative present; rarely are there fleeting references to the plane of the narrative present inserted into the rendering of the narrative past. The two sequences of the narrative past are kept structurally separate from each other, too. Only in a few instances are they mingled (pp. 85, 113, 141, and 168), with three of them constituting some of the most crucial passages of the novel. With the two levels of the past being presented right next to each other here, these passages demonstrate *in nuce* what throughout the rest of the novel has to be achieved by the integrating mind of the reader with far less guidance by the text, i.e. the interrelationship between the two sequences of the past on the one hand and, here less directly, between them and the narrative present on the other:

> His *[Judy's father's]* blue eyes faded, not so bright as she remembered them. *[Reference to the plane of the narrative present; back to father sequence:]* 'But those things don't matter, Judy, if you have the farm, if you've got animals and things to do, and you build.' . . . The train swung around a long curve and she jolted against the side of the seat. She remembered his *[her lover's]* fingers this afternoon on the small of her back, easing against her, and then the circular pattern of the room strange and upside-down from the carpeted floor. *[Lover sequence imposed on father sequence]* (pp. 84/5)[9]

Here a connection between Judith's refusal to take over her parents' pig farm and her sexual affair with her employer is alluded to. Later on Judith leaves her lover to revise her former decision against the farm and thereby against her father, who has died estranged from his beloved daughter.

> She would have to carry her mad plan through, would have to face her unavoidable reparation and escape. She wished for him *[her lover]* to take it out of her hands, to sweep her into a plan of his own so that she could abandon hers like the madness it was and so block out the shape of her father's face, stern in death as it had never been in life. *[Father sequence imposed on lover sequence]* For it was his *[her father's]* plan, after all, his design, and somewhere he must be watching her pain. To my only daughter, Judith, I bequeath all my worldly goods, for her to use in remembrance of me. (p. 141)

This second intermingling of the two strands of plot of the narrative past shows her lover's inability to keep Judith from giving in to her father's wish, after all. The hinge of the two strands of the past gives the last view or one of the last views Judith had of each of the two most important people in her life, showing the deadlock into which she had been manoeuvred with respect to both of them. The situation summarized in this episode thus constitutes the starting point for the events of the narrative present, in which Judith struggles to revise her former decision; it also demonstrates that she is still ruled by her father, at this stage to the exclusion of everybody else.

> So this is the way it happens, she thought, holding the telephone receiver in her hand like a weapon. Failing to stop at a stop sign. *[Father sequence]* And she thrust him *[her lover]* away from her, his anxious, puzzled face advancing and receding, wrested her rigid body away from his eager consolation, pushing him aside to walk to the bedroom and calmly lay some clothes in a suitcase. *[Lover sequence imposed on father sequence]* (p. 168)

This third instance of the narrative strands of the past intermingling shows that Judith's lover is not even allowed to console her in the face of the loss of the person dearest to her.

In *Judith* the past is given structural weight by taking up about a third of the novel, by the frequency of its evocation as well as by its arrangement into two fairly self-sufficiently presented sequences of action; it is given thematic significance by virtue of the fact that the novel deals with its protagonist's redemption of the past. Narrative technique and structure in *Judith* are an integral part of its thematic concern.

Whereas in *Judith* the reader has to come to an understanding of the important role which the past plays in these various respects in order to appreciate the work as a whole, in van Herk's second novel, *The Tent Peg*, the past is of subordinate importance. Here the reader is called upon to integrate the different points of view applied as elements in a mosaic rather than different time-levels. In both novels the structural units are placed next to each other without the thematic relationships between them being made very explicit in the text. In *The Tent Peg* the structural support which the reader receives as a first step towards the integration is the clear labelling of the different point of view, which make up the different sections of the novel, as well as the fact that crucial situations tend to be treated

several times from several points of view. In *Judith* the transitions
between the different units are formally abrupt because unmarked,
but in terms of content smooth because of the associative linkages,
whereas in *The Tent Peg* the transitions are marked by the name of
the character from whose point of view the particular section is told,
used as title for the section; here the passages are, however, placed
discontinuously, though largely chronologically, next to each other.
In both novels the integrative devices, such as they are, structure the
reading process rather than guide an integrative interpretation of the
works. This the reader has to achieve largely by himself.

The multiple point of view technique of *The Tent Peg* allows for
no unifying narrative voice as in *Judith*. *The Tent Peg* is divided into
105 sections, each of which is written in the first person. Altogether
fifteen different first-person points of view appear, four of them only
once. This splitting of the point of view, quite in contrast to the
homogeneous one used in *Judith,* is in keeping with the content and
theme of van Herk's second novel. *The Tent Peg* tells the story of
J. L., the woman protagonist, and nine men in a uranium
prospecting camp. The development of the relationship between
each of the men and J. L. is at the centre of the novel. J. L. takes a
pivotal place in the events, since the men's thoughts and attentions
are—directly or indirectly—increasingly attuned to her, just as her
tent is situated right in the middle of the camp. Still, through the
handling of the point of view the men's different characters,
backgrounds, and problems are revealed, in some cases just as much
as are J. L.'s.

The first-person point of view makes for a seemingly unmediated,
personal response of the characters to the situation. In *The Tent Peg*
the characteristics of this point of view are taken one step further. The
different time-levels involved in first-person narration, that of
'experiencing time' and of 'narrating time,' are not really put to use
here. Symptomatically, most of the narrative is written in the present
tense, and the reader is given the impression of participating in the
events on the spot—first-person narration approaches figural
narration. The story thus develops along with the consciousness of
the characters. Inner action predominates over outer action, more so
than in *Judith.* For the group, forced to live together in the
wilderness for a while, inner developments partly substitute for the
lack of outward distractions in the daily routine of their isolated lives.

Fifteen characters have their say in the novel, but only a few of
them are at the centre of our attention, having most of the sections

devoted to them: Mackenzie, the leader of the group, whom J. L. generally responds to most (22 sections), J. L. herself (17), and Thompson (15) ('He's the only one of them that seems sexual to me').[10] These are also the only characters in the novel who achieve some sort of roundness. We get to know a little about their pasts, especially about the relationships important to them. (Mackenzie's constant preoccupation with his wife's leaving him ten years before reminds us of the overruling influence of the past in *Judith*.) All the other characters in van Herk's second novel, however, are much more involved with the present and with the immediate situation in which they find themselves. As a result, flashbacks occur very rarely—to say nothing of their forming separate strands of plot—and essentially only in the sections told from the point of view of Mackenzie, J. L., and Thompson.

A second group of figures, from whose point of view between five and eight sections are told, consists of characters who may each be summed up with one sentence: Jerome is a digruntled, embittered person, who finds fault with everything and everybody, especially with J. L.; his assistant Hudson, a British geology student, suffers under Jerome's treatment; Milton is an immature, religious, highly inhibited person who lives by the rule that 'you don't kiss a girl until after you're married' (p. 101); Ivan is in love with his helicopter and has a deep-rooted fear of crashing; Hearne's life is ruled by photography, Cap's by sex.

Due to the number of characters appearing in the novel and due to the relative scarcity of space which may be allotted to each of them, it is not surprising that the figures in this second group are not drawn in detail. Each of them achieves an individuality of his own; we recognize them immediately on their re-appearance, but they remain flat. Each of them—gradually and to different degrees—comes under J. L.'s influence, and it is this developing attraction to her rather than their individualities which lends them their status in the novel. To be sure, Hudson, Milton, and Ivan are rudimentarily presented in the grip of problems existing independently of J. L. But she serves as a catalyst or she gives essential advice, thereby binding the men to her even more. The remaining characters—also those in a third group with only one to four sections told from their point of view—appear either exclusively as adjuncts to J. L. (e.g. Franklin, who is completely devoted to her), or serve as outside observers of the developments within the group (Roy, Bill, Zeke, P. Q.); they do not achieve an individuality of their own.

Narrative technique and structure of *The Tent Peg* thus produce a multifaceted mosaic of the changing constellation of human relationships in a group of people thrown entirely upon themselves. If several of the characters are not fully drawn, the camp situation as a whole is. This fullness is achieved, among other things, through the technical device of the same situation being treated several times from different points of view. The device is applied only to crucial events in the development of the action; for example, J. L.'s confession 'Mackenzie, I'm a girl' (p. 20) is treated first from Mackenzie's point of view, then indirectly from Zeke's, and sections later from J. L.'s; Cap's first explicit sexual approach to J. L. is first described from her point of view, then from his; the trick which is played on Jerome is seen first through his eyes, then through Mackenzie's; the first bodily encounter between J. L. and Mackenzie, one of the climaxes of the novel, is, ironically, observed by Milton, before we get Mackenzie's shortened, commented version and J. L.'s even shorter, symbolic interpretation of the same situation. The privileged reception of the reader is situated at the cross-section of these different, equally valid renderings of the same action.

One of the chief attractions of *The Tent Peg* lies in this constantly fluctuating view of the psychological as well as of the physical events which take place within the group. These events focus more and more on J. L., and we become aware of a steadily sharpening contrast between her awareness of these events and that of the men. Whereas the narrative technique in *Judith* serves to present in detail, though with a certain distance, one person's present as it derives from the past, that of *The Tent Peg* allows an immediate and subjective but multifaceted registering of an ever-changing portrait of a group of people, who in the last resort are engaged in that most difficult of human processes, that of relating to each other.[11]

University of Cologne, Federal Republic of Germany

---

[1]The only exception in the novel is to be found on p. 109, where a reminiscence of the past starts a new chapter. *Judith* (Toronto: Bantam-Seal, 1978); subsequent references to the novel in the text will refer to this edition.

[2]The term 'neutral omniscience' goes back to Norman Friedman's influential article 'Point of View in Fiction: The Development of a Critical Concept,' *PMLA*, 70 (1955), 1160-84, where he distinguishes Editorial Omniscience, Neutral Omniscience, 'I' as Witness, 'I' as Protagonist, Multiple Selective Omniscience, Selective Omniscience, The Dramatic Mode, and The Camera as the possible points of view from which a story may be told.

[3]The 'figural point of view' *(personale Erzählsituation)* is one of three points of view distinguished in the categorization of the Austrian Franz K. Stanzel. The figural point of view represents the thoughts and perceptions of a character or 'agent' in the story; 'figural point of view' roughly corresponds to 'selective omniscience' in Friedman's categorization. Stanzel's narrative theory has become influential, particularly in the German speaking countries, by means of three major publications of his: *Die typischen Erzählsituationen im Roman: Dargestellt an Tom Jones, Moby Dick, The Ambassadors, Ulysses u.a.* (Vienna: Braumüller, 1955), *Typische Formen des Romans* (Göttingen: Vandenhoeck & Ruprecht, 1964), and *Theorie des Erzählens* (Göttingen: Vandenhoeck & Ruprecht, 1979); of the first and third books English translations are available: *Narrative Situations in the Novel: 'Tom Jones,' 'Moby Dick,' 'The Ambassadors,' 'Ulysses,'* trans. J. Pusack (Bloomington: Univ. of Illinois Press, 1971), and *A Theory of Narrative,* trans. Charlotte Goedsche (Cambridge: Cambridge Univ. Press, 1984).

[4]Franz K. Stanzel in his *Theorie des Erzählens,* pp. 126ff., speaks of *Erzähler-"Ich mit Leib"* and of *Leiblichkeit des Erzähler-Ich* (narrator-'I with body') to distinguish between several degrees of presence of the fiction narrator.

[5]For a differentiation and discussion of these terms and phenomena see Helmut Bonheim, *The Narrative Modes: Techniques of the Short Story* (Cambridge: D. S. Brewer, 1982), pp. 55ff.

[6]Cp. Michel Fabre, 'Margaret Laurence on *The Stone Angel,*' in **The Stone Angel** by *Margaret Laurence: A Collection of Critical Essays,* ed. Michel Fabre, *Études Canadiennes/Canadian Studies,* 11 (Paris: Association Francaise d'Études Canadiennes, 1981), 11-22, here 20ff; Simone Vauthier, 'Notes on the Narrative Voice(s) in *The Stone Angel,*' *op. cit.,* 131-153, especially 134-138; Reingard M. Nischik, *Einsträngigkeit und Mehrsträngigkeit der Handlungsführung in literarischen Texten: Dargestellt insbesondere an englischen, amerikanischen und kanadischen Romanen des 20. Jahrhunderts.* Tübinger Beiträge zur Anglistik, 1 (Tübingen: Narr, 1981), pp. 138ff.

[7]See Reingard M. Nischik, pp. 81ff.

[8]Notice that Jim, in the narrative present, keeps calling Judith 'Judy,' i.e. by the name which her father applied to her. Significantly, Judith objects to this practice, un-successfully.

[9]It may be of help for the analysis of such passages to make use of Gerard Genette's theory of narrative, which Jonathan Culler called 'the most thorough attempt we have to identify, name, and illustrate the basic constituents and techniques of narrative.' In Genette's book *Narrative Discourse* (Oxford: Basil Blackwell, 1980), which is the English translation of a portion of his *Figures III* (Paris: Editions du Seuil, 1972), Genette distinguishes between *prolepsis* as 'any narrative maneuver that consists of narrating or evoking in advance an event that will take place later' and *analepsis,* 'any evocation after the fact of an event that took place earlier than the point in the story where we are at any given moment' (p. 40). In the quoted van Herk passage, which largely consists of *analepsis,* the phrase 'not so bright as she remembered them' constitutes a proleptic reference in the *analepsis.* In Genette's terminology, it has no 'duration'; it is merely a fleeting glimpse of the plane of the narrative present from within the *analepsis.* The analeptic passages of the childhood/father sequence and the job/lover sequence altogether have considerable 'duration' (narrative and narrated time range) and may duly be regarded as separate strands of plot. In the quoted passage we also have an instance of *analepsis* within *analepsis,* where the time sequences of the

past intermingle. Considerations of the time element, which apply in our context, may be found as early (4th/5th century) as in St. Augustine's Confessions, where he distinguishes 'three times: a present time of past things, a present time of present things; and a present time of future things.' Augustine, Confessions, with an English translation by William Watts (1631) (London: Heinemann, 1970), p. 253.

[10]Aritha van Herk, *The Tent Peg* (Toronto: McClelland and Stewart-Bantam, 1981), p. 137. Subsequent references to the novel in the text will refer to this edition.

[11]Reprinted, by permission, from *Zeitschrift der Gesellschaft für Kanada-Studien*, 3, No. 2 (1983).

Coral Ann Howells

WORLDS ALONGSIDE: CONTRADICTORY DISCOURSES IN THE FICTION OF ALICE MUNRO AND MARGARET ATWOOD

Woman's at best a contradiction still[1]

In writing about contradictory discourses of realism and fantasy in the fiction of these two women writers, I am trying to rehabilitate a much abused characteristic of women and women's writing. Arguably, contradiction may be a feature of women's writing at its best, when used in a positive way as a means of creating through the gaps of fictional discourse a new language for making visible perceptions usually relegated to the margins or entirely neglected.[2] The fictions of Alice Munro and Margaret Atwood are obsessed with discontinuities and with crucial absences of connection in society and within the self, while at the same time they also embody the opposite urge to make connections, to tell the unspoken/unspeakable in the belief that connections are vital to an integrated fully human awareness. In this essay I shall trace the interplay of contradictory discourses in the optimistic fictions of Alice Munro's *Lives of Girls and Women* and *Who Do You Think You Are?* and Margaret Atwood's *Surfacing*, contrasting these with the more threatening fiction of her *Bodily Harm*.

The relationship between realism and fantasy is one of opposition, so before looking at particular texts I shall try to describe briefly the features of both, to see where their differences lie, and to make precise distinctions between contradiction and contrariety. Whereas realistic discourse works on the assumption that the world is describable and intelligible rather than alien, fantastic discourse challenges that assumption by focusing instead on what is accidental and inexplicable. Fantasy undermines the rhetorical structures of referentiality and coherence within realism, being concerned with those areas of uncertainty and unpredictability which have been neglected in order to create those structures. Fantasy deals with what cannot easily be accommodated, with all that resists order, and in so doing exposes the blind spots of realistic discourse and the structures of thought that it expresses.[3] So realism and fantasy confront each other as kinds of fictional discourse, in a relationship of mutual opposition that may take various forms. With Alice Munro it seems to be a relationship of mutual contrariety (rather than true contradiction) where each discourse co-exists with the other; on the other hand, the relationship between them may be one of binary opposition where realism and fantasy are contradictory or mutually exclusive, as seems to be true in the fiction of Margaret Atwood. I am suggesting that Munro and Atwood exploit the discontinuities between these two kinds of discourse in order to discover through the gaps revealed in both new ways of perceiving experience and a language for such perceptions.

These are all stories about women's experiences and they share that ambivalent relation to traditional realistic fiction so characteristic of women's texts since eighteenth century Gothic novels. Not surprisingly the Gothic, that literature of female dread, repression and constraint, is the favorite fantasy form for both Munro and Atwood, though here it is Gothic critically scrutinized and updated while still retaining its original charge of menace, mystery and malignancy. Munro's Gothic landscape is within the small Canadian towns where her heroines have grown up: there are unplumbed holes in the Wawanash River which one of her heroines has known since childhood, the terrors of assault, rape and murder are in local newspapers and local gossip as part of everyday experience. Atwood's *Surfacing* hides the heroine's vital secret in the labyrinth of the text so that it can only be told after a descent into another unplumbed hole (this time a lake known since childhood) and her dilemma resolved through a kind of visionary madness and a ghost story. *Bodily Harm*, for all its modern Toronto and Caribbean scenarios, is traditional Gothic minimally transformed with its insistence on pervasive threats to the heroine and her final incarceration, the dread of every Gothic heroine. It is an interesting difference between the two writers that whereas Munro has come increasingly to see Gothic as an 'unreliable structure,' Atwood continues to explore its possibilities since *Bodily Harm* in *Murder in the Dark* (1983). What is evident in both writers' work is that the world of Gothic fantasy coexists with everyday reality, and that fantasy and realism are separate genres only in fiction, not in lived experience. Fantasy may be a way of evasion and resistance, but that is only its negative side. It may also be used creatively as a way of gaining for oneself the necessary inner space to remake images of the self and of the world outside the self so that it becomes a way of renegotiating connections. On occasions, fantasy may also function as primitive female intuition, and both writers share such moments of uncanny insight which are always perceptions of danger:

(Alice Munro)
> People say they have been paralyzed by fear, but I was transfixed, as if struck by lightning, and what hit me did not feel like fear so much as recognition. I was not surprised. This is the sight that does not surprise you, the thing you have always known was there.[4]

(Margaret Atwood)
> She's afraid of men and it's simple, it's rational, she's afraid of men because men are frightening.[5]

In Alice Munro's fictions fantasizing as a mental process coexists with a character's everyday normal living; this parallels the relation between fantasy and realism as narrative discourses in her texts. Just as the female narrators inscribe their differences of view from cultural images of 'normal women' through fantasizing and daydreaming, so fantasy challenges the limits of realism as fictional construct imposed on reality. The possibilities envisaged by fantasy do not however lie outside reality, rather they are contained/hidden within it. So in her fiction, fantasy and realism cannot exclude each other in a truly contradictory relationship; instead, they supplement each other as two kinds of discourse which together make up a fictional text which is still less than the complexity of reality itself.

As the title suggests, *Lives of Girls and Women* contains the stories of many women's lives, not just the particular narrator's story of her own life. These are the stories of 'infinitely obscure lives' that Virginia Woolf glances at in *A Room of One's Own* and they represent the 'experience of the mass behind the single voice'[6] which is that of the narrator as heroine of her own story. All these other stories or fragments are about women's secret resistance to the maxims of a male-dominated culture; often they are stories of emotional wreckage and frustrated ambition, stories of refusal, but all of them reveal women's stance as 'alien and critical' *(Room of One's Own*, p. 93), like Del's maiden aunts who 'respected men's work beyond anything; they also laughed at it.'[7] Del and Rose are the inheritors of this tradition of repression and secret resistance practised within the bounds of conformity to prevailing cultural images of women and their proper roles. (In this case, the images are those of small-town rural Ontario where the voice of public opinion is singularly authoritative with the confidence that is possible only in a small self-enclosed village community.) The difference for Munro's heroines is that through their intelligence and educational opportunities they have the chance to deviate openly from the social norms, to escape from this community, and so write their life stories in different ways from their mothers.

But what Del's and Rose's narratives also make plain is that they too, like all the women before them, are caught in a web of contradictory discourses. There is the world where they live and the discourse within which that world is encoded—the discourse of the 'doxa' in real life and of realism in fiction—versus the world that they desire or dread, which is the world of their private fantasies. What we are concerned with are the fictional forms that their fantasies take: for Del it is traditional Gothic as her perceptions, her daydreams and finally her (rejected) novel show, while for Rose it is less Gothic in its dark dreads but equally sensational, exaggerated and theatrical. Not surprisingly Rose becomes a professional actress who is always wondering if she has got the emphasis right: 'The thing she was ashamed of, in acting, was that she might have been paying attention to the wrong things, reporting antics, when there was always something further, a tone, a depth, a light, that she couldn't get and wouldn't get.'[8] The fragility of these created worlds reflects the tensions in these women, who see themselves as exiles or spies in their home towns, but who are at the same time products of that culture. Their nonacceptance of those norms is complicated by the alarming degree to which the stereotypes have been internalized by each of them. Their procedures for resisting entrapment and emphasizing their own separateness are also accompanied by the need to camouflage that resistance and to compensate to themselves for their nonconformity, so that deviousness and self-contradiction become both theme and source for the contradictory discourses within the text.

Both Del and Rose are struck by the discontinuities between the surface ordinariness of their town and of their own lives and the secret worlds that lie beneath appearances of normality. Their narratives disrupt the conventions of realism by fixing on moments of instability, when through passionate desire or rage or revolt what is usually repressed becomes visible, transforming the familiar into the unfamiliar as contradictory ways of seeing are revealed side by side in a world which to the narrator is both 'touchable and mysterious': 'People's lives, in Jubilee as elsewhere, were dull, simple, amazing and unfathomable—deep caves paved with kitchen linoleum.' ('Epilogue: The Photographer,' *Lives*, p. 210). This grammatical structure of contradictions relates to the basic structure of fantasy narrative and is close to oxymoron which, as Rosemary Jackson asserts, is the common trope of fantasy, being the figure of speech which holds together contradictions and sustains them in an impossible unity.[9] These hidden worlds challenge the comfortable assumptions of everyday life and its fictional expression through the realistic forms of chronicle history and autobiographical novel. Yet, as the real world contains those secrets, so they have to be accommodated within a fictional structure where the conventions of realism are continually disrupted.

It is the female narrators' intuitive perceptions of these hidden worlds that is the most characteristic sign of their outsider status. They both grow up on the edges of what is socially respectable, a condition exacerbated by their education, so that they see themselves as not conforming to the norms of femaleness as seen either by other women or by men. Only through fantasy can their energies create an attractive alternative to the unacceptable possibilities in their lives, for it is through language alone that transformations of the ordinary into the extraordinary can be effected. The very activity of verbalizing and writing down is a transformational process in which things are changed into words. The act of narration is an act of the creative imagination, where the mind comes to dominate things as they are, as language replaces/displaces reality. To paraphrase J. Hillis Miller, any text is a substitute for reality or a supplement to it. The creative imagination transforms things into words so that a thing ceases to be itself and becomes a sign pointing beyond itself to something absent, something existing elsewhere.[10] Language is always opening up gaps with its substitutions and splittings apart, and fantasy discourse is perhaps the most extreme example of this creative displacement of reality.

Certainly Munro's narrators glory in the transforming power of words, so creating imaginative worlds that transcend the ordinariness and the humiliations of everyday living. The opening paragraph of 'Royal Beatings' (the first story in *Who Do You Think You Are?*) is a riot of verbal fantasy in the mind of Rose, who is at this time 'nine, ten, eleven, twelve':

> *Royal Beating.* That was Flo's promise. You are going to get one Royal Beating.
>
> The word Royal lolled on Flo's tongue, took on trappings. Rose had a need to picture things, to pursue absurdities, that

was stronger than the need to stay out of trouble, and instead of taking this threat to heart she pondered: how is a beating royal? She came up with a tree-lined avenue, a crowd of formal spectators, some white horses and black slaves. Someone knelt, and the blood came leaping out like banners. An occasion both savage and splendid. In real life they didn't approach such dignity ('Royal Beatings,' *Who Do You Think You Are?*, p. 1).

It is this same quirk of mind that has got Rose into trouble in the first place, in her repetition of the nonsense rhyme:

'Two Vancouvers fried in snot./Two pickled arseholes tied in a knot.'

Rose couldn't stop herself. She hummed it tenderly . . . It was not just the words snot and arsehole that gave her pleasure, though of course they did. It was the pickling and tying and the unimaginable Vancouvers . . . The tumble of reason; the spark and split of craziness ('Royal Beatings,' pp. 12-13).

For Rose, the tumble of reason brings her moments of insight into the contradictory nature of reality, into that treachery 'on the other side of dailiness,' and though discourse holds her double perceptions together, between them 'only a formal connection could be made' ('Royal Beatings,' p. 8).

The power of fantasy to rupture the discourse of realism by pointing to its inconsistencies and repressions and then filling those gaps with a discourse of desire is keenly scrutinized in the central female fantasy of falling in love—and then falling out of love again. This fantasy recurs in remarkably similar form in at least three of Munro's stories: Del's experiences in 'Baptising,' Rose's in 'Simon's Luck,' and the unnamed narrator's in 'Bardon Bus.' As a plot configuration it accords with Nancy K. Miller's suggestion that there is a distinctive female erotics that structure the plots of women's fiction.[11] The main elements of Miller's female plot analysis are: the longing to be transported by the exquisite currents of desire, which is followed by the woman's awakening to disentangle herself from the web, and then renunciation of that love. As she remarks, 'Perhaps this renunciation, this choice to go beyond love, beyond erotic longing, is the figure that the "ambitious wishes" of women writers take?' (p. 41).

Though Munro's heroines do not all take the initiative in renouncing love, they all share that sense of self-possession that comes when love is over. All her heroines crave the self-abandonment of falling in love, crossing over into a fantasy world where 'everything we did seemed to take place out of range of other people, or ordinary consequences' ('Baptising,' *Lives*, p. 192). But they all recognize such loving as a luxury, a conforming to a female stereotype that they can indulge in only temporarily and as a fantasy from which they must awaken. Del's struggle with Garnet French in the water is the most explicit recognition that at the center of sexual love there is a woman who retains her independent selfhood: 'I felt amazement . . . that anybody could have made such a mistake, to think he had real power over me . . . It seemed to me impossible that he should not understand that all the powers I granted him were in play, that he himself was—in play, that I meant to keep him sewed up in his golden lover's skin for ever, even if five minutes before I had talked about marrying him' ('Baptising,' p. 197). Del escapes from this fantasy world and so resumes possession of the world and of herself in the language of realistic discourse: 'Unconnected to the life of love, uncoloured by love, the world resumes its own, its natural and callous importance. This is first a blow, then an odd consolation. And already I felt my old self—my old devious, ironic, isolated self— beginning to breathe again' ('Baptising,' p. 199). All of which is not to deny the pain of contradictions with which that story ends: 'Garnet French, Garnet French, Garnet French. Real life' ('Baptising,' p. 201).

Rose's fantasies of being in love with Simon are never so lyrical, though they follow a similar pattern, modified only by her mature chagrined realization that her fantasies are self-created: 'She had done it all herself, it seemed she never learned any lessons at all' ('Simon's Luck,' *Who Do You Think You Are?*, p. 170). It is the awakening from fantasy to actuality that is emphasized here in language very similar to Del's:

> It was those dishes that told her of her changed state . . . All she could have said was that she saw them in a way that wouldn't be possible to a person in any stage of love. She felt their solidity with a convalescent gratitude . . . She thought how love removes the world for you . . . It seemed to her it might not be the disappointment, the losses, the dissolution, she had been running from, any more than the opposite of those things; the

celebration and shock of love, the dazzling alteration. Even if
that was safe, she couldn't accept it. Either way you were robbed
of something—a private balance spring, a little dry kernel of
probity. So she thought ('Simon's Luck,' pp. 174-75).

The notion of love as 'misplacement' is the one that Munro returns to
in 'Bardon Bus,' her most recent critical scrutiny of the central female
fantasy: 'There I come back again and again to the center of my
fantasy, to the moment when you give yourself up, give yourself over,
to the assault which is guaranteed to finish off everything you've been
before. A stubborn virgin's belief, this belief in perfect mastery; any
broken-down wife could tell you there is no such thing.'[12] Of course
such knowledge does not prevent either her narrator or her narrator's
friends from falling in love and then having to undergo the process of
recovery. It is in the letting go of erotic fantasy that the narrator
moves to a recognition of the contradictions within reality itself,
contradictions that love has oversimplified: 'The lightness is
something to think about. It isn't just relief. There's a queer kind of
pleasure in it . . . It's an uncalled-for pleasure in seeing how the
design wouldn't fit and the structure wouldn't stand, a pleasure in
taking into account, all over again, everything that is contradictory
and persistent and unaccommodating about life. I think so. I think
there's something in us wanting to be reassured about all that, right
alongside—and at war with—whatever there is that wants permanent
vistas and a lot of fine talk' ('Bardon Bus,' pp. 127-28).
   This judgement on fantasy as an 'unreliable structure' echoes
Del's words in the 'Epilogue' of *Lives*, where she rejects her Gothic
novel about Jubilee: 'It is a shock, when you have dealt so cunningly,
powerfully, with reality, to come back and find it is still there'
('Epilogue,' p. 209). Fantastic discourse conforming as it does to
patterns of desire is shown to be as unreliable, as incomplete, as the
discourse of realism. In either case, there is always something in
addition, for reality is infinitely recessional. What then is Alice
Munro aiming for, with her presentation of worlds alongside, in
different dimensions of awareness? While one of her narrators (Del) is
aiming toward a new condition of writing where everything will be
'held still and held together—radiant, everlasting' ('Epilogue,' p.
210) and all of them are aiming toward a new condition of being, one
continuous enterprise is to expose the limits of any fictional
discourse. Fantasy and realism confront each other in a supple-
mentary relationship, for as both are inevitably incomplete

structures imposed on reality, neither discourse ought to be privileged over the other.

In Margaret Atwood's fiction the exposure of contradictions together with attempts to disengage from the kind of realistic discourse that enshrines and masks them seems to be central. Her fiction has strong didactic elements both feminist and humanist as her novels engage directly with life in a scrutiny of prevailing cultural images and assumptions. As her (male) porn artist says in *Bodily Harm*, 'What art does is, it takes what society deals out and makes it visible, right? So you can *see* it' (p. 208). The importance of making things visible through writing about them as a way of raising consciousness is explicitly stated in *Bodily Harm* where the heroine Rennie Wilford, a Toronto journalist doing a holiday piece on 'lifestyles' on a Caribbean island, is exhorted to write about the hidden lifestyles on the island by its one political idealist: 'Here, nothing is inconceivable . . . I wish you to write about it' (p. 133). His plea is echoed later in the prison by Rennie's fellow victim Lora, who says, 'When you get out . . . Tell someone I'm here . . . Tell someone what happened' (p. 282). Both these are pleas for realistic reportage, but this leaves an important space for fantastic discourse as a way to go further by imagining change, alternative possibilities which do not as yet exist. It is in this sense that fantasy has an important function, a point which Margaret Atwood makes herself in her essay on 'Witches': 'When you are a fiction writer, you're confronted every day with the question: What kind of world shall you describe for your readers? The one you can see around you, or the better one you can imagine? If only the latter, you'll be unrealistic; if only the former, despairing. But it is by the better world we can imagine that we judge the world we have. If we cease to judge this world, we may find ourselves, very quickly, in one which is infinitely worse.'[13]

Surfacing and *Bodily Harm* are not developmental fictions about girls' education like Alice Munro's, but instead they are stories about grown-up women for whom self-division, repression and marginality have become a condition of being. Sexual relationships are at the center of crisis and conflict, but these novels do not share the female plot configurations of Munro's fiction. Both Atwood's heroines have already examined the fantasy of being in love, and what is scrutinized here are women's fantasies of irresponsibility as responses to the recognition of female powerlessness. In *Surfacing*, the woman's role as victim is itself shown to be a harmful fantasy: 'This above all, to refuse to be a victim. Unless I can do that I can do nothing. I have to recant, give up the old belief that I am powerless and because of it nothing I can do will ever hurt anyone. A lie which was always more disastrous than the truth would have been.'[14] *Bodily Harm* presents a more threatening scenario altogether. Modelled on the traditional female Gothic plot, it is also an astute analysis of the two main components of Gothic fantasy: the heroine's fears of assault and capture versus her hopes of rescue by the hero. It bleakly confirms female dreads and starkly denies fantasies of rescue, for Rennie is not 'exempt' from physical danger any more than she is exempt from moral responsibility. What is shown most plainly in *Surfacing* and *Bodily Harm* is the incompatibility between the world of desire and the world of reality: 'There was such a gap between what she wanted and where she was that she could hardly stand it' (p. 196).

Many critics have written about women's sense of duality and alienation in Atwood's poems and novels,[15] so in writing about *Surfacing* I shall merely note that it is a novel about deconstruction—of cultural stereotypes of Canadianness as well as of women—worked out through the story of the efforts of one woman to examine contradictions within herself in her process of self-revision. I shall focus here on how such a process of change is imaged through changes of discourse within the novel. *Surfacing* uses both realism and fantasy, and the way to fantasy is signalled through breaks in the realistic part of the narrative—in the hints of dislocation, in deliberate blanks in the story, and in gaps of chronological sequence, as in many images of bodily dismemberment. What all these disruptions signal and conceal is the lie at the center of the narrative: for the narrator, there was no conventional love and marriage story but only an abortion and its consequent guilt which has shaped her story up to its climax in Chapter 17. Lying is an abuse of fantasy, but lies may also be necessary fictions, necessarily makeshift and needing to be revised: 'I couldn't accept it, that mutilation, ruin I'd made, I needed a different version . . . A faked album . . . but a paper house was better than none and I could almost live in it, I'd lived in it until now' (pp. 143-44).

The language of recognition is always the language of realistic discourse, but the process of recognition has perhaps to be the language of fantasy, involving the deconstruction of the familiar in order to perceive something new. Certainly for this heroine the familiar childhood places become the unfamiliar places of spiritual quest and ritual. The discourse breaks decisively with realism as she enters the climactic stages of her psychic quest: 'Now I understand the rule. They [the spirits of her parents] can't be anywhere that's marked out, enclosed . . . They can move only in the spaces between them, they are against borders. To talk with them I must approach the condition they themselves have entered' (p. 180). As Atwood has remarked, *Surfacing* is a ghost story, and the narrator in her hallucinatory state assumes the 'transparency' of a ghost herself, as she transcends the limits of individual identity via her vision of undifferentiated existence: 'I lean against a tree, I am a tree leaning . . . I am not an animal or a tree, I am the thing in which the trees and animals move and grow, I am a place' (p. 181). If this is a mystic vision it is also a state of madness, and the narrator's psyche according to the self-regulating principle of binary opposition immediately goes into reverse, working back through the image of the tree: 'I have to get up, I get up. Through the ground, break surface, I'm standing now; separate again' (p. 181). It is with the psychic strength generated by that experience that the narrator is able to see the ghosts of her parents, in visions that become revisions of her relationship to them both. Her recovery 'to live in the usual way' is signalled by her return to realistic discourse, as she 're-enters her own time,' the world of mirrors, clothes, relationships and language, compromise and negotiations, for 'withdrawing is no longer possible, and the alternative is death' (p. 191).

Surfacing is an optimistic fiction, for it affirms the possibility for a woman's self-forgiveness and self-revision; it also looks toward futures through the female biological image of the narrator's pregnancy. Fantasy has played a double role: escapist female fantasies have been exposed, while female vision drawing its power from chthonic sources has become the way to revision—of the self and of cultural stereotypes. No such release is envisaged in *Bodily Harm*, where attempts to disengage from contradictions merely project them onto a wider screen. Indeed the same contradictions between freedom and submission, responsibility and irresponsibility, authority and powerlessness which women perceive in their personal lives are shown to be magnified in the political situation of the Caribbean island. Women are not an isolated case but only one example of an oppressed group. This novel shows that disengagement and escape may be possible only in fantasy.

This story is a more extreme version of the split between the real world and the self than we have in *Surfacing,* for here metaphors become literal. Amputation is no longer a figurative expression but the central fact of the narrator's mastectomy which has happened before the narrative begins: the female dread of male sexual assault is figured in the discovery of the rope on her bed, and her sidestep from real life is no escape but lands her in a truly unfamiliar place where she does not know the rules and cannot find them out; she is not on home territory in any sense and she is truly powerless. The narrator is forced to re-evaluate her cherished marginality as a guarantee of security: 'Most of the people she knew thought Rennie was way out ahead of it, but she saw herself as off to the side. She preferred it there' (*Bodily Harm*, p. 26); and 'Massive involvement, said Rennie. It's never been my thing' (p. 34). By the end of the novel, Rennie is literally 'off to the side' (in prison) and she does **not** prefer it, for marginality, though it may confer invisibility, does not prevent 'massive involvement.'

The narrative is told almost entirely in the third person, a form that the narrator of *Surfacing* explicitly rejects (*Surfacing*, p. 14).[16] There is a dramatic shift from the early Toronto section (the first five pages) when the narrator still feels herself responsible and speaks as 'I' to the third person narrative which takes over at the point where she escapes to the Caribbean island:

> I want you to believe me, *I* said.
>
> *
>
> There's a two-hour stopover in Barbados, or so they tell **her** (p. 15; my emphasis).

The narrator is still the subject, but the shift in focalization images the disjunction between the self and the outside world. We realize by the end that there is a total break between the narrator's story and what is actually going on, and that this is how the world feels to one particular woman caught up in a mesh of political events where she is absolutely powerless. As Atwood has said, 'I was writing a spy story from the point of view of one of the ignorant peripherally involved women.'[17] Here, contradiction defines the conditions of possibility for this woman's writing, and fantasy narrative is her only way of resistance, of 'covering her eyes' to what is actually happening.

I said earlier that *Bodily Harm* is traditional female Gothic minimally transformed. Images of female dread are pervasive, radiating out from the icons of the coiled rope on the bed and the absent faceless stranger who had put it there: 'In itself it was neutral, and useful too, you could use it for all kinds of things' (p. 41). But the rope is also a message, and what would happen if you pulled on the rope? 'What would come up? What was at the end, *the end?* A hand, then an arm, a shoulder, and finally a face. At the end of the rope there was someone. Everyone had a face, there was no such thing as a faceless stranger' (p. 41). This is the story of a woman's discovery of what is at the end of the rope, and the revelation that female fantasies of male threat are founded in fact. It echoes Alice Munro's perception in an earlier story, 'Images': 'Our fears are based on nothing but the truth' (*Dance of the Happy Shades*, p. 43). In a curious way the man at the end of the rope conflates with Rennie's images of the men in her own life: Jake, her lover, with his power fantasies of rape, Daniel with all his ordinary human decency who had done the mastectomy, and Paul, the X factor, with his 'kindly threatening smile' (p. 150). Paul is, after all, 'the connection' (p. 182, 206)—between what and what? Looked at simply, he runs drugs and guns by boat in the Caribbean, but less simply he is the connection between the men Rennie has known and the faceless stranger. All this only becomes clear to her in her prison dream in the transformations of the faceless stranger, which come to rest on an earlier image of Paul in his mirror sunglasses:

> Rennie is dreaming about the man with the rope, again, again. He is the only man who is with her now, he's followed her, he was here all along, he was waiting for her. Sometimes she thinks it's Jake . . . sometimes she thinks it's Daniel . . . But it's not either of them, it's not Paul . . . The face keeps changing, eluding her, he might as well be invisible, she can't see him, this is what is so terrifying, he isn't really there, he's only a shadow, anonymous, familiar, with silver eyes that twin and reflect her own (p. 287).

Rennie is almost at the end of the rope, and confronted with the naked exercise of police power in the prison courtyard, she has her climactic moment (in common with every Gothic heroine) where fantasy and reality fuse in an uncanny insight into past, present and future: 'She's afraid of men and it's simple, it's rational, she's afraid of men because men are frightening. She's seen the man with the rope, now she knows what he looks like. She has been turned inside out, there's no longer a *here* and a *there*. Rennie understands for the first time that this is not necessarily a place she will get out of, ever.

She is not exempt. Nobody is exempt from anything' (p. 290).

As if to confirm this perception, the prison guards beat up Lora. All Rennie wishes is that someone would cover her eyes, something she achieves for herself through fantasizing about her own release from prison: 'This is what will happen' (p. 293). The rest of Rennie's story of her release and return to Toronto is, I suggest, fantasy, signalled in the text by the flickering of verb tenses between present, past, future. In this 'massive involvement' (not to say 'terminal') situation, only through fantasy can she distance herself from the intolerable present. And yet it is in these unpropitious circumstances that Rennie makes her one truly moral gesture: she takes Lora's hand and holds it 'with all her strength' (p. 299) trying to will Lora back to life.[18] Through that effort Rennie releases herself from the slavery of fear, and it is with the energy of her imagination that the novel ends: 'She will never be rescued. She has already been rescued. She is not exempt. Instead she is lucky, suddenly, finally, she's overflowing with luck, it's this luck holding her up' (p. 301).

The massed contradictions of the final section make it difficult for the reader to reach a finalized hypothesis. Does Rennie get out of the prison or doesn't she? Instead of closure, there is oscillation between two opposite possibilities. However, I suspect this undecidability is only an illusion (very much like the double ending of Charlotte Brontë's *Villette*, another woman's novel about the incompatibility of the world of desire and the world of reality), for if we take a retrospective look we see contradiction as Rennie's verbal mode in earlier crisis situations, and if we go back to the first framing sentence of the novel, 'This is how I got here, says Rennie,' we begin to wonder 'Where is here?' The whole story may be read as a prison narrative, written from the other side of ordinariness by a narrator who is literally confined to an obscure private existence. In this novel there is a sharp confrontation for the reader (as for the narrator) between the expected and the actual. Our expectations from Gothic literature coincide with Rennie's expectations from mid-twentieth century Toronto life that she will be rescued. However, it becomes clear from the narrative that there is no male rescuer for Rennie, as there never has been. Our expectations like Rennie's have been culturally conditioned, and they are disproved. All of which raises interesting questions about the dynamics of the reader's expectations, no less than the heroine's. The contradictions of the ending lead to a re-examination and a necessary modification of our (and Rennie's) former assumptions about art and about life: 'In any case she is a subversive. She was not one once but now she is. A reporter. She will pick her time; then she will report' (pp. 300f.). Her report is her silenced prison narrative, which does get told through the novel itself.[19]

All these fictions use a double discourse where fantasy is not the subtext, because realism is in no way privileged. Instead, contradictory discourses generate the multiple meanings of these texts. Fantasy challenges realism so that realism itself comes to look like a convenient fiction as the surface world begins to fissure, to look very uncommon indeed. Fantasy and realism both exist, but they do not necessarily connect. These women's texts contain both ways of seeing, and their language insists on the contradictions. Alice Munro: 'So lying alongside our world was Uncle Benny's world like a troubling distorted reflection, the same but never at all the same' ('The Flats Road,' *Lives*, p. 22). And Margaret Atwood: 'From the surface you can feel nothing, but she no longer trusts surfaces' (*Bodily Harm*, p. 48).

University of Reading, England

[1]Alexander Pope, 'Epistle to a Lady,' I. 270, *The Poems of Alexander Pope: A Text with Selected Annotations*, ed. J. Butt (London: Methuen, 1963), p. 569.

[2]This essay is situated within a context of feminist criticism, the parameters of which are indicated by the following: *Women Writing and Writing about Women*, ed. Mary Jacobus (London: Croom Helm, 1979); Annette Kolodny, 'Some Notes on Defining a Feminist Literary Criticism,' *Critical Inquiry*, 2 (Autumn 1975), 75-92; *Writing and Sexual Difference*, ed. Elizabeth Abel (Brighton: Harvester, 1982).

[3]For full length discussions of fantasy and realism, see Christine Brooke-Rose, *A Rhetoric of the Unreal: Studies in Narrative and Structure, Especially of the Fantastic* (Cambridge: Cambridge Univ. Press, 1981), and Rosemary Jackson, *Fantasy: The Literature of Subversion*, (London and New York: Methuen, 1981).

[4]Alice Munro, 'Images,' in *Dance of the Happy Shades* (Toronto: McGraw-Hill Ryerson, 1968), p. 38.

[5]Margaret Atwood, *Bodily Harm* (London: Virago, 1981), p. 290. All further references to this work appear in the text.

[6]Virginia Woolf, *A Room of One's Own* (London: Panther, 1977 [1929]), p. 63.

[7]Munro, 'Heirs of the Living Body,' in *Lives of Girls and Women* (Scarborough, Ontario: New American Library of Canada, 1974 [1971]), p. 27. All further references to *Lives* appear in the text.

[8]Munro, 'Who Do You Think You Are?', in *Who Do You Think You Are?* (Scarborough, Ontario: New American Library of Canada, 1979 [1978]), p. 209. All further references to this work appear in the text. This book was published in England under the title, *The Beggar Maid: Stories of Flo and Rose* (London: Allen Lane, 1980; Harmondsworth: Penguin, 1981).

[9]Jackson, p. 21.

[10]J. Hillis Miller, 'The Stone and the Shell: The Problem of Poetic Form in Wordsworth's Dream of the Arab,' in *Untying the Text: A Post-Structuralist Reader,* ed. Robert Young (London: Routledge & Kegan Paul, 1981), pp. 244-65.

[11]Nancy K. Miller, 'Emphasis Added: Plots and Plausibilities in Women's Fiction,' *PMLA,* 96 (1981), 36-48.

[12]Munro, 'Bardon Bus,' in *The Moons of Jupiter* (Toronto: Macmillan, 1982), p. 111. All further references to this story are in the text.

[13]Atwood, 'Witches,' in *Second Words: Selected Critical Prose* (Toronto: Anansi, 1982), p. 333.

[14]Atwood, *Surfacing* (London: Virago, 1979 [1972]), p. 191. All further references to this work appear in the text.

[15]See Sherrill Grace, *Violent Duality: A Study of Margaret Atwood* (Montreal: Véhicule, 1980); Kolodny, *op. cit.*; James Harrison, 'The 20,000,000 Solitudes of *Surfacing,*' *Dalhousie Review,* 59, 1 (Spring 1979), 74-81; Barbara Godard, 'My (m)Other, My Self: Strategies for Subversion in Atwood and Hébert,' *Essays on Canadian Writing,* 26 (Summer 1983), 13-44.

[16]There is one other short section in the first person, Rennie's memories of her Griswold childhood, pp. 53-58.

[17]Quoted from Atwood's address delivered at a conference, 'Imagined Realities in Contemporary Women's Writing,' Dyffryn House near Cardiff (October 1982), organized by the Welsh Arts Council.

[18]This gesture of female bonding is also a revision of Rennie's relationship with her mother and grandmother where 'hands' are very important. It may be compared with the narrator's final vision of her mother in *Surfacing.* For a fascinating reading of women's relations with women in *Lady Oracle,* see Godard, *op. cit.*, pp. 24-37.

[19]In this reading of the ending I am indebted to the theoretical analysis of the dynamics of reading in Shlomith Rimmon-Kenan, *Narrative Fiction: Contemporary Poetics,* (London New York: Methuen, 1983), pp. 121-22.

Paul Goetsch

MARGARET ATWOOD'S *LIFE BEFORE MAN* AS A NOVEL OF MANNERS

At one point in Margaret Atwood's novel *Life Before Man*
Elizabeth reacts to the moral lecturing of her aunt Muriel as follows:

> Elizabeth puts her hand against the pine sideboard to steady
> herself. She closes her eyes briefly; behind them is a network of
> elastic bands. With everyone else she can depend on some
> difference between surface and interior. Most people do
> imitations; she herself has been doing imitations for years. If
> there is some reason for it she can imitate a wife, a mother, an
> employee, a dutiful relative. The secret is to discover what the
> others are trying to imitate and then support them in their belief
> that they've done it well. Or the opposite: *I can see through you.*
> But Auntie Muriel doesn't do imitations; either that or she is so
> completely an imitation that she has become genuine. She is her
> surface.[1]

Since Elizabeth likes to see her aunt as a grotesque fossil from
prehistoric times, she is wrong about her. Shortly before Muriel's
death, it becomes clear that even in her case there is some difference
between 'surface and interior.' Throughout the novel Atwood
exploits this discrepancy between self-presentation of the individual
and hidden emotional life, between public behavior and private
experience. She examines the contemporary norms of human
behavior and depicts the difficulties resulting from them. In
addition, she demonstrates that the code people live by is of little help
when they are faced with existential problems. *Life Before Man*
combines, as it were, two types of novel: as a novel of manners the
work offers a rather bleak view of human interaction and relationships in the so-called age of sexual liberation; as a psychological
novel it plays variations upon standard themes of Atwood's fiction,
such as extinction and survival, victimization, rebirth, and
metamorphosis.

In terms of narrative technique the author produces a fusion of the
novel of manners and the psychological novel with the help of a
third-person, center-of-consciousness narrative. By shifting the point

of view from Elizabeth to her husband, Nate, and to his friend, Lesje, and by moving freely from the external behavior of the characters to their inner experiences, Atwood is able to contrast their civilized standards and norms with their emotional needs and difficulties. Her rather dispassionate analysis,[2] which goes along with the third-person point of view, is in keeping with the self-control expected of characters in a novel of manners. Nevertheless, the reader is in a position to find out where this self-discipline becomes a burden for the protagonists and how they try to cope with problems such as the longing for passion, love, and understanding, and the experience of time and death. While it is true that the main characters are preoccupied with the same problems, it is wrong to argue that 'the very necessity for separate points of view is ironically undercut by the boring sameness of these people.'[3] When they go through the motions of everyday life and stick to their civilized routines, they may resemble automatons or (to use a characteristic image of the novel) fossils; but their inward lives are interesting and varied.

The discrepancy between outward behavior and the world of subjective feelings and reflections has been a distinguishing feature of the novel of manners ever since the time of Jane Austen, the first novelist to make frequent use of the indirect interior monologue in order to counterbalance the deceptive nature of civilized behavior. The following genre-oriented analysis is an attempt to show that *Life Before Man* draws on the novel of manners and probes its limitations.

As in the novels of Austen, Trollope or James, and of course as in real life, the norms of behavior have the function of regulating and at the same time facilitating social interaction between different human beings. *Life Before Man* focuses on the guidelines that concern relationships between the sexes. In contrast with the traditional novel of manners, the rules accepted by the characters have not been handed down by the previous generation. As in some of the novels of the 1960s, say in John Updike's *Couples,* the characters, as members of the pill generation, make use of new possibilities of conducting their sexual affairs and set up rules of their own. Nate and Elizabeth grew up in the 1950s and turned their backs on the moral attitudes of the older generation when they went through the sexual revolution of the 1960s. However, unlike their contemporaries in Updike's novels, they do not seem to experience any joyful sense of discovery and exploration. Similar to the characters in Doris Lessing's *The Summer Before the Dark,* they turn to the new rules not so much in relief as in a perfunctory spirit, wishing simply to exchange old habits for new.

When Elizabeth sleeps with another man for the first time and informs Nate, both of them are shocked: 'The first time, she told him and they both cried, holding each other closely, consoling each other for some violation they felt as mutual. Then they discussed their problems, sitting up till four in the morning, whispering across the kitchen table. They promised reforms, repairs, reparations, whole new sequences of events, a new order. And the second and the third time' (p. 175). As time goes by they come to an understanding: they agree to accept each other's affairs and to keep the marriage going for the sake of the children. Among the rules which have been developed from these premises are agreements on the division of housework, regulations for going out and staying at home, and the promise of frankness and honesty about their sexual arrangements: 'It's the rule that when Elizabeth cooks, Nate does the dishes. One of the many rules, subrules, codicils, addenda, errata. Living with Elizabeth involves a maze of such legalities, no easier to understand because some of them are unspoken. Like an unwary pedestrian, he only realizes he's violated one of these when the bumper hits him, the whistle blows, the big hand descends. Ignorance of the law is no excuse' (p. 163). Elizabeth extends these rules, as far as possible, to other people as well. For her, mutual tolerance implies the obligation to have close contacts with her husband's lovers. She tells Martha: ' "Why not be friendly? . . . We might as well behave like reasonable adults" ' (p. 106). It is true that her ulterior motive may be to discover whether her marriage is in danger or not; but as the self-appointed advocate of good manners—' "I believe in being civilized about these things" ' (p. 147)—she is, ironically enough, successor to her aunt Muriel. The puritanical spinster Muriel represents the ethical code of a bygone age and, as Elizabeth remembers only too well, used to be so strict and miserly that she even forbade the children to go out on Halloween. Because Elizabeth resembles her hated aunt so much, she comes to stand for the 'enlightened' manners of the age of sexual liberation. However, she has acquired some sense of responsibility from Muriel and wishes therefore to maintain her marriage at all costs. Martha, who has no such scruples, summarizes the effect of Elizabeth on other people: ' "You wanted to *supervise* us. Like some kind of playground organizer" ' (p. 147).

Though Martha and other characters are against supervisors, they are not against rules in general. For example, Lesje and William have promised 'to give each other a lot of room' (p. 20). Lesje patiently suffers his long absences and accepts the fact that he does not introduce her to his conservative parents in London, Ontario. She treats his wish that she should not change her hairstyle as one of the rules which she has to accept during the period they live together. In a very short time the relationship with William has become so much a matter of routine for her that, like Elizabeth with respect to Nate, she might compare her lover with a comfortable old shoe.

As in the traditional novel of manners, the rules which the people in *Life Before Man* have given themselves shape their interactions in many different ways. In contrast with the novels of Jane Austen and others, they are supposed to promote, rather than prevent, the initiation of sexual affairs and the exchange of partners. The basic function of these rules, however, remains the traditional one of ensuring the civilized behavior of the people involved. They help Martha and Nate, then Lesje and William, to get over their separations. They facilitate the encounter of potential rivals, for instance when Nate, who cannot quite suppress his jealousy, meets Chris, his wife's new conquest, and plays chess with him instead of venting his aggressions in another way. Usually, the prevailing code manages to channel emotions and render potentially explosive situations harmless. Thanks to it, couples, ex-lovers, would-be lovers, and divorcees can meet each other. At parties even truth games, for instance 'Lifeboat,' may be played without incurring too much risk, although someone might try to use the games for selfish reasons. The fact that Lesje does not know how to play the games at the party given by Elizabeth and Nate presents no serious problem within the framework of the novel of manners: like Elinor in *Sense and Sensibility* or Anne Elliot in *Persuasion,* Lesje hides her humiliation and leaves the room quickly in order to give free rein to her feelings in solitude. Usually, Lesje of course knows how to behave in harmony with the code: 'she doesn't like being irritating, so she tries to control herself even when nobody else is with her' (p. 20). How highly self-discipline is esteemed is proven by people's admiration of the poise Elizabeth displays after Chris's suicide.

In comparison with traditional novels of manners, the contemporary code described in *Life Before Man* is a liberal one. It is not necessarily simple and without complications. While it makes it possible even for a shy woman like Lesje to entertain sexual relations with various men, as a system of rules it is closely related to the seemingly more involved courtship rituals and social manners in the novels of Jane Austen. A symptom of this is that the principal characters long for uncomplicated relationships in vain. In spite of his experiences with Elizabeth and other women, Nate imagines Lesje 'to be without rules' (p. 163), but his eyes are soon opened. On one occasion Elizabeth wants to have sex with no strings attached and falls victim to a man who abuses her to satisfy his grotesquely exhibitionist needs. Lesje, for her part, nostalgically recalls the times when her affair with William was 'simple-minded and joyously adolescent' (p. 221), and daydreams of a relationship without involvement: 'she very much wants one of them, either of them, to say, "Come out for a beer." She would watch baseball games on television with them, eating potato chips and drinking from the bottle. She would hold their hands, roll on the carpet with them, make love as an afterthought, attaching no more meaning to that than to any other healthy exercise, a swim, a jog around the block. It would all be friendly and without any future. She wants actions, activities, with no significance and no hidden penalties' (p. 221). Such wishes cannot be fulfilled. 'China' (p. 317), that utopian country where one's wishes are not thwarted, does not exist, as Elizabeth regretfully tells herself at the end of the novel. Even in a so-called liberated age, every kind of human relationship, including sexual, is subject to rules. And wherever rules exist, complications and open or hidden penalties, as the traditional novel of manners has shown, are bound to follow. The price one has to pay for good manners is high. It may cause a general discontent with civilization, suffering, and loneliness. *Life Before Man* illustrates this in various ways.

Although frankness and honesty are principles of the code the main characters have accepted, their relationships function only because the partners repress individual wishes and longings time and again and hide what goes on in their minds. One leitmotif of the book is the pose of the attentive listener, a masquerade that allows the individual to take refuge in the private world of thoughts, memories, and dreams while pretending to be available for communication. Though prostrated by grief for Chris, Elizabeth forces herself to act surprised, and admire the costumes her children have thought up for Halloween. Playing a role before Muriel is much more difficult for her, but when she visits her aunt, who has cancer, she succeeds in repressing her hatred and posing as the understanding niece. Lesje bears the endless ecological comments of her lover William with 'a studiously attentive face' and 'murmurs applause' (p. 27), thinking of other subjects in the meantime and dreaming of having children of her own.

Insecure as she is, she is usually afraid of saying the wrong thing anyway and likes to play the role of the appeaser (p. 62). Her self-denial goes so far that she does not like to speak about herself and wishes to become the woman Nate believes she is:

> The fact is that she's addicted to Nate's version of her. Sometimes, when he touches her, she feels not naked but clothed, in some long unspecified garment that spreads around her like a shimmering cloud. She's realized with something close to panic that the picture he's devised of her is untrue. He expects her to be serene, a refuge; he expects her to be kind. He really thinks she is, underneath. . . . He ought to be able to tell by now that she isn't like this at all. Nevertheless she wants to be; she wants to be this beautiful phantom, this boneless wraith he's conjured up. Sometimes she really does want it. (p. 267)

Nate, too, is often willing to adjust to people's expectations of him. Under the influence of his mother, a political crusader, he became a lawyer. With Elizabeth supporting him against his mother, he gave up his position in order to find his self-fulfillment in making wooden toys. Since this work is less creative than he thought and is not remunerative either, he returns, with Martha's help, to his old law firm. Sometimes Nate feels trapped by women and is afraid of losing his identity. 'Occasionally, though by no means all the time, Nate thinks of himself as a lump of putty, helplessly molded by the relentless demands and flinty disapprovals of the women he can't help being involved with. Dutifully, he tries to make them happy. He fails not because of any intrinsic weakness or lack of will, but because their own desires are hopelessly divided. And there's more than one of them, these women. They abound, they swarm' (p. 41).

All in all, the major characters are players of different roles, thus repressing or controlling their desires and aggressions and deceiving their partners. In order to keep their relationships going, they also avoid discussing the problems which they have in common. For Nate and Elizabeth the word 'divorce' has for a long time been an unspeakable word (p. 84). They do not talk about Chris's suicide either, though both of them have been shocked and moved by it. Lesje, who is of Jewish and Ukrainian descent, soon notices that she cannot speak to 'William Canadian' (p. 28) about visiting his parents (who are of good British stock) or about marriage and children. Easily intimidated, she hesitates to inform William about her new lover or to broach the subject of divorce and children with Nate.

As in the traditional novel, good manners tend to veil facts and feelings and to taboo the discussion of certain problems. Though honesty is expected, insincerity has become habitual with everyone. As a result the characters begin to feel guilty and to have doubts about the code. For example, from a rational point of view, Lesje does not worry about intruding into a marriage; she has discussed the pros and cons of the question in her women's lib group and believes that as far as her own case is concerned, 'Nate no longer seems like Elizabeth's husband' (p. 127). But when Nate and she use Elizabeth's bed, she 'feels for the first time that she has wronged Elizabeth, that she has trespassed' (p. 169). Similarly, Elizabeth at first pushes the idea of responsibility for Chris's suicide far back into her mind. Though assuming that Chris, by killing himself, wanted to make her feel guilty, she tells herself that the dismissal of her lover was justified in terms of her code. Later, she is no longer sure about this (p. 98) and admits to herself that she enjoyed her power over him and then dropped him as if he had not been anything but a vacation dream: 'She thinks: I treated him the way men treat women' (p. 161). In spite of this insight she does not know whether to regard him as a weakling or an object of pity. This is in character. Since she is worried that Nate might leave her at any moment, she feels that she has to remain controlled and so, unlike Chris, keep up appearances and save face.

In order to protect themselves and stay civilized, the characters lie to each other and avoid discussing their problems. What they think and feel often remains hidden from their partners. In a certain sense everyone lives the essential part of his life all by himself. One formal expression of this is the way in which Atwood has organized the chapters of the novel: as a rule the depiction of the emotions and reflections of the protagonists takes up much more space than the external action. Another formal expression of the importance of the hidden life of the characters is the discrepancy between the external and internal actions in the novel as a whole. Within the context of the novel of manners the external action can be described as a repeated variation of the themes of losing and finding partners. Elizabeth loses Chris and Nate, has brief affairs with William and a chance acquaintance, and then remains alone with her children; Lesje leaves William and joins Nate; before Nate can live with the younger woman, he has to discard Martha and Elizabeth. What, apart from Chris's suicide, seems to be a frictionless process in accordance with the contemporary code, is in psychological terms a very complicated development. Forced to come to terms with loss and change more or less all by themselves, the characters resort to a number of strategies.

They seek refuge in memories and private fantasies, invent games, try to justify their past behavior and wish to redefine their identity in the light of their experiences.

The discrepancy between appearance and subjective reality is especially striking in the case of Elizabeth. Because of her versatility in managing impressions she intimidates others even after the death of Chris. To Lesje she appears as a 'bereft queen out of a Shakespearean play' (p. 64), a woman with 'competent maternal manners' (p. 21), a 'shark,' 'a Jurassic toad' (p. 265), and only once, near the end of the novel, does she seem to be simply 'worn, ordinary; mortal' (p. 309). Martha calls her an 'haute Wasp' (p. 96), 'Nate's mother,' a 'playground organizer' (p. 147), and a 'bitch' (p. 223). Nate, who at the beginning of their love affair adored Elizabeth as 'Madonna in a shrine' and a second Florence Nightingale (p. 49), comes to see her more and more as 'the lady with the axe' (p. 49) who threatens to outmanoeuver and corner him. Only when he feels that she is playing the martyr (p. 15) and presenting 'a dying swan look' (p. 16) does he get a glimpse of what is going on in her mind.

Elizabeth has to cope with her grief for Chris and face the problem of death in general. This forces her to live through the traumatic experiences of her life again—the death of her mother, a drinker, by fire, the suicide of her sister Caroline in the bathtub of an asylum, the strict puritanic education she received from Muriel, and her aunt's death. Taking a bath herself, Elizabeth toys with the idea of committing suicide. Death seems to be a suitable way out of the mess of her life on other occasions too. But finally she decides against imitating other victims. In a private game which might bear the title 'Why I don't need to go to the psychiatrist,' she tells herself: 'I am an adult and I do not think I am merely the sum of my past. I can make choices and I suffer the consequences, though they aren't always the ones I foresaw' (p. 99). Gradually she learns how to accept both her past and her future. Though she does not love Nate any longer, she sticks to their marriage for a long time. As R. D. Laing has observed,[4] some people are more disturbed by giving up a habitual game than by the loss of the partner: Elizabeth does not worry about Nate's relationship with Lesje, but she minds his breakaway from her rules (p. 251). She accepts his independence only when the burden of the past seems to be lifted from her after the burial of Muriel. Rationally, she regards her aunt's death as a kind of liberation. Subconsciously, however, she identifies with Muriel. As her blackout at the grave and her awakening indicate, Muriel is, virtually, reborn in her.[5] And like

Muriel in her lifetime, Elizabeth is going to raise two children, 'single, alone' (p. 316).

While Elizabeth clings to her marriage almost until the end of the novel, Nate for the first time thinks of leaving Elizabeth when observing her rejected lover Chris. Nevertheless the separation from his wife and his children is a painful and long trial for him, comparable to the imminent dissolution of his country. He does not understand why his wife does not watch the television news about the country falling apart (p. 70), and he bores his new friend Lesje with comments on the state of the nation. When René Lévesque and his Parti Québécois win the election in 1976, Nate is secretly exultant because he reads the threat of the separation of French Canada subjectively as an expression of the possibility of breaking with Elizabeth (p. 70).[6] Before he can leave his wife though, he has to learn to jettison old habits and accept the old house, where he and Lesje live, as his new home.

At the beginning of the novel Lesje feels that because of her multicultural and racial background 'William Canadian' and his family do not fully acknowledge her as an individual. In order to get over this and other disappointments she retreats into dreams of a time she has been familiar with from childhood and from her work at the Royal Ontario Museum, the age of the dinosaurs.

> Lesje knows she's regressing. She's been doing that a lot lately. This is a daydream left over from her childhood and early adolescence, shelved some time ago in favor of other speculations. Men replaced dinosaurs, true, in her head as in geological time; but thinking about men has become too unrewarding. Anyway, that part of her life is settled for the time being. Settled, as in: the fault settled. Right now *men* means William. William regards them both as settled. He sees no reason why anything should ever change. Neither does Lesje, when she considers it. Except that she can no longer daydream about William, even when she tries (p. 19).

The sterility of her relationship with William is reflected in their frequent conversations about the end of life. Whereas she usually speaks of the extinction of the dinosaurs, William, an environmental engineer, talks about the destruction of nature and mankind. Though Lesje soon begins to long for a change in her life and falls in love with Nate, it takes her a long time to get used to the idea of a separation from William. Since Nate also finds it difficult to sever connections with his family, she is quite depressed, remembers William nostalgically and, like Elizabeth, thinks of committing suicide: 'She ran up to the bathroom. . . . On the spur of the moment she'd decided to kill herself. She was amazed by this decision; she'd never considered anything remotely like it before. People like Chris had merely puzzled her. But at last she could see why Chris did it: it was this anger and the other thing, much worse, the fear of being nothing. People like Elizabeth could do that to you, blot you out; people like Nate, merely by going about their own concerns. Other people's habits could kill you' (pp. 292f.). Finally, however, she decides to try and get Nate to make her pregnant and thus force him to choose between her and Elizabeth. During her pregnancy Nate is 'displaced, if only slightly, from the center of her universe' (p. 309). She stops dreaming of the extinct dinosaurs and is willing to face the future. Though she believes that a pregnant paleontologist is a contradiction in terms (p. 308), her behavior is in harmony with the prehistoric past, for, as she knows, the dinosaurs once wished to survive too (p. 290). Therefore it makes sense that the guardian of the past (p. 308) develops into a guardian of the future and joins the many mothers and mother figures of the novel.

As the discrepancy between the external and internal actions, between the elements of the novel of manners and the psychological novel, illustrate, even the liberal code of the 1970s cannot solve the standard problem of the novel of manners—how to impose order on feelings, passions, human relationships. Like the manners of the Lintons in *Wuthering Heights*, the code cannot protect anyone from the kind of passion that drives Chris to suicide. Even milder forms of love are attended by frustrations and aggressions that undermine the code and suddenly come to the surface. Examples are the rape of Lesje by her neglected lover William, Elizabeth's grotesque experience with her chance acquaintance, and Martha's outburst of jealousy when she suspects Nate of flirting with one of the party guests.

The code of the people in *Life Before Man* is questionable because it is difficult to regulate passions and emotions socially and rationally, and also because the protagonists rely on the code so much and use it as a mainstay in their lives, even as a kind of *ersatz weltanschauung*. They certainly know, and pay lip service to, other sets of norms current in their society, but these other codes mean less to them. Let us take, for example, their attitudes to their professions and jobs. Lesje has occupied herself with prehistory and paleontology since her childhood and likes her job at the Museum;

she is, however, aware that her work is only a kind of 'glorified filing' (p. 183), and does not fully identify with it. While Elizabeth mourns for Chris, she carries on with her work at the Museum like a somnambulist and does not find any consolation in it. Atwood also makes it quite clear that religion is no longer a support for the protagonists. The characters still participate in rituals, such as family Christmas, or funerals, that have become meaningless for them. According to Elizabeth, everything is worse at Christmas (p. 99), and yet she goes on celebrating the day. So do Nate and Lesje, who consider Christmas spent with the family terrible (p. 115). As Arnold Davidson notes, 'In *Life Before Man*, the traditional holidays and holydays are mainly unwelcome ties to a personal history that most of the characters would prefer to forget, occasions for another depressing encounter with some "Auntie Muriel".'[7]

Since religion, puritan ethics, and other traditional values have lost their hold, the characters place too heavy a burden on love and sexual relationships. When disappointed and left by their partners, they learn that their code of behavior is not of much help. The will to go on living and make a new start can only come from within. Ironically, the mother figures of the older generation, whom the protagonists have rejected as role models, demonstrate the ability to survive. At first sight, Lesje's grandmothers, Auntie Muriel, and Nate's mother appear to be ridiculous fossils from a distant past. The continuous bickering of the grandmothers, which Lesje remembers, the puritanical zeal of Muriel, and the eager, but ineffective political crusades of Nate's mother may indeed seem grotesque; yet compared to the apathy and indifference of the younger generation, their commitment to values and care for their children are impressive, even if the protagonists would hesitate to admit this.

As in her other works, Atwood sympathizes with those who are easily victimized, but finally sides with the characters who struggle to survive and commit themselves to life. Elizabeth succeeds in overcoming her melancholy. She accepts Chris's death and the dissolution of her marriage, takes over the responsibility for her children, and, losing her husband to a younger woman, faces the problem of age. Her development is reminiscent of the central character of Doris Lessing's *The Summer Before the Dark* and anticipates Atwood's own *Bodily Harm*, where a somewhat older woman, who resembles Elizabeth, is confronted with the possibility of dying of cancer. Another main character in *Life Before Man*, Lesje, leaves her regressive phase behind and grows up by willing herself to become a mother (a theme reminiscent of *Surfacing*) and accepting the future even if it should bring about the extinction of life. Nate gives up making wooden toys, works as a lawyer again, though in a minor position, and decides to stay with Lesje. The decisions of the characters and their development are neither spectacular nor surprising. Elizabeth, Lesje and Nate remain very ordinary people. And it is not unlikely that they will soon become creatures of habit again, trying to live on the surface of life. On the other hand, they have not given in to despair and resignation and so may perhaps leave some traces in the life of the next generation, as did Lesje's grandmothers, Auntie Muriel, and Nate's mother in theirs.

Life Before Man, the title of the novel, links the world of dinosaurs, as reconstructed in the Museum, to human life in the 1970s. As the many comparisons with animals, statements about evolution, and Lesje's daydreams show, human beings are as clumsy as dinosaurs. They have difficulties in communicating with each other and regulating their relations, and, like some types of dinosaurs, they have special problems in connection with love and sexuality (pp. 143f.). In Lesje's regressive fantasies the dinosaurs sometimes represent life before humans, but in other daydreams of the young woman they also stand for passion or for extinction. Whether mankind is doomed or not, or even if it has become too 'big' for life on this earth, it must follow the example of the dinosaurs and struggle for survival (p. 290).

In this respect, *Life Before Man,* like the traditional novel of manners, points out that manners alone create only a superficial kind of order unless they are made subservient to the aims of life. The energy and imagination that enabled the Museum people to make their exhibits appear to be alive are also required whenever the individual copes with his own life. For Lesje the Museum has at a very early age become a substitute for the synagogue (p. 95). Perhaps it is possible to learn something from the Museum, the 'mausoleum of lost life forms,'[8] if one realizes that the recreation of past life is analogous to, but finally less important than, the creation of new life and new life forms.

University of Freiburg, Federal Republic of Germany

---

[1]Margaret Atwood, *Life Before Man* (Toronto: Anansi, 1979), pp. 216f.

[2]Cf. Cathy N. and Arnold E. Davidson, 'Prospects and Retrospect in *Life Before Man,*' in Davidson/Davidson (eds.), *The Art of Margaret Atwood: Essays in Criticism* (Toronto: Anansi, 1981), pp. 205-21, here p. 207.

[3]Sherrill Grace, *Violent Duality: A Study of Margaret Atwood* (Montreal: Vehicule, 1980), p. 136.

[4]Cf. R. D. Laing et al., *Interpersonelle Wahrnehmung* (Frankfurt: 1971), pp. 18f. For the notion of private games see also E. Berne, *Transactional Analysis in Psychotherapy: A Systematic Individual and Social Psychiatry* (New York, 1961), and *Games People Play: The Psychology of Human Relationships* (New York, 1964); and A. H. Chapman, *Put-Offs and Come-Ons* (New York: 1968).

[5]Cf. Linda Hutcheon, 'From Poetic to Narrative Structures: The Novels of Margaret Atwood,' in *Margaret Atwood: Language, Text and System*, Sherrill E. Grace and Lorraine Weir (eds.), (Vancouver: University of British Columbia, 1983), pp. 17-31, here p. 24.

[6]Cf. Davidson, p. 213.

[7]Davidson, p. 221.

[8]Davidson, p. 221. For a negative reading of the ending of the book and the development of the characters see the studies by Cathy N. and Arnold E. Davidson and Sherrill Grace.

Michel Fabre

'ORPHANS' PROGRESS,' READER'S PROGRESS: VOICE AND UNDERSTATEMENT IN MAVIS GALLANT'S STORIES

The short stories of Mavis Gallant are characterized by their great thematic diversity as well as by their variety of narrative techniques, so much so that it is difficult to take into account all of the techniques that make her style distinctive. Its uniqueness seems to flow from a voice which for the most part refuses to pass judgement, and then suddenly, when it is least expected, takes responsibility for the confrontation of different points of view. What Mavis Gallant herself says about 'style'—or about spiral-shaped stories which circle around a central event—hardly enlightens us.[1] Nor do the critical studies—as yet far too few, given the importance of Gallant's literary production—for they focus more on themes or on spatial and temporal categories than on textual analysis.[2] When Donald Stephens writes that a certain short story operates 'by the subtle implication of selected isolated incidents,'[3] he may account for some of the stories, but not, among others, for 'Orphans' Progress.' I propose to use this short story as the principal example in my analysis—an admittedly problematic and fragmented attempt to clarify what makes for, in my opinion, the uncontestable success of Mavis Gallant.

In its original version,[4] 'Orphans' Progress' is divided into three parts. In the first part, the Collier girls, aged six and ten, are taken away from Montreal and their mother, a widow who is judged incapable of looking after them properly; the girls are entrusted to their paternal grandmother in Ontario. The second part begins a year later, after the grandmother's death: at first the girls live with their mother's brother in a Montreal suburb, then, at the ages of eight and twelve, are sent to a Catholic convent school. The last part of the story takes place seven years later. Adopted by an aunt on her mother's side, Mildred comes back from Chicoutimi for a brief reunion with her older sister, who has become a nurse but is still closely attached to the convent. Their meeting marks the end of the orphans' 'progress' towards the socially acceptable norm, a progress characterized by the sisters' emotional growing apart and by the complete rupture of the younger girl with her past and with the memory of her mother.

Certainly, it is the choice of significant details which serves to reveal emotions or to sum up the children's reactions at each stage in their evolution. For example, the goat's milk brought in at great expense and which passes, in the grandmother's house, for especially nourishing food, becomes in the children's world a most disquieting element. This is expressed in the text by the unease of a man at a service station who is frightened by the goats, and by the fact that the animals' eyes do not reflect the children's faces as do human eyes.[5] The 'scissors episode' works in the same way: Mildred is forced to carry a sign around her neck saying 'I am a liar' after she declares, deceived by memory, that she has seen her mother's house over the rooftops. But, more than the choice of incidents, it is their juxtaposition in a relationship of resemblance or contrast that counts. One of the story's central themes is the opposition between interior and exterior, between feeling and public opinion, between intimate experience and reality as conceptualized by society—a society which uses language to impose its norms. Seen from this point of view, the various incidents serve above all to mark the stages of the evolution towards these norms. As social constraints progressively take hold, the orphans' image of a maternal home disappears and their affective memory regresses. The wiping out of the girls' past is reinforced, during the course of their wanderings, by their being rejected by one branch or another of their family, of either French-Canadian or English-Canadian background. In the end, Mildred Collier (officially renamed Desaulniers), having been punished several times for using the words 'maman' or 'mummy,' so effectively represses nostalgia for her childhood that she has no apparent reaction on seeing the apartment where she once lived: 'The parents [Desaulniers] craned at a garage and at some dirty-legged children with torn sneakers on their feet. Mildred glanced up, and then back at her book. She had no reason to believe she had seen the place before or would ever again.'[6]

This ending reveals by its cold factuality the dehumanizing horror of the orphan's progress into alienation. But the horror is not named, it must be supplied by the reader from what is left unsaid by the narrator, who carefully refrains from taking sides or passing judgement. It is in this sense that the author's narrative strategy takes it originality from the use of voice rather than from the rejection of the conventions of the short story form.

One would be inclined, in fact, to define Mavis Gallant's style not by a specific narrative 'chain' but rather by a characteristic voice. By 'chain' I mean the use of echoes and variations, more or less evident, that mark the development of a theme at each stage in the syntagmatic, linear development of the plot. In 'Orphans' Progress' this partial reiteration certainly exists and is marked by the recurrence of thematic motifs against the background of events constituting the story's plot. For example, the motif of the bed indicates attachment to the mother and the relative absence of individuality in the two girls. The three sleep together at first, which brings warmth and comfort to the children even when their mother is beaten down by anguish and alcohol. When they go to live with their uncle, the girls sleep together on a pull-out divan and argue about the covers: 'Cathie wanted them pushed down between them in a sort of trough, because she felt a draught, but Mildred complained that the blankets thus arranged were tugged away from her side' (p. 192). This is the beginning of their growing apart. At the convent, not only does each girl have her own bed for the first time in her life, but they are also in different dormitories. The recurrence of the bed motif evidently marks, by its variations, the growing individuation of Cathie and Mildred.

At a deeper linguistic level, verbal recurrences weave a chain reconstituting affective connotations which the omniscient narrator, on occasion, does not hesitate to define. Thus, the stay in the grandmother's house ends: 'What they remembered afterwards of this period when they were living with their grandmother was goat's milk, goat eyes and the frightened man' (p. 191). The text underlines the crucial value of 'goat' which, in the children's minds and as a result of their experiences, carries the connotation, firstly, of a disgusting liquid which symbolizes their grandmother's home; secondly, of opaque eyes which bar communication (while on the other hand, the girls' eyes mirror each other and make them 'twins'); and thirdly, of the uneasiness that overtakes the man in the service station. It is at this linguistic level that 'frightened man' echoes the phrase 'they attract frightened men' (applied to widows like the girls' mother) and also recalls directly 'seeming so sexually innocent that one is frightened' (p. 191). As a result, the value of 'goat' in the text is necessarily ambiguous: it is linked in the childrens' minds to unpleasant memories of Ontario, but it is also, by the same system of verbal echoes, implicitly linked to the mother and the negative image that the social workers have of her. The repetition of 'fright' suggests the possibility of a double reading, giving two meanings from two opposite points of view.

This story is effectively structured by the introduction of meanings which echo throughout the narrative to create an aesthetic result.

The progression of the story is marked by the changes in the children's ages. This insistence on chronology, on the passing of time, however, signals the permanence of one theme as much as it does the succession of events. Nevertheless, Mavis Gallant seems less preoccupied by the plot details than with the creation of a point of view from which events can be interpreted simultaneously from the exterior and from the interior, according to the social norm and according to the children's vision, until finally the norm triumphs over emotion.

Often, in a short story, a point of view is established from the beginning—indicated or suggested by the narrative voice and by enunciative modes that establish communication. The narrator supposes the connivance of the reader. Mavis Gallant, by her repeated recourse to indirection and understatement, seems to refute the involvement of the author/narrator who effaces herself more often than she lets herself be seen in most of the short stories. And, paradoxically, in 'Orphans' Progress,' it is when she seems to reveal herself most openly that the narrator is furthest from the 'voice,' that she is least sympathetic to the profound vision of the author.

In its original version, 'Orphans' Progress' begins *in medias res* with the announcement that welfare officials have taken the Collier girls away from their beloved mother. This is a statement of objective fact, even if the sentence contains an 'aside' by the omniscient narrator: 'they were taken away from their mother, whom they **loved without knowing what the word implied, or even that it existed,** and sent to their father's mother in Ontario' (p. 191). There follows a series of independent clauses which excites in the reader a need to find the missing logical links: 'Their father was dead. Their mother was no longer capable of looking after them properly' (p. 191) must implicitly be read, '**because** their father was dead **and** their mother was no longer capable.' It seems that the basis in truth of 'their father was dead' differs from that of 'their mother was no longer capable of looking after them properly,' which merely reflects an opinion, even though the parallel construction of the two statements presents them as equivalent. The passage from fact to opinion is not marked by any reference to a speaker/narrator who might take responsibility for this opinion. Curiously enough, the following sentence, by generalizing the statement into an observation, turns the so-called incapacity of the mother to look after her children into a general rule, an almost inevitable consequence derived from indubitable premises: 'When women turn strange, it happens very rapidly. The first sign is lack of care about clothes and hair, and all at once they are sluts. Drinking slides in. They attract frightening men. . . . At the end, the men around them are almost respectable (by contrast) but very unkind' (p. 191). The present tense of reality and of repetitive occurrence replaces here the preterite of fiction; 'women' (a general and undefined term) replaces 'the mother.' The enunciation of an intra-diegetic fact by the omniscient narrator thus shifts towards the enunciation by an extra-diegetic commentator of a general rule about the deterioration of a husbandless woman. This sends the reader to the referential code of 'what people usually believe.' At this stage, no indication permits the reader familiar with psycho-social semiology to recognize signs of connivance, for the statement does not reveal what we might call its 'emotional tone.'

In a no less astonishing manner, the impersonal statement thus given the value of a psychological law is now reclaimed by a first-person subject (an intrusion of the self which Gallant totally erases in the later version of the story): 'I have more than once seen women get into this state, and the common factors were drink, and dirt, and weeping, and rages, and being preyed upon, and finally seeming so sexually innocent that one is frightened' (p. 191). The 'I' authenticates the remark and implicitly defines the speaker as belonging in the camp of the conforming majority and welfare officers; at the same time, the statement demands the reader's connivance by using the indefinite 'one' at the end of the sentence. 'One' is all-englobing, in the same way that 'frightened' is strongly inclusive because of the undefined nature of the fear (fear produced by the mother? felt by her and taken up by the narrative voice? fear felt for her?). Be that as it may, the use of the indefinite draws the reader into a reaction of fear—fear of the behavior that is supposed to characterize the ineluctable fall of a woman alone. When we read: 'One says she is alcoholic, she is manic-depressive, the children should be taken away' (p. 191), the indefinite is more closely linked to an intra-diegetic speaker whose words are passed on by the narrator than it is to the reader; and the reference to the children brings us back to Mrs. Collier's plight. Nevertheless, the reader finds himself trapped: he has become, in spite of himself, one of the voices of opinion defining the social norm. Then, as if to fight the reader's possible reticence (his desire to dissociate himself from the statement about Mrs. Collier), the text responds by reiterating and insisting on the point: '*Yes,* they [the children] are seeing things they shouldn't, and not getting proper food, and in moral and perhaps physical danger (someday she will set the place on fire)' (p. 191). Here, the use of the present progressive tense to make us 'see' the reality of the danger posed to the children goes well beyond the simple expression of a possible ('perhaps') or probable ('someday she will') threat.

An entire critical study should be devoted to Mavis Gallant's use of the parenthesis, and the statement inserted between dashes: their recurrence seems to signal a desire on the part of the narrator to hold back his narration, to remain master of it by giving only the information he judges necessary with the tone of someone who always knows more than he says, thus obliging the reader to trust him. The last example, ('Someday she will set the place on fire') seems to be a free-form quotation of the words of another observer. The 'duplicity' of the narrator is such that he may be considered to have a double identity, for he seems to express the doubts of the skeptical reader when he continues: 'but if the mother still has her qualities . . . do you take them [the children] away for their own good?' (p. 191). The second-person pronoun designates both the representative of public opinion and the skeptical reader—or rather, its use is meant to engage this narratee by personalizing the dilemma. The return to the indefinite 'someone,' used to designate people other than the narrator—a 'janitor's wife, an anonymous friend of the husband'—avoids the necessity for the reader to take sides, for it is another character who decides to denounce the mother to the welfare authorities. But at the same time, the narrator is absolved from having accepted the orthodox point of view, for the denunciation is presented as inevitable, as part of the human order of things, and yet as the product of jealousy which the narrator implicitly pretends to condemn.

The analysis reveals that the object of this type of *a parte*, of these extra-diegetic fragments, was first and foremost to offer a key for 'decoding' the short story. This key is the 'interior/exterior' opposition which constitutes, we might say, the story's metafictional theme: 'the life that seems safe from the inside (to the children) but perilous from without is destroyed. Whether it is the right thing or the wrong thing as far as the children are concerned, it is the end of love' (p. 191).

It may appear scandalous that the narrator is thus able to dispose of the moral dilemma ('the right thing or the wrong thing') with a discussion which sets off against each other the points of view of the welfare authorities and of the children. But this announcement of the diegetic theme ('it is the end of love') probably counts less than the proposition of a technique for analyzing points of view, (the inside and the outside) in the text; this interplay of points of view, to the exclusion of all moral judgement, will dominate the dramatization and successive echoes of the progressive stifling of love. The story itself proposes that we read it as a refusal to judge and as a simple affirmation of gradual alienation. The absence of the emotional reactions that we might have expected from the narrator obliges the reader to look for clues between the lines, in what is not said; to this end, understatement and attenuation are used both to obscure and to reveal.

In more than one of Gallant's stories, the linearity of the plot and the relative thematic unity are noteworthy, even when the story extends over a period of years or decades. However, this relative thematic unity is always accompanied by the presence of several narrators, or at least of juxtaposed statements which come from different sources, even if each 'source' does not appear as a character. Side by side with the characters exists an omniscient narrator and/or an observer more often objective than involved; and there is also the narrative voice, which is created through a complex mechanism based largely on enunciative strategies. Mavis Gallant's ˙ tone indicates a refusal of a single totalitarian point of view, perhaps through fear of losing surface control; this sometimes leads to the creation of a polyphonic voice, a collective voice born from the overlapping of points of view. Certainly, in her short stories, the frequent use of indirect speech facilitates the disappearance of the author to make way for a sort of anonymous, unemotional recounting, whether the characters are explored from without or from within.

Yet it seems that Gallant pushes the use of implication further than do most short story writers. In the first version of 'Orphans' Progress,' the only intrusion of the narrator (the passage we have analyzed) occupies about twenty lines and is inserted between the opening ('When the Collier children were six and ten, a social worker came to the place where they were living in Montreal, and shortly after that they were taken away. . . . Their mother was no longer capable of looking after them properly') and the second paragraph, which begins: 'The children's grandmother was scrupulous about food, and made them drink goat's milk' (p. 191). This introductory strategy serves above all to set the story in a slightly problematic context. Subsequently, the narrator's refusal to take responsibility for other people's opinions is continual. Statements are rejected onto the characters who make them, as reflected in the recurrence of expressions like 'said the maid,' 'she said that,' 'said the social worker,' 'the children were told,' 'so they were told.' These multiple yet converging statements seem little by little to force the Collier girls to interiorize other people's visions of them and of their mother. Whether through so-called 'emotional deprivation' or through the denigration of their mother tongue, the girls submit to these visions until they finally become passive and manipulable beings. 'One says' thus become the creator (or deformer) of reality, subjective though it might be, without the narrator having taken sides. Once the digression we have analyzed above is over, nothing in the text intervenes to defend love against the imperialism of the orthodox 'truth.'

This narrative technique is often complemented, especially in Gallant's most recent stories, by recourse to a complex juxtaposition of points of view which does not, however, exclude the voice of the author. An interesting example is to be found at the end of the short story 'Luc and His Father,' published in *The New Yorker* on October 4, 1982.[7] With a great deal of humor, the story treats of the disappointments of a middle-class Parisian family in which the son seems more inclined to 'live and let live' than to pass the entry examination to an engineering school which graduated his father, a highly placed civil servant sent into early retirement after a heart attack. Near the end of the story, Roger Clairevoie, having been alarmed about Luc's liaison with a young woman with a non-French name, suddenly finds himself almost as upset as his son when Luc and Katia break up. Attempting to comfort Luc, Roger evokes his own youthful memories, his problem with girls in the pre-pill era, when the best solution consisted of a house of prostitution in the rue Spontini: 'There were Belgian girls, Spanish girls from Algeria. Some were so young—oh, very young. One told me I was like a brother. I asked Cousin Henri what she meant. He said he didn't know' (p. 73). Then suddenly abandoning forever the idea of Luc and Katia as a couple, Roger comes back to the subject of his wife: 'How real Katia and Luc had seemed; how they had touched what was left of Roger's heart; how he had loved them. Giving them up forever, he said, "I always admired that picture of your mother" ' (p. 73).

This visual transition, by reminding Roger of his fate as a husband, permits the narrator to introduce a flashback which seems to come out of Roger's thoughts; this flashback provides information essential to the decoding of the whole story and to our appreciation of this aging man (whom Cassandra, a brainless English girl who is the family's guest, describes in her diary as obsessed with sex):

Simone and Roger had become engaged while Roger was still a lieutenant in Algeria. On the night before their wedding, which was to take place at ten o'clock in the morning in the church of Saint-Pierre de Chaillot, Roger paid a wholly unwelcome call. Simone received him alone in her dressing gown, wearing a fine net over her carefully ballooned hair. Her parents, listening at the door, took it for granted Roger had caught a venereal disease in a North African brothel and wanted the wedding postponed; Simone supposed he had met a richer and prettier girl (pp. 73-74).

Coming after a minutely detailed account of Roger's pompous wedding, this scene of Roger's unwelcome visit (who takes responsibility for the judgement 'wholly welcome' if not the omniscient narrator who expresses the bourgeois idea of acceptable behavior?), with its juxtaposition of the future parents-in-law's opinion and that of the fiancée, completes the picture of Roger as lacking in decorum and breeding.

A few details suffice to create the social satire: Simone receives her fiancé alone, without being dressed; her parents hope to be discreet but listen at the keyhole and immediately think of a shameful disease. Simone herself, preoccupied with keeping every hair in place, is a narrow-minded daughter of the bourgeoisie obsessed with wealth and beauty as the bases of marriage. What, then, did Roger want? 'All Roger had to say was that he had seen an Algerian prisoner being tortured to death'—this prisoner perhaps becomes his 'brother' if we think back to the Algerian girl who saw Roger as her brother. At this point, Roger has not yet been swallowed up by his wife's family and the respectable bourgeoisie. He has doubts and questions that he would like to bring up with his future spouse, but Simone is incapable of understanding. By a return forward in time to the moment when Roger is speaking to Luc, the narrative will make clear the incomprehension that exists between husband and wife and the irresponsibility of a whole portion of the French population symbolized by Simone, who does not feel involved in the matter: 'Simone had often asked Roger, since then, why he had tried to frighten her with something that had so little bearing on their future. Roger could not remember what his reason had been.' This text thus also indicates Roger's incapacity to remember or to distinguish his own motives once they have been repressed—once he has stifled his existential doubts. One recalls, from the same story, 'He [Cousin Henri] said he didn't know'; or, from the end of 'Orphans' Progress':

'Mildred had no reason to believe she had seen the place before, or would ever again.'

The impossibility of analyzing experience once the propitious moment has passed is what Roger will vainly try to overcome at the end of 'Luc and His Father': 'He tried now to think of something important to say to Luc, as if the essence of his own life could be bottled in words and handed over.' Here, the doubt introduced by 'as if' is less Roger's doubt than that of a hidden narrator; the remainder of the text is organized to hint that Roger's message does not get across. A dog wanders onto the scene and finishes it off: 'Sylvestre, wakened by a familiar voice, came snuffling at the door, expecting at this unsuitable hour to be taken out. Roger remarked, "Whatever happens, don't get your life all mixed up with a dog's".' The unlucky appearance of the dog echoes Roger's unwelcome visit to his fiancée; and surely, his refusal to get 'mixed up' with a dog echoes Simone's refusal to think about torture in Algeria. Thus, after decades of conjugal life, Roger has learned by heart the bourgeois pattern of good breeding and detachment. But the text insists less on this point than on the absurdity of a message reflecting the absurd life of Roger Clairevoie, whose passivity (in spite of his good intentions) and whose wife (but one gets the wife one deserves) have made him, long before his heart attack, into a 'dog-walker' on the sidewalks of respectable neighborhoods.

It would be presumptuous to draw conclusions from these two analyses about narrative techniques, the uses of point of view, and of voice, or enunciation, in Gallant's short stories as a whole. These remarks may, however, serve to draw attention to the complexity of her art. In contrast to interviews with the author,[8] in which she refers frequently to inspiration (perhaps because her skills are so highly developed as to function unconsciously), we may conclude that Gallant's deliberate way of hiding and revealing herself at the same time accords a major role to understatement. It is not always easy to break through to what the author has left unsaid, but the reward is great for the reader who chooses to become involved.[9]

University of Paris III, France

[1]See Geoffrey Hancock, 'An Interview with Mavis Gallant,' *Canadian Fiction Magazine*, 28 (1977), 67.

[2]Grazia Merler, *Mavis Gallant: Narrative Patterns and Techniques* (Ottawa: The Tecumseh Press, 1978; 82 pp.)

[3] 'The story is [no longer] told by carefully engineered plot but by the subtle implication of selected isolated incidents.' This statement is quoted and applied to Mavis Gallant by Anna Rutherford in her introduction to 'Orphans' Progress' in *Commonwealth Short Stories* (Aarhus: Dangaroo Press, 1979), p. 190.

[4] The *Commonwealth Short Stories* version appeared in *The New Yorker*, XLI, 7 (3 April, 1965). In *Home Truths* (Toronto: Macmillan, 1981), the story begins thus: 'When the Collier girls were six and ten they were taken away from their mother, whom they loved without knowing what the word implied, or even that it existed, and sent to their father's mother' (p. 56), i.e. very much like the original version; but the following development of their mother's deterioration after their father's death and the ensuing first-person comments (twenty odd lines) are completely left out, so that the narrative resumes with the children's stay with their grandmother. The original 'The children's grandmother was scrupulous about food and made them drink goat's milk. Two goats were brought by station wagon from fifty miles away. The girls went with the driver to get them. A man in a filling station was frightened by the goats, because of their oblong eyes' is changed to: 'Their grandmother was scrupulous about food, particularly for these underfed children, and made them drink goat's milk. Two goats bought specially to supply the orphans were taken by station wagon to a buck fifty miles away, the girls accompanying them for reasons of enlightenment. A man in a filling station was frightened by the goats, because of their oblong eyes' (p. 56).

[5] The reference to sexuality (the goats' being taken to a buck) in the latter version seems to counter the explicit claim that the man was frightened by the animals' oblong opaque eyes and to link his fear with that of the children's vague anguish about their mother and her men, more explicit in the earlier version.

[6] In *Commonwealth Short Stories*, p. 197. Further page references in the text are to this edition.

[7] 'Luc and His Father,' *The New Yorker*, LVIII, 33 (4 October, 1982).

[8] See Geoffrey Hancock's interview referred to in note 1.

[9] This essay is a translation by Eva Schacherl and Michel Fabre from the French, published in *Recherches Anglaises et Américaines*, 16 (1983), 57-67.

Giovanna Capone

A BIRD IN THE HOUSE: MARGARET LAURENCE ON ORDER AND THE ARTIST

In Margaret Laurence's *A Bird in the House* the distance between the real and the imaginary is the ordering theme of the cycle of stories, built as they are on the spaces between experience and its imaginative reconstruction. In these stories time constantly stretches both ways, and the future is mirrored in the past while dwelling in it. This special sense of 'memory' is underlined in the words spoken in silence by the narrator near the end of the last story: 'The memory of a memory returned to me now. I remembered myself remembering . . .' (p. 206).[1]

As the stories follow one another the confrontation of the narrator's reconstructions with her childhood vision of the world gradually becomes more explicit. The importance of childhood and adolescence from the creative viewpoint is indicated in Laurence's essay, 'A Place to Stand On,' when she cites Graham Greene: 'The creative writer perceives his world once and for all in childhood and adolescence, and his whole career is an effort to illustrate his private world in terms of the great public world we all share.'[2]

In *Heart of a Stranger* Laurence writes of her own life in Neepawa:

> When I was eighteen I couldn't wait to get out of that town, away from the prairies. I did not know then that I would carry the land and town all my life within my skull, that they would form the mainspring and source of the writing I was to do, wherever and however far away I might live.
>
> This was my territory in the time of my youth, and in a sense my life since then has been an attempt to look at it, to come to terms with it. Stultifying to my mind it certainly could be, and sometimes was, but not to the imagination. It was many things, but it was never dull.[3]

Margaret Laurence's leaving of Neepawa has its parallel in Vanessa MacLeod's leaving of Manawaka in *A Bird in the House*. The leaving is like an emergence from the womb, a long and exhausting birth. Not unlike Rachel in *A Jest of God*, Vanessa too seems laboriously to emerge 'from the tomb-like atmosphere of her extended childhood'

(17), and here too the protagonist-author refers to her emergence as 'partial defeat' and 'partial victory.' She attempts to break 'the handcuffs of her own past,' but her insight makes her understand that there will never be such a thing as total liberation from her ancestors. And it will therefore be a problem of freedom which is at stake: political freedom for a country and a people, personal freedom for an individual, the victory always being only partial anyway.

Freedom and birth represent substantially the same theme. Every birth in Laurence's writing is difficult, starting with Vanessa's brother's in the story 'To Set Our House in Order,' down to the dubious one in *A Jest of God:* everything 'struggles into life,' as the entrance into life is hard. And it is all the fault of order—the house to be kept in good order at all costs—that Vanessa's mother risks losing her baby and her own life. Life and birth are closely related to order, and order means, above all, beginning and knowing where to begin from. Knowing where to begin from is one of the recurring themes of the Canadian intellectual: does one begin from Canada, from England or one's European mother-country, from one's own region, from somewhere else? Where should one locate one's own birth?

The place of order then is *par excellence* the house. In *Bird* there are various houses, all ancestral, not only the more orderly ones belonging to the MacLeods and the Connors, but also the less orderly ones of the Tonnerres and of Uncle Wilf at Shallow Creek. Each house represents an epic of its own, with its own story and dramas; each world, inside each house, remains separate from the others in both time and space, 'a world separated by aeons' (p. 121). This is especially true of the Tonnerres' and Uncle Wilf's houses, which represent remote worlds, forever rejected and hopeless, worlds still to be got in touch with, but whose separateness and disorder have led what once were youthful hopes of life to death and destruction. That is why not far from Uncle Wilf's house the menacing 'footprints in the rocks' (p. 135) can be seen, evidence of the past permanently imprinted in the bedrock on which the country is based, traces of that remote past which it is imperative to get in touch with.

The established order within Vanessa's maternal and paternal grandparents' houses is rigidly hierarchical and patriarchal, governed as it is by the severe figures of the grandparents, the young parents being frail, almost inexistent, figures, crushed by life and too soon dead, weaker than the patriarchs, and their true victims. Of Margaret's frail real mother, who died when she was still a child, and her father's remarriage to her aunt, there remains no trace in *Bird*.

Once the heroic chapter of the pioneer grandparents is over, the parents succumb before external forces—the Depression that holds the country in these years—and internal ones inherent in everyday life. In the houses of order the task of keeping things in their place is by tradition assigned to women. Aunt Edna and the mother are relegated to doing nothing but set the house in order. As for the grandparents, Grandmother MacLeod and Grandfather Connor, order is something they simply expect, each one in his or her own image. All this reflects the conflict between two generations: here the parents' generation is sacrificed to guarantee a screen against external reality that changes precipitously, forced by the economic climate, and the immutable and 'ordered' reality of family background. Whatever hardships they may have suffered, the pioneer grandparents' sacrifice was a more celebrated epic and acknowledged as heroic, not like the middle generation's obscure attempt to set things in order. Order is equally to be found in the immutability of traditions, in the cliché-ridden immobility of the Scottish clans to which each belongs, in family mottos to be followed, almost impersonated. For Grandmother MacLeod each person must correspond to the everlasting fixity of her own heraldic motto: *'Be then a wall of brass. Learn to suffer. Consider the end. Go carefully'* (p. 46). Though reassuring to her grandmother, none of these slogans reassures Vanessa.

Order is negated freedom, and freedom is often seen as being denied to creatures of nature, whether men or animals. There is a bird in Margaret Wemiss Laurence's family coat of arms, and it is perhaps no mere chance that images of birds run throughout her work. In 'To Set Our House in Order' Grandmother MacLeod's hair looks like white-feathered wings. A sparrow that has fled into the attic troubles Vanessa's sleep. As Vanessa tidies up while her mother is in hospital risking her life, this is the way she depicts herself: 'I stood there holding the feather duster like a dead bird in my hands' (p. 50). The MacLeod house has never seemed like home to the child, with its too formal appearance, its turret decorated with ferns, its verandah embellished with a profusion of wrought-iron scrolls and well-composed curls, and its circular rose-window.

Here all is alien territory, forbidden to the games and the inevitable disorder of the child, who is invited by Grandmother to use the back stairs and to stay upstairs so as not to make a mess, and induced by her own craving for freedom to seek secluded corners, quaint nooks, hidden places in the house. In this double microcosm the disposition of the inhabitants of the house is precise: grand-mothers live in the living-rooms, mothers—that is Mother and Aunt Edna—in the kitchens, Grandfather and the child concealed, Father outside.

Grandmother MacLeod lives in the myth of the aristocracy, and with each step recollects her late husband, a successful doctor who was well-off in the community and who remains a silent implied reproach to her son Ewen. Ewen counts just a few scrawny birds in payment for his work, and so little money that he cannot afford to hire a maid to keep the house in order. 'My accounts were always in good order, and so was my house,' Grandmother MacLeod insists, as she adopts her own father's warning, 'God loves Order,' with which she afflicts Vanessa: 'You remember that, Vanessa. God loves Order—he wants each one of us to set our house in order' (p. 46). The warning extends far beyond housecleaning, but cleaning the house stands for keeping life's moral order, caring for one's soul. This warning about order suggests the equation of order and death. For Vanessa, precociously conscious that her mother is risking her life to give her a brother, the equation is ominous.

In the houses, however, order is always elusive. No one there is in the place where he or she would like to be, everyone would have preferred to be someone else and to live somewhere else. Grand-mother MacLeod wished she could have been an aristocrat, Father a traveller and a sailor, Roderick a doctor, Grandfather MacLeod a Greek scholar; Aunt Edna would have liked to marry young and work in town, Mother to take a degree and continue her education and Cousin Chris to go to the university and to pursue life. Each one is out of place and each finds it difficult to perceive the uneasiness of the other. Vanessa's father refers to Grandfather MacLeod, remarking that he must always have been a lonely man, and that he himself in his own youth had not been able to understand his father. 'Sometimes a thing only hits you a long time afterwards' (p. 51) is Vanessa's father's comment regarding his relationship with his father, and this of course applies as well to Vanessa's personal experience; only years later will she be able to see this world of her childhood with different eyes. As for Grandmother MacLeod, the father's comment is that 'the house is still the same, so she thinks other things should be, too. It hurts her when she finds they aren't' (p. 53). The conclusion that Vanessa reaches, after having experienced so many emotions and sensed so many contrasts during the span of a few days, is not so much to understand rationally as to feel deeply and permanently from then on the disarray, and to sense the sinister associations of the word 'order': 'I could not really comprehend these things, but I sensed their strangeness, their disarray. I felt that whatever God might love in this world, it was certainly not order' (p. 59).

This is perhaps a good point at which to remark on Vanessa's choice of language. Here all is founded on the vocabulary of intuition. The child depicts herself as a 'professional listener' (p. 11), she has the vocation of the observer; as in Laurence's novels to come, it is almost an artist's credo which Vanessa voices regarding her childhood: 'I had long ago discovered it was folly to conceal oneself. The best concealment was to sit quietly in plain view' (p. 11). The refined use of the vocabulary of intuition reflecting the child's sensitivity and sensibility rather than plain rational understanding is worth noting. Vanessa is a juvenile storyteller by vocation; and side by side with the life she is living, she lives the story she is currently making up, so that at times a word from reality evokes a literary atmosphere, a sentence, or a paragraph from a would-be story. More often than not these are stories with a tragic ending, like the ones about the old man dying of pneumonia while assisted by a beautiful Métis lady, or the baby that drowns while being baptized by total immersion in the Wachakwa River. One of the stories she is writing is about pioneer life, entitled *The Pillars of a Nation*, but when she is told that Grandfather Connor in his day had been a pioneer, she feels disappointed and abandons it.

Using the language of intuition, she portrays her apprenticeship. The sadness of her mother and Aunt Edna is 'such a new thing, not to my actual sight, but to my attention,' that a sudden and almost physical pain gives her the sense of having lost something: 'some comfort had been taken from me' (p. 22). Progressively she learns perceptiveness. The acquisitive, accumulative process of these lessons constitutes the profound motivation beneath these stories, loose like all the apprenticeships of life, fragmentary like all the dictates of experience, and, like the natural and vital disorder of things, hard to set in order. But the artist has an order of his own. The pace of his imagination is the pace of the mind moving through memory in a quest for meaning, not for an explicit abstract order, but rather for the shape, sense, and sentiment—the vital pulsation—of the past. Laurence chooses to narrate what memories endure in her, what is part of her. In the end order coincides with the individual, and the measure of order is the artist herself, in her internal imaginative reality.

Time **is** Vanessa, a developing creature; time is with her, in her advancement towards her own life. Time is movement, everything changes incessantly; and through the theory of things glimpses of meaning, truth, and divinity will be perceived. As for the rest, all is fragmentary, like the structure and so-called 'order' imposed by men, captured by the fragmentary order of memory. Only imagination is able to grasp order and time without their coming to signify death.

The time of the beginning of a story exemplifies the time of the story; the short story is thus akin to poetry. More than showing her reader that symbols do exist, Laurence shows that things are in themselves symbolic, and that they are especially so when connected with the theme of freedom. Almost everything in her writing points toward some sort of negated freedom, first and foremost the bird pattern in the title. The theme of negated liberty recurs in the theme of birds and other animals seen as being trapped, menaced or extinct: Grandmother Connor's canary Birdie, the caged wild bear that represents Grandfather Connor, the half-husky that stands for the Métis such as the Tonnerres, the loons, representing the original Indian inhabitants of the country eradicated by so-called civilization, the dinosaurs to which Grandfather Connor and Grandmother MacLeod are equated, and finally the bird in the house, emblem of the father. Though born to be free, to travel and see the world, the father's only freedom may have been confined to the season of the war. The world he saw then was only a Europe of trenches and destruction and death: his death symbol will be the bird in the house, trapped like him, generous and beaten, and destined to die young.

The caged bear is Grandfather Connor. When offended he withdraws from the living-room and retreats to his cavern in the basement, where he sits cross and mute in his rocking chair, squeaking out a reproachful warning for the whole house, which almost trembles from it, so oppressive is his irritated, intolerant presence down there: 'From his cave . . . the angry crunching of the wooden rockers against the cement floor would reverberate through the house, a kind of sub-verbal Esperanto, a disapproval which even the most obtuse person could not fail to comprehend' (p. 62). Vanessa associates the Bear-Grandfather with the never-seen Great Bear Lake, perceived only on the maps like an imagined vastness of black water that lies in an unknown place beyond the known prairies and the fenced fields, a place where nature is indomitable and impregnable. Grandfather may be an intermediary to the world that is aeons away, where still 'there was no feeling about the place' (p. 148). This sets the 'savage' Grandfather Connor in contrast to the extremely 'civilized'

Grandmother MacLeod, so that a fight between the two would be nothing less than 'like a brontosaurus running headlong into a tyrannosaurus' (p. 63).

In this period Vanessa is writing her hundredth story, *The Silver Sphinx.* A passionate story of love and death, it is inspired by the Bible, which is her only reading experience and only source for such feelings; her love scenes are spoken in the hieratic language of the Song of Solomon. The story is an exotic pastiche set in ancient Egypt, and its auburn-haired heroine, when left by her lover, can feed only on avocados. The love and death scenes have the sombre splendor of Ecclesiastes. However, though 'Both death and love seemed regrettably far from Manawaka and the snow, and my grandfather stamping his feet in the front porch of the Brick House' (p. 65), it is in the Brick House that Vanessa for the first time encounters experiences of love and death.

Her first perception of what real love is reaches her during a visit of Aunt Edna's boyfriend and occurs as a story of conflicting sentiments and renunciation linked to the difficulty of finding a job during the Depression. Grandfather is unkind and rough towards the guest, hurting Edna. The couple withdraws to another room while Vanessa, the eternal eavesdropper, approaches her listening post. The conversation between the lovers is bitter and painful, and in the end pitiless reality overwhelms affection. That night Vanessa overhears Aunt Edna crying in her loneliness, whispering the name of the man she will no longer be able to love. All of a sudden Vanessa is struck by the absurdity of what she thought was love in her barbaric queen, and she sees that like every human image, that of human love and suffering is made up of contrasts: 'I could not reconcile this image with the known face, nor could I disconnect it,' she thinks. 'I thought of my aunt, her sturdy laughter, the way she tore into the housework, her hands and feet which she always disparagingly joked about, believing them to be clumsy. I thought of the story in the scribbler at home. I wanted to get home quickly, so I could destroy it' (p. 78). The image of passion, the reality of love, true pain, Aunt Edna's sacrifice to solitude—this superior order—will linger from now on in the narrator.

Another life experience that Vanessa apprehends here is death— Grandmother Connor's death. Left in the care of Grandmother MacLeod in the house-museum, she has not been able to visit the Connors' house-monument so frequently: 'Without my mother, our house seemed like a museum, full of dead and meaningless objects, vases and gilt-framed pictures and looming furniture, all of which had to be dusted and catered to, for reasons which everyone had forgotten' (p. 79). At the death of her beloved Grandmother Connor, Vanessa is again caught eavesdropping; but the season of spying is almost at an end: 'I could no longer eavesdrop with a clear conscience, but I justified it now by the fact that I had voluntarily removed myself from the kitchen' (pp. 84-85), the adults' place. It is here that she realizes how complex the reality of pain can be, and how unexpected, unexplored, and unfathomable feelings of guilt and merit link the quick and the dead in inscrutable ways.

That *Bird* is an extraordinary celebration of clichés finds its confirmation in the title story, the story of the death of Vanessa's father. The country-girl, hired at last by the MacLeod household to 'make order,' announces a death when she sees a sparrow trapped indoors: 'A bird in the house is a death in the house.' The scene is full of horror, but what dominates the story is above all grief and the comprehension of grief. Vanessa justifies herself to her grandmother for not having gone to the Remembrance Day parade by formally telling her she is sorry. Then, after thinking over again what the parade means to her grandmother—the remembrance of her son Roderick's death—Vanessa repeats: 'I'm sorry'; but it is only when she is fully aware of why she is saying it that she really feels she means what she says, attaining the comprehension of grief. In an analogous episode occurring during the Second World War, when she is seventeen and herself in love with an officer, Vanessa casually discovers the photograph of a girl, whom her father may have briefly loved during his service in Europe; only then will she really feel the acute pain for the whole of her father's life, which was so ungenerous towards him. She finds herself hoping that the brief moment he lived with that girl had meant freedom to him. And only then can she really feel her father's death. The whole book is her way of saying a protracted 'I'm sorry' and of revisiting the clichés and digging out their meanings, both mysterious and charged with confirmation.

After the death of her father the house-monument, the mythical 'Sunday place,' becomes the 'everyday place.' Grandmother Connor is no longer there. Grandfather Connor has been debunked: 'The rocking chair trick was used fairly often, and when my mother and Michael and I were doing the dishes we would hear the reproachful *screee-scraaw* coming from Grandfather's cavern' (p. 198), his prison-refuge. And there is now a Michael in Vanessa's life, a presence of short duration, rapidly eliminated from the scene by Grandfather, as in Aunt's time. (Edna has meanwhile succeeded in marrying a bolder boyfriend who in the eyes of the grandfather has the merit of having prevented the house from catching fire, daring to invade his territory and desecrate his cave by laying hands on the furnace located there). Michael leaves, but Grandfather has been clear-sighted: the young man, it turns out, was married after all. Vanessa must of course suffer because of this, but she will cure her own sorrow, although about this as about everything that happens to her during these years, she will later have to observe: 'and yet, twenty years later it was still with me to some extent, part of the accumulation of happenings which can never entirely be thrown away' (p. 202). Like Edna before her, she now becomes frantic to get away from Manawaka and the Brick House—'Jericho's Brick Battlements,' as she will humorously call this place, as remote and embattled as an outpost.

She leaves to go to town and study at the university, and will come back only for Grandfather's death two years later; during the funeral oration for him she hears the story of a pioneer by the name of Connor as if it were an entirely new person, a 'stranger,' a persona, a fictional character:

> He had come from Ontario to Manitoba by the Red River steamer, and he had walked from Winnipeg to Manawaka, earning his way by shoeing horses. After some years as a black-smith, he had enough money to go into hardware business. Then he had built his house. It had been the first brick house in Manawaka. Suddenly the minister's recounting of these familiar facts struck me as though I had never heard any of it before (p. 204).

After twenty more years Vanessa will again come back, but she will not go to visit her grandfather's tomb: 'There was no need. It was not his monument.' She will go instead to his true monument, the Brick House, symbol of the man's immortality, which Vanessa feels proclaiming itself in her veins, while the immortality of the mother—the deep reason perhaps why the mother in this collection outlives the father, whereas Laurence's own real mother dies when she is still a girl—will be found in the imperishable 'clichés of affection' (p. 207).*

Bologna University, Italy

[1]Margaret Laurence, *A Bird in the House* (New York: Alfred A. Knopf, 1970). Further references to this book appear in the text.

[2]Graham Greene, *Collected Essays,* quoted in 'A Place to Stand On,' in Margaret Laurence, *Heart of a Stranger* (Toronto: McClelland and Stewart, 1976), p. 13.

[3]*Heart of a Stranger,* p. 217.

*This research was carried out with the financial assistance of the Ministero della Pubblica Istruzione.

Karla El-Hassan

REFLECTIONS ON THE SPECIAL UNITY OF STEPHEN LEACOCK'S *SUNSHINE SKETCHES OF A LITTLE TOWN*

I

The number of books, articles and essays written on Stephen Leacock, the man, his political and economical writings, and his literary works, is legion. This applies in particular to Leacock's most popular book, *Sunshine Sketches of a Little Town*. When I too in this essay deal with *Sunshine Sketches*, I do so in order to investigate an aspect which up to now has not been treated in detail: the special character of *Sunshine Sketches* as a composition of several independent pieces of short prose, which by means of special unifying patterns form an artistic whole. I believe this topic to be of general interest because *Sunshine Sketches* may be considered one of the predecessors of the linked short stories or short story ensembles which at present are very common in Anglo-Canadian literature. Nonetheless only a few critics have probed into the genre-character of these ensembles.

In 1912 Leacock accepted a commission from the *Montreal Star* to write a series of contributions 'which would have a distinctive Canadian setting.'[1] Between February 17 and June 22, 1912, twelve sketches appeared at intervals in the magazine's weekend edition. In the same year the sketches were published in a slightly regrouped form as a book. With *Sunshine Sketches of a Little Town* a literary work had come into existence the genre-character of which could not be classified easily. Critics paraphrased it as a 'loosely episodic book,'[2] as 'a series of loosely interrelated sketches' which complement one another to form a 'whole.'[3] Robertson Davies asks the reader of *Sunshine Sketches* to read the book 'as a novel, and all the characters fall into a coherent pattern.'[4] At the same time he states that *Sunshine Sketches* form a whole without being a novel.[5] Arthur Phelps claims that 'the book is really no more than a collection of sketches.'[6] These different classifications indicate a dilemma which has become symptomatic. Critics are still at a loss as to how to define the genre-character of today's short story ensembles, for this is by no means merely a question of terminology.

It is worth remarking that closely linked short story ensembles—books like Ray Smith's *Lord Nelson Tavern*, Margaret Laurence's *A Bird in the House*, or Alice Munro's *Lives of Girls and Women* and *Who Do You Think You Are?*—are often referred to by critics as 'para-novels,' 'disjointed novels,' 'episodic novels,' 'loosely episodic novels,' 'story-novels,' 'open structured novels,' or just 'novels.' This terminology indicates that many critics presume that there exists a similarity between novels and tightly connected short story ensembles. Although *Sunshine Sketches* has not directly been called a 'novel,' it has been considered to be a promising attempt leading to the writing of a novel. Douglas Bush expands on his statement that *Sunshine Sketches* is 'not a novel' by commenting that 'Leacock's talents did not stretch to that.'[7] Elsewhere Leacock is judged to be an author who never got to the 'heights' of literature (i.e. the novel) because, according to David M. Legate, of a lack of talent, desire and incentive.[8] Already with reference to *Sunshine Sketches* a widely held valuation of closely linked short story connections appears: they are considered to be first steps in the process of writing a novel, experiments or exercises of future novelists, or just failed attempts to write a novel.[9]

The assertion that Leacock was a failed novelist loses its basis as soon as one understands the special structural patterns of his longer works. His entire literary production proves that he regarded short prose forms as best suited to his perception of reality and to his talents. This corresponds with his understanding of the function of literature which in his opinion has to react quickly to the outside world, does not have 'to observe nature but to improve nature,'[10] and which should cause the reader to recognize social problems in an inconspicuous and indirect manner. Leacock maintains that in view of the fact that time is moving fast short prose is especially suited for this task: 'The habit and custom of a long introduction has come down to us from other and more leisurely times. We have no time for it now.'[11] In his introduction to *Sunshine Sketches* he stresses—certainly not accidentally—the fact that he does not write his short pieces 'in idle moments when the wearied brain is unable to perform the serious labours.'[12] He emphasizes the concentrated and intensive activity which is necessary to the writing of short stories. An adequate analysis of *Sunshine Sketches* requires an evaluation of each single part as a separate, autonomous and self-contained piece of short prose and of its relationship to the other sketches.

Before writing the single parts of *Sunshine Sketches* Leacock had outlined a plan. Legate mentions in his biography of the author a manuscript containing detailed information on 'plans and ideas' of the sketches.[13] These notes confirm my hypothesis about the genesis of closely linked short story ensembles: they must be either 'composed' or 'completed.' (The term 'composed' characterizes—with reference to Helen M. Mustard[14]—the fact that the single parts of an ensemble have been conceived from the beginning as elements of a larger unit; the term 'completed'—introduced by Forrest L. Ingram[15]—indicates that independent stories showing unifying patterns have been revised or completed by the author with the intention of combining them into an artistic whole.)

II

As Leacock outlined the sketches beforehand and wrote them within a few months, he fulfilled some of the most essential preconditions for the creation of closely linked short story ensembles. All of the sketches reflect the same *weltanschauung*, the same perception of reality, and the same view of the function of literature. The fact that Leacock's view of the world is affected by contradictory or at least paradoxical opinions, ideals and judgements is of paramount importance for an evaluation of the contents and the structure of *Sunshine Sketches*. This ambivalence—resulting from a mixture of rational understanding and emotional interpretation, from realistic and from wishful thinking, from objectively and subjectively motivated standpoints—is logically related to the author's sense of humor, which has it basis in the incongruities between the real and the ideal. Embodied imaginatively in *Sunshine Sketches*, the ambiguity of Leacock's view of life permeates the central theme of the whole ensemble. Individually and as a whole the sketches show a thematic tension set up between contradictory or paradoxical views caused by acknowledged differences between rural and urban, traditional and modern ways of life and practices in business and politics, between standards and norms characteristic of small towns and of cities.

This central theme which weaves through the book on many levels turns out to be the result of Leacock's inability to opt unconditionally for one side or the other concerning the process of disintegration and the widening of the gulf between country and city. To describe life in Mariposa as an idyll would have been an attempt to turn back the clock of history, and thus it would have been inconsistent with Leacock's recognition of the positive sides of the political and economical development in Canada. Simply criticizing the goings-on and the atmosphere in Mariposa is in contrast with the author's special desire to live in the country. Thus the particularity of the central theme of *Sunshine Sketches* explains why this book 'seems to have become all things to all men'—including literary critics.[16] But it is just this thematic ambivalence which in various ways becomes the essential unifying pattern of the whole book.

The inconsistencies in the description and interpretation of life and the atmosphere of Mariposa find their expression mainly through the specific nature and function of the narrator. As a literary device which, according to its manifold functional possibilities, is qualified to interweave the single parts of an ensemble on many levels, the narrator requires thorough attention in the analysis of the structure of short story connections.

The unity of *Sunshine Sketches* is supported neither by a narrative sequence nor by a central figure who undergoes a development. It is the narrator who above all takes part in shaping the single pieces into a whole. He is a Mariposan who also stands outside the fictional world, who repeatedly communicates with an imaginary 'reader' and comments upon events and persons, who always refers to himself as 'I,' and whose point of view is partly omniscient and partly limited. These features are typical of the narrative medium throughout the whole book, and assist the unity of the sketches, due to their recurrence.

Of much greater relevance for the integration of the single pieces, however, is the function of a narrator, who by interfering and evaluating, focuses the reader's attention on 'an experiencing mind whose views of the experience will come between us and the event.'[17] This perspective tends particularly to entice the reader because the narrator's comments—his opinions on events, persons and certain standards of evaluating men and things—are as a whole a complex interweaving of ambiguous views reflecting traits of Leacock's ambivalent perception of the world. For instance, in the narrator's judgement of the 'sinking' of the Mariposa Belle the following points of view are contradictory:

> Safe! Oh, yes! Isn't it strange how safe other people's adventures seem after they happen? But you'd have been scared, too, if you'd been there just before the steamer sank, and seen them bringing up all the women onto the top deck (p. 50).

Really, it made one positively laugh! It seemed so queer and, anyway, if a man has a sort of natural courage, danger makes him laugh. Danger? pshaw! fiddlesticks! everybody scouted the idea. Why, it is just the little things like this that give zest to a day on the water (p. 50).

The characterization of the inhabitants of Mariposa shows clearly the narrator's balancing between sympathy and distance: Josh Smith—to single out one figure—acts according to the (im)moral practices of modern businessmen: he bribes his enemies, pockets additional profit under the cloak of charity, plans his transactions with cool deliberation and does not shrink from trickery. But Josh Smith also supports Jefferson Thorpe after his misinvestment; he is the leader of the 'salvage operation' for the Mariposa Belle and of the fire-brigade when the church is ablaze. According to his political and business practices Smith is a 'citizen' among the people of Mariposa but he also makes efforts to their credit. His characterization proves that the narrator—as well as Leacock—appreciates the able businessman whom he, at the same time, condemns or at least criticizes.

Money and wealth are of great importance to the ups and downs of life in Mariposa. Here, just as in the big cities, man is valued by his worldly possessions: 'it was a favourite method in Mariposa if you wanted to get at the real worth of a man, to imagine him clean sold up, put up for auction, as it were. It was the only way to test him' (p. 34). The rural idyll of Mariposa is open to the infiltration of capitalist standards of value: Smith's leading role among the Mariposans results essentially from his financial success; Thorpe becomes famous for his suddenly accumulated wealth; Dean Drone is forgiven when it is discovered that he had—subconsciously—overinsured the church; Pupkin is allowed to marry the daughter of the judge after his salary has been raised. Seen from a different angle, wealth is for Smith a means to corrupt and to manipulate people, Pupkin's marriage is threatened because he is not rich enough, Dean Drone loses prestige and is pensioned off because he is made responsible for the indebtedness of the new church.

The ambivalent attitude of the narrator towards his subject also affects his portrayal of the town. He states that, according to how long one stays in Mariposa, the town seems to be still and sleepy or else busy and exciting. The streets are described as being wider than the avenues of big cities. The high facades of the houses, however, turn out to be only wooden imitations. Corresponding to the change of seasons, Mariposa is either 'dark enough and dull' (p. 4), or 'a fierce, dangerous lumber town' (p. 5). In winter the Mariposa Belle appears as a 'little thing the size of a butternut' (p. 39). In summer there seems to be 'no difference between the Mariposa Belle and the Lusitania' (p. 39). Obviously the contrasts and comparisons between Mariposa and the neighboring 'city,' between small-town, metropolitan and world-wide standards are favorite elements in the narrator's description of Mariposa. They continuously provoke the reader to pay close attention to the values of life in Mariposa. But it is these values which remain vague: sometimes the peculiarities of life in the 'city' seem to be more desirable, sometimes the 'blossoming' life in Mariposa is equal to the life in the 'city' or even preferable to it.

These examples serve to illustrate my assertion that one of the means to link the single sketches is the repetition of the narrator's incongruous opinions of Mariposa. At the same time they suggest the expanding dimensions of these ambiguities. In each of the following sketches, the narrator, while describing Mariposa, touches upon new aspects of the town. The diverging judgements and opinions complement one another; thus step by step a picture of the Little Town is created the interior inconsistencies of which are gradually revealed to be its most intrinsic feature. This thematic expansion forms one of the strongest unifying links.

In this connection it should be pointed out that the thematic core of the whole book cannot be perceived when the single sketches are read separately. Contrary to short story cycles in which the 'Mittelpunktsbezogenheit' (J. Müller) or the central theme is clearly recognizable in each single story, and in which each part is an illustration of the main theme, in ensembles that are linked more closely than cycles—*Sunshine Sketches* being one of these—the theme is developed gradually in the succession of the single pieces. It reaches its final dimensions in the last sketch only.

In the final part of *Sunshine Sketches*, 'L'Envoi. The Train to Mariposa,' the contrast between small-town life and life in the 'city' leads to the question 'Where is home?' At this point the narrator has already been living in the 'city' for thirty years, and compared to the length of time he spent in Mariposa, he therefore deems the 'city' to be his 'home.' Emotionally, however, he feels rooted in Mariposa. This is proved by his imaginary journey there by train. During this tour, about which the reader is told in the final sketch, comparisons between the big and the small town multiply. They relate to modern and old-fashioned clothes, to the impersonal and friendly behavior of the passengers, to the exchange of a locomotive run by electricity for a dated steam-engine, to urban environments and farms, woods and windmills. Evidently the narrator's longing for Mariposa comes to the fore, signaling his emotional bonds to this town. Thus the imaginary journey is to some extent an answer to the question posed above. But it is not the Mariposa of the present time which the narrator is yearning for. It is rather his recollections of 'the little Town in the Sunshine that once we knew' (p. 153). Such an interpretation of 'home' includes that nostalgic trend which Leacock ascribes to all reminiscences: 'Seen through this refracting prism of past distance all the harsh outlines are blurred and softened, the colours mingle to a mellow richness.'[18] In *Sunshine Sketches* the narrator indicates explicitly this aspect when saying: 'the whole town was irradiated with sunshine, and there was such a singing of the birds, and such a dancing of the rippled waters of the lake, and such a kindliness in the faces of all the people, that only those who have lived in Mariposa, and been young there, can know at all what he [Pupkin] felt' (p. 96).

The final sketch reveals a point of view which is relevant to the eleven preceding sketches: as a whole they are those recollections—described from a temporal and spiritual distance—through which 'comes into being the peculiar legend of the "good old times of the past".'[19] The sketches are antedated thirty years. This temporal distance gives the single parts coherence, for it characterizes them as constituents of a whole complex of memories. Seen from the perspective of the last sketch it becomes clear that the narrator wants his recollections of Mariposa to correspond to his idealized imagination of this town. But it can also be noticed that his intellectual distance from the place where he spent his youth does not tally with this ideal. His recollections therefore reflect an outlook upon the past which on the one hand is tinged with a sentimental attitude towards Mariposa and on the other hand is strongly realistic, sharpened by thirty years of experience. Both aspects are combined to create a picture of the Little Town the pros and cons of which run through the sketches like a red thread forming a strong associational pattern.

Another aspect revealing the consistency of the point of view in the final sketch is given by signaling the distance between the narrator experiencing the events and narrating them. The narrator who, throughout eleven sketches, seems to be no different from the average Mariposan, is revealed in 'L'Envoi' as a person who has recognized the cause of his ambiguous view of his home-town: it was an ideal place for spending one's youth, but it is no place to stay forever. Once the reader has grasped this he is able to understand flashes of witty and intelligent remarks which the narrator included unobtrusively in the preceding sketches. Thus 'L'Envoi' elucidates the ambiguous attitude of the narrator as a deliberate, conscious dichotomy. Seen from this perspective, each sketch can be distinguished as an autonomous piece of short prose, which within its contradictory expression is entire in itself. Much more effective, however, are those aspects of the point of view which shape all the separate sketches into a whole. The mere fact that the ambiguity of the point of view pervades all pieces and connects them by means of recurrence is thereby only of secondary importance. The most efficacious unifying force emerges from the fact that the special dichotomy of the point of view comprises in itself the central theme of the whole book, thus including its own gradual development: sympathy and distance towards the Mariposans, their life, their town and their values are thesis and antithesis converging step by step into a kind of synthesis. This process is completed in the last sketch where a certain tendency of the narrator's point of view, his attitudes and judgements, is sustained.

The sketches are a constant provocation for the reader to form his own opinion. In the sequence of the single pieces it becomes evident that they all have a 'good' ending. The reminiscences of Mariposa stay in mind as something pleasant not meant to be forgotten. Jefferson Thorpe is, at the end of his story, the sympathetic man he was at the beginning; Dean Drone is looked after by his parishioners; the Mariposa Belle does not really 'sink'; Pupkin gets married to Zena; Josh Smith regains his licence for selling liquor and wins the election. The temporary difficulties of the figures are settled in such a way that in the end they all are at peace with themselves, with the narrator, and with the reader. Their belief in the righteousness of men is maintained, in the moral tendency of Leacock's view of the world as well as in the attitudes of the narrator.

Yet the ambiguous descriptions of Mariposa are not all similarly convincing. Those delineations of the town which show a sympathetic picture pass the narrator's lips more easily than descriptions in which he—to all appearances subconsciously—doubts the ideal picture of Mariposa. While the aspects of small-town life are integrated harmoniously into the sketches, the metropolitan dimensions of Mariposa seem to be slightly out of place. Not seldom is Mariposa depicted as being inadequate if compared to large cities, so that the reader accepts unreservedly its provinciality but agrees only reluctantly to the aspects of its urbanization. Despite the substantial incongruities of the evaluation of life in Mariposa, in the end the reader gets the impression of having read sketches which show on the whole a 'sunny' picture of the Little Town.

The emergence of such a picture is also backed up by the use of comical methods of delineation which, according to the moral traits in Leacock's perception of reality, reflect a conception of humor based on 'kindliness' and 'humanity.' The humorous aspects of Leacock's comedy coincide with an affirmation of the ideal, and thereby with a decision favoring the pleasant reminiscences of the narrator. Being, however, a combination of humorous and ironical devices, Leacock's comedy in *Sunshine Sketches* produces unifying effects above all by applying the narrator's ambiguous attitude to Mariposa and its inhabitants. While the humorous descriptions, causing affirmative laughter or a sympathizing smile, support the acceptance of the idealized picture of the past, the ironical representations—unmasking silliness, falsehood and conning shrewdness, and affecting a disquieting, mocking smile—jeopardize the ideal and illuminate the real picture of the past. Both variants of comical delineation merge into a portrayal of the Little Town the purpose of which is to avoid any unequivocal evaluations.

The comical depictions of Mariposa unfold on two levels: in the direct portrayal of figures, things, and actions, and in the narrator's comments. It is characteristic of both that the narrator's pretended belief in an ideal Mariposa is de-idealized by a perspective which is known as 'eye of innocence.' Leacock explains the effect of the 'eye of innocence of the Westerner' which he observed in the writings of Mark Twain as follows: 'And to this eye, contrasts and incongruities are revealed never suspected before.'[20] The narrator of *Sunshine Sketches* relates and elucidates in a way which is meant by him to be serious. But his simple-minded, sometimes innocent naivety produces a comical tension between his seriousness and the nonsense told. The weaknesses and faults of the Mariposans become especially evident because they are depicted by the narrator as being normal. Here and there they are even interpreted as virtues. Although the literary device of the 'eye of innocence' includes different comical means of description, it possesses on the whole a certain homogeneity which, effecting stylistic conformities, also assists to strengthen the unity of the sketches.

The special features of comical portrayal in *Sunshine Sketches* are part of that pattern of the comic which Leacock describes as 'amusing all through, not the end alone but the steady current of the narrative. We laugh as we listen . . . the listener . . . comes to a boil and stays there. The story is interesting, and even amusing, all through.'[21] While the narrator does not seem to regard the inhabitants of Mariposa as funny, the reader is a permanent witness to the incongruities which derive from their provincialism and their imitation of urban ways of life, from the goals aimed at and reached by their actions, from the purpose of their deeds and the means used, from what they really are and what they want to be like. The reader is stimulated to smile all the time, reacting to an inner conformity of the comic devices. Thus the latter, too, contribute to creating an impression of unity. As a special component of the point of view, the comic side of *Sunshine Sketches* accentuates the continuous provocation, making the reader want to know the true face of Mariposa and the true opinion of the narrator. Being thus conducive to the expression and to the gradual development of the central theme, it also brings about pervasive linking strands.

Besides the unifying forces emerging in the process of reading, through the communication between reader and narrator, additional connections between the single sketches are effected by the addresses of the narrator to an imaginary 'reader.' The latter is considered throughout the whole book to be a like-minded and trusty partner of the narrator. Occasionally the narrator interrupts the flow of his narrative to arouse this 'reader' to pay attention to important facts, to encourage him to think over what has been related, to respond to imaginary questions of the 'reader.' As the 'reader' seems to share the narrator's discrepant opinions and judgements, they both are united in a certain way on the level of the main theme, the fictive communication underlining the thematic conception of the sketches. The constant presence of a 'reader' and the use of such a noticeable fictitious rhetoric bring about futher integrating effects emphasizing a way of narration which is characteristic of all the pieces of the book. The narrator of *Sunshine Sketches* also comments on his story-telling. He criticizes his anticipation of future events, he confirms the repeated descriptions of certain details, or he asks whether he has already mentioned special facts. His explicit remarks on the handling of the flow of narrative draw the single sketches together, not only by the mere repetition of such comments but mainly by the fact that fragments of the contents are repeated at the same time.

Some of the pieces of *Sunshine Sketches* form a separate unity within the ensemble. Strictly speaking, Leacock's narrator does not tell twelve but seven 'stories.' Apparently the author was compelled by the relatively fixed size of magazine articles to subdivide his more extensive contributions. The sketch 'The Ministrations of the Rev. Mr. Drone' and the following texts 'The Whirlwind Campaign in Mariposa' and 'The Beacon on the Hill' actually form one story. 'The Extraordinary Entanglement of Mr. Pupkin' constitutes an entity together with 'The Fore-Ordained Attachment of Zena Pepperleigh and Peter Pupkin' and 'The Mariposa Bank Mystery.' 'The Great Election in Missinaba County' and 'The Candidacy of Mr. Smith' are also parts of a single 'story.' The fact that some of the sketches belong together is made clear not only by their content but also by the special ending of all but the last sketch of a group. 'The Ministrations of the Rev. Mr. Drone,' for instance, ends with the narrator's remark: 'I must pause and tell you in another chapter of the Whirlwind Campaign in Mariposa' (p. 69). This sentence refers directly to the following sketch, 'The Whirlwind Campaign in Mariposa,' which is interrupted in the midst of events and is carried on—only after a formal break—in 'The Beacon on the Hill.' In this part the incidents revolving round Dean Drone and his church are brought to an end in a conclusive way. Also in the other two groups of sketches one can distinguish between formal, not logical, 'indirect' endings, and a conclusion motivated as such by its contents and its form.

The beginnings of the single parts of a group of sketches, however, have hardly any reference to the larger 'story' they belong to. Seen from the perspective of the whole ensemble, neither the beginnings nor the endings of the single pieces of a 'story' are of relevance to constituting an entity comprising all of the sketches. On the contrary, the fact that some sketches form one 'story' seems to indicate that they withstand an integration into a tightly linked ensemble. To point out that the narrator tells seven 'stories' is important only with regard to the autonomy of the single pieces. If we proceed from the assumption that each part of a short story ensemble must be complete in itself, *Sunshine Sketches* apparently does not belong to such a composition. The sketches 'The Ministrations of the Rev. Mr. Drone,' 'The Extraordinary Entanglement of Mr. Pupkin' and 'The Great Election in Missinaba County' require a completion by further texts. However, since they are characterized as 'chapters,' these sketches do not necessarily have to be independent. They are parts of 'stories' which in their turn form the required autonomous whole.

Within the sketches belonging to one 'story' the order of the single pieces cannot be changed without destroying logical, causal and correlative interrelations. This is valid also for the sequence of the 'stories' and of the other separate sketches within the ensemble. A detailed analysis reveals such correlations between the sketches— references to preceding and forthcoming events, repetitions of incidents and facts already known to the reader—that a modification of their order would be confusing for the reader. It is, however, characteristic of *Sunshine Sketches* that the references mentioned do not cause an enrichment of the contents of the separate pieces. They are rather functional means signalling that the single texts are parts of a larger context, and thus are meant to arouse the reader's desire to learn about further sketches.

Within the fixed order of the single pieces the first and the last sketches function as corner-stones embracing the main theme, the contents and the composition of the whole ensemble. The first pages of the first sketch in which Mariposa is introduced extensively serve as an introduction to the following texts. The ambiguity which is symptomatic of the description of the Little Town is revealed here: the central theme is taken up and the reader's attention is drawn to the special attitudes of the narrator.

The final sketch, giving an answer to a question which includes the main theme of the whole book and ultimately elucidates the point of view, rounds off all the preceding pieces of the ensemble. So the first and the last sketches strengthen the stability of the unity of *Sunshine Sketches* due to the fact that they have an opening and a concluding function and that they bring together the end and the beginning of the ensemble concerning the evaluation of small-town life. although the final sketch rounds off the central theme and therefore resembles the composition of short story cycles, this does not mean that *Sunshine Sketches* constitutes a cycle. This ending merely tends to corroborate the validity of Forrest L. Ingram's statement that the rounding off of short story ensembles is not restricted to cyclical compositions.

Within the single sketches the events are told in chronological order, but as to the whole book a straight course of narrative is more or less missing. There is no plot running through all of the sketches, there is no common protagonist whose character is unfolded gradually, and furthermore the town is characterized by its unchangeableness. The fact that shared and repeated references suggest events which occur one after the other is of secondary importance only. In *Sunshine Sketches* the chronolgical order of narrative is superimposed by a cross-section of Mariposa shown in horizontal as well as in vertical dimensions. The conception of the particular setting and the handling of the ensemble of figures are especially conducive to this end.

The title of the book, although referring anonymously to a Little Town, hints at the specific role of a common setting. The reader expects to learn about events that occur in the same Little Town, and he begins to read the book stimulated in this way. The opening sentence of the first sketch, therefore, strikes him as a confirmation of this anticipation: 'I don't know whether you know Mariposa' (p. 1). Notwithstanding the fact that the first sketch has its own unique plot, Mariposa is introduced in an opening passage covering several pages. Thus the significance of the location is already signalled at the outset of the book, and Mariposa is integrated functionally into the ensemble from the very beginning. Besides the associational effects emerging from the fact that all of the sketches are set in the same town, their unity is strengthened by the constant expansion of the spatial picture of Mariposa. The mentioning of more and more local details gradually gives rise to a complex topographical portrayal of the town and simultaneously brings about a certain narrative sequence. This is supported by the fact that the integration of those parts of the setting which are indispensable to the understanding of the action is often bound to the knowledge of details already noted. These mutual relations, emphasizing the complexity of the outward appearance of Mariposa, form a further connective pattern.

All the self-contained units of *Sunshine Sketches*, excepting 'The Marine Excursions of the Knights of Pythias' and the last sketch, have a main character who is an inhabitant of Mariposa. If one imagines the Mariposans arranged in a row according to their share in action, Josh Smith takes the lead. He is the central figure of two sketches or 'stories.' Smith is followed by Jefferson Thorpe, Dean Drone, and Peter Pupkin, who are the protagonists of one text each. As main characters of single pieces, these figures underline the independence of the separate parts. But since at the same time they belong together with Pepperleigh, Macartney Mullins and Gingham to that group of figures which is of central importance for all of the sketches, their story becomes part of the goings-on in Mariposa and of experiences typical of its inhabitants. As there is no common protagonist for all of the sketches, the portrayal of a whole community becomes the central point. This community, however, is no undifferentiated mass, but a collective unit having representative individual characters. Thus on the one hand the main characters stand out from the majority of the Mariposans; on the other hand they are embedded into a larger circle of figures which in its turn is incorporated into the whole population of the town. The ensemble of figures is arranged and presented in such a way that it shows the double character of separation and unification which—the emphasis lying on unification—is symptomatic of all short story connections.

The more than fifty figures in *Sunshine Sketches* are characterized with unequal intensity. If one imagines them, in this connection, arranged in a row again, the lack of distinguishing features increases towards the end of the row until the presence of some characters is reduced to a mere mentioning of their names and professions. Correspondingly, the position of the protagonists at the start of the row reflects a more detailed characterization, which is typical of all members of the central group of figures. They appear in nearly all of the sketches, they are shown in various situations, and their features are illustrated more or less elaborately. Altogether a great number of figures is portrayed in a way which cannot be realized in a single short story.

It is worth mentioning that all the figures who are at the center of interest with regard to the whole book are already present in the first sketch (function of an introduction). In the following texts the ensemble of figures is supplemented little by little, paralleling the gradual expansion of the setting, and thus bringing about further unifying links between the separate pieces.

In *Sunshine Sketches* the intention of the author to portray the Little Town as an entirety, as a 'total' world, becomes evident. Besides its topographical and geographical dimensions, Mariposa also shows aspects of a social and intellectual landscape and as such helps significantly to shape the separate parts into a whole. The inhabitants of Mariposa appear as members of a special society. Projects and activities of individual characters counterbalance social enterprises and apply sooner or later to wider sections of the population. Their experiences and doings are revealed in the sequence of the sketches more and more clearly as components of a way of life typical both of Mariposa and of small towns in Canada at the turn of our century. Besides the unifying effect caused by the outward description of the Little Town, its depiction generates connective strands by showing relationships that exist between the particular atmosphere at Mariposa and the life style and habits of its population. The enrichment of the setting obtained by a continuous addition of local details, the gradual extension of the ensemble of figures and a great number of events associate themselves closely with an intensive enlargement of the townscape. The setting not only functions as the background for actions but it also corresponds with the peculiarities of the figures living in it. Mariposa is embodied in its population whose individual experiences are reflections of the specific atmosphere and living conditions of Mariposa. The latter therefore appears to be a compound of different conditions of existence interdepending and combining to form that idea of the Little Town which imparts to Mariposa a symbolic meaning transcending the dimensions of the literary work.

University of Jena, German Democratic Republic

[1]David M. Legate, *Stephen Leacock: A Biography* (Toronto, New York: Doubleday, 1970), p. 61.

[2]William H. New, 'In Defence of Private Worlds: An Approach to Irony in Canadian Fiction,' *Journal of Commonwealth Literature*, 10 (December 1970), 132.

[3]Douglas Spettigue, 'A Partisan Reading of Leacock,' *The Literary Half-Yearly*, 13, 2 (1972), 173.

[4]Robertson Davies, *Stephen Leacock* (Toronto: McClelland and Stewart, 1970), p. 21.

[5]*Ibid.*, p. 31.

[6]Arthur Phelps, 'Stephen Leacock,' *Canadian Writers* (Toronto: McClelland and Stewart, 1951), p. 75.

[7]Douglas Bush, 'Stephen Leacock,' in *The Canadian Imagination*, ed. David Staines (Cambridge, Mass. and London: Harvard Univ. Press, 1977), p. 134.

[8]Legate, *Leacock*, p. 63.

[9]In this paper I will not engage in detailed arguments about a comparison between short story ensembles and novels; I do so in an as yet unpublished manuscript in which I argue that such an assumption is very questionable if not wrong.

[10]Stephen Leacock, *Humour: Its Theory and Technique* (London: John Lane, 1935), p. 175.

[11]*Ibid.*, p. 199.

[12]Stephen Leacock, *Sunshine Sketches of a Little Town* (Toronto, Montreal: McClelland and Stewart, 1970), p. xv. All citations will refer to this text.

[1³]Legate, *Leacock*, p. 256.

[14]Helen M. Mustard, *The Lyric Cycle in German Literature* (New York: King's Cross Press, 1946).

[15]Forrest L. Ingram, *Representative Short Story Cycles of the Twentieth Century: Studies in a Literary Genre* (The Hague, Paris: Mouton, 1971).

[16]Malcolm Ross, 'Editor's Preface,' in Leacock, *Sunshine Sketches*, p. ix.

[17]Wayne C. Booth, 'Distance and Point-of-View: An Essay in Classification,' *Essays in Criticism*, 11 (1961), 65.

[18]Leacock, *Humour*, p. 281.

[19]*Ibid.*

[20]*Ibid.*, p. 110.

[21]*Ibid.*, p. 69.

Waldemar Zacharasiewicz

THE INVENTION OF A REGION: THE ART OF FICTION IN JACK HODGINS' STORIES

Jack Hodgins' art of fiction taps the resources common to the modernist rather than the postmodernist writers of the twentieth century. He shares their preoccupation with a locale modelled on the milieu of the writer's own past and, unlike leading Canadian fiction writers such as Margaret Laurence and Alice Munro, resists the autobiographical impulse. It is no coincidence that while the interconnected stories in Laurence's *A Bird in the House* or Munro's *Lives of Girls and Women* make use of the first-person perspective, Hodgins seems to have avoided first-person narration. In his first collection, *Spit Delaney's Island*,[1] it is used only once. His favorite mode has been the fairly consistent use of the figural narrative situation,[2] which suits his tendency to immerse himself in the roles of characters through whose senses and minds the physical setting—the 'feel'—of region and its social structures—are largely filtered. In several interviews Hodgins has referred to his early habit of watching other people and of being 'supersensitive to the way they might feel,' and he has plausibly claimed that unlike many contemporary writers he is not writing about himself.[3]

His stories bear the stamp of his native region which, since it is spared the winters afflicting most other regions of Canada, seems to provide a milieu basically favorable to an optimistic or even Edenic picture of human life. The regional literature from British Columbia and Vancouver Island in particular is thus molded on a pattern very different from that which Margaret Atwood sees as characteristic of Canadian literature—the concept of survival.

Only one of the stories in *Spit Delaney's Island*, 'After the Season,' through its atmosphere and setting, corresponds to what has come to be regarded as typical of Canadian fiction. Characteristic themes and mythical patterns are present in the story of Hallie Crane's exile from her family and her former life in the isolated tourist camp on the coast in the north of Vancouver Island and her strange sexual relationship with Morgan, the camp owner. For the intruding representative of civilization, Mr. Hamilton Grey, this relationship during the winter months significantly resembles the victimization of Proserpina by Hades. It seems appropriate that in such a 'typical' Canadian story the death of the intruder in an accident caused by powerful natural forces should be foreshadowed at the beginning of the text which, in contrast to other stories by Hodgins, opens with the mode of pure description. Helmut Bonheim in his examination of 'Topoi of the Canadian Short Story' has shown this device to be a technique still particularly dear to (male) Canadian writers.[4]

The other stories in Hodgins' first collection, while showing a strong regional touch, seem to be more closely related to fiction from other regions of North America than to the patterns allegedly characteristic of Canadian fiction. A careful analysis, in fact, reveals that Hodgins' use of the specifically regional material in order to convey stories of general human significance was shaped and inspired by masters of short fiction from the American South. In this respect he seems to have shared several models with his compatriots from other provinces of Canada, in particular Alice Munro, whose debt to Southern authors like Eudora Welty and James Agee has been demonstrated by Tim Struthers.[5]

Hodgins himself has admitted to an intense admiration for William Faulkner which, at least for a while, even prevented him from finding his own voice. Among his collected stories, 'Other People's Troubles' (the original title of the story published in 1969 was 'Yesterday's Green Summer)[6] might illustrate the debt to his model from Mississippi. One could almost mistake the opening paragraph of this story of the initiation of a ten-year-old boy for the oblique beginning of a Faulkner story.

> In those early years, it seemed that she often dressed in green as pale and just as gentle as the wild mint patch growing not too far from the house. Oh, they would tease her for it; first he (born Barclay Miles but called Duke then for riding the haywagons like some kind of royalty) and then Dora and Mary too—all her children—saying maybe she was blind to any other colour and afraid of wearing red by mistake, which was her only hate, but saying it beyond her reach for safety just in case this once she didn't want to laugh. (p. 123)

Time markers suggesting anteriority ('In those early years'),[7] nonsequential sequence-signals (the ambiguous 'she,' 'he,' and 'they'),[8] and the parenthesis placed in the relatively long sentence combine to create the semblance of a Faulknerian opening. Yet the events of this critical summer, which are largely filtered through the mind and senses of the boy, and the memory of the adult who looks back at his youth, strike one as distinctly Hodgins' own.

Hodgins' receptivity to literary influences is also reflected in his assimilation of situations and types of characters from the work of other writers from the American South, in particular Eudora Welty and Flannery O'Connor.[9] While most of the characters in *Spit Delaney's Island* are fairly ordinary though somewhat eccentric people, one story in the book confronts the reader with figures who become allegorical types. 'At the Foot of the Hill, Birdie's School' dramatizes the initiation of a seventeen-year-old lad after his descent from the seclusion of the deserted utopian community once presided over by the 'Old Man.' One encounters several bizarre figures who are willing to teach Webster Treherne their 'counter-lore'—for instance their negation of love. Their new disciple is eager to learn and to rival the villainies of a gang of three (the 'McLean gang') and desires to be quickly corrupted. The depiction of the prompt satisfaction of this desire which, however, involves painful encounters and quickly ends in illness and death, gives this unique story a Kafkaesque touch. Its opening also echoes situations familiar from Flannery O'Connor's work, especially her second novel, *The Violent Bear It Away*. Usually Hodgins anchors his stories more clearly in everyday reality than he does in this surreal text, though 'At the Foot of the Hill' also achieves a degree of contemporaneity through the dependence of Webster Treherne's original fantasies on his familiarity with comic strips and modern adventure romances.

The way Hodgins normally conveys a persuasively realistic picture of a fictional milieu reminds one of Flannery O'Connor, to whose stories he is clearly indebted in his grouping of characters or the introduction of some similar topics. This fact, which has so far largely escaped the attention of his readers,[10] is underlined here not in order to belittle his achievement as a writer. Instead, the intention is to point out the complex relationship between the regional subject matter and fictional models, and to illustrate a creative impulse that can assimilate motifs, themes and situations from other literary contexts.

The first story Hodgins ever published, 'Every Day of His Life,' parallels in its depiction of the prospective bridegroom and his wooing of the somewhat grotesque bride O'Connor's 'The Life You Save May Be Your Own.' Both the title of the story and the interest the visitor takes in the neighboring mountain and in the bride's car echo elements of O'Connor's work, which, however, does not project the sparkling vitality of a central character like 'Big Glad Littlestone.' The story, indeed, strikes the reader who is familiar with the narrative tradition of the American South as a successful blend of narrative patterns and modes common in Welty and O'Connor.

An even closer connection between Hodgins' and O'Connor's fictions can be established by an analysis of Hodgins' early story, 'Three Women of the Country.' This haunting novelette dramatizes isolation and loneliness; its effect hinges on the consistent application of the multiple point of view, the consecutive illumination of the private dilemmas of three female characters in the three chapters of the text. The delay in the provision of expositional matter in the interest of suspense and maximum impact necessitates the use of flashbacks. They reveal the factors determining the day-long crisis in the life of Mrs. Edna Starbuck, a middle-aged widow with a retarded child she has concealed from her neighbors. The narrative technique chosen also underlines the problems faced by the other two female characters, Charlene Porter and Mrs. Milly Wright.

The fact that the initial chapter is largely rendered from the angle of Mrs. Wright does not preclude some satirical strokes by the authorial voice. Strikingly idiomatic dialogue is framed by the silent and mostly negative evaluation of the other figures by the self-satisfied Mrs. Wright, a busybody whose rational judgements fail, however, to recognize the hidden factors moulding the behavior of her neighbors in the rural community named 'Cut-off.' She remains completely unaware of the tragic dilemma of the seemingly incompetent Mrs. Starbuck, whose unexpected death-blow for a calf which has fallen into an abandoned well alienates Mrs. Wright still further. Mrs. Starbuck's peculiar action perplexes Charlene, for whom she has been a mother substitute for the last year but whose trust in her is now shaken by the recent discovery of the retarded boy. Charlene's attempt to come to terms with her experiences prompts not only her ruminations, which are frequently rendered in narrated monologue, but also her seemingly decisive action—she tries to take the sick boy from his hiding place in the attic—which in turn precipitates Mrs. Starbuck's behavior in the third chapter. The moving portrayal of Mrs. Starbuck's solitary nightly search for a solution after abortive attempts to get help and end the nightmarish concealment of the boy derives its impact partly from the combination of summarized reminiscence and narrated monologue. It culminates in her desperate effort to save the boy from being hit by Mrs. Wright's car after he has run away during her preparations for a new beginning by making another move. She is killed by her own car, crushed to death in the ditch into which she has been pushed by the vehicle.

It is at this point that the reader who has been reminded of O'Connor's work by the title, the grouping of characters, and the graphic description of the rural setting,[11] will inevitably notice Hodgins' closeness to one of O'Connor's favorite strategies, the depiction of a dying human being with the broken eyes seemingly suggesting a message of general importance.[12] Yet the reader will also observe that the story is not concluded by this accident, possibly a quasi-sacrificial act, but by a coda which emphasizes the shock of the two female survivors now finally aware of the narrow limits of their knowledge. A so-called 'mirror-look,' popular among short story writers,[13] dramatizes this incipient awareness of Mrs. Wright and the shattering of her self-confidence.

This is but one example suggesting an attitude towards the art of fiction different from that of avant-garde or postmodern writers.[14] For Jack Hodgins, the fictional communities that he depicts clearly have more stability than they would have in postmodern fiction. Yet while being concerned less with verbal surfaces and games exposing the problematical nature of language and communication and more with the 'comedy and tragedy of human life'[15] and the 'mysteries in human beings,' Hodgins similarly derives intense pleasure from the act of writing.

His art often entails the representation of a fictional world from the angle of somewhat freakish individuals. Hodgins has in fact recently admitted that there are striking parallels between even his more freakish or grotesque characters and the people inhabiting his region, and he has maintained that he repeatedly observes and recognizes people he had regarded as figments of his imagination.[16] While this experience puzzles him slightly, as it seems to undermine his sense of having invented his world and its characters, one can support his claim that these strange encounters with individuals 'in all their nuttiness' are due to his instinctive truthfulness to the region in which he and his fiction are rooted.

University of Vienna, Austria

---

[1]*Spit Delaney's Island* (Toronto: Macmillan, 1976). All page references in the text are to the First Laurentian Library edition, 1977.

²The term is F. K. Stanzel's in *Narrative Situations in the Novel,* trans. Charlotte Goedsche (Vienna, 1971; Chicago: Univ. of Chicago Press, 1971).

³Cf., e.g., Jack Hodgins' interview with Alan Twigg, 'Western Horizon: Jack Hodgins,' in *For Openers: Conversations with 24 Canadian Writers* (Madiera Park, B.C.: Harbour Press, 1981), pp. 185-95, esp. pp. 185f.

⁴Helmut Bonheim, 'Topoi of the Canadian Short Story,' *Dalhousie Review,* 60 (1981), 659-69, esp. 663.

⁵Cf. J. R. (Tim) Struthers, 'Alice Munro and the American South' (1974); rev. in *The Canadian Novel: Here and Now,* ed. John Moss (Toronto: NC Press, 1978), pp. 121-33. I am indebted to Tim Struthers' forthcoming bibliography of Jack Hodgins' work for information about uncollected stories.

⁶The original version appeared in *Descant,* 13, 4 (Summer 1969). Cf. *Spit Delaney's Island,* pp. 123-33.

⁷The term is borrowed from Helmut Bonheim's *The Narrative Modes: Techniques of the Short Story* (Cambridge: Brewer, 1982), pp. 101-07.

⁸Joseph M. Backus, ' "He Came Into Her Line of Vision Walking Backward": Non-sequential Sequence-Signals in Short Story Openings.' *Language Learning,* 15 (1965), 67-83.

⁹Cf. the somewhat simple-minded female character of Crystal Styan in 'By the River,' who has a counterpart in several figures in Welty's early stories who succumb to male charm.

¹⁰Only Margaret Laurence's review, 'Hodgins At Last Collected,' *The Globe and Mail* (8 May, 1976), p. 38, contains a passing reference to the similarity between Hodgins' 'At the Foot of the Hill' and O'Connor's work.

¹¹The reader is alerted to aspects of intertextuality by several allusions to Shakespeare's *The Tempest,* references to which are acknowledged in the author's interview with Jack David in *Essays on Canadian Writing,* 11 (Summer 1978), 142-46, and in the commentary contained in Jack Hodgins and Bruce Nesbitt, *Teaching Short Fiction: A Resource Book to Transitions II, Short Fiction* (Vancouver: CommCept, 1978), pp. 10-14.

¹²Cf. p. 68: 'One of Mrs. Starbuck's eyes was under water; the other, a dull plastic ball, stared swollen and incredulous up at Mrs. Wright as if Mrs. Starbuck in the last failing moment had seen something she badly needed to tell about.'

¹³Cf. Bonheim, *The Narrative Modes,* pp. 96f.

¹⁴I have explored in a longer article the development of Jack Hodgins' art of fiction and his increasing preoccupation with the problems of the artist in his later stories.

¹⁵Cf. Hodgins' recent interview with Peter O'Brien in *Rubicon,* 1 (Spring 1983), 34-71, esp. 63.

¹⁶Cf. *Ibid.,* pp. 39f. for his claim to have met one of the major figures of *The Resurrection of Joseph Bourne,* the ex-stripper Jenny Chambers (with her pink hair and plastic raincoat), after having invented her.

Cedric May

FORM AND STRUCTURE IN *LES ILES DE LA NUIT* BY ALAIN GRANDBOIS

Les formes de la nuit vont et viennent dans l'ombre.
Victor Hugo[1]

Alain Grandbois, arguably Québec's greatest poet, had the elegant and world-weary detachment of the expatriate globetrotter. His first poems were published privately in Hankow in 1934, when Grandbois was on an abortive trip to Tibet.[2] Like Malraux, he felt the spiritual temptation of the East, and this is reflected in his short stories, which recreate the air of luxury tinged with the foreboding of the inter-war years.[3] When in Europe, he put down roots briefly in Paris where there was a group of Canadian artists, and on the Mediterranean island of Port-Cros where he met fellow-poet, Jules Supervielle. Grandbois has none of Supervielle's humor, none of his power of minute observation of the immediate, tangible world of objects which solitude drives him to befriend. But the solitude is the same, as is the cosmic spatial breadth of reference and the tragic sense of borrowed time. Apart from poetry, Grandbois wrote rather special travel books (some the texts of broadcasts made in Canada in the 1950s).[4] His restless quest for a haven and a landfall is common to both kinds of writing. The challenge which Grandbois and his footloose generation (Scott Fitzgerald, Hemingway, Supervielle, Malraux, Cendrars, Morand, Saint-Exupéry, Callaghan, some of whom he knew personally) throw out to their readers is posed by their disregard for landmarks, their waywardness, their openness to the provisional and the inchoate.

Poetry plays on ambiguity and multiple meaning. It creates images and sensations using techniques which invite the imaginative participation of the reader. When, as well as accepting these variables of tolerance, the poet chooses a subject as elusive and amorphous as night, then the challenge of form and control is real indeed.

Night as Figure of the Absurd

Night, for the author of *Les Iles de la nuit,* provides a respite. It is a refuge from the 'mortelle incohérence' revealed by dawn and the dazzling profusion which the light of day unrolls before us. The created world, mirror of the inner world of sensation and experience, is plethoric and bewildering and the poet finds few keys to this box of marvels, 'la nuit était moins épaisse que mon silence et mon aveuglement' (77).[5]

The few 'signes de l'étoile' that there are, shedding a tolerable gleam of apparent significance on an infinitely varied world of circumstance, leave the poet 'muet et paralysé.' His natural response to the challenge of meaning in what otherwise is absurd and defies rationalization is not words but silence and stillness. 'Songe' and 'mensonge,' the veil of unreality which the imagination constantly draws over the tangible, is tantalizingly deceptive and mocks our best efforts to comprehend.

The poet defines himself by his insatiable appetites, and one of these is a thirst for illumination: 'Et moi cherchant la clarté comme un homme//de faim' (61). And yet, all the world can offer him is malicious indifference and stony derision: 'et ce grand rire de pierre inattaquable' (61).

The Disproportion of Man and His World

The impermeability of man's environment, both physical and psychological, is made more intense by the scale of this environment. The poet's protests and his appeals are lost in vastness and amorphousness:

> Et nos cris désormais
> N'auront plus que le tremblant écho
> Des poussières perdues
> Aux gouffres des néants. (68)

In language strongly reminiscent of the French Romantic poets, particularly Victor Hugo and Alfred de Vigny (in an interview Grandbois named Vigny and the Bible amongst his sources), Grandbois offers us the spectacle of man as the 'prisoner of space,' a playfully antithetical term Georges Poulet once used of the

Romantic imagination. By means of superlatives and a vocabulary of general categories rather than of specifics, Grandbois creates a backdrop of formless immensity: 'Nous allions plus loins que les plus lointains horizons' (66);

> Voice l'archipel du désir
> Convoitant les fenêtres fraîches
> Des aubes d'immensité. (48)

(Several words here such as 'immensité' have a high frequency in the poetry of Victor Hugo.) The haunting first lines of *Les Iles de la nuit* sum up this theme of incoherent space, cheating us of sense, denying us a foothold:

> ô tourments plus forts de n'être
>   qu'une seule apparence
> Angoisse des fuyantes créations
> Prière du désert humilié. (15)

The stance here is, without forcing the material, the austere, aristocratic stance of Vigny's prophet in the desert, Moïse (Moses) 'puissant et solitaire,' relying on the occasional burning bush to interpret an otherwise silent and cryptic universe. ('Tu savais la torche implacable des buissons allumés.') (31)

The Need for Form

If I begin with this rapid survey of the themes of *Les Iles de la nuit*—man's isolation in an absurd universe, the vast disproportion between self and world, and the incompatibility of the two, and to these must be added the themes of time and death, final proof for Grandbois, if any be needed, of the sick joke of man's condition—it is merely to make evident the need Grandbois has of form and structure. Paradoxically, to convey effectively the amorphous, the incoherent, the non-specific, the vast formlessness of the cosmic depths of night mirrored in boundless oceans, the poet needs a sure hand and eye, a cool control of form and structure. And as with the Romantics, the challenge is a double one—the cosmic is but a patiently worked analogy paralleling the world of dream. The seven Hankow poems of 1934, published by an acquaintance during a visit the poet made to

China, had as a frontispiece a sketch of a man lying on his back and holding in his hands an opium pipe. The dreams turns out to be as cruel and as hollow as life itself.

Charting the Unfathomable

'Comment architecturer le vide?' Is is in these terms that Jean Gaudon spells out in his study of Victor Hugo's cosmic and apocalyptic verse the challenge the poet faces.[6] How is Grandbois to structure the void? We should dispel immediately a false impression created earlier by the quotation which showed the poet struck dumb by the enigma. And the quotation is not an isolated one. Here he is again seemingly reduced to silence, lost for words, this time before the sudden, tantalizing intimation of beauty and perfection:

> Mais une fois j'ai vu les trois cyprès parfaits
> Devant la blancheur du logis
> J'ai vu et je me tais
> Et ma détresse est sans égale. (96)

This silence is not the silence of despair about words. Grandbois does not write off poetry as a means of grappling with the intangible and the inexpressible. This is rather the silence of extreme circumspection in which poetry can begin. Speaking of Mallarmé, Jean-Paul Sartre said that 'la poésie commence au-delà du bavardage.'[7] Grandbois has his 'chatter poems,' poems which by their sheer verbal facility transmit to the reader a feel for the overpowering profusion of emotional and sense experience which crowds our hours, 'Parmi les heures mortes et les heures présentes...' (25) (and indeed the whole of poem IV), and which throng especially the streets of our urban selfhood: 'Ah toutes ces rues parcourues dans l'angoisse//de la pluie...' (75) (and the whole of poem XXV). Beyond this chatter lies the world of silence punctuated by the clipped, hieratic utterance, 'Je suis seul et nu//Je suis seul et sel' (38), or by the soul's lilting song of life:

> Mais toi ô toi viens hâtons-nous
> Courons volons
> Replie en pointe de flèche tes longs
>   cheveux d'étincelles

Ah jetons du lest fuyons . . .
Pour que morte la mort et
   morte son ombre
Elle ne puisse nous saisir (63)

Using Words to Disturb

Grandbois seems to scorn the easy props of language. Language is automatically experience structured, structured by syntax, by its own logic, by the constraints of meaning on which the conventions of language depend. Without being quirky or wayward, Grandbois uses language to stir rather than to lull us. One poem (XIX), eighteen lines in length, manages without a single finite verb. Poem XIII of twenty-four lines has only two finite verbs, though this is by no means a characteristic feature of this poetry where we find more often a succession of independent clauses and a lack of subordination. Absence of punctuation,[8] another of the comforting props Grandbois eschews, creates ambiguity and a brief uncertainty which checks our complacency. Poem III has the arresting title: 'Au delà ces grandes étoiles. . . .'[9] The word 'au-delà,' conventionally written with a hyphen, exists as an adverb and as a rare poetic noun—'l'au-delà,' the after-life or the beyond—and as a preposition in the form 'au-delà de.' Here we expect the preposition but then it becomes clear that 'au delà' is an adverb in its frequent (seven) appearances in a poem of 48 lines. Or is it perhaps an elliptical use of the preposition?

Au delà ma main
o mon pressentiment
Au delà mon talisman. (23)

More ellipsis in the same poem, 'Mais où mon deuil,//Mais où mon seuil' (23), and this time the device is a favorite of the poet. But Grandbois takes only rare liberties with the conventions of language. What he does do is to avoid making a convenience of convention. He makes frequent use of accumulation but avoids cadencing. By that, I mean that he does not signal to the reader when the accumulation is ending. The word 'et' is not a cosy signal that the accumulation is finite and that the world has order. It is used often as an urgent, insistent reminder of a fragmented, contingent universe:

> Ces murs protecteurs
> et ce plafond fraternel
> et ces trous d'ombre et cette
> grande ombre
> et ce plancher de fer
>
> et moi sous mes seuls cheveux (60);
>
> Pris et protégé et condamné par la mer. (38)

(See also poem IV for a further example of the use of this concatenatory 'and'.) The language of Grandbois is taut, sinewy, disturbing, rarely comforting. It is the language of anguish and protest.

Grandbois' Eloquence

But it is informed by rhetoric. Accumulation has just been mentioned. Anaphora is so prevalent that it does not need illustration. Anaphora, the device of the litany which repeats the first words of each phrase with incantatory effect, is the chief device in poems I, III, IV, V, VI, XII, XV, XVI, XVIII, XXI, XXIII, XXVII, XXVIII, and there are frequent echo effects in other poems.

Word Frequency as a Key

More helpful in this process of structuring the void is Grandbois' use of key words. Vocabulary frequency in his poetry has been systematically studied.[10] The list is headed by words with a high frequency by any standard, but such a comment merely reveals the limitations of word counts. No account is taken of levels of metaphorization or of contexts. Look, for example, at the transformation the poet gives to parts of the body in these lines from poem XI, making nonsense of any attempts at simple categorization:

> Les mille abeilles de ta paupière
> Cette chevelure jusqu'à ton doigt bagué
> Ce qui hier existait
> Ce qui nous est aujourd'hui accordé. (43)

Word counts work for nouns. Here the context is created by the bold use of a preposition ('jusqu'à' meaning either 'and this is even true of,' 'not excluding' or, more literally, 'down as far as'), by the general 'ce qui,' by the time frame of 'hier' and 'aujourd'hui,' and the further insight into the theme of time contained in the contrast between the verbs. Innocent parts of the body—the emphasis is on what is fragile, fluttering, restless, ephemeral, scintillating, impermanent—become symbols of mortality and keys to the hidden inner life, and a precious gift to be savoured while there is still time.

What the key words, simple as they are, reveal is that *Les Iles de la nuit,* beyond the incantatory effects we have described, is structured thematically. The most frequent can be arranged as follows:

nuit	être	main	silence
ombre	savoir	oeil	dernier
étoile	voir	doigt	seul
pluie		homme	songe
jour		coeur	mort[11]
heure		pas	

What we discover is mortal man, reduced to the basic elements of his physicality, pitted against the vast, vague permanency of time and space. The Romantic polarities of self and world could not be starker. It is the patient sustaining of this stance, this defiant confrontation, which underpins *Les Iles de la nuit.* Poem XIX, which reads like an extended version of poem VIII, and which was one of the Hankow poems of 1934, says it most clearly: the non-self taunts man with promise of hope and salvation, with promise of purpose and illumination: 'Quand par la fenêtre déjà cette//aube hypocrite et généreuse' (60). The self is hemmed in with these taunts, these apparent clues offered fleetingly by interpersonal relationships, these apologies for communication: 'et leur bruit dans mon silence//et leur effrayant silence dans mon désert' (61). Yes, the non-self is human, too. Other people are part of the omnipresent, absurd otherness. Thrown back on his own resources, the self is reduced to the sum of his appetites, the present participles common in Grandbois 'cherchant,' 'criant' characterizing the hungry soul crying out for light, love and reality, and finding death and darkness. The non-self has the last laugh, stony and implacable. Self and non-self alternate in a dialogue of the deaf, but the triumph of poetry is signalled in the changing proportions:

ll. 1-4	non-self	4 lines
l. 5	self	1 line
ll. 6-8	non-self	3 lines
ll. 9-12	self and non-self in conflict	4 lines
ll. 13-16	self	4 lines
l. 17	non-self	1 line

The self grows in confidence and experience, asserts itself through the word whose value is rarely that of communication, of inter-personal communion already proved impossible, but rather that of prophetic protest:

> Parmi tous et toutes ou seul avec soi-même
> Nous lèverons nos bras dans des appels
>   durs comme les astres. (28)

Dimension as Structure

The poems of *Les Iles de la nuit* are further structured by a clear use of dimension. In the lines just quoted, there is an urgent desire for transcendence and the poem concludes: 'cherchant en vain au bout de nos doigts crispés//ce mortel instant d'une fuyante éternité' (29). Horizontality is regularly an image of entrapment: 'Je flotte à la dérive sur la mer' (38); 'Le flux de la mer me noie' (22); 'Nous guidant vers les routes//ne conduisant nulle part' (26);

> o vous tous ensevelis derrière les
>   murs des chambres vides . . .
> o vous tous sur ce chemin
>   perdu de mon passe (35);

'Les lois éternelles//Galopaient comme des chevaux fous' (41); ô toi mortel instant de l'éternel fleuve' (52); 'et ce plancher de fer' (60); 'Les grands espaces sont abolis//Nous sommes sans évasion' (74); 'Ah toutes ces rue parcourues//dans l'angoisse de la pluie' (75); the whole of poem XXV; 'Tu disparaissais et ma recherche//s'égarait en vain dans les derniers labyrinthes' (88). This desperate horizontality is intensified by closing doors, the finality of parting, forgetting and dying.

Verticality is not automatically a contrastive sign of escape and transcendence.[12] The cyclones and spirals of poem XXVII threaten devastation, and the pillars of heaven in poem VIII weigh heavy on the poet, pinning him to the sea. But in the main, man's Promethean quest skyward is what marks the poet's stance: 'Je sais cet élan retrouvant le ciel du mât' (17), he says with weary recognition. The word 'colonne' recurs several times and, though the context restrains the poet's optimism, the force of this upward thrust can be joyful and liberating: 'Et ces hautes colonnes de joie//souvenirs ô SOUVENIR' (20);

> Tes deux mains sur ton visage
> M'apportaient les miraculeux enchantements
> Les colonnes se dressaient
> Comme les géométries totales. (73)

Grandbois even intimates that man's upward leap, his hunger scouring the heavens, is destructive in its intensity. Verticality brings vertigo.

> Voici l'archipel du désir
> Convoitant les fenêtres fraîches
> Des aubes d'immensité . . .
> D'un espace égorgé
> Par le vertige de l'homme
> Dont le songe dévore le ciel. (48)

Poem V, 'le feu gris,' is the poet's horrified response to the tyranny of his desire. He recoils from the compulsive upward thrust of his whole being, once he is aroused, recoils from the threat of being engulfed in 'l'immense incendie des volcans,' and even denies his nature by begging for the oblivion of night: 'Qu'une nuit sans fin déroule sur moi//ses voiles de plomb' (32). The structure of *Les Iles de la nuit* is, in part, that of the 'total geometry' of poem XXIV just quoted. Rare, fleeting joys, miraculous enchantments, lift us out of our entrapment in the grim horizontality of linear time.

Absence of Other Organizing Features

So far, we have seen broadly two sets of technical devices organizing Grandbois' poems. Rhetoric and themes, voice and message, inform and shape and give coherence to what threatens always to be intangible and elusive. What else? Can we detect in the arrangement of the twenty-eight poems of *Les Iles de la nuit* patterns of significance? Are there other external indications of the author's intention? We have noted that there are only *incipits*, but no titles proper. No help is given in the form of the useful mnemonic devices that titles of poems can be. The title of the whole collection is a quotation from poem XXVI, 'ô fiancée.' From the context, we gather what is everywhere apparent in the collection, that love is a dubious gift. The release it gives from the dark phantasms of man's inner world is short-lived and illusory. The stars, like islands in the night, are the feeble, flickering relics of ecstasy overwhelmed by solitude, silence and space.

Significant Groupings

Intriguing for the structure of the book as a whole is the presence within the collection of the seven Hankow poems. Grandbois, in accounts of their publication, gives the impression that they were a few poems he happened to have by him when asked for them on one of the stops he made in a planned journey to Tibet. It is most surprising that the seven poems, when reprinted in *Les Iles de la nuit*, do not remain as a group or retain their original order even. The seven poems appear in *Les Iles de la nuit* as numbers V, VII, XXII, VI, XIX, IV, I.

What we can notice about these seven poems is that with one exception they appear in the first and last quarters of the later collection: I, IV, V, VI, VII and XIX, XXII. These opening and closing quarters, seven poems in each case, I-VII and XXII-XXVIII, have, as Jacques Blais has pointed out, several distinctive features. He detects, in fact, four groups of seven poems, the first and last groups marked by the use of the first person and the tragic predominance of the theme of night. The second and third groups are barely distinguishable, though on average group two, poems VIII to XIV, contains shorter poems with the fewest syllables per line. Blais points, too, to the curious fact that the anguished poems of the first and last sections are the most prolix with the most lines and the longest lines. Blais makes a good case for a cyclic structure to the collection *Les Iles de la nuit*, the torment, the cosmic *angst* of the opening giving way to a false calm, a respite—'cette aube hypocrite et généreuse' (60)—before night once again crowds out hope, happiness, tenderness in the concluding section from poem XXII to the end. The respite is introduced at the end of the first section in poem VII by the word itself: 'Pourquoi ce répit favorable' (37). Jacques Blais identifies as 'sursis' (stay of execution) poems numbers XIV, XVIII and XXI. To these might be added other references in this middle section, where the terror is assuaged by the evocation of childhood (poem XIV) and the consolation of the angel (54), references to 'sanctuaires' (56) and 'refuge' (59).

A Sense of Ending

The other recurring technical feature, again discussed by Jacques Blais, is the detachment of the final line or the rather abrupt conclusion which Grandbois gives poems in other ways. The islands in the night are but brief 'sursis,' brief pauses on the hurried journey down linear time. At the end of the experience, the poet recoils in a burst of dreadful lucidity. 'C'est du moins ce qu'indique avec constance le dernier vers de la majorité des poèmes, vers final souvent mis en retrait, incisif, comme figé dans l'effroi ou l'incredulité face a l'inflexible destin.'[13] The final lines (detached from the body of the poem), producing a particularly chilling and strident note of finality, are these: 'Tout le reste est mensonge' (44); 'Le soleil était fermé' (50); 'et ce grand rire de pierre inattaquable' (61); 'mais son âme était glacée' (83); 'Et tu me laissais seul avec une âme perdue' (89). The technique is one dear to Victor Hugo. Hugo's poem 'on vit, on parle, on a le ciel et les nuages' (Book IV, poem XI in *Les Contemplations*) makes very interesting comparison in structural terms with poem XXV, 'Ah toutes ces rues.' Grandbois creates here a stark opposition between experience and perception, between the subconscious and lucid realization, between the flux of linear time, soothing and persuasive, and the moment of truth. And this is one of the deep structures of his work revealed by the form, the themes, and the poet's attitude.

Discerning the Unifying Principle

Jacques Blais is properly cautious about the signs of coherence which he finds in *Les Iles de la nuit*. 'On ne trouve pas que (l'agencement des thèmes) vise à quelque démonstration, suive un ordre progressif. . . . Pourtant, au sein même de *l'éclatement labyrinthique*, il est possible de discerner un principe unificateur. . . . L'interdépendance *d'éléments disparates et distants* est voulue par l'action unificatrice du mouvement même de la vie et de l'expérience humaine.'[14] The cosmic intangibility, nocturnal amorphousness, and labyrinthine profusion of experience in *Les Iles de la nuit* is shaped by certain themes such as that of time but above all by the presence of the poet in his work, by his consistent voice and stance. From the opening words 'O tourments plus forts de n'être qu'une seul apparence' (45) which bid fair to becoming as sonorous and indispensable to Québec literature as Valery's 'Harmonieuse Moi' or 'Le Ciel fut par-dessus le toit' for French literature, Grandbois, calmly and with no illusions except those he knowingly cherishes, defies the inevitable, against all the evidence. It is his truculent rhetoric, his muted melancholy, which inform the material of *Les Iles de la nuit.*

Grandbois' Range of Utterance

Let us attempt, in conclusion, to identify the different notes of this voice: the poet laments his condition: 'ô tourments . . . je sais je sais . . . pourquoi' (15-17); celebrates its tragic disproportion: 'ces hautes colonnes de joie' (20); defines it with lapidary and lucid concision: 'je suis le veuf de la nuit' (23); enumerates the chaotic profusion of his world: 'Parmi tous et toutes' (28); celebrates the rare gift of beauty and love: 'le paysage ultime de ta beaute' (44); and cries stoically his defiance: 'Nous lèverons nos bras dans des//appels durs comme les astres' (28), 'Moi criant mes cris glacés dans ce vide inhumain' (61). This enumeration of a range of styles also sums up the range of themes in *Les Iles de la nuit.* Grandbois successfully takes up the challenge of the minimal ordering of his material by achieving a fine fusion of theme and form and stamping his work with a signature which becomes essential as it becomes familiar. 'O coeurs bouleversés de cris//Depuis si longtemps arrachés' (47).

University of Birmingham, England

---

[1]Victor Hugo, *Les Contemplations*, Book VI, poem 14, 'O gouffre! l'âme plonge et rapporte le doute' (Paris: Édition Garnier Frères, 1962), p. 286.

²See Jacques Blais, *Presence d'Alain Grandbois* (Québec: Presses de l'Université Laval, 1974), pp. 61 and 241.

³Alain Grandbois, *Avant le chaos* (Montréal: Les Editions Modernes, 1945; ed. augmentée, Montréal: Editions HMH, 1964).

⁴Alain Grandbois, *Visages du monde: Images et souvenirs de l'entre-deux-guerres* (Montréal: Éditions HMH, 1971).

⁵The numbers after each quotation in the article are page references to the edition of Alain Grandbois' *Les Iles de la nuit*, published by Fides, in the Bibliothèque canadienne-française, in 1972 [1st appearance Montréal: Parizeau, 1944].

⁶Cf. Jean Gaudon, *Le Temps de la contemplation*, (Paris: Flammarion, 1969), particularly pp. 279-326.

⁷Cf. Jean-Paul Sartre, 'Orphée noir,' in *Anthologie de la nouvelle poèsie nègre et malgache de langue française*, ed. Leopold Sedar-Senghor (Paris: P.U.F., 1948). The phrase quoted here sums up Sartre's argument on pp. xix-xx.

⁸Contrary to popular belief, Grandbois was not the first Québec poet to abandon regular verse forms and punctuation. Jean-Aubert Loranger, who had clearly read the early Eluard with profit, wrote excellent free verse in *Les atmosphères* (1920) and *Poèmes* (1922).

⁹'Title' is a misnomer. There are no titles in *Les Iles de la nuit* though Grandbois uses them in his later collections. Here we have only *incipits*.

¹⁰Jean A. Beaudot, *Dictionnaire du vocabulaire d'Alain Grandbois*, 2 vols. (Centre de calcul de l'Université de Montréal, 1966).

¹¹List given in Jacques Brault, *Alain Grandbois* (Paris: Pierre Seghers, 1968), p. 71, n.l.

¹²The reader is referred to an essay by Père Ernest Gagnon in *L'Homme d'ici* (Montréal: Éditions HMH, 1963), p. 51, which offers a striking parallel with the poetic vision of Grandbois examined here. This profound resemblance with the writing of another Québecois who saw his province from the privileged viewpoint of someone who had lived abroad (Gagnon was a missionary in Africa) encourages us to accept gratefully Georges-André Vachon's astonishing reference to the 'inspiration fortement autochtone de Grandbois,' in *Europe* (fevrier-mars, 1969), 26.

¹³Jacques Blais, p. 127.

¹⁴*Ibid.*, pp. 125-26; my italics.

Wolfgang Klooss

NARRATIVE MODES AND FORMS OF LITERARY PERCEPTION IN RUDY WIEBE'S *THE SCORCHED-WOOD PEOPLE*

Whereas Sam Solecki spoke of Rudy Wiebe's *The Scorched-Wood People* as 'the great novel about Riel that we all knew would eventually be written,'[1] basing his judgement primarily on the narrative structure of the novel, George Woodcock called it 'a disappointing book for those whose expectations are at the level of *The Blue Mountains of China.*'[2] What was highly praised by Solecki became one of the major targets for Woodcock's harsh criticism. In his eyes, Wiebe had failed to employ a convincing technique. Even worse, he had given an insufficient portrayal of Riel's military leader, Gabriel Dumont, whom Woodcock saw totally misrepresented as 'a crude and violent figure.'[3] R. P. Bilan on the other hand has not hesitated to call Wiebe's Dumont 'a warm and appealing figure.'[4] It is interesting to note that these early conficting reviews were published almost simultaneously. Reviewers and literary critics have always felt inclined either to comment very enthusiastically on *The Scorched-Wood People*, or to condemn it for what Donald Swainson, following Woodcock's line, has characterized as 'progressive propaganda,' 'bad history,' and 'bad allegory.'[5]

Since Wiebe has not only decided to deal with a politically turbulent and controversial period of Canadian history, where Louis Riel and John A. Macdonald represent two competing economic and cultural systems, but has also confronted the reader with a narrator who can speak from beyond the grave, it seems natural that his novel has caused serious confusion. At the same time, however, it should be acknowledged that while the complexity of *The Scorched-Wood People* is responsible for its ambivalent reception, the controversy about the novel is also based on diverging political and historical viewpoints.[6] In order to assure *The Scorched-Wood People* fair treatment, one must see the work in its context. Thus, any detailed study of the novel should include a proper consideration of Wiebe's Mennonite background, his idea of a genuine Western fiction, and the influence of the Canadian prairies as a 'state of mind'[7] on Wiebe's historical perception, all of which are reflected in the sophisticated narrative structure of *The Scorched-Wood People*.

Wiebe's interest in the Plains Indians and the Métis is manifold in its origin. In an interview given in November 1977 he describes how he discovered that the prairies have their own past, and how they have become an important part of his writing: 'It was only when I began to write about a land much like the one I'd grown up in that I began to think about the aboriginals who had lived there. And then I discovered that Big Bear and Wandering Spirit and all these other easily identifiable historical figures had actually lived in this area. As a matter of fact General Strange had chased Big Bear around Turtle Lake which was seven miles from where I was born. So I got this incredible sense of a *past.*'[8] This happened while Wiebe was working on his first novel, *Peace Shall Destroy Many* (1962). Since then, Métis and Indians have been central to his work. Apart from *The Scorched-Wood People,* the Métis leader is either directly mentioned, referred to, or appears at least in the background of *Peace Shall Destroy Many, First and Vital Candle* (1966), *The Temptations of Big Bear* (1973), and also Wiebe's latest novel *My Lovely Enemy* (1983). As a Saskatchewan Mennonite, Wiebe has become especially sensitive to a minority people who have not only shared similar experiences, like alienation and exile, but whose history is also geographically linked to that of his own.

Despite the fact that the Indians lived in the West long before the arrival of the first white man, they were largely ignored by official historiography. Wiebe was first introduced to Big Bear in university, where he read William Bleasdell Cameron's *The War Trail of Big Bear* (1926), an account of the Frog Lake Massacre by the only survivor. Although he went to school with Métis children, he was never confronted with their dramatic history in the classroom. It was only in later years that he discoverd that 'the world of my childhood had stories too, stories I had never heard: of Big Bear and Wandering Spirit and Gabriel Dumont and Almighty Voice and William McKay and the Frenchman who was carved up by Indians for trading crookedly and whose memory, not even his name, is still commemorated by the strange geological formation called Frenchman Butte; . . . And when I gradually discovered that there were fascinating stories about my Canada, I also discovered that they were most often told badly.'[9] Wiebe may have been thinking of such popular writers as Ralph Connor and John Mackie, who used Indians and Métis solely to give their novels and adventure stories local color. Elsewhere, Wiebe has expressed his strong dislike for the portrait of natives given in the Canadian Depression novels, where they are shown as drunkards and thieves.[10]

After his frustrating experiences with Canadian historiography and Western fiction, it is hardly surprising that Wiebe turned to historical fiction to present his own view of the prairie past. Asked about his specific interest in Riel and his decision to make Riel and his people the object of his writing, he says:

> as a Western Canadian, it is clear to me how important the acquisition of the Northwest was to the history of Canada. Manitoba is indeed the keystone province in the sense that it was an essential element in the construction of the country. . . . Riel is important as the leader of a group of people who had the power to prevent the acquisition of Manitoba by Canada. The second point is that the Métis played a crucial role as intermediaries between the Indian and the white civilizations. They were, then, at the centre of the process by which the Northwest—which, we must remember, belonged by right of habitation to the Indians—was taken over by the whites. This in itself makes the Métis and their leader worth writing about. . . . I should mention a third matter. The story of Louis Riel is one of the great stories of the Canadian West, and for me as a novelist, that's reason enough.[11]

One point is missing in this list. As a Mennonite, Wiebe is also fascinated by Riel's messianic self-understanding and the prophetic appeal to his people. In contrast to the traditional Anglo-Canadian view of the Métis leader as an eternal troublemaker and a madman, Wiebe accepts both Riel's political and his spiritual leadership and tells the story of a visionary. More than Riel's political appeal, it is really his inward religious struggle that attracts Wiebe's attention.

Yet, although Riel serves as protagonist, he does not entirely dominate the novel: 'While he appears on one level as an heroic individual, on the other he is the epic representative of his race.'[12] Thus, *The Scorched-Wood People* is also a novel dealing with the rise and fall of a nation. Wiebe demonstrates how the economic imperialism of the Canadian expansionists and 'Canada First' not only challenged the semi-nomadic way of life of the Métis, but easily destroyed the old order in the West. Since Wiebe knows about the historical development following the Northwest Rebellion, his Métis novel, like *The Temptations of Big Bear*, offers the reader more than just the author's comment on two antagonistic views of Canada and their impact on the prairies during the second half of the 19th century. It relates to contemporary Canada too. David L. Jeffrey has remarked that the further Wiebe goes back into the past, the more his characters are turned into prophets and martyrs whose message is directed at their own people as well as at 'us, now in our time.'[13] Thematically and ideologically, *The Temptations of Big Bear* and *The Scorched-Wood People* are therefore closely linked with each other. According to Sam Solecki's observations, Wiebe is saying, 'this is how it was, and it could not have been otherwise. Wiebe's approach translates history into eschatology; Creighton's Eastern economic vision is stood on its head and turned into Riel's Western religious one. . . . It is almost impossible, given what we know of subsequent Canadian history, not to see Riel, the Métis and their history as representative, almost symbolic, of something larger than themselves, as being at the centre of socio-political issues—local autonomy, west against east, Ontario against Québec, minority rights—that remain problematic even today.'[14]

Historical figures like Big Bear and Riel fascinate Wiebe, who believes in human greatness and in people who think in 'large, and superhuman terms'[15] like the prophets and the saints. Whereas he had yet to discover Big Bear as 'an incredibly great man, who had never been talked about, almost totally unknown,'[16] Riel offered himself as an ideal protagonist immediately. With his remarkable political record, he had quickly established himself in Western Canadian consciousness. It was not the actual discovery of the Métis leader as a character for fiction that concerned Wiebe, but rather the kind of ideological perspective that dominated the literary treatment of Riel. As W. J. Keith put it: 'What Wiebe ha[d] to combat . . . [was] not ignorance but prejudice.'[17]

Overwhelming in his historical, political and spiritual proportions, Riel represents the kind of human greatness which Wiebe is so keen to explore in his novels. Even more, the Métis leader corresponds ideally to the criteria on which Wiebe has founded his idea of 'giant fiction' through his outstanding role in the shaping of the Canadian West—and the West is really what has determined Wiebe's literary conception: '[T]o touch this land with words requires an architectural structure; to break into the space of the reader's mind with the space of this western landscape and the people in it you must build a structure of fiction like an engineer builds a bridge or skyscraper over and into space. A poem, a lyric will not do. You must lay great black steel lines of fiction, break up that space with huge design and, like the fiction of the Russian steppes, build giant artifact. No song can do that; it must be giant fiction.'[18] After Gutteridge's 'Riel: A Poem for Voices' or Pratt's *Towards the Last*

Spike, a radical statement like this could only result in irritation. Wiebe has therefore been (falsely) accused of being prejudiced against poetry and song. What Wiebe really meant has been explained by him on various occasions. He advocates a concept of literature which is truly regional. Unlike Edward McCourt, for instance, whose definition of a Western Canadian literature is based on the white experience of the prairies and is thus limited in its historical and cultural scope,[19] Wiebe makes it his goal to include the indigenous tradition of the West. In this way, he is quite distinct from a centralist understanding of Canadian regionalism as it is reflected in McCourt's Hardy-like vision of the prairies. According to Wiebe, the prairies as a landscape are simply so different from Egdon Heath that they demand an entirely modified approach:

> If you stand on Bull's Head Hill where the South Saskatchewan and the Red Deer rivers meet you see nothing but sky and the curve of the earth. You don't write about Bull's Head Hill the same way you do about Egdon Heath. And as for McCourt's bemoaning the lack of tradition in the West, well let's face the fact that there isn't much white tradition. It's awfully short. What we have to do is dig up the whole tradition, not just the white one. It's not a recorded tradition, it's a verbal one. It would be an absolute farce to compare Saskatchewan's tradition, for example, with that of Egdon Heath.[20]

The degree to which Wiebe has freed himself from the traditional Eastern way of looking at the West is suggested by one of his critical articles, entitled 'In the West, Sir John A. Is a Bastard and Riel a Saint. Ever Ask Why?',[21] which indicates a complete reversal of the conventional images associated with both men. As a Westerner Wiebe is also bold enough to attribute a greater innovative quality to prairie literature than to the writing in Eastern Canada. For him 'the landscape of the prairies is much more alien to the landscape of England than the landscape of Ontario. You can see a parallel to this in Australia. They're still grappling to come to grips with an alien landscape because they had less varied immigration. But you can't build a little England in a land of marsupials. We learned that in the prairies because we had more varied immigration than Ontario.'[22] Wiebe's pride in his land and literature resembles the kind of change in the attitude towards culture which Canada has experienced in recent years. Although it may seem paradoxical at first, regionalism—which is originally and by definition opposed to any ideology that fosters the dominance of a particular center—has not only become a distinct feature of Canadian life, but also essential to the formulation of a Canadian identity. Wiebe's perspective is as much Western as it is Canadian, regardless of how little it has in common with the Eastern view of the all-Canadian experience, but above all it is Christian.[23]

Regionalism and Christianity are both so central to Wiebe's thinking that they become distinctly visible in the background of his philosophy of history. As a Mennonite who admits openly that his 'faith in Jesus Christ is . . . the foundation stone of all . . . [his] thought patterns,'[24] Wiebe takes sides with the underdogs. At the same time, the presentation of prairie history from the natives' point of view reflects Wiebe's interest in a perspective that is peculiar to his own region. In this way, *The Temptations of Big Bear* and *The Scorched-Wood People* contribute literally to an understanding of the Canadian West which is associated only with the writings of scholars like W. L. Morton. Reinterpretation of Western history in Canada becomes therefore not only a major feature of historical studies but also of Wiebe's fiction.

In *The Scorched-Wood People*, this reinterpretation of history leads to an especially favorable picture of the Métis leader. Riel is no longer the religious fanatic and irresponsible politician of Canadian mainstream historiography. Instead, he is turned into a credible visionary who pursues the cause of his people in a reasonable and humanitarian way. Wiebe's Riel in *The Scorched-Wood People* derives more or less directly from his ideas on a 'possible film treatment'[25] of the Métis leader which were originally published two years before the novel appeared. At that time, the author listed a number of characteristics which he regarded as essential to a portrait of Riel. He focused on Riel's 'religious piety and hope,' his 'sense of freedom and the sense for his own peculiar people,' Riel's 'knowledge of music, song, story-telling, and the rhetoric of great speeches'; in addition, Wiebe referred to Riel's awareness of being a member of a strange minority and his 'sense of aloneness,' his 'recognition that his calling is political' and 'religious.'[26] Like the Metis and like 19th century Québec, Wiebe simply accepts Riel as a victim of Ottawa's expansionist policy in the West. He conceives of him as a martyr and develops him into the hero of his novel. Moreover, as a result of his Christian orientation Wiebe has no problem in demonstrating how Riel the man of spirit can dominate Gabriel Dumont the man of action who, despite all his practical experience in the buffalo hunt and brilliant military leadership, surrenders himself to Riel's autocratic decisions. Wiebe later justified his Christian idea of heroism in a rather polemic reply to George Woodcock's criticism of character presentation in *The Scorched-Wood People:* 'I don't know why a martyr can't be a hero. . . . It may be difficult for some people, such as Woodcock, to conceive of a martyr as a hero but that's of course the whole picture of Christ. . . . Martin Luther King is a far greater hero in my eyes, even though he wouldn't have raised a hand to defend himself, than some almighty general. I think that's a false dichotomy to say that there are heroes and there are martyrs. . . . We don't have many of those heroes, by which I mean someone who has a vision of mankind that is greater than society's.'[27]

While 19th century Franco-Canadian poets like Louis Fréchette turned Riel into a 'Jeanne d'Arc of the Prairies' or saw in the Metis leader another Papineau,[28] the Riel of *The Scorched-Wood People* is of Christ-like stature. From here it is only a small step to suggest that Riel's moral integrity and political honesty became serious obstacles in his negotiations with Macdonald's unscrupulous political administration. Canada's Prime Minister, on the other hand, 'emerges as a dishonest and shrewd political schemer who preaches morality and justice, but who lives a continuous lie.'[29]

As he did in his sympathetic description of the Indian way of life in *The Temptation of Big Bear*, Wiebe tries to convince the reader in *The Scorched-Wood People* that the Métis *weltanschauung* makes a lot more sense than does the Canadian perception of it. When Wiebe's narrator Pierre Falcon summarizes Riel's famous speech in the Regina courtroom, for instance, he emphasizes for the reader how substantially Riel's vision of the Canadian West and its future differed from that of the official land companies and private speculators:

> Riel's careful explanation of how five sevenths of the North-West should go to the landless believers of the world to create a new Bavaria and a new Italy. . . ; how British Columbia . . . should likewise become a new Norway . . . of beautiful mountains and sea; how . . . rich, landless lords of finance would find a new Judaea of consolation for their centuries of wandering in the sweet chanting music of the Pacific lapping against the mountains; to build a paradise for the world's deprived on the thousands of square miles of the North-West: this was barely interesting, especially since the Hudson's Bay Company . . . and private speculators already knew exactly what they were going to do with all the land, endlessly large though it

seemed; it would never be too large for their developed white ambitions. (*SWP*, pp. 324, 325)[30]

Riel's humanitarian, almost romantic approach to the land is effectively contrasted to the property-bound thought patterns of the Canadian speculators. Regardless of how unrealistic or even strange Riel's ideas may seem, the reader can hardly escape preferring them to those of the Anglo-Canadian capitalists from Ontario. Yet, Canadian progress cannot be stopped. The transcontinental railway, its most powerful tool and symbol, advances rapidly. It brings not only Middleton's army to the West, but serves as a forceful instrument in the hands of the expansionists who do not hesitate to rigorously subdue nature at all costs. The CPR leaves deep scars on the untouched prairie ground, and when Gabriel Dumont's Métis delegation returns with Riel to Saskatchewan, Wiebe has their horses rebel symbolically against the hated railway tracks. Scenes like this are repeatedly employed in *The Scorched-Wood People* to suggest the difficulties which the Métis had to face as a result of the cultural confrontation. Wiebe's belief in the superiority of the ethics of Canada's indigenous people is evident throughout the novel. Whereas the military actions of the Métis are interpreted as an unavoidable form of self-defence, the author at the same time does not refrain from depicting the Candians as brutal intruders who seem to enjoy the destruction of Métis life and property. 'Thus, in terms of the ethics of war, . . . the adjective "savage" fits the "democratic," "humanistic" whites much more appropriately than it fits the Métis.'[31] From the textual evidence, Alan Dueck's comparison reaches even beyond Wiebe's view of the actual military performance of Métis and Canadians in the Northwest Rebellion. After the violent destruction of the old order in the West entered the history books as just another necessary step towards social progress, *The Temptations of Big Bear* and *The Scorched-Wood People* can be defined as 'an elegy for a way of life.'[32] Wiebe shows at once how it really was and how it should have been. He is eager to correct the prejudices which have shaped historical as well as literary writings on the Manitoba Resistance and the Northwest Rebellion, and which have also influenced the Métis' perception of themselves. Wiebe presents a novel which is written from a Métis point of view.

Critics have generally claimed that *The Scorched-Wood People* provides a completely revised interpretation of Métis history. This proves to be an adequate assessment as long as one sees the novel primarily in terms of its overwhelming bias. On the other hand, compared to some of its less radical forerunners, Wiebe's image of Riel and the Métis is less innovative than some readers may wish to believe. When Wiebe wrote *The Scorched-Wood People*, readers had not only been offered Coulter's and Langley's plays, Gutteridge's documentary poem, fiction by McNamee and Laurence, and Newlove's found poem, to name only some of the numerous and contemporary works which are more or less sympathetic to the Métis leader, but also a number of 19th century literary accounts that are exceptional in their ideological implications. Unfortunately, most critics have failed to consider novels like Forrest Crissey's *Rodney Merton, the Young Newspaper Scout* (1892), or Anne Mercier's and Violet Watt's *The Red House by the Rockies* (1896); nor have they dealt satisfactorily with a short story like Roger Pocock's 'Eric' (1888). Whenever Mercier and Watt, for example, refer to Riel, they show him in a truly positive light. They even call him 'a brave man and a patriot'[33] and comment very favorably upon his devotion to his people. Published by the 'Society for Promoting Christian Knowledge' in London, *The Red House by the Rockies* proclaimed a Christian humanism which included 'rebels' like Louis Riel at a time when the Protestant extremists of Eastern Canada, notably Ontario's Orangemen, showed no tolerance for the Métis leader. Following as it did the popular formula for sensational romance, *The Red House by the Rockies* certainly cannot stand any serious comparison with *The Scorched-Wood People*. Yet, it is worthwhile noting how the English novel links ideologically with Wiebe's portrayal of Riel. Perhaps it is even legitimate to suggest that *The Red House by the Rockies* offered as much a challenge to the chauvinistic Riel image of late Victorian Imperial Canada as Wiebe's novel 'challenges most of our received notions about this crucial period of Canadian history.'[34]

As far as Wiebe's actual historical sources are concerned, the novelist has confirmed his respect for George F. G. Stanley's *Louis Riel* (1963), which is generally accepted as the authorized biography of the Métis leader. Joseph Howard's *Strange Empire* (1952) also comes to mind. It may be regarded as a historiographical counterpart to *The Scorched-Wood People*, since it too provides a Métis perspective. In order to find out how the novelist's perception and treatment of historical evidence differs from that of the historian, it would be revealing to compare Wiebe's novel to Howard's historical analysis.

In contrast to the professional historian who has to work under the premise that historical data can be perceived and conveyed objectively, Wiebe rejects any concept that prolongs belief in historical authenticity. According to him, the original recording of historical facts and their interpretation are biased. Whenever he writes about Indians and Metis, for instance, Wiebe sees himself primarily as a recreator of history who does not at all aim at an exact reproduction of the past.[35] As an artist Wiebe acknowledges the imaginative intention of his work. He presents history not as document but as story, told from a subjective point of view. In his eyes, 'unless they are very carefully handled, facts are the invariable tyrants of story.'[36] Since Wiebe usually tries to focus on the human side of historical events, he has really no other choice but to prefer 'a created image of truth' to 'police-court facts.'[37] Nevertheless, facts remain essential to Wiebe's historical fiction. His 'image of truth' is as much a product of his narrative talents as it is the result of very careful historical research, or, as the novelist himself put it in a discussion with Eli Mandel, 'The act is in the past. The fact is always in the past, but a fiction is what you make of it. And you have to have a certain amount of facts to make a fiction out of them. Something that will last.'[38] What makes Wiebe feel uneasy about the perception of history is the diversity of possible approaches, that is, the presentation of one and the same historical incident in a variety of forms and ways. Consequently, the transformation of fact into fiction becomes a central issue in Wiebe's artistic conception, which is most clearly formulated in 'Where Is the Voice Coming From?', a short story about creating a story. As the author states in the opening sentence of his 'aesthetic programme,' 'the problem is to make the story.'[39] It is significant that Wiebe does not talk about **writing** a story, but **making** it. Applying his literary concept to historical fiction, he conceives of the writer's task as a process in which the artist gets so closely involved in the events he deals with that a real separation between the writer as subject and history as his object is no longer possible: 'If ever I could, I can no longer pretend to objective, omnipotent disinterestedness. I am no longer *spectator* of what *has* happened or what *may* happen: I am become an *element* in what is happening at this very moment.'[40] This then is Wiebe's distinction between the historian's and the novelist's handling of history.

'Where Is the Voice Coming From?' propagates an almost indigenous, orally defined concept of historical writing or narrative, in which fact and fiction do not appear as an antinomy but are treated like synonyms. Subsequently, Wiebe's tasks are basically reduced to the selection of an adequate viewpoint and the presentation of the story in a narratively convincing way. As Wiebe neither trusts the official documentation of native Canadian history nor its depiction by a centralist Eastern historiography, he chooses the Métis point of view and the Métis poet Pierre Falcon to give *The Scorched-Wood People* an appropriate ideological as well as narrative scope: 'Although we see the Riel rebellions from all sides, the mediating vision is that of Pierre Falcon, poet-singer of the Métis. The white historian has given the white perspective often enough, but a resurrected Pierre Falcon can place Riel within the context of his own people, can force us to see the whole uprising through the eyes of those who were impelled to take up arms. Wiebe's achievement is not merely to comprehend this vision (the word is needed) in himself but to communicate it to others.'[41] Furthermore, Wiebe's choice of Falcon is supported by the fact that the Métis culture was primarily an oral one in which historical data, facts and events were communicated verbally. It is through Falcon's narrative that Riel and the Métis come to life in the novel. Falcon is Riel's voice; at the same time he is the mouthpiece of the Métis as a whole people, and yet it is still Wiebe who talks. Throughout the novel, **voice** in its abstract notion and in its linkage to an individual person becomes a major clue to an understanding of *The Scorched-Wood People*. A glance at the opening paragraphs reveals Wiebe's 'obsession' with voices. Riel hears Dumont's 'voice boom in the next room.' It is 'Gabriel's huge voice in the Company mess' (*SWP*, p. 10) that is covered by laughter, while Riel later shouts in a 'tremendous voice' or catches the attention of a church congregation as he 'thunder[s]' (*SWP*, p. 222) at them. It is again Wiebe's scheme for 'Riel: A Possible Film Treatment' which gives an idea why the novelist puts such a striking emphasis on Riel's rhetorical abilities: 'The traditional arts of his illiterate people move Riel deeply and when he achieves literacy in several languages he becomes an almost compulsive writer . . . almost as if he would inscribe forever all those unrecorded thoughts of his people. His writing proves his veneration for the word, for the *written* word which speaks though the speaker be dead. He wants his people to gain a permanent voice—and, in a profound way, he accomplished just that.'[43]

In what follows, Wiebe also employs Riel's voice to have the Metis leader tell his people about their own past. Riel tries to give the Métis an identity in a situation where their existence is seriously endangered. Thus, storytelling becomes a defence strategy. History on the other hand has disclosed only too well how little effect this strategy actually had. In this respect, *The Scorched-Wood People* can be seen as a novel which demonstrates how a sophisticated, literate society like the Anglo-Canadian was able to lay its hands on the aboriginal world of the Métis and Plains Indians who needed no written records since they believed in the truth of the spoken word. It is by the way part of Riel's tragic fate that amnesty was granted him only verbally. How little the spoken word is valued in a literate society is indicated by the fact that Ottawa quickly reneged on this promise when it proved politically no longer convenient.

Voice then has a specific meaning for the Métis leader. Whenever he hears a voice, it signals his doom. A narrative device borrowed from García Márquez makes this clear from the very beginning of the novel: 'Sixteen years later Louis Riel would be dressing himself again, just as carefully. And he would remember then this dressing in Fort Garry.' (*SWP*, p. 10). *The Scorched-Wood People* opens with a sentence which resembles the opening of *One Hundred Years of Solitude*. Both novels begin with a reference to the protagonist's death: that is in terms of the chronology, the story commences with its end. Since Riel's story is well known to the reader, this does no harm to the narrative. There is no particular need for suspension. Robert Kroetsch has pointed out that Wiebe's opening reflects 'an important part of the oral tradition. We're told stories we know.'[43]

As Wiebe selects a particular narrative formula to portray the oral tradition in Métis society, the reader becomes aware immediately that the narrative aspect plays a predominant role in *The Scorched-Wood People*. In the course of the novel one is constantly reminded of it. It takes not only considerable reading before one can identify the narrator as Pierre Falcon, the Métis poet singer, but also Falcon turns out to be a narrator who changes identities. Once, for instance, a mere observer of the Métis unrest in 1869, he suddenly emerges as Riel's own voice, then speaks with the voice of Riel's 'grandfather,' or is even turned 'into Wiebe, himself, the voice of the Métis in the novel.'[44] The following quote may give an idea how broad Falcon's narrative scope is:

> I know of no historian who has commented on this to say the least strange legal distinction that the men who shot and killed Canadian soldiers only *intended* to wage war while Riel, whom no witness had ever seen with anything more than a cross or a pen in his hand, that he and he alone had actually waged war. I presume everyone in Canada accepts, as even the dullest Quebec backbencher did in 1885, that blessings shouted to men being

shot at or hand-written letters which can be laid as facts before a judge are far more lethal to the Queen, her crown and dignity, than outright lies or even Winchesters. (*SWP*, pp. 316, 317)

Wiebe uses this passage as an introduction to Falcon's subsequent description of Riel's trial in Regina. Since Wiebe's narrator knows how the trial has been treated in the history books, he can no longer be the Métis poet Pierre Falcon. Falcon has indeed been converted into a distanced commentator who speaks ironically from the present. Later he changes back into the oral poet who must then pretend that 'that is all the story I can tell you' (*SWP*, p. 348).

At first, Wiebe's technique is rather irritating. Then it becomes obvious what he had in mind when he chose the multivoiced Falcon as narrator. The miscegenation of the actual Pierre Falcon, whose experience reaches as far back as the Battle of Seven Oaks, with a 'fictitious Falcon' who outlives his historical model by many years, provides Wiebe with a narrator who can justly claim to have insight into an otherwise incomprehensibly wide span of history. Wiebe's narrative possibilities are additionally extended through Falcon's alternating identities. As the voice of Riel's 'grandfather,' for example, he is a trustworthy witness of Riel's own experience. Just how flexible Wiebe is, is shown by Falcon's ability to simultaneously comment on the Northwest Rebellion of 1885 and his own funeral which had already taken place in 1876: 'how can I sing this sad, last act of our people when I found my greatest strength at the altar of our merciful Lord in St. Francois Xavier and when I died was buried with the full blessing of Holy Mother Church and every priest within two days' travel? The word and understanding is very near you: you need no revelation from beyond the grave; as our Jesus said when he was on earth, if you will not believe what is already discernible on earth, then neither will you believe that which comes extraordinarily from beyond' (*SWP*, p. 284). Viewed within the context of the whole novel, this passage serves as a key to Wiebe's peculiar narrative conception. The novelist tries to create a structure which at once conveys immediacy as well as distance. Accordingly, Falcon has to appear as a single and yet multivoiced narrator. Whenever he speaks in the voice of a particular character, he communicates the kind of direct viewpoint which only a Métis eyewitness can have and which Wiebe needs in order to make his narrative sound authentic. At the same time, Wiebe cannot be satisfied with an individual, limited perspective, since he wants to tell the story of a whole people, which asks for an omniscient narrator. At first glance, 'the two viewpoints are mutually exclusive.'[45] Wiebe, however, solves the problem by having Falcon tell the story of Riel and his people from an 'omniscient Métis heaven.'[46] He thereby surprises his readers with what W. J. Keith has called 'a new fictional convention.'[47]

It is first of all due to this newly invented narrative mode that *The Scorched-Wood People* gains the dimensions of a Métis epic. Moreover, with a resurrected Pierre Falcon as the voice of a whole people, the novel transforms history into myth. Wiebe's narrator confirms Kroetsch's notion that all tale-telling derives from 'a very serious movement toward, a need for, myth-making.'[48] Myth, of course, includes an element of distortion. Gabriel Dumont's presence at Fort Garry in 1869, for example, shows how Falcon's narration transcends factual evidence, how historical reality is turned into mythical truth. As Wiebe admits, it is not his point 'that Dumont actually was at Red River dancing on a buffalo robe, but that this is that *[sic]* he would have done.'[49] Critics have also attributed an almost prophetic quality to *The Scorched-Wood People*, which they have again explained with Pierre Falcon's double perspective: 'when Pierre Falcon speaks both from lived history and from beyond the grave, we have moved one step further to a position from which prophetic witness, though ostensibly "generated" in an historical movement *(chronos)* can gain an eternal or trans-historical value and authority; the interpretative prospect is more than that of mere history (it suggests a *chairos*). [...] History provides the interpretative commentary on the prophetic message, rather than the other way round.'[50]

Because of Wiebe's rather casual treatment of historical accuracy and his continuous violation of established novelistic conventions, it seems quite natural that the question whether *The Scorched-Wood People* can be legitimately classified as historical fiction has caused serious arguments. George Woodcock simply denies the novel this quality. In his understanding Wiebe has proved himself completely unable to distinguish between historical fiction and historical moralism. Woodcock goes so far as to claim that in all of Wiebe's books 'the moralist has been predominant over the historian, which means that the facts of the past, and even its essential character, are subordinated to dogmatic purposes that lie outside history and perhaps outside art.'[51] Woodcock sees the Riel of *The Scorched-Wood People* as a Christ-like figure who is taken out of his genuine Métis context and made a prophetic visionary beyond time and space. For W. J. Keith, however, Wiebe's Métis novel is a successful book which combines an 'epic mode with fictional form and historical reconstruction.'[52] Using George Lukács' definition of the historical novel, Keith concludes that *The Scorched-Wood People* gives an even better illustration of Lukács' theory than do Walter Scott's *Waverley* or *Old Mortality*.

University of Kiel, Federal Republic of Germany

[1]Sam Solecki, 'Review of *The Scorched-Wood People*,' *The Fiddlehead*, 117 (Spring 1978), 120.

[2]George Woodcock, 'Riel and Dumont,' *Canadian Literature*, 77 (Summer 1978), 100.

[3]*Ibid.*

[4]R. P. Bilan and Sam Solecki, 'Two Reviews of *The Scorched-Wood People*,' in W. J. Keith (ed.), *A Voice in the Land: Essays by and about Rudy Wiebe* (Edmonton: NeWest Press, 1981), 173.

[5]Donald Swainson, 'Rieliana and the Structure of Canadian History,' *Journal of Popular Culture*, 14, 2 (Fall 1980), 294.

[6]With his exciting book on Gabriel Dumont—*Gabriel Dumont. The Métis Chief and His Lost World* (Edmonton: Hurtig, 1975)—Woodcock, for instance, has made a remarkable contribution to a hitherto widely neglected part of Métis biography and history. He has proved convincingly that Gabriel Dumont deserved more attention than he had so far been granted by either historians and writers of fiction. On the other hand, this well-justified reconsideration of Dumont's place in Métis history seems to have led Woodcock himself to a rather specific way of viewing the Northwest Rebellion and its protagonists. He has become a committed spokesperson for Dumont on all possible occasions, as his smashing review of Thomas Flanagan's *Riel and the Rebellion: 1885 Reconsidered* (1983) has recently confirmed. Cf. George Woodcock, "Not Guilty," *Books in Canada*, 13, 1 (January 1984), 10ff.

[7]Cf. Henry Kreisel, 'The Prairie: A State of Mind,' in Eli Mandel (ed.), *Contexts of Canadian Criticism* (Chicago: The Univ. of Chicago Press, 1971), pp. 254-66.

[8]Brian Bergman, 'Rudy Wiebe: Storymaker of the Prairies,' in W. J. Keith, *A Voice in the Land*, p. 165.

[9]Rudy Wiebe, 'A Novelist's Personal Notes on Frederick Philip Grove,' in *A Voice in the Land*, p. 217.

[10]Cf. George Melnyk, 'The Western Canadian Imagination: An Interview with Rudy Wiebe,' in *A Voice in the Land*, p. 205.

[11]Anon., 'An Interview with Rudy Wiebe,' *Riel Project BULLETIN du Projet Riel*, 6 (1981), 4.

[12]W. J. Keith, *Epic Fiction: The Art of Rudy Wiebe* (Edmonton: Univ. of Alberta Press, 1981), p. 83.

[13]David L. Jeffrey, 'A Search for Peace: Prophecy and Parable in the Fiction of Rudy Wiebe,' in *A Voice in the Land*, p. 181.

[14]Sam Solecki, 'Review of *The Scorched-Wood People*,' 118, 119.

[15]Eli Mandel and Rudy Wiebe, 'Where the Voice Comes From,' in *A Voice in the Land*, p. 154.

[16]*Ibid.*, p. 154.

[17]W. J. Keith, *Epic Fiction*, p. 85.

[18]Rudy Wiebe, 'Passage by Land,' *Canadian Literature*, 48 (Spring 1978), 26f.

[19]Cf. Edward A. McCourt, *The Canadian West in Fiction* (Toronto: Ryerson, 1949; rev. ed. 1970).

[20]George Melnyk, 'The Western Canadian Imagination,' p. 206.

[21]This article first appeared in the *Toronto Globe and Mail* of 25 March 1978; it is reprinted in *A Voice in the Land*, pp. 209-11.

[22]Alan Twigg, 'Public Eye: Rudy Wiebe,' in Twigg, *For Openers: Conversations with 24 Canadian Writers* (Madiera Park, B.C.: Harbour, 1981), p. 209.

[23]Cf. in this context Sam Solecki, 'Giant Fictions and Large Meanings: The Novels of Rudy Wiebe,' *The Canadian Forum*, 60 (March 1981), 5-8 and 13, especially 5.

[24]Rudy Wiebe, 'The Artist as a Critic and a Witness,' in *A Voice in the Land*, p. 41.

[25]Cf. Rudy Wiebe, 'Riel. A Possible Film Treatment,' in *A Voice in the Land*, pp. 158-62.

[26]*Ibid.*, pp. 158, 159, 160, 161.

[27]Anon., 'An Interview with Rudy Wiebe,' p. 5.

[28]Cf. Louis Fréchette, *La légende d'un peuple* (Paris, 1887).

[29]Alan Dueck, 'Rudy Wiebe's Approach to Historical Fiction: A Study of *The Temptations of Big Bear* and *The Scorched-Wood People*,' in John Moss (ed.), *The Canadian Novel: Here and Now*, vol. 1 (Toronto: NC Press, 1978), p. 189.

[30]The quote is taken from *The Scorched-Wood People*, New Canadian Library No. 156 (Toronto: McClelland and Stewart, 1977). All subsequent quotes refer to this edition.

[31]Alan Dueck, 'Rudy Wiebe's Approach to Historical Fiction,' p. 190.

[32]W. J. Keith, *Epic Fiction*, p. 74.

[33]Anne Mercier, Violet Watt, *The Red House by the Rockies* (London, 1896), p. 57.

[34]Sam Solecki, 'Review of *The Scorched-Wood People*,' p. 117.

[35]For a better understanding of Wiebe's concept of historical authenticity see his article 'On the Trail of Big Bear,' *Journal of Canadian Fiction*, 3, 2 (1974), 45-48.

[36]*Ibid.*, 45.

[37]W. J. Keith, 'From Document to Art: Wiebe's Historical Short Stories and Their Sources,' *Studies in Canadian Literature*, 4, 2 (Summer 1979), 108.

[38]Eli Mandel and Rudy Wiebe, 'Where the Voice Comes From,' p. 152.

[39]Rudy Wiebe, 'Where Is the Voice Coming From?,' in David Helwig and Tom Marshall (eds.), *Fourteen Stories High* (Toronto: Oberon, 1971), p. 112.

[40]*Ibid.*, p. 119.

[41]W. J. Keith, *Epic Fiction*, pp. 8, 9.

[42]Rudy Wiebe, 'Riel: A Possible Film Treatment,' p. 159.

[43]Shirley Neuman, 'Unearthing Language: An Interview with Rudy Wiebe and Robert Kroetsch,' in *A Voice in the Land*, p. 241.

[44]Alan Dueck, 'Rudy Wiebe's Approach to Historical Fiction,' p. 196.

[45]W. J. Keith, *Epic Fiction*, pp. 98, 99.

[46]*Ibid.*, p. 99.

[47]*Ibid.*

[48]Quoted from Barbara Godard, 'The Oral Tradition and Contemporary Fiction,' *Essays on Canadian Writing*, 7/8 (Fall 1977), 58.

[49]Anon., 'An Interview with Rudy Wiebe,' p. 4.

[50]David L. Jeffrey, 'A Search for Peace,' pp. 193, 194.

[51]George Woodcock, 'Prairie Writers and the Métis: Rudy Wiebe and Margaret Laurence,' *Canadian Ethnic Studies*, 14, 1 (1982), 14.

[52]W. J. Keith, *Epic Fiction*, p. 2.

Rudolf Bader

FREDERICK PHILIP GROVE AND NATURALISM RECONSIDERED

In 1932, Robert Ayre compared Grove with the great American master of literary naturalism, Theodore Dreiser: 'If the analogy be not pressed too closely, he might be called the Theodore Dreiser of Canada; these two austere spirits, these two men with the clumsy tongues, have much in common.'[1] The obituary tribute to Grove written by Northrop Frye for *The Canadian Forum* took up Ayre's reference to Dreiser.[2] Ronald Sutherland doubts whether Grove ever had the opportunity or the inclination to read such American authors as Crane, Dreiser, Norris, and others,[3] but he agrees that Grove was a naturalistic writer, pointing out the 'naturalistic emphasis upon the ultimate futility of individual self-reliance.'[4] Sutherland sees Grove's presentation of the individual as placed on a wave of evolution, inevitable and irrepressible, and the role that the individual plays as essentially predetermined. However, he does not believe that Grove ever channelled his ideas into any philosophical framework. Raymond Knister writes about 'Mr. Grove's whimsical naturalism.'[5] Desmond Pacey also writes of Grove's naturalism: 'Like Hardy, Grove oscillates between conceptions of a universe controlled by forces deliberately malignant towards man and one controlled by forces which are simply ignorant of or indifferent to human aspirations.' He compares him not only to Hardy, but also to Zola and Dreiser, and concludes: 'But Grove's conception . . . resembles rather the Greek conception of Fate than the scientific determinism of the naturalists.'[6] The idea is that man not only has to fight hidden forces but must also contend with his fellows and with himself. Pacey also asserts that Grove was as much a surrealist as a realist. Thus, with relatively slight variations, the early Grove critics accepted the naturalistic label for Grove.

After the revelation of Grove's real past by Douglas Spettigue,[7] it was George Woodcock who first realized that the question of Grove's indebtedness to naturalism was dependent on his European background, at least to a certain extent; and the two significant literary movements in Europe on the eve of Grove's departure were those of naturalism and symbolism.[8] Douglas Spettigue also tried to differentiate more carefully in his assessment of Grove's allegiance to naturalism.[9] He finds that there is a difference between the early Grove and the late Grove, and that most of Grove's novels can be called tragic rather than naturalistic. Spettigue shows how Grove, especially in his late novels, tried to follow an ethical orientation.

However, even before Spettigue's spectacular revelations, the interpretation of Grove's novels in the light of naturalism was met by an opposing view. In an article in *Canadian Literature*, Frank Birbalsingh, in 1970, asserted that Grove's characters did not respond passively but followed personal values: 'In stressing the pre-eminence of personal values, Grove's novels in fact counteract the naturalistic overtones which some have found in his writing.'[10] Birbalsingh finds that Grove, unlike the major American naturalist writers, did not have a Marxist background, his views being more open rather than narrowly political, and he concludes that Grove was neither a socialist nor a naturalist, but an existentialist.

Walter Pache, who states that Grove has read novels by Dreiser, Norris, and Sinclair Lewis, 'which leave their traces in his concept of realism,'[11] for the first time goes beyond the mere controversy about whether or not Grove was a naturalist. Pache agrees that there is a deterministic approach in Grove's main novels, but he also points out Grove's distance from the European literary movement of naturalism.[12] Pache's solution is to link the psychological analysis in Grove's writings with 'a new kind of social realism.'[13]

Grove himself had something to say about naturalism. In an essay on 'Realism in Literature' (1929), in which he divides some outstanding works from world literature into two major categories ('Realistic' versus 'Romantic') according to his own literary tastes rather than any scholarly criteria, he reminds his Canadian readers of the original meaning of the term 'naturalist': 'We are used to think that the word naturalist denotes, in English, something entirely different from what it connotes in French. That is an error. A naturalist, in English, means a scientist; but no more emphatically so than in French.'[14] And he adds a footnote quoting from Littré and Beaujean: '*Naturaliste (dérivé du latin naturalis).* Celui qui s'occupe spécialement de l'étude des productions de la nature.' In this sense, of course, the pure naturalist does not belong to the realm of creative literature but to that of science, or possibly journalism. Grove himself, indeed, loved the productions of nature and took a very keen interest in science. His marriage certificate, for example, gave his profession as 'professor of science'; he liked to teach science, and at least one of his novels shows his close connection with nature and its phenomena: *Consider Her Ways* (1947), which is full of scientific information on the physiology, behavior, and social habits of ants, and in which the ants, in turn, set out on an expedition to study the ways of man. In an article on Grove and his audience, Janet Giltrow obviously refers to this scientific naturalism when she writes: 'Before the twentieth century, the naturalist's art in America had traditional connections with a European audience.'[15] And it seems that Grove was still very much the scientist when he set forth into literature. The reviews of his first published work in English show this. One reviewer of *Over Prairie Trails* (1922), for example, catches Grove's state of transition from science to creative writing when he says, 'There is combined the naturalist's scientific accuracy and attention to detail with the poet's interpretative affection.'[16] It seems obvious then that any assessment of Grove's naturalism would be incomplete without giving due consideration to the original, scientific meaning of the term. The observant eye of the scientist must remain the starting point for any interpretation of Grove's view of the world.

Scientific observation of nature proper, in our modern sense, goes back to the eighteenth century. Margaret Stobie appropriately approaches Grove's work from the background of Rousseau and his philosophy. In this context, she writes that Rousseau's theme of unequal opportunities had a particular fascination for Grove, exemplified in his novel *The Yoke of Life* (1930).[17] Unequal opportunities do not only have a socially determined component but are also dependent on the laws of the characters' own natures. Thus Mrs. Vogel of *Settlers of the Marsh* (1925) or Edmund Clark of *The Master of the Mill* cannot act in any other way than according to the laws of their own natures. These laws, while including psychologically determined forces, are also linked to man's physical existence—for instance, the state of Grove's own disability due to an injured back and a failing eyesight, as described in *In Search of Myself* (1946)—and his position within the overwhelming dominance of nature. 'Not society but nature is the destroyer of the pristine freedom.'[18] In this sense nature must be seen as one. And it is this view of nature as a unity that recalls Thomas Hardy's *Jude the Obscure,* to which Grove's *The Yoke of Life* has been compared.[19] Grove himself stressed that he did not believe in a personal god who ordered his life. Yet he added: 'But I believe in the unity of all life; in the unity of the urge which compels the atoms of quartz to array themselves in the form of a crystal; with the urge which holds the stars in their courses or which made me sit down to write this last will and testament of my life.'[20] As it appears, the terms 'life' and 'nature' were practically synonymous for Grove, and the unity of nature/life in the tradition of Rousseau and Hardy, whether considered in connection with the theories of Darwin and the philosophical concepts of determinism or not, do indeed leave little room for the individual's free will. The parallels drawn between atoms of quartz, the courses of the stars, and the creative impulse of the author show Grove's perception of man within nature and his basis in the scientific view of nature.

If we try, then, to look at some of the most important works by Grove with all those critical views in mind, it seems reasonable to trace some of the generally acknowledged features of literary naturalism against the background of which Grove's particular kind of naturalism ought to emerge more clearly.

One of the obvious features of literary naturalism, whether applied to European or to American novelists, is the indebtedness to psychological determinism. Elizabeth Waterston has pointed out how Grove followed Freudian psychology by writing about the secret springs of actions and ideas, and by venturing forth into the analysis of fetish and taboo, inhibition and sublimation.[21] Grove himself, in *A Search for America*, mentions 'the myth of our own free will.'[22] At the end of Book One of *Our Daily Bread*, John Elliot puzzles over his relation to his children, thus introducing one of the major themes of the remaining parts of the novel. At the time, photography is just becoming a fashionable pastime:

> One day he had seen Cathleen develop prints. She immersed an apparently blank sheet of paper in a solution contained in a tray. A few irregular patches appeared on its surface. These patches gradually arranged themselves into a picture, each one assuming a definite, purposeful significance.
>
> Thus his children appeared to him. The developing solution was life itself. They had been mere blanks, more alike in the lack of distinguishing features than differentiated by the small deviations in texture. Like those first patches on photographic prints certain peculiarities had asserted themselves in each of them, mysterious in their significance. Development went on; and suddenly character and fate became readable as the features connected themselves to each other.
>
> Correct them? How can you correct what you do not know? Blame them? The picture on the blank sheet appeared because the hidden chemistry of the underlying strata had been influenced in some incomprehensible way. Only that appeared which was already invisibly traced in its layers. There was

something uncanny about it. We can but become what we are. . . .[23]

The metaphor of photography establishes the fixedness of the emerging character. Life itself (which, for Grove, also means nature) appears as the developing solution. If character and fate can become readable, they must be understood as fixed and predetermined. The force that has determined them, however, remains incomprehensible. And since only that appears which is already invisibly traced in the layers of the photographic sheet, there is no room for new features or radically significant outside influences. Though this passage reshapes psychological determinism, it is interesting to see that this uncanny and mysterious quality in the characters of men and women does not appear to John Elliot as a philosophical or psychological phenomenon, but as a religious one: he comes to call it God.

Although *Our Daily Bread* and *Fruits of the Earth* have a great deal in common, one can feel a difference in their attitudes to the relative significance of free will. Whereas the former has an atmosphere of inevitability throughout, the latter seems to start from the same idea but manages to proceed towards a protest against this inevitability imposed by some hidden force and to recognize the existence of man's own power of judgement based on free will. Towards the end of the novel, Ruth Spalding consults Abe's brother-in-law, Dr. Vanbruik, on the question of depriving Abe of his right to punish the man who has deceived their daughter. The doctor's emotional involvement is immediate: 'He was voicing a protest against the violation of a fundamental right: the right of every human being to determine his own course of action.'[24] In this light, determinism becomes an impediment for the development of a fundamental human right. Senator Clark, in *The Master of the Mill*, is never quite sure if he has acted upon this fundamental human right or under some compulsion within his own psyche: 'He could never get away from the feeling that, whatever he had done, he had done under some compulsion. Yet it was he who had determined the development of the mill. . . .'[25] Throughout the novel, the reader is never quite convinced of the senator's true and honest psychological position, though long passages are presented from his perspective.

At the bottom of psychological determinism there is, of course, biological determinism. In Grove's quasi-autobiographical account, *In Search of Myself*, young Phil has a revelation: 'All these humans . . . represented mere wavelets on the stream of a seminal, germinal life which flowed through them, which had propagated itself, for millennia, through them, almost without, perhaps even against, their will and desire. They had done what they must do; and from their doings life had sprung' (p. 153). This is Phil's revelation upon meeting a travelling clan of Kirghiz herdsmen, when riding through the hostile barrenness of the Siberian steppe with his uncle. The question remains whether men in Western Europe or North America, through civilization more removed from the natural state of man, can still do what they must do. Or are they more than mere wavelets on the stream of life? On the level of psychological determinism Grove seems to view man as independent from social influences, as some sort of superior animal functioning according to set rules of nature. 'Even when dealing with human beings, I have always been somewhat of a naturalist' (p. 262), meaning a scientific observer. Thus, when man fails, he can be defeated not only by circumstance but also by his own nature. This is what Phil feels when he comes to a dead end in his career as a school principal, on the eve of meeting his future wife on a more intimate footing: 'I felt poignantly that circumstance had once more defeated me; circumstance and my own nature' (p. 272).

Proceeding to social circumstance, then, we can find a good deal of social interest in Grove's work in general. Already in *Over Prairie Trails,* which deals with the confrontation between man and nature more than with anything else, there is a small reference to the social question. On one of his trips between Gladstone and Falmouth, the narrator comes across a human habitation that looks like a veritable hovel: 'In the door of the hovel there stood two brats—poor things!'[26] It is this exclamation of 'poor things!' which opens up a whole vista of the possible chances in the lives of those brats, and these chances are obviously very meagre in view of the surrounding poverty.

After this tentative approach to the social question, Grove enters into a colorful treatment of social determinism with the odyssey of his alter ego as an immigrant, in *A Search for America.* The immigrant, Phil Branden, is a person of some social prestige in Europe, and when he arrives in America he is conscious of his social position. On finding that it is not easy to get a job in Toronto, he starts to wake up to the new social reality when he asks himself: 'Could a man starve in this great country?' (p. 30). He finds that social class in America does not mean what it means in Europe. With the absence of the aristocratic order, social class first of all merely means social environment. And the immigrant experiences this as a step down into 'utter chaos' (p. 39). He sees that this difference in the social structure has another basis in the different attitudes towards culture. But he acknowledges the indifferent social atmosphere in America as a healthier one, and soon he recognizes the existence of social strata in America, too.

Having learnt and accepted those basic facts about the social background, Phil proceeds to comment upon individual situations that show an influence of social determinism. He finds that the waitress Ella is a girl 'missing her destiny through no fault of hers' (p. 99), and of himself he says: 'I felt as if I were in the hands of powers beyond my own or any human control; as if the gods were grinding me into their grist and grinding me exceedingly small' (p. 136). These individual observations lead him to the investigation of the reasons behind them. He starts to look at social practice with a more critical eye, and eventually he sees through some of the evil aspects of the social system, for example the generally accepted American business methods, which he compares to the killing methods of cats, hawks, and snakes: 'What was America then? Graft and cruelty, nothing else!' (p. 160). In New York and then in the whole Northeast of the United States, Phil even plays this cruel game himself for a certain period, without recognizing his own contribution to the racket; but when he recognizes his position he leaves the city and heads West as a tramp. His experiences in the city and his subsequent descent into the depths of the social system, which leads him to the verge of death, make him despise the power of money: 'Money is slavery' (p. 299). This leads him into a general reassessment of the American social system: 'There are three classes of men engaged in the industries of the nation: born leaders, born servants, and the rest of them who are neither the one nor the other but who work for others because they cannot help themselves. Nothing needs to be said about the first two classes; if all men belonged to them, there would be no industrial troubles' (p. 301). And he adds several pages of inquiries into the situation of the third class and into the driving forces behind the social actions of man. He recognizes the driving forces as those of chance and destiny. When he experiences the social inequality predetermined by the American system again on a personal level— the incongruous and preposterous wealth among the landowners of Dakota—he leaves the United States for Canada, hoping to find a less cruel social environment. He completely rejects the United States, a country where social iniquity is perpetrated systematically, and where poker, the symbol of much that is horrible in modern life, is the national card game.

Social determinism, after having found such ample treatment in *A Search for America*, is less important in Grove's prairie novels. *Our*

Daily Bread contains some social observations that might have a slightly cynical undertone for many modern readers, but there is no doubt that, for Grove, they were straightforward observations, based on long experience of the prairies. For example, there is the observation on marriage, when Henrietta drives her bargain with Pete: marriage, at least on the prairies, is not a partnership, but 'mostly slavery' (p. 64). In many ways, the novel confirms this view. The novel also contains some details of the social difference between city life and prairie life. When old John Elliot visits Cathleen and Woodrow Ormond in Winnipeg, he sees that they have to live up to their social positions because their servants expect them to do so. This absurd situation, seen against the background of *A Search for America*, almost appears as a return to the social pretensions of the old world. Thus *Our Daily Bread* presents social life in the city as an alienating force. John Elliot asks himself why he has been so deeply antagonized by what he has seen in the city: 'Because, within his own seed, he has seen a departure from that great purpose. Because his own child and her chosen husband saw the end of their lives—if they saw any at all—in what he considered to be inessentials. . . . Empires rose and fell: kings and high priests strove with each other: wars were fought: ripples on the sea of life. . . . The city with its multifarious activities was nothing but a bubble on that sea' (p. 190). This alienation from the real purpose in life, conditioned by the inessentials of social pressure in the city, is what comes to disturb Abe Spalding in *Fruits of the Earth*. When Abe gets his first foretaste of public business in his rural district he realizes that he likes power. A city evil, the alienation from the real purpose in life, threatens to lead this pioneer of the prairies astray. Thus the prairie novels merely underline and illustrate what *A Search for America* has put forward on social determinism and the alienating force of city life.

The latent criticism of the American capitalistic system emerging from the investigation of social determinism at last breaks loose with full force in Grove's masterpiece, *The Master of the Mill*. It is in this novel that the power of Grove as a naturalist can be seen most clearly. Published in 1944, the novel makes good use of almost everything that was treated in earlier novels, and of a lifelong experience. The mill that is at the center of the novel is much more than a mere leitmotif for the intricate narrative pattern. This is the only novel in which Grove deviates from a chronological plot. The mill is a symbol on several levels:

> To many people, as the old man was aware, that mill stood as a symbol and monument of the world-order which, by-and-large, was still dominant; of a ruthless capitalism which had once been an exploiter of human labour but had gradually learned, no less ruthlessly, to dispense with that labour, making itself independent, ruling the country by its sheer power of producing wealth.
>
> To others, fewer these, it stood as a monument of a first endeavour to liberate mankind from the curse of toil; for it produced the thing man needed most, bread, by harnessing the forces of nature. . . .
>
> To still others, fewer again, the old man among them, it was the abode of gnomes and hobgoblins, malevolent like Alberich, the dwarf of the Rhinegold, but forced, by a curse more potent than their own, to do man's work . . . binding man to their service in turn, or to the service of the machines. (p. 21)

Senator Clark, who, together with Maud Dolittle, has been trying all his life to realize some of his socialist ideas, such as improving the bad living conditions of the mill-hands and introducing less cruel business methods than his father had been employing—'It was the American game to "put one over on the other fellow" ' (p. 101)—finds himself unable to tear his thoughts away from the mill when he gets very old. These retrospective thoughts in old age reveal the mill in all its aspects. While the senator is aware of the ruthlessness of the capitalistic world-order, epitomized by the mill, he has also realized that this same mill, originally designed to ease man's labor, has grown independent and can now produce wealth by itself. Industrialization thus becomes a deal with the devil, and once engaged in this deal, man cannot withdraw because the deal involves man's basic need, bread. The senator, in view of this gigantic mechanism, realizes that, as socialists, he and Miss Dolittle have been dreamers. (Is this why she is called Do-little?)

The mill's capacity to produce wealth was already symbolized at an early stage by the character of Bob Stevens, a rapidly promoted protégé of the senator's father: 'Brief as the life of the mill had been, Bob Stevens represented its tradition; and that tradition had resumed itself in one aim: profit. Profit was his god; not *his* profit; not anyone's; profit in the abstract' (p. 90). So if the mill produces profit and wealth by itself, the idea of the workers and growing trade union movements, namely that they can stop 'the whole show' (p. 134), becomes a dangerous fallacy that merely speeds up the process of mechanization. Also, if this process runs its course by itself once mechanization has been introduced, the profiteers can somehow no longer be blamed, though, as numerous episodes in the novel show, some of their excessive demonstrations of wealth and privilege remain unwarranted and inappropriate. Because there is nothing that the working classes can do about this, they are ever so ready to pounce upon what they consider the immoral behavior of those 'overhead.' The weird expulsion of Sybil Carter at the hands of the workers' wives (p. 160) must be seen in this context. The inevitability of the whole system is elaborated upon by Maud Dolittle at the end of the novel, when she puts the events into a larger context of a cyclic pattern. At this point, man has been diminished to the smallest possible size within Grove's work, and social determinism cannot go any further. Or perhaps there is one step further: to depict the social behavior of a species from the perspective of another species, in a scientific way. And this is what Grove attempts in his ant book, *Consider Her Ways*, thus returning to the original meaning of the term 'naturalist.'

Taking the novels in the order of publication—thus disregarding some of Grove's claims in *In Search of Myself*—we can define the development as proceeding from a psychological interest in the individual to the social quest, on to the limits of social determinism, and from there back to the origins of naturalism in scientific writing. The peak within this development is clearly marked by *The Master of the Mill*. It is this novel that must be at the center of any more detailed analysis of Grove's naturalism, more particularly the sections that deal with man and industrialization.[27] Grove himself seems to have been aware of the importance of this novel. He apparently worked through several revisions of it, and about these revisions he writes: 'I know of only one other writer whose technique, in building the hidden background of his work, resembled my own; Henrik Ibsen' (*In Search of Myself*, p. 437).

However, as this study attempts to show, it is not a simple matter to transfer European naturalism to Canada. Grove's naturalism is more descriptive, while Ibsen's (like that of many other European naturalists) was more satirical and directed to social reforms. In this comparison, Grove emerges as a very modest writer. Naturalism, in his case, does not suggest a desperate cry for social reform, but rather a close observation of the individual pioneer in the new world, an attempt to understand the general pattern of social life, a pattern larger than life when seen in terms of industrialization, and a way of seeing the world with the eyes of a scientist. It seems obvious that such a commitment to naturalism does not leave much room for a flourishing imaginative style. Readers with such expectations will always find Grove a little clumsy and dull, just as some are bound to dismiss him for his lack of any sense of humor. And some Canadian readers might find him too European, although his social criticism is largely directed against American capitalism and thus paves the way towards a Canadian nationalism based upon values of a higher social justice. Thus, Grove's naturalism can been seen as one aspect of what constitutes the Canadian element in Canadian literature.

University of Bern, Switzerland

[1]Robert Ayre, 'Frederick Philip Grove,' *The Canadian Forum*, 12 (April, 1932), 255.

[2]Northrop Frye, 'Canadian Dreiser,' *The Canadian Forum*, 28 (September, 1948), 121f.

[3]Ronald Sutherland, *Frederick Philip Grove* (Toronto: McClelland and Stewart, 1969), p. 25.

[4]*Ibid.*, p. 36; see also Ronald Sutherland, 'What Was Frederick Philip Grove,' in *The New Hero: Essays in Comparative Quebec/Canadian Literature* (Toronto: Macmillan, 1977), pp. 39-50.

[5]Raymond Knister, 'Frederick Philip Grove,' *Ontario Library Review*, 13, 3 (1928), 60-62. Quoted from Desmond Pacey, ed., *Frederick Philip Grove* (Toronto: Ryerson, 1970), p. 15.

[6]From Desmond Pacey, *Frederick Philip Grove;* reprinted in Pacey (ed.), *Frederick Philip Grove*, pp. 45-55, here 46ff.

[7]Douglas O. Spettigue (in a first futile attempt), *Frederick Philip Grove* (Toronto: Copp Clark, 1969); (then successfully) 'The Grove Enigma Resolved,' *Queen's Quarterly*, 79 (1972)   ; and *FPG: The European Years* (Ottawa: Oberon, 1973).

[8]George Woodcock, 'Possessing the Land: Notes on Canadian Fiction,' in David Staines (ed.), *The Canadian Imagination* (Cambridge, Mass. and London: Harvard, 1977), p. 86. See also Walter Pache, 'Der Fall Grove—Vorleben und Nachleben des Schriftstellers Felix Paul Greve,' *(German-Canadian Yearbook*, 5 (1979), 131.

[9]Spettigue, *Frederick Philip Grove* (1969), p. 87.

[10]Frank Birbalsingh, 'Grove and Existentialism,' *Canadian Literature*, 43 (Winter 1970), 70.

[11]Walter Pache, 'The Dilettante in Exile: Grove at the Centenary of his Birth,' *Canadian Literature*, 90 (Autumn 1981), 189.

[12]Pache, 'Der Fall Grove,' 133.

[13]Pache, 'The Dilettante in Exile,' 187.

[14]Frederick Philip Grove, *It Needs to be Said* (Toronto: Macmillan, 1929), p. 55.

[15]Janet Giltrow, 'Grove in Search of an Audience,' *Canadian Literature*, 90 (Autumn 1981), 103.

[16]Unsigned review of *Over Prairie Trails*, in *The Canadian Forum*, 3 (May 1923), 250.

[17]Margaret R. Stobie, *Frederick Philip Grove* (New York: Twayne, 1973), p. 28.

[18]*Ibid.*, p. 97.

[19]For the first time in William Arthur Deacon's review of *The Yoke of Life*, in *The Ottawa Citizen*, October 11, 1930, p. 15. Grove himself also mentions Hardy's novel in *In Search of Myself* (Toronto: Macmillan, 1946), p. 357.

[20]*In Search of Myself*, New Canadian Library, No. 94 (Toronto: McClelland and Stewart, 1974), p. 230. Further references to this book will appear in the text. Cf. the discussion of this aspect in Henry Makow, 'Frederick Philip Grove,' in Jeffrey M. Heath (ed.), *Profiles in Canadian Literature*, 1 (Toronto: Dundurn, 1980), p. 51.

[21]Elizabeth Waterston, *Survey: A Short History of Canadian Literature* (Toronto: Methuen, 1973), p. 120.

[22]*A Search for America*, New Canadian Library, No. 76 (Toronto: McClelland and Stewart, 1971), p. 93. Further references to this book will appear in the text.

[23]*Our Daily Bread* (Toronto: Macmillan, 1928), p. 135. Further references to this book will appear in the text.

[24]*Fruits of the Earth*, New Canadian Library, No. 49 (Toronto: McClelland and Stewart, 1965), p. 257. Further references to this book will appear in the text.

[25]*The Master of the Mill*, New Canadian Library, No. 19 (Toronto: McClelland and Stewart, 1961), p. 22.

[26]*Over Prairie Trails*, New Canadian Library, No. 1 (Toronto: McClelland and Stewart, 1970), p. 9. Further references to this book will appear in the text.

[27]See *The Master of the Mill*, pp. 21, 108, 168, 171, 192-94, 226-46, 280, 330f.

Eva-Marie Kröller

NINETEENTH-CENTURY CANADIANS AND THE RHINE VALLEY*

On April 26, 1838, Joseph Howe sailed aboard the ten-gun brig *Tyrian* to England to visit, together with his friend Thomas Chandler Haliburton, the land of his forefathers and to make an abbreviated *Grand Tour* of the European continent. Records of the journey survive in Howe's articles in *The Novascotian*, in entries noted in 'a small, worn, brown leather diary,'[1] and in a number of poems inspired by some of the sights witnessed *en route*. Among these travel-poems, one in particular suggests an extended comparison between Howe's homeland Canada and a European scene: in 'The Rhine' the poet juxtaposes 'the noble stream . . . by nations loved, by poets sung' with the 'gentle streams' in his native Nova Scotia. Although his own country does not boast ancient castles and legends, he loves it better because it is free (and always has been) of feudalism and monarchical oppression:

> Then, German, keep your Drachenfels,
> Vine-clad and foaming Rhine,
> The taint of bondage on them dwells,
> Far happier streams are mine.[2]

Howe's poem is only one item among a number of others concerning the Rhine in nineteenth-century Canadian writing. Although of mostly modest literary merit, these pieces provide important insights into Canadians' search for cultural role models, especially if complemented by discussions of the Rhineland in travel diaries, letters, sketches, and essays. Perceptive travellers 'read' this region of Germany as if it were a history book with lessons to be embraced, refuted, or modified in their own growing nation. As such, Canadians' fascination with the Rhineland is to be compared with their even stronger interest in Italy's fight for nationhood under Cavour, Mazzini and, above all, Garibaldi, a fight undertaken against the backdrop of the ruins of previous historical splendor. Both the city of Rome and the Rhineland projected an uncanny proximity of ancient past and revolutionary future. In doing so, they issued both warning and inspiration, although it depended very much on the ideology of the observer whether it was the past that issued the warning or the future.[3]

Like the Lake District and Switzerland, the Rhine Valley—particularly the narrow passage between Mainz and Bonn—was discovered in the early nineteenth century by German and English Romantics to be one of Europe's most quintessentially sublime regions, and it acquired considerable popularity enhanced by its convenient location as a *pays de passage* on the journey to Italy. Steep rocks and dangerous rapids, together with vine-clad ruins, monasteries and cemeteries, made the Rhine Valley an ideal ground for Romantic contemplation of Nature the Divine as opposed to the insignificance of man.

In 'nature's nation,' i.e. America, landscape painters of the Hudson River School absorbed concepts of the German Romantics into their art and soon compensated for the initially deplored lack of historical associations by celebrating the virtues of their 'virgin land.'[4] The untouched grandeur and spectacular coloring of the Hudson River in the fall competed successfully with the crumbling ruins of the Rhine Valley. Innocence and size—an unlikely pair—became criteria to be matched against history and scenic variety. Canadians too made claims on the Hudson as a means of assuring themselves that the American continent was as good a place as Europe to contemplate natural beauty. Thus Edmund Allen Meredith (1817-1899), principal of McGill College between 1846 and 1847 and Assistant Provincial Secretary, Canada West, at the time of a journey through the Rhine Valley in 1853 noted that, stripped of its castles and legends, the Rhine was altogether inferior to the Hudson in scenic beauty.[5] Others compared the Rhine to the Saguenay and the St. Lawrence and once again remarked with exhilaration that the latter was 'as large as half a dozen Rhines.' In the late 1870s, William H. Withrow (1839-1908), editor of the *Canadian Methodist Magazine* and the prolific author of patriotic works, religious tracts and historical novels, contemplated with disdainful glee the Rhine Falls near Schaffhausen, scoffing at Ruskin for 'going into raptures' over them: 'He ought to see Niagara and the Yosemite.'[6] More perceptive than Ruskin, Peter Kalm—the widely travelled Swedish scientist in William Kirby's *The Golden Dog* (1877)—assures his Canadian hosts that the view from Québec City's Cape Diamond is more beautiful than 'moonlight over Drachenfels on the Rhine.'[7] In comparing European and American landscapes, Canadian travellers furthermore realized that their natural environment was a commodity well worth taking meticulous care of.[8] As for transport and convenience, America was considered far ahead of Europe: the Rhine steamers were thought to be inferior to the vessels plying the Hudson, not to mention the cuisine offered on board the ships.

Yet while North American rivers seemed so much more grandiose, Canadian travellers appreciated similarities between the fortress of Ehrenbreitstein near Koblenz and the cities of Québec and Edinburgh, similarities reminding Canadians that German nationhood, like their own (and, at one time, Scotland's) demanded self-defense against hostile neighboring powers. Romantic fascination with the Rhine's scenery was closely connected with the emergence of national consciousness in Europe, and Canadian travellers were usually quick to apply such ideological implications to their own situation. In keeping with Herder's advice, German Romantic poets explored the legends and customs of the Rhineland in an attempt at capturing and thus strengthening the German national character. Isolated from world politics until the Napoleonic Wars and split up into 150 small states until approximately 1790, the Rhine Valley paradoxically both offered a particularly rich field for folkloric study **and** represented the German region most obviously in need of national unification. Again paradoxically, the advent of the French under Napoleon provided both the basis for administrative and legal consolidation **and** the incentive for growing assertiveness, hence hostility toward the French.

The poet who illustrated through his life and work most admirably the dilemma of the German Romantic was Heinrich Heine, a writer Canadian periodicals seem to have been more interested in than any other German author. In 1894, *The Week* printed an article assessing Heine's achievement and personal tragedy as symptomatic of Germany's political and cultural situation and concluded in a rapturous sentence: 'Not entirely in vain had he sung, if often, when the twilight clasps the earth in dusk and falls in quiet restfulness on German homes and hearts, when the snowflakes gently fall upon the cottage roof, and old Father Rhine rolls his waters without and the fitful fireside flames within fall on the tearful eyes of those that lift the harp to sing a song that touches human hearts through the ivied lattice of the German cottage there bursts the melody of perfect song, and fathers and mothers and men and maidens twine their arms around each other's necks and sing the songs of Heine.'[9]

The seemingly harmless cottage idyll in German Romantic poetry about the Rhine often connotes increasing hostility toward the French, an attitude feeding into an equally growing antagonism between Britain and France. English travellers were inclined to look upon the Rhine as an allegory of their own situation. So, needless to say, were Canadians. In 1847, the *Literary Garland* printed a series of long poems by the Scottish author Andrew L. Picken (1788-1833), entitled 'Ballads of the Rhine,' at first sight sentimental pieces evoking the romantic ambiance of towns and castles like Oberwesel, Stolzenfels, and Ehrenbreitstein, in reality, however, invectives against 'these scum of France,' who, having failed to realize that 'the wounded Rhenish boar has still got iron teeth' are in for an unpleasant surprise.[10] Anglo-Canadian imperialists watched the outcome of the Franco-Prussian War in 1870-71 with some satisfaction because it seemed to confirm the belief of men like Sir George Robert Parkin in the superiority of the 'northern,' i.e. energetic and healthy, over the 'southern,' i.e. effeminate and slothful, race.[11] William H. Withrow, never one to mince words, admired a regiment of 'large, well-built, blue-eyed, full-bearded Teutons' marching along to the strains of 'Die Wacht am Rhein,' finding them 'far superior in physique and intelligence to the average French soldier.'[12]

In a series of travel sketches entitled 'Down the Rhine,' an author in the 1877/78 issue of *Belford's Monthly Magazine* signing herself 'Erin' describes with disgust the 'Parisian cafés with all their tawdry paraphrenalia [*sic*]'[13] crowding the Place Broglie in Strasbourg. The annexation of Alsace-Lorraine following the Franco-Prussian War was observed with some interest; complete and peaceful assimilation of its population might give renewed hope for the solution of the French-Canadian problem at home. Although 'Erin' admits that it is difficult for a foreigner to assess the natives' feelings adequately, her own bias is fairly clear: 'Colmar, in its streets, the names of the shops, the old corner windows is as German and as antique . . . as Nuremberg or Aügsburg [*sic*].'[14] The Niederwald monument, a sculptural monstrosity erected high above the vineyards of the Rheingau to remind the French of their defeat, incites—like the bronze lions at Waterloo—'Erin's' admiration; she seems obsessed with the Franco-Prussian War to the point of tracing its developments to their inception in the spa of Bad Ems where Bismarck received (and fatally altered) the cable triggering the confrontation.

French-Canadians looked upon the annexation of Alsace-Lorraine much less benignly.[15] France's humiliation was also theirs, although J. F. Dubreuil, identified by the *Revue canadienne* as a former student of the Collège Sainte Marie and as a burgeoning author, addressed the Union Catholique de Montréal in 1872 in a speech entitled 'La France et les châtiments de Dieu,' in which he reported with horror on 'scandales babyloniens'[16] witnessed in Paris during the 1867 *Exposition universelle,* assuring his audience that God had justly punished the French for their impiety and decadence. However, Dubreuil was certain that France had been shocked into repentance, although he did not go as far as others did in suggesting that France look to Québec for a model of impeccable Christianity.[17]

To inform its readers further about the events in Alsace-Lorraine, the *Revue canadienne* also printed travel reports by Frenchmen like Jean-Jacques Weiss (1827-1891), editor of the *Journal de Paris,* a periodical which attracted the Québec journalists Elzéar Gérin and Oscar Dunn to work briefly in the French capital. French-Canadian readers were bound to sympathize when they read 'De l'alouette gauloise, de l'aigle prussien, du léopard anglais, qui régnera sur les continents et sur les mers? Le léopard a la mer, et l'aigle de Prusse aura le continent. Il ne restera à la pauvre alouette que sa chanson.'[18] Many probably agreed with the author that plans for revenge were in order.

French-Canadians' responses to the Franco-Prussian War were exacerbated by the religious conflicts between Protestants and Roman Catholics in the *Kulturkampf;* in 1898, Wilfrid Laurier incensed Sir Thomas Chapais and Jules-Paul Tardivel, both ultramontanists, by ranking Bismarck, together with Cavour, Lincoln and Gladstone, as one of the four greatest men of the century.[19] English-Canadians were somewhat more in agreement with Laurier; *The Saturday Reader* printed a sympathetic portrait of the Count in 1866, recommending him to its readers as having 'the air of a true gentleman, and a constitution of iron,'[20] but also characterizing him as a Macchiavellian statesman intent on enlarging Prussian power at all cost.

Whereas Prussian imperialist politics on the Rhine were eyed with anger and alarm by French-Canadians and with a mixture of consent and wariness by the English, the German educational system seems to have incited considerable admiration, although once again the Rhineland proved to be an area in which feudal practices and democratic innovation existed in close proximity. Between 1844 and

1846, Egerton Ryerson (1803-82), then Chief Superintendent of Education for Canada West, travelled through Europe in order to study educational facilities, stopping over in Berlin where he visited numerous elementary, secondary, trade and military schools, and conferred with the Prussian Minister of Public Instruction.[21] Subsequently Ryerson boarded a Rhine steamer, calling at the cities of Cologne, Bonn, Mainz, Wiesbaden, Frankfurt, Darmstadt and Strasbourg on the way and dividing his time equally between enjoying the scenery and visiting addition schools. Ryerson lauded German education institutions for their systematic approach to teacher training—a goal he was to pursue with particular application in his own work as Superintendent—and their collections of 'apparatus and specimen'[22] to facilitate teaching. From each of his numerous trips to the continent, Ryerson brought back maps, scientific equipment, and other educational materials; it was partly due to his efforts that Canada distinguished itself through superb educational displays at world expositions in Paris, Philadelphia and elsewhere.

While Ryerson was impressed with Prussia's democratic approach to education, 'Erin' in *Belford's Monthly Magazine* deplored remnants of feudal elitism in German universities. Visiting Heidelberg university during her trip 'Down the Rhine,' she commented with revulsion on the custom of duelling and deliberate scarring in some fraternities; W. H. Seymour, in 'Impressions of a Canadian in Germany,' a sketch published in *The Week* in 1894/95, confirms 'Erin's' view, but adds that 'it has nevertheless a good element in it, for to this may be attributed much of the gentlemanly bearing which here characterizes the relation of student toward student.'[23]

Seymour's somewhat ambiguous position between loyalty toward the democratic principle on the one hand and fascination with elitism on the other is replaced by an unabashed devotion to old-time aristocracy in the letters written in the 1890s by the daughters of Robert Bell, between 1901 and 1906 Acting Director of the Geological Survey of Canada, from a finishing school in Karlsruhe.[24] Here, under the guidance of one Fräulein Nödel, the Bell sisters were introduced to the mysteries of German idioms, grammar, composition and conversation, but also received instruction in chemistry, physics, history and sports, besides being thoroughly prepared for their role as débutantes in London and Ottawa with lessons in music, drawing and comportment. The day was planned from nine in the morning till eight at night, with breaks for meals and walks, all of which still seems to have left enough time for Margaret Bell to read the occasional trashy novel by Eugenie Marlitt, a nineteenth-century Germany best-selling author, or to attend a performance of a Wagner opera. The Bell sisters, extremely well-connected teenagers who sent greetings to Wilfrid Laurier and the Fréchettes[25] through their father, were as anxious as Fräulein Nödel to keep the Karlsruhe school an enclave for the elite. In a letter of May 6, 1897, Margaret Bell reports that the granddaughter of the Chancellor of Edinburgh University has been admitted, whereas another girl is refused entry because Nödel deems her socially undesirable. The Bell letters contain numerous school-girlish descriptions of outings in and around Karlsruhe; in their view, shaped by class and age, Germany remains a romantic country with quaint villages and princesses—albeit eccentric, 'emancipated' ones, as Margaret points out to her father—stationed at every street corner.

Besides exploring the German education system for evidence of both democratic and aristocratic principles and, in doing so, establishing criteria for the nature of instruction in their own country, Canadians were interested in German schoolbooks for yet another reason. In *The Week*, W. H. Seymour complained that German geography books were grossly inadequate in describing Canada, for they represented it as 'an inhospitable wilderness which bears a decidedly Siberian character.'[26] No wonder, Seymour concludes, that 'the Dominion has so few of these honest, industrious law-abiding German farmers who are acknowledged to make such good settlers.'

Germany, the new nation, created mixed, sometimes contradictory response among its Canadian visitors. More unanimously positive were their comments on its art treasures, its literature and music, although the occasional tourist noted in his diary that he found Cologne cathedral to be inferior to Milan's, complained that he had expected its tower to be much higher, or was repelled, like William H. Withrow, by the 'livid Christs, stained with gore,'[27] adorning Roman Catholic churches in the Rhine villages in general. In his guidebook *The European Tour* (1899), Grant Allen suggested that his readers not bother with the modern Germany and its symbol, the city of Berlin, 'the artificial and complex capital of a brand-new modern Empire.' Allen announced categorically that 'all that is oldest and best worth seeing for its native art in the region we now call Germany . . . is to be found in and around the Rhineland—the noblest cathedrals, the finest churches, the thickest clustered castles, the most exquisite paintings.'[28] The buildings and paintings most admired by

Canadian tourists were medieval or neo-gothic art, partly because of
a strong tendency in Canada, especially after the building of the
Houses of Parliament, to identify the new Canadian nation with the
virtues represented by the Gothic as opposed to classicism in its
various expressions, such as the 'miserable Renaissance mania'
angrily condemned by 'Erin' because she considers it anti-Christian
in spirit.[29]

The most important gothic monument in the Rhine Valley was, of
course, Cologne cathedral, the more so after it had become a symbol
of national cooperation following the decision, in the 1840s, to
complete the building using the rudimentary East Choir and South
Tower with its crane, both of which had been left standing since 1322.
Once again, it was the French who were ultimately responsible for
the completion of the cathedral. In the winter of 1797, they held
Austrian prisoners of war in the choir; parts of the wooden interior
decorations were burnt, and ammunition and horses were sheltered
in the building. Incensed, the population of Cologne who had done
nothing to save the building for hundreds of years, initiated and
supported the nation-wide effort to restore the cathedral to its
original purpose. Edmund Allen Meredith describes the site of the
building in 1853, comparing the old tower and crane, both over-
grown with grass, with the new nave looking, to him, as pristine as
one of Washington's new marble edifices. Medieval art embodied a
combination of craftsmanship, humility and cooperative spirit
attractive to men like George Munro Grant (1835-1902), Presbyterian
minister and principal of Queen's University, who in 1860 reinforced
the favorable impression Cologne cathedral made on him by visiting
Nürnberg, Albrecht Dürer's town, and noting in the painter's self-
portrait a face more noble than, he thought, a Greek's could ever be.

The authors of an essay on 'Les Nazaréens' and of a travel sketch
entitled 'Les Bords du Rhin' in the *Revue canadienne* advised their
readers to study the murals in the St. Apollinaris Chapel near
Remagen, built between 1839 and 1843 by the chief architect of the
Cologne cathedral project, Ernst Zwirner; to visit Stolzenfels castle, a
medieval ruin presented in 1823 by the city of Koblenz to King
Friedrich Wilhelm IV of Prussia whose architect Karl Friedrich
Schinkel refurbished it in neo-gothic style; and to look at the
collection of Nazarene paintings in Frankfurt's Städel Museum.[30]
For French-Canadian travellers, the idealization of medieval art took
on an additional ideological significance because it formed part of
ultramontanist propaganda with strategies outlined in Alexis-
Francois Rio's *De l'Art chrétien* (1855): art was to be strictly symbolic

in subject matter and technique, emulating the ascetic flatness of Fra Angelico's work rather than the sensuous forms of Rafael's paintings, and it was to submit itself at all times to a greater theological and nationalist purpose. As a result, French-Canadians pursued with considerable interest the careers of the German Nazarenes who, in the early nineteenth century, attempted to imitate in their life and work a medieval monastic community in Sant' Isidoro in Rome. Napoléon Bourassa (1827-1916), one of Canada's most versatile artists and a founding member of the Royal Canadian Academy, is reputed to have been influenced by Johann Friedrich Overbeck (1790-1869), the mentor of the Nazarene brotherhood, in his use of fresco techniques in Québec churches like the Nazareth chapel in Montreal (demolished for the construction of Place des Arts), Notre-Dame-de-Lourdes in Montréal and the Cathedral of St.-Hyacinthe. Bourassa probably met Overbeck during a sojourn of study in Italy in 1853 and although the Nazarene painter's influence on the French-Canadian has been the subject of debate,[31] there is sufficient evidence in Québec periodicals of the time that the Nazarene concept of art was considered a model well worth following. For those of its readers who were not fortunate enough to go travelling through Europe, the *Revue canadienne* printed from the 1890s onwards engravings of paintings by Overbeck, Cornelius, Kaulbach, Plockhorst and others, each picture accompanied by a detailed biographical sketch and analysis of the painting. Pictures were commended for their devotional value rather than brilliance of execution; the long-time art critic of the *Revue*, Eugène Aubert, criticized the work of Carl Becker, Director of the Berlin Academy of Arts and a fashionable painter patronized by the imperial court, as dwelling unduly—like the Venetian painters of the Renaissance—on the rendition of surface and texture in his 'Ave Maria in Venice.'

In 1805, when the Elector Jan Wellem inherited the rank of a Bavarian duke, a collection containing rare paintings by Rubens, Rembrandt and van Dyck was transferred from Düsseldorf to Munich where they formed the core collection of the Old Pinakothek. The transfer added to the depletion of the Rhineland of its art treasures due to territorial strife and lack of common purpose,[32] but ironically contributed to making the Munich of Ludwig I an exemplary artistic center illustrating to Canadians the importance of official support for the arts. Nazarene fresco painting re-introduced art into (and onto) buildings accessible to the public; art assumed once more the role of helping to educate the people toward a common national and religious goal. French-Canadians were somewhat more fervent than their English compatriots in their realization that all cultural efforts must be streamlined to support a patriotic ideal;[33] not surprisingly then, *Revue canadienne* published a long and well-informed essay on German literature, underlining the necessity of comparative studies because 'pour le politique, le moraliste, aucune n'est plus instructive et n'offre un plus haut intérêt.'[34] Although the general tone of the essay is appreciative, its author does not fail to point out that German literary historians like Georg Gottfried Gervinus have not sufficiently acknowledged the role of Divine Providence in history, and he admonishes the prospective writer of a French-Canadian literary history not to commit the same error.

Nineteenth-century Canadians' response to the Rhineland reveals itself to be the complex evaluation of a role model which is, in many ways, perceived to be an allegorical version of Canada's own situation. Exploring these responses moreover provides a backdrop to such contemporary pieces as Irving Layton's 'Rhine Boat Trip' and Mavis Gallant's stories in *The Pegnitz Junction* on the one hand, and Margaret Laurence's use of Heinrich Heine's 'Ich weiss nicht was soll es bedeuten' in *The Stone Angel* and its parody in Paul Hiebert's *Sarah Binks* on the other. According to these, Canadians have shifted from fascination with the history and romanticism of the Rhine Valley to wariness and irony. This change implies nothing so simple as a rejection of a previously admired ideal, but the realization that Western civilization as a whole has come to a watershed in which the symbols of humanism have generally proven to be deceptive. Gallant's image of a train-journey without arrival across the Rhine near Strasbourg is, at the same time, a mockery of nineteenth-century faith in technological progress, progress developing in close proximity with natural beauty and cultural achievement: 'The German train crossed the Rhine at snail's pace and then refused to move another foot.'[35]

Studying Canadian literature as part of developments in art, architecture, education, the sciences, and other areas seems to be an approach particularly suited to nineteenth-century Canadian writing. In my research, I have often been struck by the cosmopolitan, almost encyclopedic outlook of eminent Victorians in Canada, for whom an ideal education embraced extensive knowledge in both the humanities and the sciences, and for whom neither could exist without the inspiration of the other. Thus, in his inaugural speech to the Royal Society of Canada, J. M. Dawson—geologist, botanist, and President of the RSC—affirmed that the Society's purpose was to usher in 'a new era in the progress of Canadian literature and science' and that 'culture of the higher grade' must be made to 'keep pace with the headlong rush of material progress.'[36] If it is impossible for us to duplicate the Victorians' faith in the advance of civilization, we can still be inspired by the astounding breadth of their intellectual inquiry and bear witness to their achievements by using an approach going beyond the confines of purely literary study.

University of British Columbia, Canada

---

*This essay was in part researched with the help of a SSHRCC Postdoctoral Fellowship.

[1]James A. Roy, *Joseph Howe: A Study in Achievement and Frustration* (Toronto: Macmillan, 1935), p. 63.

[2]Joseph Howe, 'The Rhine,' in Joseph Howe, *Poems and Essays* (Toronto: Univ. of Toronto Press, 1973), p. 80.

[3]Cf. Angelo Principe, 'Il Risorgimento visto dai Protestanti dell'Alto Canada 1846-1860,' *Rassegna storica del Risorgimento*, 66 (1979), 151-63; Pierre Savard, 'Voyageurs canadiens-français en Italie au dix-neuvième siècle,' *Vie française*, 16, 1-2 (1961), 15-24; 'L'Italia nella cultura franco-canadese dell'Ottocento,' in Luca Codignola (ed.), *Canadiana 3: Problemi di Storia Canadese* (Venezia: Marsilio Editori, 1983), pp. 91-106; and my 'Viaggiatori canadesi-inglesi nell'Ottocento in Italia,' forthcoming in a special issue on Italo-Canadian relationships of *Il Veltro: Rivista di civiltà italiana*.

[4]Cf. Barbara Novak, *Nature and Culture: American Landscape and Painting 1825-1875* (New York: Oxford Univ. Press, 1980); Dennis Reid, *Our Own Country Canada* (Ottawa: The National Gallery of Canada, 1979).

[5]Meredith papers, Public Archives of Canada. For a biography of Edmund Allen Meredith within the context of Victorian Canada, cf. Sandra Gwyn's superb *The Private Capital: Ambition and Love in the Age of MacDonald and Laurier* (Toronto: McClelland and Stewart, 1984).

[6]William H. Withrow, *A Canadian in Europe* (Toronto: Rose-Belford, 1881), p. 270.

[7]*Ibid.*

[8]Cf. an article in *The Canadian Spectator*, 1 (1878), 273-74, entitled 'The St. Lawrence Route and Our Tourists.'

[9]Ethelbert F. H. Cross, 'Heine,' *The Week*, 11 (Dec. 1893-Nov. 1894), 780.

[10]Andrew L. Picken, 'Ballads of the Rhine,' *The Literary Garland*, n.s. 5 (January 1847-Dec. 1847), 252.

[11]Cf. Carl Berger, *The Sense of Power: Studies in the Ideas of Canadian Imperialism 1867-1914* (Toronto: Univ. of Toronto Press, 1970). Even a Canadian novel is based upon the events of the Franco-Prussian War. James De Mille's *A Comedy of Terrors* (1872) describes a sensational balloon escape during the Siege of Paris.

[12]Withrow, *op. cit.*, p. 270.*

[13]Erin, 'Down the Rhine,' *Belford's Monthly Magazine*, 3 (December 1877-May 1878), 364.

[14]*Ibid.*, p. 359.

[15]Cf. Pierre Savard, 'Voyageurs canadiens-français dans l'Allemagne de Bismarck et de Guillaume II,' *Zeitschrift der Gesellschaft für Kanada-Studien*, 3, 1 (1983), 55-64; I have refrained from discussing texts already covered by Savard, e.g. Ernest Gagnon's *Notes de voyages*, Victor-Alphonse Huard's *Impressions d'un passant*, and Henri Cimon's *Aux vieux pays*, but I do expand on his references to material about Germany in the *Revue canadienne*.

[16]J. F. Dubreuil, 'La France et les châtiments de Dieu,' *Revue canadienne*, 10 (1873), 514. For further information, cf. Alfred Rambaud, 'Québec et la guerre franco-allemande de 1870,' *Revue d'Histoire d'Amérique française* 6 (1952-53), 313-330. The Siege of Paris was described by Octave Cremazie, then living in exile in Paris, in a journal kept for his family in Québec.

[17]Cf. some of the motivations explaining the participation of Québec *zouaves* in Pius IX's defense against Garibaldi, e.g. in René Hardy, *Les Zouaves: une stratégie du clergé québécois au XIXe siècle* (Montréal: Boréal, 1980).

[18]Jean-Jacques Weiss, 'Huit Jours en Alsace en 1884,' *Revue canadienne*, 21 (1885), 735.

[19]Cf. Savard, 'Voyageurs canadiens-français dans l'Allemagne de Bismarck et de Guillaume II,' 56.

[20]Anon., 'Count Bismarck,' *The Saturday Reader*, 2 (March 1866-September 1866), 343.

[21]Egerton Ryerson, *The Story of My Life* (Toronto: Briggs, 1884), p. 364.

[22]*Ibid.*

[23]W. H. Seymour, 'Impressions of a Canadian in Germany,' *The Week*, 13 (Dec. 1895-Nov. 1896), 613.

[24]Robert Bell papers, Public Archives of Canada.

[25]Cf. James Doyle, *Annie Howells and Achille Fréchette* (Toronto: Univ. of Toronto Press, 1979).

[26]Seymour, p. 613.

[27]Withrow, p. 261.

[28]Grant Allen, *The European Tour* (New York: Dodd, Mead, and Co., 1899), p. 141.

[29]Erin, p. 364.

[30]Eugène Aubert, 'Les Nazareens,' *Revue canadienne*, 30 (1894), 529-37; P.B. Mignault, 'Les Bords du Rhin,' *Revue canadienne* 18 (1882), 329-41; 385-94.

[31]Cf. especially Roger Le Moine, *Napoléon Bourassa: l'homme et l'artiste* (Ottawa: Editions de l'Universite d'Ottawa, 1974).

[32]Cf. Horst-Johs Tümmes, *Rheinromantik* (Cologne: Greven, 1968).

[33]The proceedings of early meetings of the Royal Society of Canada are an especially interesting source for comparisons, because both English and French speakers at the

RSC's meetings made an effort to view literature within the context of developments in history and science. Cf. for instance John George Bourinot's 'Our Intellectual Strength and Weakness' of 1893, reprinted in the 1973 edition prepared by the University of Toronto Press.

[34]Albert Lefaivre, 'La littérature allemande,' *Revue canadienne*, 17 (1881), 68. The French consul in Québec presented a lecture entitled 'Esquisse sur la littérature allemande' to students and faculty of the Séminaire du Québec in 1879-1880 printed in volumes 13 and 14 of *L'Abeille du Petit Séminaire du Québec*. The lecture breaks off as soon as it reaches 1870/71 because the consul feels that no literature of any value can come out of Germany while it suffers from 'cette infatuation nationale' and while it listens to the 'leçons empoisonées du matèrialisme.'

[35]Mavis Gallant, *The Pegnitz Junction* (Toronto: Macmillan, 1973), p. 16.

[36]Cf. *Proceedings and Transactions of the Royal Society of Canada for the Years 1882 and 1883*, vol. 1 (Montréal: Dawson, 1883), pp. VI and VII.

II

CANADIAN LITERATURE IN EUROPE: PROGRAMS AND PUBLICATIONS

Reingard M. Nischik

NEW HORIZONS: CANADIAN
LITERATURE IN EUROPE

I

In a review entitled 'Sins of Omission' of *The Cambridge Guide to English Literature* (1983),[1] Wayne Grady calls the inclusion of *'only eight Canadian entries in a volume that is supposed to represent the accumulated wisdom of one of the two greatest universities in the English-speaking world . . . a myopic insult to the immense body of writing that has come from Canada since the end of the Second World War.'*[2] Grady shows that even these eight entries on Canada are partly erroneous, some of them embarrassingly so. He concludes: 'With courses on Canadian literature being taught in some 40 universities in Germany alone, with Canadian novelists invited to be writers-in-residence at universities in Italy, with at least three Canadian writers having been nominated for the Nobel Prize, surely one has reason to expect more than this from so grand an undertaking.'[3] Grady is correct in his argumentative drift. But his references to the status of Canadian literature in Europe are themselves somewhat misleading. True, Canadian literature is taught at several German universities; but with some 55 universities in the Federal Republic of Germany, the inclusion of Canadian literature at 'some 40' of them in the beginning 1980s would be an academic wonder (some 20 would be an accurate and probably still surprising figure). Then too, although Germany belongs to the European vanguard in Canadian literature studies, France or Italy might have been named here with similar justification. Furthermore, Grady's statement about German universities may suggest that Canadian literature is an integrated part of the curricula in English departments in Europe—which in most cases it is not. As to Canadian writers-in-residence in Europe, Grady might have mentioned Germany, England, or Scotland as well as Italy.

Grady's review highlights some of the difficulties that may arise when an emerging literature is studied outside its national borders—on the one hand, problems when a hitherto not much known, not much studied foreign national literature is first approached, problems ranging from lack of reference materials to differences in cultural background; on the other hand, Grady's review indicates the relative lack of knowledge in Canada about the state of Canadian literature studies across the Atlantic, and the difficulty Canadians may have in assessing the treatment of Canadian literature abroad.[4]

The present project sets out to make better known to an international audience how Canadian literature is treated in Europe today. It assembles some of the strands which make up the developing texture of Canadian studies in Europe. It will of necessity be incomplete, not least because this is the first endeavor of its kind; but past developments and current trends may be highlighted at this stage nevertheless. The following complexes will be considered:

—academic, institutional and political aspects of the treatment of Canadian literature in Europe
—extent of treatment of Canadian literature in Europe
—specific European contributions to the study of Canadian literature.

The fact that Canadian literature like the more established British and American is a foreign literature in Europe has kept the thematic approach from becoming as important as it has been in Canada itself. There the native literature has frequently been regarded as a means of 'seeing ourselves.' In Europe the critical approach to Canadian literature, by contrast, has more often been textual. Individual works have been regarded as aesthetic artefacts rather than as sociological and socio-psychological documents. This critical methodology is especially evident in France and the Federal Republic of Germany. Perhaps the analysis of narrative strategies, or, more generally, of structural and technical rather than thematic aspects is a specific contribution of European scholarship to the accumulating criticism of Canadian literature.

At the same time European scholars have subjected Canadian literature to comparative or generic study. More distant from the works in point of language, cultural background, and personal concern, European scholars have felt freer from the beginning to put specific Canadian works into a larger international context than has been the habit in Canada itself. In order to give an authentic impression of the current research interests of European scholars working in Canadian literature, the editors of *Gaining Ground* did not ask the contributors for specific contributions; rather they let the current research interests of the individual scholar determine genre, period, author and topic.

The factors which influence the development of Canadian literature at European universities also have to be seen in the wider context of the study of other literatures. The Federal Republic of Germany may serve as a case in point: up to the 1930s English Studies was practically monopolized by British literature. It was only in 1936 that the first professorship for American Studies was established.[5] After World War II U.S. American cultural policy supported the growing interest in the second great English-language literature. Thus in most English departments in Germany today, 'English Philology' consists of two strands of studies, the literature and language of Britain and of the United States. Any new literature written in English has to compete with at least fifty years of this academic tradition.

With an increase in self-awareness, in output and quality, the literatures of other English-speaking countries have encroached increasingly on the traditional bastions of English Studies. Since the early 1970s African, Canadian, Australian, West Indian, Indian, and New Zealand literatures have made a cautious entry into some English departments in Germany. In the second half of the seventies several articles called into question the continuing predominance of British and American literature in research and teaching; they suggested an increasing consideration at universities and grammar schools of other literatures written in English.[6] Essay collections appeared, giving introductory surveys of Commonwealth literature.[7] In linguistics, too, English was put into a wider, international context.[8]

In 1976 the first two German professorships with a specialization in Commonwealth literature (here the anglophone and francophone literatures of Africa) were advertised by the University of Bayreuth (i.e., significantly, by one of the new universities), an important first step towards institutionalizing the new development. Since 1977 annual international conferences on Commonwealth literature have taken place in Germany.

In principle, then, the academic reception of Canadian literature in Germany developed within the wider framework of a cautious opening up towards Commonwealth literatures in general. Concentrations and specializations have, however, taken place from the beginning: thus Tübingen and Heidelberg focussed on Asian, especially Indo-English, literature, Bayreuth on African literatures, Wuppertal concentrated on Australian literature. But today Canadian literature has the widest circulation of any Commonwealth literature in Germany. At Kiel and Trier it is a regular part of the curriculum. At some twenty other universities Canadian literature is offered more or less regularly—although one has to keep in mind that much is dependent on the activities of individual scholars; the number is growing steadily.

There are other signs of a further integration and institutionalization of Canadian studies in Europe. In the 1970s and 1980s seven national or multinational European associations for Canadian studies were formed next to those in the United States (1971), Canada (1973), Japan (1978), Australia/New Zealand (1981), and China (1984):

1975: The British Association for Canadian Studies (BACS)
1976: L'Association Française des Etudes Canadiennes (AFEC)
1978: Associazione Italiana di Studi Canadesi (AISC)
1980: Gesellschaft für Kanada-Studien (GKS)
1982: The Association of Canadian Studies in Ireland (ACSI)
1984: The Nordic Association for Canadian Studies
1985: The Association for Canadian Studies in The Netherlands (ACSN).

The main aim of these associations is to further Canadian studies and facilitate communication among members and institutions. All of these associations are members, in turn, of the International Council for Canadian Studies, founded in 1981 with headquarters in Ottawa; the Council gives an organizational framework to member associations (newsletter, international conferences, information exchange, etc.). All of the European associations are interdisciplinary, as is the conception of the journals several of the associations edit (in France, West Germany, Italy, and England). In West Germany and France the interchange within the associations between diverse disciplines has been furthered in the choice of a single inclusive theme for the annual conferences.

Another auspicious sign for the further development of Canadian studies in Europe is that positions for visiting Canadian scholars and/or writers have been established; financial and organizational cooperation of Canadian and West German political authorities has helped create such positions in Kiel, West Berlin, and Augsburg; there are similar arrangements in Scotland (Centre of Canadian Studies in Edinburgh), France, England (Leeds), and Italy (Bologna, Rome). Without such determined political and financial support, particularly through Canadian international cultural policy, Canadian studies in Europe could not have developed as they have. The Commission on Canadian Studies, chaired by Professor Symons, reported in 1976 that the general neglect of Canadian studies at Canadian universities was paralleled by a neglect of Canadian studies abroad. But even in April 1975, before the Symons report had recommended that a sustained interest in Canada be created abroad, particularly in the humanities and the social sciences, the Department of External Affairs in Ottawa had officially established a Canadian Studies Program. The first fruits of this program were harvested too late to be noted in the Symons Report. In the later *Reflections on the Symons Report: The State of Canadian Studies in 1980,* the section on 'Canadian Studies Abroad'[9] no longer sounds as bleak as it did in the first report. It shows the crucial role which Europe plays in implementing the program. The priority support countries are those with which Canada has close political and economic ties: these are the U.S.A. and Japan on the one hand, and Britain, France, Germany, Italy and Belgium on the other. In these, and to a lesser extent in other European countries (like Scandinavia) as well, generous Canadian financial and organizational assistance made possible systematic acquisition and growth of library holdings in Canadiana. In a period of severe reductions of government spending at universities in Europe, many institutions would otherwise have found the acquisition of even the most fundamental publications in Canadian literature next to impossible. Another effective method of strengthening the beginning interest in Canadian studies in Europe has been the so-called Faculty Enrichment Program; in the Federal Republic of Germany alone, for example, it enables fifteen scholars from various fields each year to travel to Canada for up to six weeks; there they do research with the aim of introducing Canadian material or new Canadian material into their teaching. The connections established this way between European and Canadian scholars have in general proved to be invaluable for the furthering of Canadian studies in Europe. Then too, Canadian authors and scholars have been helped to participate in European conferences, give readings and lectures. Last but not least, Ottawa gives financial support to the diverse Canadian studies associations in Europe. Between 1982 and 1984, $3.8 million were spent by Ottawa for the Canadian Studies Program altogether; for the years 1985-87 the amount made available has been tripled to $11.7 million.

One of the barriers to an institutionalization of Canadian studies in Europe is the predicament of young scholars looking for tenured university positions. A significant proportion of European Canadianists belongs to the younger academic generation. In Germany alone at least four young scholars have chosen, against all odds, to specialize in Canadian literature in postdoctoral studies. Some of these scholars will perhaps reach a secure academic position eventually, and hand on their interest in Canadian literature, but others may well have to look for work elsewhere.

The state of Canadian literature studies in Europe thus proves to be a complex web of influences, restrictions and encouragements. Canadian literature is still of minority interest in Europe; this interest is academic rather than general in kind. But as a closer look at the state of Canadian literature studies in the individual countries will show, Canadian literature has arrived in Europe to stay.

II

Canadian literature is now taught at least occasionally and sporadically in almost all European countries, most frequently in France, the Federal Republic of Germany, and Italy. MA theses, doctoral dissertations, and the occasional postdoctoral thesis are devoted to it and young scholars may specialize in it. Some established scholars have added Canadian literature to their research interests, like Paul Goetsch and Helmut Bonheim in Germany and Franz K. Stanzel in Austria; others have turned to it in the 1970s and 1980s as their at least temporarily predominant research area, like Pierre Spriet and Simone Vauthier in France and Giovanna Capone in Italy. Some universities in France, Italy and Denmark have established interdisciplinary Canadian Studies Programs. Canadian literature is also occasionally taught at grammar schools in France, Germany, Great Britain, Switzerland, Denmark, and Norway.

Of the eleven world-wide associations for Canadian studies, two thirds are situated in Europe. Scholars interested in English-Canadian literature tend to form the largest groups in these associations. Thus even in France, more research is done today in English-Canadian than in French-Canadian literature.[10] In Britain, however, in contrast to the overall trend, there is a stronger interest in French-Canadian literature, perhaps surprisingly so. The following individual surveys are largely alphabetically arranged by the names of the various countries to be considered:[11] Austria—Belgium and the Netherlands—Denmark—Eastern   Europe—England—Federal Republic of Germany—France—Ireland and Wales—Italy—Norway—Scotland—Spain and Portugal—Sweden and Finland—Switzerland.

Austria

The reception and study of Canadian literature in Austria is still in its initial phase. Organizationally, Austrian interest has been fostered through the multinational Association for Canadian Studies in the German-Speaking Countries *(Gesellschaft für Kanada-Studien);* of the 254 members of this association in 1984, 17 are Austrians. Since the foundation of the association in 1980, an Austrian has been one of the three members of the executive center: from 1980 to 1984 Professor Franz K. Stanzel of the University of Graz, from 1984 onwards Professor Waldemar Zacharasiewicz of the University of Vienna. A palpable interest in Canadian literature has been largely restricted to these two universities, where Professors Stanzel and Zacharasiewicz have included Canadian literature in their research and teaching for some years; in 1981 a doctoral dissertation on Margaret Laurence's novels was completed in Graz.[12] But interest in Canadian literature is also developing in Salzburg and Klagenfurt, where the first course on Canadian literature was taught in 1983. French-Canadian literature is occasionally treated at the Institute for French Studies at the University of Vienna, where Professor F. P. Kirsch teaches.

In May/June 1984 Professors Stanzel and Zacharasiewicz organized a symposium on English-Canadian literature near Vienna; one of the aims of this conference was to broaden the interest and knowledge in Canadian literature in this particular part of Europe, including the neighboring East European countries. Some sixty scholars from ten countries participated, among them representatives from Hungary, Yugoslavia, Poland, Romania, Switzerland, Belgium and Austria. The Canadian participants were Margaret Atwood, Graeme Gibson, Robertson Davies, Jack Hodgins, Rudy Wiebe, and Fred Cogswell.

Belgium, The Netherlands

In **Belgium** there has been a growing interest in Commonwealth literature, the main exponent of which is Dr. Hana Maes-Jelinek at the University of Liège, who specializes in Australian and West-Indian literatures. She is the current secretary of the European Branch of the Association for Commonwealth Literature and Language Studies (EACLALS). As early as in 1974, Dr. Maes-Jelinek organized the Liège Conference on Commonwealth literature, one of the first conferences in Europe of its kind, where Canadian literature was represented among others.[13] Liège is the only Belgian university where a course on Commonwealth literature is officially recognized. English-Canadian literature is treated in Liège, and there is also a considerable interest in Québécois literature, as the founding of a 'Centre d'études québécoises' in 1977 suggests.[14]

English-Canadian literature is mainly treated at the Free University of Brussels, where a Centre for Canadian Studies was established in 1982. It conducts comparative studies of Canada and Belgium in literature, linguistics, history, sociology and communications. In November 1983 the Director of the Centre, Mme. G. Kurgan-van Hentenryk, organized a conference on Canada entitled 'Des Grands Voisins,' which comprised sections on literature and linguistics, media and culture. (The first Belgian conferences on Canada had been held in the early 1970s.) The literature section was headed by Professor Jeanne Delbaere-Garant of the English Department of the Free University of Brussels, who has included Canadian literature in her teaching and research for some years. Under her supervision several Belgian students have written theses on Canadian literature.[15]

There is a Canada-Belgium literary prize, established in 1970, which annually makes a $2,500 award to French-language writers in Canada in one year, and in Belgium the next.

In *The Netherlands* English-Canadian literature has been taught regularly in the English Department of the Free University in Amsterdam by Professor August J. Fry since 1980. The French Department includes Francophone Canadian novels in their contemporary novel course. There is also some interest developing at the Universities of Groningen, Leiden and Nijmegen. In October 1984 the first Canadian studies conference was held in the Netherlands, and a few months later, on February 1, 1985, The Association for Canadian Studies in The Netherlands was established.

Denmark

The University of Aarhus in Denmark has been developing into a center of Canadian studies in northern Europe. This fits into the Aarhus Commonwealth tradition inaugurated by the late Greta Hart, who introduced Australian, Canadian and New Zealand literature to Aarhus. In 1967, the year that Hart died, Inger Hastrup, a

student of hers, was completing what became the first Scandinavian
MA thesis on Canadian literature; Hastrup went on to do further
postgraduate work on Canadian literature at Queen's University in
Kingston, Canada, and has been active in the field in Denmark ever
since.

The Commonwealth tradition of Aarhus has been carried on
especially by Anna Rutherford, Chairperson of the European Branch
of the Association for Commonwealth Literature and Language
Studies (EACLALS), editor of the journal of the branch, *Kunapipi*
(formerly called *Commonwealth Newsletter*), and associate editor of
World Literature in English, Ariel, and *The Journal of Commonwealth Literature*. In April 1971 she organized the first conference on
Commonwealth literature outside the Commonwealth in Aarhus.[16]
Rutherford occasionally includes Canadian literature in her
teaching. In fact, Canadian literature has been taught at Aarhus since
the early 1960s, and since the late 1970s each term; in 1976 Jørn
Carlsen began to specialize in it and has been teaching it regularly
ever since. A growing number of students write their MA theses on
Canadian literature. Once every year a seminar on Québécois litera-
ture is offered by the Department for Romance Languages. The
Department of English, French, Political Science, and the Greenland
Institute have cooperated in establishing a two-year interdisciplinary
Canadian Studies Program.

In April/May 1984 Jørn Carlsen and Knud Larsen (Department of
Romance Languages) organized a Canadian Studies Conference at
the University of Aarhus, with Margaret Atwood, Rudy Wiebe,
Aritha van Herk, Anne Hébert, Peter Buitenhuis, Patricia Smart,
Elizabeth Waterston, and Frank Birbalsingh among the speakers.
The conference also saw the inaugural meeting of the Nordic
Association for Canadian Studies/L'Association Nordique des
Etudes Canadiennes, which consists of a Danish, Swedish and
Norwegian section. Simultaneously, a wide-ranging Canadian Arts
Festival, organized by Anna Rutherford and Kirsten Holst Petersen,
took place at Aarhus University.

Aarhus is the center of Canadian studies in Denmark, but
Canadian literature has also been taught at Copenhagen and Odense
universities; at Copenhagen University Canadian writers have been
treated in the North American Studies Programme and the Feminist
Studies Programme.

Canadian literature is also entering Danish high schools; in
November 1982 secondary school teachers from Jutland attended an
introductory course on Canadian literature at Randers, and in

December 1982 secondary school teachers of English, French, History
and Geography from all over Denmark discussed the interdisciplinary
possibilities of Canadian studies at a seminar at Liselund, Slagelse.
Inger Hastrup compiled and edited *Canada: Native Peoples and
Immigrants* (Copenhagen: Gyldendal, 1981), a collection of fiction
and non-fiction texts for use in Danish schools. Another textbook on
Canada is being prepared by Merete Bjørn. There have also been
three school radio programs about Canada with a student's textbook
prepared by Paul Levine (Copenhagen University) and Steen
Johansen.[17]

Eastern Europe

In Eastern Europe interest in and studies of Canadian literature
are less developed than in the west. There are, however, several
scholars who treat Canadian literature, or have recently started to do
so.

The German Democratic Republic has been spearheading this
development. There Canadian literature is the object of teaching and
research at the Humboldt University of Berlin and the Friedrich-
Schiller-University in Jena. In Berlin Canadian literature is an
integrated part of literary studies; as a result, many MA theses in
Canadian literature have been written there. Two scholars are
working on postdoctoral theses in Canadian letters: Dr. Karla
El-Hassan (Jena) on Canadian short story ensembles, and Dr.
Marianne Müller (Berlin) on Northrop Frye. Several GDR academics
have attended the annual conferences of the Association for
Canadian Studies in the German-Speaking Countries. In 1981 an
interdisciplinary academic research group on Canadian studies was
formed in the GDR, one of whose aims is to make Canada known to a
broader public in East Germany. In 1974 an anthology of Canadian
stories appeared in translation. Some of Norman Levine's short
stories have been read over East German radio; Reclam in Leipzig has
published a selection of his stories in German translation.[18]

In **Hungary,** several Canadian short stories have appeared in
Hungarian translation in *Nagyvilàg* ('The Great World'), a monthly
magazine directed at the general public; this journal has also printed
a few introductory articles on Canadian literature. In 1978 an
anthology of Québécois poetry appeared (see bibliography). In 1979
the University of Budapest received a book grant from the Canadian
government, and later a course on Canadian literary history was

established here. Interest in Canadian literature is also developing at the University of Debrecen, where it was first taught in the English Department in the autumn of 1984, and at the University of Szeged, where Canadian drama is treated.

In **Yugoslavia** Canadian literature is gradually and sporadically taught at the Universities of Ljubljana and Zagreb. Some Québécois poetry has appeared in Serbo-Croatian translation in an anthology in 1972 and in a journal in 1973. In **Czechoslovakia** eight French-Canadian novels appeared in Czech translation in the 1970s, but this is not matched by any noteworthy critical attention as yet. In **Romania** English-Canadian literature is occasionally taught at the University of Bucharest, in **Poland** at the University of Cracow, and some theses have been written on Canadian literature in this country. A recent issue of the Polish journal *Literatura na Świecie* ('Literature Around the World'), No. 7 (1984), is the first Polish publication devoted entirely to Canadian literature; it includes translations from works by Jacques Ferron, Claude Jasmin, and of Québec poetry, as well as a few scholarly articles on Québec literature. Several Canadian professors have visited Poland and given lectures (Elisabeth Bednarski, Jean-Marcel Paquette, Jean-Cléo Godin).

One of the most important studies of French-Canadian literature in Eastern Europe appeared in the **Soviet Union** in 1969 (see bibliography); it is an attempt at an analysis of ideological elements in some French-Canadian poetry and novels up to 1960. Apart from this one knows of hardly any critical studies and translations of Canadian literature in the Soviet Union (a collection of Morley Callaghan's short stories, some of his novels, Yves Thériault's *Agaguk* and parts of Gabrielle Roy's *Bonheur d'occasion* have been translated into Russian).[19]

The major barrier to a development of Canadian literature studies in the Eastern European countries is state interference in research and teaching as well as the highly restricted book situation; both severely hinder a free development and exchange of ideas.

England

With a strong Commonwealth literature tradition in Britain, the British Association for Canadian Studies (BACS), established in 1975, was, not surprisingly, the first European association for Canadian studies. By 1985, the development of Canadian studies in England is not quite as strong as in France, West Germany, or Italy.

The British association is multidisciplinary and counts some 219 members, with a predominant interest in Canadian geography, history, politics and literature. In 1984 a 'Literature Group' within the association was formed. Since 1975, the association has been organizing an annual interdisciplinary conference; it provides a quarterly *Newsletter*, and publishes its *Bulletin of Canadian Studies* twice a year—a scholarly journal featuring articles on an inter-disciplinary basis. A concentration of teaching and research in the Universities of Leeds and Birmingham is recognized by the designation 'Regional Centre for Canadian Studies,'[20] but teaching of Canadian literature also goes on elsewhere in England (at the Universities of Reading, Exeter and Hull, and the Polytechnic of North London). The French Department of the University of Birmingham has been offering a course on Québec for twenty years. The University of Leeds has an annual visiting professorship in Canadian studies. Under the visiting writers programs of the Canadian High Commission and the Québec Delegation, writers recently welcomed in England have been Irving Layton, Anne Hébert, Nicole Brossard, Margaret Atwood, and Michel Tremblay.

In April 1984 Shirley Chew and Tim Bilham organized a conference entitled 'Re-Visions of Canadian Literature' at the University of Leeds, with John Moss and Fred Cogswell among the speakers.

Special endeavors are being made in England to introduce Canadian material, especially Québec literature, in the established secondary school program;[21] successful seminars for secondary school teachers have been held from time to time.

British publishers are beginning to publish Canadian titles: Alice Munro was, next to Indian writer Anita Desai, the first woman writer to be included in the King Penguin series (*Lives of Girls and Women, The Beggar Maid, Dance of the Happy Shades,* and *The Moons of Jupiter*). Penguin England also published Mordecai Richler's *The Apprenticeship of Duddy Kravitz,* Joseph Skvorecky's *The Cowards, The Penguin Book of Canadian Short Stories* and *The Penguin Book of Modern Canadian Short Stories* edited by Wayne Grady, *The Penguin Stephen Leacock,* Hugh MacLennan's *Voices in Time,* and Robertson Davies' *Deptford Trilogy, The Rebel Angels,* and *High Spirits.* Methuen England published *Making It New: Contemporary Canadian Short Stories,* edited by John Metcalf, and commissioned a book on Canadian woman writers of the 1970s, to be written by Dr. Coral Ann Howells of the University of Reading. Margaret Atwood's *Edible Woman, Surfacing, Lady Oracle, Life Before Man,* and *Bodily*

Harm have all been published by Virago. Michael Ondaatje's *Collected Works of Billy the Kid: Left Handed Poems,* and *Rat Jelly and Other Poems, 1963-78* have been published by Boyars, London, *Coming Through Slaughter* and *Running in the Family* by Picador. Nine titles by Farley Mowat are available in Pan Books. Novels by Marie-Claire Blais (Jonathan Cape) and Réjean Ducharme (Hamilton) have appeared in translation, and Dent has published an English version of Anne Hébert's *Les Fous de Bassan.*

Federal Republic of Germany

In Germany treatments of Canadian literature started to appear in the 1920s.[22] At the time literary studies were regarded as part of the 'cultural studies' then in vogue, and thus were predominantly interested in the national characteristics of literature, yielding few critical insights into individual texts. The first study of Canadian literature published in Germany was Gösta Langenfeldt's comparative article 'Die Literaturen des britischen Kolonialreichs,' which appeared in 1926.[23] Nine years later the first German PhD theses on Canadian literature were written, Ursula von Megenkampff's *Die 'Grenze' in der anglokanadischen Literatur* (1935), and Helene von Kieseritzky's *Englische Tierdichtung: Eine Untersuchung über Rudyard Kipling, Charles G.D. Roberts und Ernest Thompson Seton* (1935). World War II put an abrupt end to the early German interest in Canadian literature, and it took more than twenty years before it was revived.[24]

The first German scholar who became intensively involved in Canadian literature after World War II was Paul Goetsch, whose dissertation on Hugh MacLennan, published in 1961, was one of the first critical monographs on a Canadian writer published in Europe;[25] Goetsch taught in Marburg and Cologne before he went to Freiburg in 1971, where he continues to include Canadian literature in his research and teaching. In the early 1970s Goetsch introduced Eva-Marie Kröller, now Assistant Professor at the University of British Columbia, to Canadian literature. Another former student of his, Konrad Gross, has become a well-known German Canadianist; in 1980 Gross was made Professor of English and American literature at the University of Kiel and in 1984 President of the Association for Canadian Studies in the German-Speaking Countries.

Another pioneer of Canadian literature in Germany was Walter Pache, who in the early 1970s made Cologne University one of the first places in Germany to teach Canadian literature. He also started building up a section of Canadian publications (especially within English-Canadian literature) in the English Department library. It is today one of the best stocked in Germany. In cooperation with the University Library of Cologne it also supports a centralized journal program, financed by the provincial government of Northrhine-Westphalia, which for Canadian studies means the subscription to some forty Canadian journals; these may be borrowed by scholars throughout the Federal Republic.

In 1977 Professor Pache's inaugural lecture at Cologne University (on the Canadian novel and the pastoral tradition) was the first to treat Canadian literature in Germany. In 1981 he became Professor for Comparative Literature at the University of Trier, where there is also a strong interest in Québécois language and literature and in Canadian geography. The organization of an interdisciplinary Canadian Studies Program, the first one in Germany, is under way there. In 1981 Pache published *Einführung in die Kanadistik;* it is the first critical survey of Canadian literature in book form published in Germany, the second in Europe.

The assistant professorship position at Cologne University was taken over by Reingard M. Nischik, who since 1981 has included Canadian literature in her research and teaching. Nischik might be said to belong to the second generation of Canadianists in Germany. Her dissertation on single and multiple plotting, published in 1981, includes Canadian literature together with English and American literature as text material for theoretical analysis almost as a matter of course, a fact which would have been unthinkable ten years or even five years earlier.

Four projects of hers were partly directed to teaching Canadian literature at German high schools. *Short Short Stories: An Anthology*, which includes six Canadian short stories, and the accompanying volume of interpretations and additional material[26] represent altogether the third undertaking to include Canadian short stories in English teaching at West German secondary teaching institutions. The first anthology had appeared as early as 1969, the second one in 1971.[27] In the 1980s, however, the circumstances for this are more favorable, not least because in several of the West German federal states the Commonwealth literatures have been explicitly included in the curricula as potential teaching material.[28] Another important support may be expected from the second part of the revised regulation of the final examination (*Staatsexamen*) at universities in Northrhine-Westphalia, which are currently under discussion; in all the relevant models international literatures in English apart from those in Great Britain and the USA are scheduled to be one of five special subjects from which students may choose.

As regards tertiary education, Canadian literature is taught at least occasionally at some twenty of fifty-five West German universities: Kiel, Trier, Cologne, Freiburg, Augsburg, Mainz, Hamburg, West Berlin, Bonn, Regensburg, Würzburg, Siegen, Frankfurt, Munich, Erlangen-Nürnberg, Dortmund, Göttingen, Paderborn, Eichstätt, Düsseldorf and Marburg. French-Canadian literature is taught at Trier, Paderborn, Frankfurt, Augsburg and Kiel.[29] Theses on Canadian literature are now written at the BA and MA level, and occasionally at the doctoral and postdoctoral level.

An organizational frame for this spreading interest is the Association for Canadian Studies in the German-Speaking Countries (*Gesellschaft für Kanada-Studien*). It was founded relatively late within the European context, in 1980, but had been preceded by annual Canadian studies conferences in Gummersbach, Federal Republic of Germany, from 1977 on.[30] Then too, the Association has developed so rapidly that in 1985 it has the largest membership (360) of any of the associations in Europe, and is, after the US (over 1000 members) and the Canadian association (over 500 members), the third largest in the world. In 1984 about 80% of the members came from the Federal Republic, 9% from Canada, 7% from Austria, and 2% came from Switzerland. A large proportion is interested in English-Canadian literature (34%), followed by geography (21%), political science and sociology (15%), French-Canadian language and literature (8%), and Canadian history (7%). The annual conference of the association in Grainau in the Bavarian Alps in 1984 hosted more than 270 Canadianists from 18 countries.

Three positions for Canadian visiting professors exist at German universities, established in cooperation between German and Canadian authorities and all interdisciplinary in orientation: at the Free University of Berlin (since 1981), at the University of Kiel (since 1982), and at the University of Augsburg (since 1983); Aritha van Herk was in Kiel in 1983, Rudy Wiebe in 1984, Margaret Atwood in Berlin in 1984, Ronald Sutherland in Augsburg in 1984, George Bowering in Berlin in 1985.

As to activity at the student level, the German Academic Exchange Service sends West German students to Canada for a year on scholarships in the North America Program, and as a result of the teaching activities in West Germany in recent years students' preference for Canada rather than the USA is increasing.

Because of the book donation program of the Canadian Department of External Affairs, the libraries at West German universities where Canadian literature is taught are becoming increasingly better stocked. Some university libraries stand out: the State and University Library of Göttingen has been assigned English-language Canadiana as one of its special areas, the University Library of Bonn the area of French-Canadian literature. The Free University of Berlin holds some 15,000 books, periodicals, government documents, and microfilm materials on Canada; it has also ordered 'Pre-1900 Canadiana,' a microfilm collection of 50,000 titles. The University Library of Augsburg has ordered the Anglo-Canadian literature part of this collection (some 5,000 titles). A Québec Archive has been established at the University of Trier.[31]

Due to the combined efforts of Canadian and German authorities, institutions, societies and individuals, Canada is also introduced to the German general public all over Germany through so-called Canada days, a mixture of speeches, readings, concerts, exhibitions, films, dances, tourism, etc. Among the more recent ones were those in Trier (November/December 1983), Stuttgart (February/March 1983), and Berlin, where 'OKanada' (December 1982 to March 1983) was the largest and most costly cultural event about Canada ever organized outside Canada itself.

A recent study of Canadian literature in German translation[32] showed that the works of more than 100 Canadian writers have been translated into German since 1837, when Catharine Parr Traill's *The Backwoods of Canada* was published as *In den Wäldern Kanadas* in Leipzig. By and large the image of Canada provided the German-speaking general public has been a distorted one, based on the too well-known clichés with which Canada was long associated; animal stories, adventure stories, and stories about Indians, often addressed to the juvenile market, abound, at the cost of more sophisticated texts. In recent years, however, this imbalance has been somewhat righted.

As regards French-Canadian literature, the following works are among those translated into German: the first one translated was Ringuet's *Trente Arpents* (transl. 1940), followed by Gabrielle Roy's *La Petite poule d'eau* (1953; paperback edition in 1959), *Alexandre Chenevert* (1956), and *La route d'Altamont*, Marie-Claire Blais' *L'Hiver Noir* (1967; paperback edition 1970), Anne Hébert's *Kamouraska* (1972) (which was printed the same year in the feuilleton pages of the *Frankfurter Allgemeine*, one of the most respected newspapers in Germany), and Yves Thériault's *Agaguk*.[33] There have been no translations of French-Canadian plays or poetry collections into German as yet.[34]

France

France is next to the Federal Republic of Germany and Italy one of the three countries in Europe where interest in Canada and, specifically, in Canadian literature is most developed. The interdisciplinary French Association for Canadian Studies (Association Française des Études Canadiennes) was founded in 1976, one year after the British one and thus the second association for Canadian studies in Europe and, with some 200 members, the second largest. The French association boasts almost equally high levels of activity in the various disciplines; if there are any areas of concentration, they are literature, history and sociology. Oddly enough, today, in contrast to earlier phases, more French scholars concentrate on English-Canadian than on French-Canadian literature. The association organizes yearly conferences centered on a theme wide enough to interest the various disciplines, and edits two publications: the *Bulletin d'Information*, and since 1975 *Études Canadiennes/ Canadian Studies*, the official scholarly journal of the association edited by Pierre Spriet and Jean-Michel Lacroix at Bordeaux, where the association has its headquarters.

Courses with Canadian content were taught in several French universities even before the foundation of the association, especially in French-Canadian literature. In fact, interest in French-Canadian literature goes as far back as 1830.[35] The first articles on the subject in France appeared in the 1830s, the first course on Québécois literature in France was given at the University of Poitiers in 1911, the first special issue of a French journal on French-Canadian literature appeared in 1923 (*Le Monde nouveau*); 1923 was also the year the first doctoral thesis on French-Canadian literature appeared in France (at the Sorbonne), with four more theses following in the 1930s.[36]

The first (and today the largest) Centre d'études canadiennes was founded at Bordeaux in 1975. It includes academics teaching courses in, among others, the Departments of French, English, Political Science, Economics, Information and Communication, and the School of Law in an interdisciplinary Canadian studies program. These courses do not lead to a degree but provide elements of specialization at various educational levels. Research in Canadian literature is partly integrated into the Centre de recherches sur l'Amérique anglophone of the University of Bordeaux III; the centre organizes regular symposia on North American literature and culture and publishes the proceedings in its journal. Other Bordeaux activities connected with Canadian literature are linked to the Centre d'études et de recherches théâtrales.

A second Centre d'études canadiennes, also multidisciplinary, was established in Grenoble in 1979, a third one at the University of Dijon in 1982, where French-Canadian and English-Canadian literature is treated, and a fourth one, in 1983, at the University of Rouen, which specializes in literature and culture in the Commonwealth context.

Canadian literature is also treated at the University of Toulouse-Le Mirail, in coordination with Commonwealth and American studies, at Paris I and IV, Strasbourg II, Lille III, Caen, Pau, and other institutions. In fact, Canadian studies are now recognized in most French universities.

Apart from the annual interdisciplinary conferences organized by the French association, several conferences have been specifically devoted to Canadian literature. Among the more recent ones was the Strasbourg conference on the Canadian short story, organized by Professor Simone Vauthier in May 1983, with Mavis Gallant, David Arnason, Laurie Ricou, and scholars from France, West Germany and England attending.[37] In March 1984 Professors Rocard and Pons from the University of Toulouse-Le Mirail organized a conference on the colonial legacy in Canada and Australia as it is mirrored in literature; scholars from France, England, Belgium, Canada and Australia attended the conference.

The degree to which Canadian literature has been acknowledged in France is also shown by the fact that in 1980 Margaret Laurence's *The Stone Angel* was selected as one of the ten works of English language literature to be taught in depth (meaning that up to a dozen one-hour lectures may be devoted to the work) within the syllabus for the *agrégation,* the nation-wide competitive exam for the recruitment of French high school teachers.[38]

Ireland, Wales

The Association of Canadian Studies in *Ireland* was established in 1982 with twenty founding members; it is open to membership from both Northern Ireland and the Republic. Up to that time Irish interest in Canada had been organizationally taken care of through the British Association for Canadian Studies. The Irish association, too, is interdisciplinary; its present membership of about fifty is drawn principally from geography, history and French literature departments; other interests are in law, sociology and economics. The association plans a biennial conference; a newsletter is issued regularly. French-Canadian literature has been taught at Trinity College, Dublin, and at University College, Cork, since the late seventies.

Recently Northern Telecom, Canada's largest manufacturer of telecommunications equipment, has presented awards totalling $40,000 to four Irish universities to provide for the expansion of Canadian studies programs in their curricula. The universities are: the National University of Ireland at St. Patrick's College, Maymooth; University College, Cork; Trinity College, Dublin; and University College, Dublin.

In *Wales,* too, interest in Canadian studies is developing, especially at the Department of English of the University College of Wales, Aberystwyth. 1983 saw the establishment of the Canadian Studies in Wales Group, which plans biennial Canadian studies conferences.

There is also a Canada-Wales Writers' Exchange, a program founded by the Canada Council and the Welsh Academy of Writers in 1979.

Italy

In Italy there has been a striking development of Canadian literature studies in recent years. The Italian Association for Canadian Studies (Associazione Italiana di Studi Canadesi, AISC) was founded in 1979, and counts more than 200 members, most of them in literature; the largest group is made up of scholars interested in English-Canadian literature, followed by smaller groups interested in French-Canadian literature, in history, geography and political science.

Academic interest in Canada had, however, developed in Italy before the establishment of the Italian association. The pioneer in Canadian literature studies in Italy was Professor Giovanna Capone of the University of Bologna, the oldest European university.

Professor Capone became interested in Canadian literature in the early 1970s, and in 1976 organized a conference on Canadian literature in Bologna (with Irving Layton among the participants), the first conference with an exclusively Canadian focus in Italy and anywhere in a country where English or French are not the native languages. Professor Capone was also the first Italian scholar of English to start teaching Canadian literature and has supervised numerous MA theses as well as some doctoral dissertations in the field. 1978 saw the appearance of Capone's *Canada: il villagio della terra: letteratura canadese di lingua inglese* (Bologna: Patron), which received considerable critical attention and constituted the first critical survey of Canadian literature to appear outside Canada.[39] When Northrop Frye toured Italy in 1979, he met with an enthusiastic response; several of his books have been translated into Italian. The biannual interdisciplinary conferences[40] organized by the Italian association have brought many other Canadian writers and scholars to Italy. Canadian literature is now taught at some ten Italian universities (Bologna, Turin, Rome, Pisa, Messina, Genoa, Bari, Padua, Venice). In collaboration with the Canadian Embassy in Rome, the Universities of Bologna and Rome established a Canadian-Writers-in-Residence Program.

Although some thirty Canadian books are available in Italian translation,[41] interest in Canadian literature is still—as in the other European countries—of an academic rather than of a general kind. Canadian literature in Italy has been supported by Amleto Lorenzini, who has been called 'a one-man cultural embassy.' A civil servant in the Ontario government before moving to Rome to work as an information officer at the Canadian Embassy for several years, he participated in the translation and publication of every one of these books, translating most of them himself and finding publishers for them; he also organized seminars on Canadian literature and cooperated with Italian scholars. The Canadian Academic Centre in Italy (Rome) and the Canadian Cultural Institute in Rome, too, have been supporting the gradual spread of Canadian literature in Italy.

The center of Italian studies of French-Canadian literature is the University of Bologna, where Professor Liano Petroni, currently president of the Italian Association for Canadian Studies, has been teaching it since 1973. He started a regular course of French-Canadian literature in 1976. He also edits *Francofonia*, devoted to all literature in French and thus including Québec literature. French-Canadian literature is also taught by Professor Franca Marcato Falzoni, Bologna University, and by Professor Pasquale Janini,

University of Rome, who has organized several conferences on the subject.[42] Altogether it may be said that in Italy today, as in France, Canadian literature courses are offered at all the major Italian universities.

Among French-Canadian works translated into Italian are Gabrielle Roy's *Rue Deschambault* (transl. in 1957), Yves Thériault's *Agaguk* (1962), Marie-Claire Blais' *Une saison dans la vie d'Emmanuel* (1967) and *La Belle Bête* (1970), Réjean Ducharme's *L'Avalée des avalées,* and poems by Gaston Miron.[43]

Norway

In 1946 the University of Oslo created the first chair in American Literature in Norway (and one of the first ones in Europe). When Professor Per Seyersted took over the chair in the 1970s, he gradually introduced Canadian literature as well. A ceremony in 1978 marked the official opening of Canadian studies in Norway: a book gift by the Canadian Embassy laid the ground for some 1,500 books on Canada held in the American and French Institute of the University of Oslo; an up-dated list of the library holdings is sent out regularly to sister institutions in the five Scandinavian countries.

In 1979 the first course on Canadian literature in Norway was given by Professor Seyersted; others followed in 1981, 1983 and 1984, so that Canadian literature may be regarded as a regular part of teaching at the University of Oslo. Several theses by Norwegian students on Canadian literature have been written as a result.

There have been two so-called Hovda Canadian Seminars in 1981 and 1982 in Norway, both organized by Professor Seyersted; the first one was meant to introduce more students to Canadian literature, the second one, with Alice Munro participating, was to create interest in Canadian literature and was attended by professors from other universities in Norway, Sweden and Finland. Previously, Oslo University had been the only institution in Scandinavia next to Aarhus, Denmark, where Canadian literature was taught.

Professor Seyersted also includes Canada in Oslo University's yearly refresher course for high school and junior college teachers. In the Spring of 1982 he gave a ten-week lecture course on Canada as part of the University of Oslo's Adult Education Program.

At Bergen University, Professor Lars Hartveit has promoted Commonwealth Studies; he has started to treat Canadian literature in recent years.

Some thirty-five Canadian books have been translated into Norwegian. Gordon Hölmebakk, chief editor of Gyldendal, the largest Norwegian publishing house, has been an active champion of Canadian literature. Bokklubben, Norway's leading book-club, has brought out a twelve-volume history of world literature, in which a separate chapter on Canadian literature is included. In 1982 Bokklubben reprinted for its members the Norwegian translation of Margaret Laurence's *The Stone Angel* in an edition of 100,000 copies.

1984 saw an important organizational step in the attention to Canadian literature (taught at some six universities in Scandinavia now): the forming of The Nordic Association for Canadian Studies, with Jørn Carlsen, University of Aarhus, as president and executive representative for Denmark, Per Seyersted, University of Oslo, Norway, and Bengt Steijffert, University of Lund, Sweden, as executive representatives of Norway and Sweden. The association plans a first Nordic Conference on Canadian Studies in Lund, Sweden, in 1987.[44]

Scotland

Members of Scottish universities who are interested in Canadian literature belong to the British Association of Canadian Studies. The most active interest in Canadian studies in Scotland is to be found at the University of Edinburgh. It has pioneered the teaching of Canadian studies in Britain and remains the only university in the country where students can take the subject as a degree major; the Centre of Canadian Studies, founded jointly by the University and The Foundation for Canadian Studies in the United Kingdom in 1974, offers courses on Canadian geography, history, politics, economics, sociology and, recently, literature; the organization of an interdisciplinary Canadian Studies Program is under way. The Centre has appointed a Visiting Professor since 1975, till 1983 in the social sciences, and in 1983 for the first time a professor of literature, Professor Malcolm Ross of Dalhousie University. Professor Ross taught the first course in Canadian literature given at the University of Edinburgh. A similar course was given in 1984 by Professor Douglas Lochhead of Mount Allison University, New Brunswick. The visiting professorship in Edinburgh often constitutes a base for a wider spread of Canadian literature activities in Europe. Thus Professor Ross gave public lectures on Canadian literature topics in London, Birmingham, Leeds, Reading, Stockholm, Uppsala, Oslo,

Bergen, Helsinki, Turku, Paris and Rome. In 1984 the Department of English at the University of Edinburgh instituted a regular and continuing program in Canadian literature.

Since 1978 there has also been an exchange of writers between the Scottish Arts Council and the Canada Council. The writer from Canada is housed in the Centre of Canadian Studies and is often active in various events there. In 1983 Kent Thompson was writer-in-residence under this arrangement, and gave readings and conducted seminars throughout Scotland and in several English universities. Fred Cogswell of the University of New Brunswick was writer-in-residence in 1984, Alistair MacLeod of the University of Windsor in 1985.

Attention is also devoted to Canadian literature at Dundee University. At Sterling University there is a strong program in French-Canadian studies, and some English-Canadian literature is included in the Commonwealth program there.[45]

Spain, Portugal

In these countries there is hardly any sustained interest in Canadian literature as yet. Two universities in Spain have a course on Commonwealth literature in which Canada is included: the University of Barcelona and the Autonomous University of Barcelona. At the University of La Laguna, Tenerife, Canary Islands, Dr. Berndt Dietz has a special interest in Canadian literature.

Sweden, Finland

In Sweden Professor Liljegren was one of the first scholars in Europe to take up Commonwealth literature; the series he edited, 'Studies on English Language and Literature,' included not only American but also Anglo-Canadian and Australian literature.

In recent years Britta Olinder of Göteborg has been an active promoter of post-colonial literatures. Whilst her own field is Indian literature, she is careful to see that all countries are represented. She has organized two conferences, one in 1982 and another in June 1984, at which Matt Cohen, Aritha van Herk, and Rudy Wiebe were among the speakers. The latter conference also saw the launching of an essay collection edited by Olinder, based on the papers delivered at the first Göteborg conference; it includes several essays on Canadian

literature: *A Sense of Place: Essays in Post-Colonial Literatures.*
Contributions to the study of post-colonial literatures in Sweden have also come from Lund University and its English Department chaired by Professor Claes Schaar. Interest in Canadian literature is also found at the University of Uppsala and Stockholm.

In *Finland,* Professor Tuomo Laitinen from Helsinki University arranged an introductory seminar on Canadian literature in 1983. The subject is taught regularly at the University of Helsinki.[46]

Switzerland

The study of Canadian literature in Switzerland is still in its initial phase. Swiss interest has been supported organizationally through the multinational Association for Canadian Studies in the German-Speaking Countries (*Gesellschaft für Kanada-Studien*); of the 254 members of this association in 1984, four came from Switzerland.

Canadian literature has been offered since spring 1985 at the English Department of the University of Bern, where Dr. Rudolf Bader teaches. At the University of Genève Dr. Philipe Renaud, Professor of Francophone Literature outside France, also treats Québécois literature occasionally.[47] At the University of Zürich a Canadian, Peter Hughes, is Professor of Literature, but although he includes Canadian material occasionally, he concentrates on British literature. There are plans to establish a special section of Canadiana at one of the Swiss university libraries.

Outside academia, some private scholars are doing research in Canadian literature. Canadian literature is also treated at several Swiss grammar schools; several symposia for grammar school teachers have been organized.[48]

There is a Canada-Switzerland literary prize, established in 1980 jointly by the Canada Council and the Foundation Pro Helvetia of Switzerland. The prize provides $2,500 in alternate years to a Swiss or Canadian writer for a work—fiction, poetry, drama, or non-fiction—published in French during the preceding eight years. In 1984 the prize was awarded to Canadian writer Marie-José Thériault for her long poem *Invariance suivi de Célébration du Prince* (Éditions du Noroît, 1982).

III

The study of Canada by foreigners has a long history. The study of Canadian literature is a relatively recent phenomenon. As contemporary Canadian writing takes its place among international literatures written in English, more critical attention is and will be focussed on it abroad. Canadian literature has come of age if its works are not read and studied primarily because of the light they shed on the country and its people, or because it belongs to the relatively new field of international literatures written in English, but because some of the writing originating in Canada is too good to be ignored and invites critical analysis and extended study. We hope that this collection of essays conveys that this is indeed the direction in which the reception of Canadian literature in Europe is heading.

---

[1]Michael Stapleton (ed.), (Cambridge Univ. Press, 1983).

[2]Wayne Grady in *Books in Canada*, 12, No. 10 (1983), 27f., here 27. Apart from Canada, Great Britain, the United States, Australia, the Caribbean, and Africa are represented in the *Cambridge Guide*.

[3]*Ibid.*, p. 28.

[4]Similarly, Michael Cope, the Halifax *Mail-Star* London correspondent, writes in a survey article of the state of Canadian literature treatment in Europe: 'Margaret Laurence's works have been translated into Norwegian, but in Sweden literature students study her work in the original English.' (*Mail-Star*, September 30, 1982). The implication that Norwegian literature students study Laurence's novel in the Norwegian translation is clearly incorrect and does not at all fit the facts of English studies in Europe. Nevertheless, this statement is repeated in a summary report of the Cope article in the *Newsletter*, 3, No. 1 (April 1984), 41, of the International Council for Canadian Studies, published in Ottawa.

[5]At the University of Berlin.

[6]Jürgen Schäfer, 'Was ist "englische" Literatur? Wissenschaftstheoretische Probleme und curriculare Herausforderung,' *Die Neueren Sprachen*, N.F. 25 (1976), 512-24; Hans Galinsky, 'Entwicklung und Perspektiven der literaturwissenschaftlichen Forschung zu den englischsprachigen Literaturen ausserhalb Englands,' in Heinz Kosok und Horst Priessnitz (eds.), *Literaturen in englischer Sprache: Ein Überblick über englischsprachige Nationalliteraturen ausserhalb Englands* (Bonn: Bouvier, 1977), pp. 239-60; see also, more recently, Reingard M. Nischik, 'Zur Behandlung anglo-kanadischer Kurzgeschichten: Tendenzen, Materialien und Hilfsmittel,' *Literatur in Wissenschaft und Unterricht*, 15, No. 4 (Dezember 1982), 381-98.

[7]Kosok/Priessnitz (eds.), *op. cit.;* Jürgen Schäfer (ed.), *Commonwealth-Literatur,* Studienreihe Englisch (Düsseldorf/Bern: Bagel/Francke, 1981); Gerhard Stilz (ed.), *Drama im Commonwealth* (Tübingen: Narr, 1981); Dieter Riemenschneider (ed.), *The History and Historiography of Commonwealth Literature* (Tübingen: Narr, 1983); Konrad Gross/Wolfgang Klooss (eds.), *Voices from Distant Lands: Poetry in the Commonwealth* (Würzburg: Königshausen and Neumann, 1983).

[8]Manfred Görlach, now University of Cologne, focussed on varieties of English world-wide, and initiated several projects in this field. The journal *English World-Wide* was launched in 1980 and has appeared in two annual numbers; the series 'Varieties of English Around the World' was started in 1979; four volumes ranging from Cameroon to Singapore and Malaysian English had appeared by June 1984. Both projects are now published by John Benjamins, Amsterdam/Philadelphia.

[9]Ottawa: Minister of Supply and Services Canada, 1981, pp. 185-202.

[10]For a detailed survey of the reception and study of Québécois literature in Europe, particularly in France, Italy, the German-speaking countries, and Eastern Europe see *Lectures européennes de la littérature québécoise: Actes du Colloque international de Montréal (avril 1981)* (Ottawa: Leméac, 1982).

[11]The surveys partly make use of information kindly provided by colleagues from the respective countries; I would like to thank all of them here for their cooperation.

[12]Ulrike Tilly, 'Die Romane des "Canadian Cycle" von Margaret Laurence' (unpublished doctoral dissertation, Graz, 1981).

[13]The conference proceedings are collected in Hena Maes-Jelinek (ed.), *Commonwealth Literature and the Modern World* (Brussels: Librairie Marcel Didier, 1975); the first conference on Commonwealth literature outside the Commonwealth was held in Aarhus, Denmark, in 1971.

[14]For a short survey of the state of Québécois literature in Belgium see Maurice Piron, 'L'accueil réservé à la littérature québécoise en Belgique,' in *Lectures européennes de la littérature québécoise,* pp. 81-88; see also the contributions by Jean-Marie Klinkenberg, Danielle Racelle-Latin, Claudette Delhez-Sarlet, Lise Gauvin and Jacques Dubois, and Pierre Popovic, all from Liège University, in the same collection.

[15]Partly based on information kindly provided by Professor Jeanne Delbaere-Garant, Free University of Brussels.

[16]The proceedings were published in Anna Rutherford (ed.), *Common Wealth* (Aarhus, 1971); the only paper on Canadian literature included in this early collection is by Halvard Dahlie, 'The International Connection in Canadian Literature.'

[17]Partly based on information kindly provided by Professor Anna Rutherford, University of Aarhus.

[18]*Die weite Reise: Kanadische Erzählungen und Kurzgeschichten,* Ernst Bartsch (ed.) (Berlin: Volk und Welt). Norman Levine, *Der Mann mit dem Notizbuch,* ed. and with a postscript by Karla El-Hassan (2nd revised ed., Leipzig: Reclam, 1979 [1975]).

[19]For a survey of the reception of French-Canadian literature in Eastern Europe see Józef Kwaterko, 'L'accueil réservé à la littérature québécoise en Europe de l'Est,' in *Lectures européennes de la littérature québécoise,* pp. 12-22; some of the information in my survey is based on Kwaterko's paper.

[20]Leeds 1979, Birmingham 1981; the earliest British center for Canadian studies was that of Edinburgh, opened in 1974.

[21]See also *A Guide to the Study of Quebec: For Teachers and Students in Britain*, compiled by Cedric May (University of Birmingham, Regional Canadian Studies Centre, 1982; 21 pp.).

[22]For previous surveys see H. Schroeder-Lanz, 'Kanadische Studien in Deutschland—Deutsche Studien in Kanada: Ein Überblick.' *Trierer Beiträge*, 3 (1977), 11-17; Walter Pache, 'Kanadistik in Deutschland,' *Einführung in die Kanadistik* (Darmstadt: Wissenschaftliche Buchgesellschaft, 1981), pp. 112-18; Walter Pache, 'Zur Situation der deutschsprachigen Kanadistik,' *Zeitschrift der Gesellschaft für Kanada-Studien*, 1, No. 1 (1981), 9-18; Konrad Gross, 'Literary Criticism in German on English-Canadian Literature: Commentary and Bibliography,' *German-Canadian Yearbook*, 6 (1981), 305-10.

[23]*Englische Studien*, 61 (1926/27), 220-80.

[24]See also this volume, pp. 250-52.

[25]Paul Goetsch, *Das Romanwerk Hugh MacLennans: Eine Studie zum literarischen Nationalismus in Kanada*. Britannica et Americana, 9. Hamburg: de Gruyter, 1961.

[26]See the bibliography at the end of this volume; the other two publications are a teaching aid to Norman Levine's story 'By a Frozen River' broadcast by the West German Radio Station (WDR) in its series 'English for Seniors' in February 1983 and again in April 1985, and a survey of trends, text material, and secondary literature available, and critical trends in connection with the Anglo-Canadian short story ('Zur Behandlung anglo-kanadischer Kurzgeschichten').

[27]*Modern Canadian Short Stories*, ed. and with explanatory notes by W. E. Riedel. Huebers Fremdsprachliche Texte, 247. Munich: Hueber, 1969 (out of print); *Canadian Short Stories*, ed. Alfons Weber (Paderborn: Schöningh, 1971).

[28]Thus in Northrhine-Westphalia the latest curricula recommendations (1981) issued by the minister of culture postulate an adequate proportion of treatment of themes from English-speaking countries other than England and the United States; Canada is explicitly mentioned.

[29]For a survey of the reception of Québécois literature in the German-speaking countries see Renate Moisan, 'L'accueil réservé à la littérature québécoise dans les pays de langue allemande,' in *Lectures européennes de la littérature québécoise*, pp. 23-29.

[30]In 1979 the first—and to date only—symposium on Canadian literature was held at the University of Bremen; see bibliography under Martini (ed.).

[31]For further details on Canadiana holdings in West German libraries see Ingwer E. Momsen, 'Kanada-Sammlungen in Deutschen Bibliotheken,' *Zeitschrift der Gesellschaft für Kanada-Studien*, 4, No. 1 (1984), 140-44.

[32]Walter E. Riedel, *Das literarische Kanadabild: Eine Studie zur Rezeption kanadischer Literatur in deutscher Übersetzung* (Bonn: Bouvier, 1980).

[33]Three anthologies of French-Canadian texts also appeared in German translation, the first one (1967) prepared by Armin Arnold and Walter Riedel, the second one (1974) by Ernst Bartsch in East Germany, and the third one (1976) again by Walter Riedel; see Renate Moisan, *op. cit.*, pp. 25f.

[34]Renate Moisan, p. 28.

[35]For a survey of activities in Québécois literature before 1945 see David M. Hayne, ' "Cette ancienne colonie française . . .": la fortune des lettres québécoises en France jusqu'en 1945,' in *Lectures européennes de la littérature québécoise*, pp. 93-107, which

includes a bibliography; the subsequent details are taken from this article.

[36]For a survey of the reception of French-Canadian theater in Europe, essentially in France and Belgium since the early 1970s, see Michel Vaïs, 'L'accueil fait au théâtre québécois en Europe,' in *Léctures européennes de la littérature québécoise*, pp. 354-63.

[37]The papers presented at this conference are collected in a special issue of *Recherches anglaises et américaines (RANAM)*, No. 16 (1983).

[38]Partly based on information kindly provided by Professor Pierre Spriet, University of Bordeaux III.

[39]The second appeared in the Federal Republic of Germany: Walter Pache, *Einführung in die Kanadistik* (Darmstadt: Wissenschaftliche Buchgesellschaft, 1981).

[40]The proceedings of the conferences concerning Canadian literature have been published, for the English-Canadian literature section under the editorship of Alfredo Rizzardi; see the bibliography.

[41]Among the translated works are books by Margaret Atwood, Marie-Claire Blais, Leonard Cohen, Northrop Frye, Anne Hébert, Margaret Laurence, Irving Layton, Marshall McLuhan, Farley Mowat, Mordecai Richler, Yves Thériault, and Aritha van Herk.

[42]For a detailed survey, beginning with the Italian reception of *Maria Chapdelaine* in 1921, see Franca Marcato-Falzoni, 'Présence de la littérature québécoise en Italie,' in *Lectures européenes de la littérature québécoise*, pp. 45-63.

[43]For earlier surveys of Canadian literature studies in Italy see also Damiano Pietropaolo, 'The Bologna Connection: An Italian Love Affair with Canadian Writing,' *Saturday Night*, November 1979, pp. 65-68; Richard A. Cavell, 'Canadian Literature in Italy,' *Canadian Literature*, No. 87 (Winter 1980), pp. 153-56; *Canadian Literature* will be publishing an Italian-Canadian issue in the fall of 1985.

[44]Partly based on information kindly provided by Professor Per Seyersted, University of Oslo.

[45]Informant: Professor Malcolm Ross, Visiting Professor of Canadian Studies at the University of Edinburgh in 1983. An interesting article (entitled 'Canadian Literature Finding Room in European Libraries') on Professor Ross' impressions of the state of Canadian studies in the European countries was printed in the *Mail-Star* (Halifax, Nova Scotia) on September 30, 1983; the article is based on an interview of Malcolm Ross by Michael Cope.

[46]On the Nordic Association for Canadian Studies see under Norway.

[47]See also Pierre-Louis Péclat, 'La littérature québécoise dans le champ culturel suisse-français,' and Renate Moisan 'L'accueil réservé à la littérature québécoise dans les pays de langue allemande,' in *Lectures européennes de la littérature québécoise*, pp. 78-80 and 23-29.

[48]Partly based on information kindly provided by Dr. Rudolf Bader, University of Bern.

Reingard M. Nischik

EUROPEAN PUBLICATIONS
ON CANADIAN LITERATURE

This bibliography shows the kind of studies which scholars in various European countries have undertaken, especially in recent years. For the purpose of this bibliography 'European publications' were taken to be written by Europeans who have lived and worked in Europe though not necessarily published in Europe. Translations, reviews and notes are not included. The compilation was done by means of bibliographies, newsletters and, last but not least, by means of correspondence.

For surveys of 'Research in Progress', 'Publications since 1980', 'In Press', 'Papers', 'Theses', and 'Suggestions for Future Research', which also encompass France, Germany, the United Kingdom, and Italy, see Barbara Godard, *Inventory of Research in Canadian and Quebec Literatures: Prepared for the Research Committee of The Association for Canadian and Quebec Literatures* (Downsview: York University, 1983).

AUSTRIA

Jantz, Ursula. ' "Orphans' Progress" in Its Canadian and Universal Context.' In *Essays in Honour of Erwin Stürzl on His Sixtieth Birthday*, James Hogg, ed. Salzburg: Institut für englische Sprache und Literatur, Universität Salzburg, 1980, pp. 302-09.

Stanzel, Franz K. 'Acrosticountry.' *Zeitschrift der Gesellschaft für Kanada-Studien*, 4, 2 (1984), 5-10.

——————. 'Texts Recycled: "Found" Poems Found in Canada.' In *Gaining Ground: European Critics on Canadian Literature*, Robert Kroetsch and Reingard M. Nischik, eds. Edmonton: NeWest Press, 1985, pp. 91-106.

Wögenbauer, Werner. 'Le mythe de la terre dans *Trente arpents* de Ringuet.' In *Lectures européennes de la littérature québécoise: Actes du Colloque international de Montréal (avril 1981)*, Jean Cléo Godin et al., eds. Ottawa: Lémeac, 1982, pp. 229-45.

Zacharasiewicz, Waldemar. 'Auf dem Weg zur eigenen Identität: Zur Situation der anglo-kanadischen Literatur heute.' *Die Presse: Unabhängige Tageszeitung für Österreich*, 26/27 (Mai 1984), Literaricum p. 5.

——————. 'The Invention of a Region: The Art of Fiction in Jack Hodgins' ' Stories.' In *Gaining Ground: European Critics on Canadian Literature*, Robert Kroetsch and Reingard M. Nischik, eds., pp. 186-91.

BELGIUM

Delbaere-Garant, Jeanne. 'Isolation and Community in Jack Hodgins' Short Stories.' *Recherches Anglaises et Américaines*, 16 (1983), 31-44.

_____. 'Decolonizing the Self in *Surfacing, Bear,* and *A Fringe of Leaves.*' In *Colonisations: Rencontres Australie-Canada,* Xavier Pons and Marcienne Rocard, eds. Toulouse: Université de Toulouse-Le Mirail, 1985, pp. 67-78.

Delhez-Sarlet, Claudette. ' "Québécité" et "belgéité": Jacques Godbout et Pierre Mertens.' In *Lectures européennes de la littérature québécoise,* Jean Cléo Godin et al., eds., pp. 209-24.
eds., pp. 209-24.

Doyen, Victor. 'Elements Towards a Spatial Reading of Malcolm Lowry's *Under the Volcano.*' *English Studies,* 50, 1 (February 1969), 65-74.

Klinkenberg, Jean-Marie. 'Lecture de l'intertexte québécois: représentation de la culture et de la littérature du Québec auprès de quelques publics européens.' In *Lectures européennes de la littérature québécoise,* Jean Cléo Godin et al., eds., pp. 140-83.

Neetens, Wim. 'Margaret Atwood and the anti-wanhoop: *Je bent gelukkig.*' *Nieuw Vlaams Tijdschrift,* 35, 2 (1982), 215-17.

_____. 'Margaret Atwood: Tien gedichten uit *Je bent gelukkig.*' *Nieuw Vlaams Tijdschrift,* 35, 2 (1982), 218-28.

Pagnoulle, Christine. *Malcolm Lowry: Voyage au fond de nos abîmes.* Lausanne: L'Age d'Homme, 1977.

Piron, Maurice. 'L'accueil réservé à la littérature québécoise en Belgique.' In *Lectures européennes de la littérature québécoise,* Jean Cléo Godin et al., eds., pp. 81-88.

Popovic, Pierre. 'Éditer de la poésie . . . : un acte politique? Réflexions sur quelques strategies editoriales.' In *Lectures europeennes de la littérature québécoise,* Jean Cléo Godin et al., eds., pp. 312-20.

Racelle-Latin, Danielle. 'Victor-Lévy Beaulieu ou la crise narcissique de l'écrivain québécois.' In *Lectures européennes de la littérature québécoise,* Jean Cléo Godin et al., eds., pp. 188-208.

Vrebos, Pascal. 'Lecture de Michel Tremblay.' In *Lectures européennes de la littérature québécoise,* Jean Cléo Godin et al., eds., pp. 366-82.

CZECHOSLOVAKIA

Janovcová, Eva. 'Literary Problems of French Canada.' *Světová Literatura,* 1 (1967), 44-50. (In Czech.)

_____. 'Réjean Ducharme, l'homme qui ne voulait pas être avalé.' *Světová Literatura,* 2 (1968), 223-30. (In Czech.)

DENMARK

Carlsen, Jørn. 'Dorothy Livesay: Interview.' *Kunapipi,* 1, 1 (1979), 30-34.

_____. 'Aksel Sandemose and Canadian Prairie Fiction.' In *English Literature of the Dominions: Writings on Australia, Canada and New Zealand,* Konrad Gross and Wolfgang Klooss, eds. Würzburg: Königshausen and Neumann, 1981, pp. 51-59.

_____. 'Canadian Prairie Fiction: Towards a New Past (Margaret Laurence, Robert Kroetsch, Rudy Wiebe).' In *A Sense of Place: Essays in Post-Colonial Literatures,* Britta Olinder, ed. Göteborg: The English Department, Göteborg University, 1984, pp. 91-97.

Dyrkjøb, Jan Ulrik. *Northrop Fryes litteraturteori.* Copenhagen: Berlingske, 1979.

Hastrup, Inger, ed. *Canada: Native Peoples and Immigrants.* Copenhagen: Gyldendal, 1981.

Rutherford, Anna, ed. *Common Wealth.* Aarhus, 1971. (Proceedings of the first conference of Commonwealth literature held in Europe.)

Rutherford, Anna and Donald Hannah, eds. *Commonwealth Short Stories.* 1971; 4th ed., London: Macmillan, 1981.

FEDERAL REPUBLIC OF GERMANY

Arns, Karl. 'Neue anglokanadische Literatur.' *Die Neueren Sprachen,* 45 (1937), 398-403, 441-48.

Bastein, Friedel H. 'Zur kanadischen Suche nach einer nationalen Identität: Harry J. Boyles Roman *The Great Canadian Novel.*' In *Literarische Ansichten der Wirklichkeit: Studien zur Wirklichkeitskonstitution in englischsprachiger Literatur: To Honour Johannes Kleinstück,* Hans-Heinrich Freitag and Peter Hühn, eds. Frankfurt, etc.: Lang, 1980, pp. 383-400.

——————. 'Zum Fortleben Catulls in der nordamerikanischen Literatur des 20. Jahrhunderts.' In *Die amerikanische Literatur in der Weltliteratur: Themen und Aspekte—Festschrift zum 60. Geburtstag von Rudolf Haas,* Claus Uhlig and Volker Bischoff, eds. Berlin: Schmidt, 1982, pp. 231-51.

Beutler, Bernhard. *Der Einfluss des Imagismus auf die moderne kanadische Lyrik englischer Sprache.* Europäische Hochschulschriften, No. 57. Frankfurt, etc.: Lang, 1978.

Bonheim, Helmut. 'Topoi of the Canadian Short Story.' *Dalhousie Review,* 60 (Winter 1980/81), 659-69.

——————. *The Narrative Modes: Techniques of the Short Story.* Cambridge: D. S. Brewer, 1982.

——————. 'He Didn't Look Back: Literary Tradition and the Canadian (Winter 1980/81), 659-69.

——————. 'He Didn't Look Back: Literary Tradition and the Canadian Short Story.' *Queen's Quarterly,* 89 (1982), 398-403.

——————. 'Conative Solicitude and the Anaphoric Pronoun in the Canadian Short Story.' In *Sprachtheorie und Angewandte Linguistik: Festschrift für Alfred Wollmann,* Werner Welte, ed. Tübinger Beiträge zur Linguistik, 195. Tübingen: Narr, 1982, pp. 77-86.

——————. 'How Stories Begin: Devices of Exposition in 600 English, American and Canadian Short Stories.' *REAL: The Yearbook of Research in English and American Literature,* 1 (1982), 191-226.

——————. 'Narration in the Second Person.' *Recherches Anglaises et Américaines,* 16 (1983), 69-80.

Düsterhaus, Gerhard. 'Kanadische Kurzprosa für den Englischunterricht in den Sekundarstufen I und II.' *Paderborner Studien,* 3/4 (1981), 181-87.

Goetsch, Paul. *Das Romanwerk Hugh MacLennans: Eine Studie zum literarischen Nationalismus in Kanada.* Britannica et Americana, 9. Hamburg: de Gruyter, 1961.

_____. 'Die anglokanadische Lyrik: Bemerkungen zu A. J. M. Smiths *The Oxford Book of Canadian Verse.' Die Neueren Sprachen,* 10 (1961), 414-23.

_____, ed. *Hugh MacLennan.* Critical Views on Canadian Writers, No. 8. Toronto, etc.: McGraw-Hill Ryerson, 1973.

_____. 'Too Long to the Courtly Muses: Hugh MacLennan as a Contemporary Writer.' *Canadian Literature,* 10 (Autumn 1961), 13-31; rpt. in *The Canadian Novel in the Twentieth Century,* George Woodcock, ed. New Canadian Library, No. 115. Toronto: McClelland & Stewart, 1975, pp. 103-14.

_____. 'Der literarische Nationalismus in Kanada seit 1960.' In *Literaturen in englischer Sprache: Ein Überblick über englischsprachige Nationalliteraturen ausserhalb Englands,* Heinz Kosok und Horst Priessnitz, eds. Bonn: Bouvier, 1977, pp. 122-40.

_____. 'Kanada.' In *Commonwealth-Literatur,* Jürgen Schäfer, ed. Düsseldorf, Bern: Bagel, Francke, 1981, pp. 79-101, 202ff., 211-16.

_____. 'Brian Moore's Canadian Fiction.' In *Studies in Anglo-Irish Literature,* Heinz Kosok, ed. Bonn: Bouvier, 1982, pp. 345-56.

_____. 'Das Bild der Vereinigten Staaten in der anglokanadischen Literatur der Gegenwart.' *Die amerikanische Literatur in der Weltliteratur: Themen und Aspekte—Festschrift zum 60. Geburtstag von Rudolf Haas,* Claus Uhlig and Volker Bischoff, eds., pp. 476-97.

_____. 'Ökologische Aspekte der Werke von Margaret Atwood.' In *Zur Literatur und Kultur Kanadas: Eine Erlanger Ringvorlesung,* Dieter Meindl, ed. Erlangen: Palm & Enke, 1984, pp. 109-28.

_____. 'Margaret Atwood's *Life Before Man* As a Novel of Manners.' In *Gaining Ground: European Critics on Canadian Literature,* Robert Kroetsch and Reingard M. Nischik, eds., pp. 137-49.

Gross, Konrad. 'Looking Back in Anger? Frederick Niven, W. O. Mitchell and Robert Kroetsch on the History of the Canadian West.' *Journal of Canadian Fiction,* 3, 2 (1974), 49-54.

_____. 'Literary Criticism in German on English-Canadian Literature: Commentary and Bibliography.' *German-Canadian Yearbook,* 6 (1981), 305-10.

_____ and Wolfgang Klooss, eds. *English Literature of the Dominions: Writings on Australia, Canada and New Zealand.* Würzburg: Königshausen and Neumann, 1981.

_____. 'The Image of French-Canada in Early English-Canadian Fiction.' In *English Literature of the Dominions,* Gross and Klooss, eds., pp. 69-97.

_____. 'Kanada entdeckt seine Entdecker: Die Reiseberichte von "fur traders" und "explorers" und die Problematik der anglokanadischen Gründungsliteratur.' *Zeitschrift der Gesellschaft für Kanada-Studien,* 2, 2 (1982), 5-17.

_____ and Wolfgang Klooss, eds. *Voices from Distant Lands: Poetry in the Commonwealth.* Würzburg: Königshausen and Neumann, 1983.

_____. 'English-Canadian Literature in German Perspective: Commentary and Bibliography, Continued and Supplemented.' *German-Canadian Yearbook* (1983), 234-38.

——————. 'Das Verhältnis von Evolutionstheorie und Geschichtsverständnis im Dokumentargedicht E. J. Pratts.' In *Zur Literatur und Kultur Kanadas: Eine Erlanger Ringvorlesung*, Dieter Meindl, ed., pp. 67-84.

Harth, Helene. 'Hubert Aquin und der "Nouveau Roman."' In *Zur Literatur und Kultur Kanadas: Eine Erlanger Ringvorlesung*, Dieter Meindl, ed., pp. 129-48.

Kieseritzky, Helene von. *Englische Tierdichtung: Eine Untersuchung uber Rudyard Kipling, Charles G. D. Roberts und Ernest Thompson Seton.* Diss. Berlin, 1935.

Klooss, Wolfgang. 'Louis Riel and the West: Literary Images of a Canadian Myth.' *Zeitschrift der Gesellschaft für Kanada-Studien*, 2, 2 (1982), 19-36.

——————. 'Narrative Modes and Forms of Literary Perception in Rudy Wiebe's *The Scorched-Wood People.*' In *Gaining Ground: European Critics on Canadian Literature*, Robert Kroetsch and Reingard M. Nischik, eds., pp. 205-21.

—————— and Konrad Gross, eds. *English Literature of the Dominions: Writings on Australia, Canada and New Zealand.* Würzburg: Königshausen and Neumann, 1981.

——————. 'Canada's Forgotten People: The Métis in Nineteenth-Century Fiction and Drama.' *World Literature Written in English*, 24, 1 (Summer 1984), 144-57.

—————— and Konrad Gross, eds. *Voices from Distant Lands: Poetry in the Poetry in the Commonwealth.* Würzburg: Königshausen and Neumann, 1983.

Lang, Hans-Joachim. 'Joshua 1980: Mordecai Richlers Held.' In *Zur Literatur und Kultur Kanadas: Eine Erlanger Ringvorlesung*, pp. 85-108.

Langenfeldt, Gösta. 'Die Literatur des britischen Kolonialreiches.' *Englische Studien*, 61 (1926/27), 220-80.

Martini, Jürgen, ed. *Leaflets of a Surfacing Response: 1st Symposium Canadian Literature in Germany.* Bremen: Univ. of Bremen Press, 1980.

——————. 'West Indian Literature in Canada: Austin Clarke.' In *Leaflets of a Surfacing Response*, Martini, ed., pp. 42-8.

Meindl, Dieter, ed. *Zur Literatur und Kultur Kanadas: Eine Erlanger Ringvorlesung*, Erlanger Studien, vol. 54. Erlangen: Palm & Enke, 1984.

——————. 'Kanadas Verhältnis zu den USA im Spiegel Seiner Literatur.' In Dieter Meindl, ed., pp. 173-94.

Mengenkampff, Ursula von. *Die 'Grenze' in der anglokanadischen Literatur.* Diss. Riga, 1935.

Nischik, Reingard M. 'Multiple Plotting in Margaret Laurence's *The Stone Angel.*' In *The Stone Angel* by Margaret Laurence: A Collection of Critical Essays, Michel Fabre, ed., *Études Canadiennes/Canadian Studies*, 11 (1981), 121-29.

——————. *Einsträngigkeit und Mehrsträngigkeit der Handlungsführung in literarischen Texten: Dargestellt insbesondere an englischen, amerikanischen und kanadischen Romanen des 20. Jahrhunderts.* Tübinger Beiträge zur Anglistik, 1. Tübingen: Narr, 1981. [English summary in *English and American Studies in German 1981*, Werner Habicht, ed. Tübingen: Narr, 1982, pp. 23-25.]

_____. 'Zur Behandlung anglo-kanadischer Short Stories: Tendenzen, Materialien und Hilfsmittel.' *Literatur in Wissenschaft und Unterricht*, 15, 4 (Dezember 1982), 381-98.

_____. 'Norman Levine: "By a Frozen River".' *English for Seniors 1982/83*, II. Cologne: West German Broadcasting Corporation (WDR), 1982, 7-11; 2nd rev. ed., *English for Seniors 1984/85*, II, 19-23.

_____, ed. *Short Short Stories: An Anthology*. Paderborn: Schöningh, 1983.

_____. 'Literatur und Computer: *Swift Current*, die erste literarische Datenbank.' *Zeitschrift der Gesellschaft für Kanada-Studien*, 4, 2 (1984), 136-40.

_____. 'Narrative Technique in Aritha van Herk's Novels.' *Zeitschrift der Gesellschaft für Kanada-Studien*, 3, 2 (1983), 25-34; rpt. in *Gaining Ground: European Critics on Canadian Literature*, Robert Kroetsch Reingard M. Nischik, eds., pp. 107-20.

_____, ed., *Hilfsmittel im Studium der englischen Philologie (Anglistik, Amerikanistik und Kanadistik), Literaturwissenschaft, Sprachwissenschaft und Fachdidaktik*. Cologne: English Seminar of the University of Cologne, 1984.

_____. 'Hilfsmittel der Anglistik, Amerikanistik und Kanadistik: Kommentierte Auswahlbibliographie zur Literaturwissenschaft.' In *Hilfsmittel im Studium der Englischen Philologie*, Reingard M. Nischik, ed., pp. 1-23.

_____. 'Point Counterpoint in Ethel Wilson's *Swamp Angel*.' *World Literature Written in English*, 23, 2 (Spring 1984), 375-81.

_____. *Short Short Stories: Analyses and Additional Material*. Paderborn: Schöningh, 1985.

_____ and Robert Kroetsch, eds. *Gaining Ground: European Critics on Canadian Literature*. Edmonton: NeWest Press, 1985.

_____. 'European Publications on Canadian Literature.' In *Gaining Ground: European Critics on Canadian Literature*, Robert Kroetsch and Reingard M. Nischik, eds., pp.

_____. 'New Horizons: Canadian Literature in Europe.' In *Gaining Ground: European Critics on Canadian Literature*, Robert Kroetsch and Reingard M. Nischik, eds., pp. 249-76.

Pache, Walter. 'Moderne kanadische Literatur: Ein Überblick über wichtige Hilfsmittel.' *Literatur in Wissenschaft und Unterricht*, 7 (1974), 122-33.

_____. 'Auf der Suche nach Identität: Zur Situation der englisch-kanadischen Literatur.' *Akzente*, 33 (1976), 196-216.

_____. 'Der Fall Grove—Vorleben und Nachleben des Schriftstellers Felix Paul Greve.' *German-Canadian Yearbook*, 5 (1979), 121-36.

_____. 'English-Canadian Fiction & the Pastoral Tradition.' *Canadian Literature*, 86 (Autumn 1980), 15-28.

_____. 'Formen der Idylle in der modernen Erzählliteratur Kanadas.' *Arcadia*, 15 (1980), 29-43.

_____. 'Kipling in Canada: Aspects of Literary Imperialism.' In *Leaflets of a Surfacing Response*, Jürgen Martini, ed., pp. 80-87.

—————. 'The Dilettante in Exile: Grove at the Centenary of His Birth.' *Canadian Literature*, 90 (1981), 187-91.

—————. 'Die Entwicklung der Kanadistik in Deutschland und ihr derzeitiger Stand.' *Annalen*, 3 (1981), 120-34.

—————. 'Zur Situation der deutschsprachigen Kanadistik.' *Zeitschrift der Gesellschaft für Kanada-Studien*, 1, 1 (1981), 9-18.

—————. 'Wo liegt Kanada? Hinweise auf ein unbekanntes Land.' *Der Fremdsprachliche Unterricht*, 15 (1981), 84-94.

—————. *Einführung in die Kanadistik*. Darmstadt: Wissenschaftliche Buchgesellschaft, 1981.

—————. 'Geschichte und Gegenwart in der Literatur Kanadas.' In *Zur Literatur und Kultur Kanadas*, Dieter Meindl, ed., pp. 1-26.

—————. ' "The Fiction Makes Us Real": Aspects of Postmodernism in Canada.' In *Gaining Ground: European Critics on Canadian Literature*, Robert Kroetsch and Reingard M. Nischik, eds., pp. 64-78.

Peper, Jürgen. 'Paradise Regained: Marshall McLuhan's Instructive Escape from History.' In *Forms and Functions of History in American Literature: Essays in Honor of Ursula Brumm*, Winfried Fluck, Jürgen Peper and Willi Paul Adams, eds. Berlin: Schmidt, 1981, pp. 160-79.

Plocher, Hanspeter. 'Soziale Aspekte im modernen frankokanadischen Theater.' *Zeitschrift der Gesellschaft für Kanada-Studien*, 4, 2 (1984), 21-32.

Pynsent, Robert. 'Nationaler Sensualismus: Dreizehn kanadische Dichter.' *Akzente*, 23 (1976), 242-55.

Riedel, Walter E. 'Kanadische Lyrik in deutscher Übersetzung.' *German-Canadian Yearbook*, 5 (1979), 137-42.

—————. *Das literarische Kanadabild: Eine Studie zur Rezeption kanadischer Literatur in deutscher Übersetzung*. Studien zur Germanistik, Anglistik und Komparatistik. Bonn: Bouvier, 1980.

Schäfer, Jürgen, ed. *Commonwealth-Literatur*. Düsseldorf, Bern: Bagel, Francke, 1981.

—————. 'Auf dem Weg zur Nationalliteratur: Die Suche nach Symbolen.' *Zeitschrift der Gesellschaft für Kanada-Studien*, 3, 1 (1983), 29-37.

—————. 'Anglo-Kanadische Romanciers der Gegenwart.' *Die Neueren Sprachen*, 83, 4 (1984), 422-36.

—————. 'A Farewell to Europe: Rudy Wiebe's *The Temptations of Big Bear* and Robert Kroetsch's *Gone Indian*.' In *Gaining Ground: European Critics on Canadian Literature*, Robert Kroetsch and Reingard M. Nischik, eds., pp. 79-90.

Schoell, Konrad. 'Bilder der sozialen Wirklichkeit in der Québec-Lyrik.' *Zeitschrift der Gesellschaft für Kanada-Studien*, 4, 1 (1984), 83-95.

FRANCE

Albisser, Marie-Yvette. 'Aspects de la focalisation dans *A Bird in the House*.' In *Recherches Anglaises et Américaines*, 16 (1983), 21-30.

Dommergues, André. 'Order and Chaos in *The Stone Angel*.' In *The Stone Angel* by Margaret Laurence: A Collection of Critical Essays, Michel Fabre, ed. *Études Canadiennes/Canadian Studies*, 11 (1981), 63-71.

_____. 'Margaret Laurence Papers.' In *The Stone Angel* by Margaret Laurence: A Collection of Critical Essays, pp. 73-76.

_____. 'La mort dans le cycle de Manawaka.' *Études Canadiennes/Canadian Studies*, 14 (juin 1983), 81-87.

Durand, Régis. 'L'individuel et le politique: notes sur les romans de Margaret Atwood et Leonard Cohen.' *Études Canadiennes/Canadian Studies*, 1 (1975), 63-72.

_____. 'Les études canadiennes dans les universités françaises.' *Études Canadiennes/Canadian Studies*, 1 (1975), 123-28.

_____. 'La littérature canadienne de langue anglaise dans la modernité nord-américaine.' *Études Canadiennes/Canadian Studies*, 2 (1976), 63-69.

_____. ' "The Forest Path to the Spring" (Malcolm Lowry): événements d'espace.' In *Recherches Anglaises et Américaines*, 16 (1983), 121-30.

Études Canadiennes/Canadian Studies, 10 (1981). [Special issue on Louis Hemon.]

Fabre, Michel, ed. *The Stone Angel* by Margaret Laurence: A Collection of Critical Essays. *Études Canadiennes/Canadian Studies*, 11 (1981).

_____. 'Margaret Laurence on *The Stone Angel*' [interview]. In *The Stone Angel* by Margaret Laurence: A Collection of Critical Essays, pp. 11-22.

_____. 'From *The Stone Angel* to *The Diviners*: An Interview with Margaret Laurence.' In *A Place to Stand On: Essays by and about Margaret Laurence*, George Woodcock, ed. Edmonton: NeWest Press, 1983, pp. 193-209.

_____. 'Devineurs/devins: Lectures du livre du monde dans *The Diviners*.' *Echos du Commonwealth*, 7 (1981-82), 79-90.

_____. 'L'Ange et l'eau vive: réseaux métaphoriques et oppositions structurales dans *The Stone Angel*.' *Études Anglaises*, 35, 1 (janvier 1982), 57-70.

_____. 'Text, Micro-Text and Mini-Text: The Forms and Functions of Narrative Units in Margaret Laurence's *The Diviners*.' *Commonwealth Novel in English*, 1 (July 1982), 166-90.

_____. 'Words and the World: *The Diviners* As an Exploration of the Book of Life.' *Canadian Literature*, 93 (Summer 1982), 60-78; rpt. in *A Place to Stand On: Essays by and about Margaret Laurence*, George Woodcock, ed., pp. 247-69.

_____. ' "Orphans' Progress," Reader's Progress—Le "on dit" et le "non-dit" chez Mavis Gallant.' In *Recherches Anglaises et Américaines*, 16 (1983), 57-67; trans. in *Gaining Ground: European Critics on Canadian Literature*,' Robert Kroetsch and Reingard M. Nischik, eds. pp. 152-60.

Formentelli, Eliane. 'La lettre assourdissante: pour un "verbier" de Claude Gauvreau.' In *Lectures européennes de la littérature québécoise: Actes du Colloque international de Montréal (avril 1981)*, Jean Cléo Godin et al., eds., pp. 327-45.

Guillaume, Pierre, Jean-Michel Lacroix and Pierre Spriet, eds. *Canada et Canadiens*. Bordeaux: Presses Universitaires de Bordeaux, 1984.

Lacroix, Jean-Michel. 'La quête d'identité dans les romans de Hugh MacLennan.' *Annales du CRAA* (Centre de recherches sur l'Amérique anglophone), 11, 2 (1974), 5-20.

——————. 'A propos de *La Sagouine:* entretien avec Antonine Maillet.' *Études Canadiennes/Canadian Studies*, 3 (1977), 101-11.

——————. 'Les mythes fondateurs de la littérature canadienne.' *Études Canadiennes/Canadian Studies*, 8 (juin 1980), 21-32.

——————. 'Religion et société chez Morley Callaghan.' In *Le Facteur religieux en Amérique du Nord*, No. 3: *Millénium, république chrétienne aux États-Unis; religion et société au Canada*, Jean Béranger and Pierre Guillaume, eds. Talence: Maison des Sciences de l'Homme d'Aquitaine, Univ. de Bordeaux III, 1982, pp. 153-69.

——————, Pierre Guillaume and Pierre Spriet, eds. *Canada et Canadiens*. Bordeaux: Presses Universitaires de Bordeaux, 1984.

Ladousse, Gillian. 'Le Discours de la fatalité dans *Crackpot* d'Adèle Wiseman.' In *Le Facteur religieux en Amérique du Nord*, No. 2: *Apocalypse et autres travaux*, Jean Béranger, ed. Bordeaux: Maison des Sciences de l'Homme d'Aquitaine, Univ. de Bordeaux III, 1981, pp. 195-205.

Marchesson, Hélène. 'Identité et méconnaissance ou reconnaissance de l'altérité chez Margaret Laurence, Leonard Cohen, Joe Rosenblatt et A. M. Klein.' *Études Canadiennes/Canadian Studies*, 4 (juin 1978), 65-76.

Marmier, Jean. 'Le père Gustave Lamarche, pionnier du théâtre québécois.' *Études Canadiennes/Canadian Studies*, 1 (1975), 105-109.

——————. 'L'enseignement de la littérature canadienne française à l'Université de Haute-Bretagne.' *Études Canadiennes/Canadian Studies*, 1 (1975), 129-30.

——————. 'Le sabbat des enfants dans le roman québécois contemporain.' *Études Canadiennes/Canadian Studies*, 2 (1976), 25-33.

——————. 'Les personnages anglophones dans le théâtre québécois.' *Études Canadiennes/Canadian Studies*, 4 (juin 1978), 27-39.

——————. 'Maria Chapdelaine et l'avenir.' *Études Canadiennes/Canadian Studies*, 10 (juin 1978), 99-108.

——————. 'Les ouvrages d'histoire littéraire francaise et la littérature du Canada.' *Études Canadiennes/Canadian Studies*, 12 (juin 1982), 125-34.

——————. 'L'Acadie dans son théâtre.' *Études Canadiennes/Canadian Studies*, 13 (decembre 1982), 201-17.

——————. 'Trois étapes d'une découverte: *Bonheur d'occasion*, Marie-Claire Blais et Réjean Ducharme, Antonine Maillet.' In *Lectures européennes de la littérature québécoise*, Jean Cléo Godin et al., eds., pp. 108-33.

Perrot, Michel and Philippe Royer. 'Le théâtre et les médias.' In *Canada et Canadiens*, Pierre Guillaume, Jean-Michel Lacroix and Pierre Spriet, eds., pp. 343-76.

Perrotin, Françoise. 'Richler et Londres: de l'utilisation romanesque de l'éxperience.' *Études Canadiennes/Canadian Studies*, 8 (juin 1980), 93-106.

_____. *Les structures du vraisemblable dans trois romans de Mordecai Richler.* Bordeaux: Univ. de Bordeaux III, 1981.

Piccione, Marie-Lyne. 'Régards sur la littérature québécoise.' In *Canada et Canadiens*, Pierre Guillaume, Jean-Michel Lacroix and Pierre Spriet, eds., pp. 243-85.

Pitavy-Souques, Danièle. ' "Deeper Into the Forest": écriture et peinture dans *Klee Wyck.*' In *Recherches Anglaises et Américaines*, 16 (1983), 81-93.

Pons, Xavier and Marcienne Rocard, eds., *Colonisations: Rencontres Australie-Canada.* Toulouse: Univ. de Toulouse-Le Mirail, 1985.

Quivy, Mireille. 'La structure hyperbolique de *The Diviners* (Margaret Laurence).' *Études Canadiennes/Canadian Studies*, 16 (juin 1984), 11-22.

Resch, Yannick. 'La problématique urbaine dans deux romans montréalais de Gabrielle Roy: *Bonheur d'Occasion* et *Alexandre Chenevert.*' *Études Canadiennes/Canadian Studies*, 1 (1975), 79-87.

_____. 'La critique québécoise à la recherche de sa québécité.' In *Lectures européennes de la littérature québécoise*, Jean Cléo Godin et al., eds., pp. 247-58.

Ritz, Regis. 'Fête et défaite de l'ouest canadien dans *The Studhorse Man* de Robert Kroetsch.' In *Séminaires 1980*, Jean Béranger, Jean Cazemajon and Pierre Spriet, eds. Talence: Publications de la Maison des Sciences de l'Homme d'Aquitaine, Univ. de Bordeaux III, 1981, pp. 177-84.

Rocard, Marcienne. 'The Métis in Margaret Laurence's Manawaka Works.' *Études Canadiennes/Canadian Studies*, 5 (décembre 1978), 113-17.

_____. 'Margaret Laurence's Attempt at Audio-Visual Fiction.' *Kunapipi*, 1, 2 (1979), 91-100.

_____. 'Margaret Laurence s'oriente-t-elle vers un roman audio-visuel?' *Études Canadiennes/Canadian Studies*, 8 (juin 1980), 113-20.

_____. 'La Femme objet-de-consommation dans *The Edible Woman* de Margaret Atwood.' *Caliban*, 17 (1980), 111-20.

_____. 'Woman and Woman in *The Stone Angel.*' In *The Stone Angel by Margaret Laurence: A Collection of Critical Essays*, Michel Fabre, ed., pp. 77-87.

_____. 'The Dispossession Theme in Margaret Laurence's *The Diviners.*' *World Literature Written in English*, 21, 1 (Spring 1982), 109-14; rpt. in *A Place to Stand On: Essays by and about Margaret Laurence*, George Woodcock, ed., pp. 241-46.

_____. '*Who Do You Think You Are?* d'Alice Munro: un titre unifiant.' In *Recherches Anglaises et Américaines*, 16 (1983), 45-55.

_____. and Xavier Pons, eds., *Colonisations: Rencontres Australie-Canada.* Toulouse: Univ. de Toulouse-Le Mirail, 1985.

_____. 'Schèmes de la circularité dans *The Temptations of Big Bear.*' In *Colonisations: Rencontres Australie-Canada*, Xavier Pons and Marcienne Rocard, eds., pp. 155-67.

Royer, Philippe and Michel Perrot. 'Le théâtre et les médias.' In *Canada et Canadiens*, Pierre Guillaume, Jean-Michel Lacroix and Pierre Spriet, eds., 343-76.

Spriet, Pierre. 'La mythologie canadienne dans l'oeuvre de Margaret Atwood.' *Annales de Centre de Recherche sur l'Amérique Anglophone*, 3 (1974), 21-38.

_____. 'Parole et terre dans la poésie canadienne contemporaine.' *Études Canadiennes/Canadian Studies*, 1 (1975), 89-103.

_____. 'Le renouveau littéraire contemporain en Canada anglais.' *Études Canadiennes/Canadian Studies*, 4 (1978), 77-84.

_____. 'Frye et la théorie des genres.' In *Théorie des genres et communication*. Bordeaux: Maison des Sciences de l'Homme d'Aquitaine, 1978, pp. 43-86.

_____. 'Margaret Atwood et la condition de l'écrivain au Canada: réflexions d'un témoix privilégié.' *Annales du Centre de Recherche sur l'Amérique Anglophone*, 5 (1980), 131-40.

_____. 'L'homme de *Lady Oracle*.' *Études Canadiennes/Canadian Studies*, 9 (1980), 63-73.

_____. 'Les poètes juifs de Montréal et le christianisme.' *Le Facteur religieux en Amérique du Nord. Annales du Centre de Recherche sur l'Amérique Anglophone*, 5 (1980), pp. 177-93.

_____. '*Beautiful Losers:* une technique de l'éclatement ou la cohérence de l'incohérence.' *Annales du Centre de Recherche sur l'Amérique Anglophone*, 6 (1981), 165-75.

_____. 'Narrative and Thematic Patterns in *The Stone Angel*.' *Études Canadiennes/Canadian Studies*, 11 (1981), 105-19.

_____. 'Écart et conjonction dans *The Diviners*.' *Echos du Commonwealth*, 7 (1981-1982), 39-57.

_____. 'Formes du récit et vision religieuse du monde dans les romans de .R. Wiebe.' *Le Facteur religieux en Amérique du Nord*, 4 (1983), 13-32.

_____. 'Les formes du refus dans les nouvelles de Rudy Wiebe.' *Recherches Anglaises et Américaines*, 16 (1983), 105-19.

_____, Pierre Guillaume and Jean-Michel Lacroix, eds. *Canada et Canadiens*. Bordeaux: Presses Universitaires de Bordeaux, 1984.

_____. 'Une littérature canadienne d'expression anglaise en gestation.' In *Canada et Canadiens*, pp. 287-342.

_____. 'Haliburton, victime de Sam Slick: les mésaventures d'un écrivain colonial en Amérique du Nord Britannique.' In *Colonisations: Rencontres Australie-Canada*, Xavier Pons and Marcienne Rocard, eds., pp. 287-342.

_____. 'Structure and Meaning in Rudy Wiebe's *My Lovely Enemy*.' In *Gaining Ground: European Critics on Canadian Literature*, Robert Kroetsch and Reingard M. Nischik, eds., pp. 53-63.

Vauthier, Simone. 'Names and Naming in *The Stone Angel*.' *Recherches Anglaises et Américaines*, 14 (1981), 237-54.

_____. 'Notes on the Narrative Voice(s) in *The Stone Angel*.' In *The Stone Angel by Margaret Laurence: A Collection of Critical Essays*, Michel Fabre, ed., pp. 131-53.

—————. 'A Transatlantic Conversation with Carol Shields.' *Études Canadiennes/Canadian Studies*, 12 (1982), 165-74.

—————, ed. (Special issue on 'La Nouvelle Canadienne Anglophone.' *Recherches Anglaises et Américaines*, 16 (1983).)

—————. 'Notes sur l'emploi du présent dans "The Road to Rankin's Point" d'Alistair MacLeod.' In *Recherches Anglaises et Américaines*, 16 (1983), 143-58.

—————. 'Photo-Roman: *The Wars* of Timothy Findley.' *Études Canadiennes/Canadian Studies*, 14 (juin 1983), 101-19.

—————. 'An interview of Norman Levine.' *Études Canadiennes/Canadian Studies*, 16 (juin 1984), 5-10.

—————. 'Structure and Antistructure in Margaret Laurence's *The Stone Angel*.' *Zeitschrift der Gesellschaft für Kanada-Studien*, 4, 2 (1984), 11-20.

—————. 'L'écrivain comme colon: Martin Avery et la conquête d'un espace fictionnel.' In *Colonisations: Rencontres Australie-Canada*, Xavier Pons and Marcienne Rocard, eds., pp. 119-36.

—————. 'The Dubious Battle of Storytelling: Narrative Strategies in Timothy Findley's *The Wars*.' In *Gaining Ground: European Critics on Canadian Literature*, Robert Kroetsch and Reingard M. Nischik, eds., pp. 11-39.

Viatte, Auguste. *Histoire Comparée des Littératures Francophones*. Paris: Nathan, 1980.

GERMAN DEMOCRATIC REPUBLIC

El-Hassan, Karla, ed. and Postscript. Norman Levine, *Der Mann mit dem Notizbuch*. 2nd rev. ed., trans. by Gabriele Bock, Annemarie and Heinrich Böll, Reinhard Wagner. Leipzig: Reclam, 1979.

—————. 'Zum Problem des Nationalen und des Internationalen in der zeitgenössischen bürgerlichen Literaturkritik Anglokanadas.' *Zeitschrift für Anglistik und Amerikanistik*, 28, 2 (1980), 139-47.

—————. 'Die Kurzgeschichten Norman Levines: Ein Beitrag zum Problem des literarischen Zyklus.' *Zeitschrift für Anglistik und Amerikanistik*, 29, 2 (1981), 154-66.

—————. 'Voraussetzungen und Ursachen für die Entstehung von Kurzgeschichtenensembles in der anglokanadischen Literatur.' *Zeitschrift für Anglistik und Amerikanistik*, 32, 1 (1984), 49-58.

—————. 'Reflections on the Special Unity of Stephen Leacock's *Sunshine Sketches of a Little Town*.' In *Gaining Ground: European Critics on Canadian Literature*, Robert Kroetsch and Reingard M. Nischik, eds., pp. 171-85.

Misgin, Marianne. 'Aspekte imperialistischer Massenliteratur in Arthur Haileys Roman *The Moneychangers*.' In *Antiimperialistischer Kampf und Funktion der Literatur in den USA*, Heinz Wüstenhagen, ed. Potsdam, 1979, pp. 61-166.

Müller, Marianne. 'What Is the Matter with Canadian Literature?' *Wissenschaftliche Zeitschrift der Humboldt-Universität zu Berlin*, 30 (1981), 629-35.

HUNGARY

Kopeczi, Béla and Eva Kushner, eds. *Óda a szent löring folyóhoz: Québec mai Francia kölyeszete*. Budapest: Europa, 1978.

ITALY

Andreani, Patrizia. 'Lettura di *Bear* di Marian Engel.' In *Canada: l'immaginazione letteraria*, Alfredo Rizzardi, ed. Abano Terme: Piovan Editore, 1981, pp. 247-56.

Angloamericana, 2, 7 (Primavera 1981). Special issue 'La dimensione canadese.'

Bertinetti, Roberto. 'L'integrazione programmata.' In *Canada: l'immaginazione letteraria*, Alfredo Rizzardi, ed., pp. 263-70.

——————. '*Fifth Business* di Robertson Davies.' In *Canada: metafora per la letteratura: saggi sul romanzo canadese del 1900*, Alfredo Rizzardi, ed. Abano Terme: Piovan Editore, 1981, pp. 62-71.

Bonanno, Giovanni. 'Il Canada e le sue 'due solitudini' in du romanzi di Hugh MacLennan.' In *Canadiana: Aspetti della storia e della letteratura canadese*, Luca Codignola, ed. Venice: Marsilio, 1978, pp. 133-56.

Bruni, Valerio. 'La crisi della comunicazione in *Surfacing* di Margaret Atwood.' In *Canada: metafora per la letteratura*, Alfredo Rizzardi, ed., pp. 106-16.

Capone, Giovanna. 'Il realismo mitico di Hugh MacLennan.' *Spicilegio moderno. Saggi e ricerche di letterature e lingue straniere*, No. 6. Imola: Grafiche Galeati, 1976, pp. 79-102.

——————. *Canada: il villaggio della terra: letteratura canadese di lingua inglese*. Bologna: Pàtron Editore, 1978.

——————. 'Introduzione all'edizione italiana.' In Northrop Frye, *La scrittura secolare*. Bologna: Società Editrice il Mulino, 1978, pp. 7-14.

——————. 'Arcipelago della memoria: *The Diviners* di Margaret Laurence.' *Lunarionuovo*, 1 (1979), 3-19.

——————. 'Margaret Laurence: la tentazione autobiografica.' *Angloamericana*, 2, 7 (Primavera 1981), 85-121.

——————. 'Northrop Frye.' In *I Contemporanei—Novecento americano*, vol. II, Elémire Zolla, ed. Roma: Lucarini, 1983, pp. 559-65.

——————. '*A Bird in the House*: Margaret Laurence on Order and the Artist.' In *Gaining Ground: European Critics on Canadian Literature*, Robert Kroetsch and Reingard M. Nischik, eds., pp. 161-70.

Casotti, Francesco M. '*The Golden Dog* di William Kirby.' In *Canada: l'immaginazione letteraria*, Alfredo Rizzardi, ed., pp. 177-92.

Cena, Adele. 'Arte e Teatro nei romanzi di Robertson Davies.' In *Canada: l'immaginazione letteraria*, Alfredo Rizzardi, ed., pp. 215-32.

Cocchi, Raffaele. '*The Edible Woman* ovvero "L'uomo da mangiare".' In *Canada: metafora per la letteratura*, Alfredo Rizzardi, ed., pp. 90-105.

Codignola, Luca. 'Gli studi canadesi in Italia.' In *Atti del I congresso internazionale di storia americana*. Genova: Tilgher, 1978, pp. 225-33.

_____, ed. *Canadiana: Aspetti della storia e della letteratura canadese.* Venice: Marsilio, 1978.

Comellini, Carla. 'Il paesaggio come simbolo nei romanzi messicani di D. H. Lawrence e di M. Lowry.' In *Canada: metafora per la letteratura,* Alfredo Rizzardi, ed., pp. 29-47.

Crisafulli Jones, Lilla Maria. 'Il viaggio nella grande guerra di Robert Ross.' In *Canada: metafora per la letteratura,* Alfredo Rizzardi, ed., pp. 117-30.

De Rosa, Renato Tullio, ed. *Francia,* 24 (ottobre-dicembre, 1977).(Special issue on Québec.)

Domenichelli, Mario. 'Il mito di Frye.' In *Canada: l'immaginazione letteraria,* Alfredo Rizzardi, ed., pp. 75-106.

Fortier, D'Iberville. 'I rapporti tra l'Italia e il Canada.' In *Canadiana: Aspetti della storia et della letteratura canadese,* Luca Codignola, ed., pp. 11-19.

Fortunati, Vita. 'Il primo studio italiano sulla letteratura canadese.' *Lettore di Provincia,* 39 (1979), 84-87.

Fratangelo, Mario. *Realismo e Simbolismo in alcune opere di Yves Thériault.* Campobasso: Casa Molisana del libro, 1978.

Fratta di Primio, Carla. *'Bonheur d'Occasion* di Gabrielle Roy.' In *Canada: l'immaginazione letteraria,* Alfredo Rizzardi, ed., pp. 193-201.

Giacobelli, Francesco. 'Identità e tradizione nello *humour* di Stephen Leacock.' In *Canada: l'immaginazione letteraria,* Alfredo Rizzardi, ed., pp. 155-76.

_____. 'I *Sunshine Sketches of a Little Town* di S. B. Leacock ovvero: una piccola proposta per fondare alcuni elementi del mito canadese.' In *Canada: metafora per la letteratura,* Alfredo Rizzardi, ed., pp. 11-28.

Gorlier, Claudio. 'La commedia gotica di Margaret Atwood.' In *Canadiana: Aspetti della storia e della letteratura canadese,* Luca Codignola, ed., pp. 121-32.

_____. 'La narrativa breve di Morley Callaghan.' In *Canada: l'immaginazione letteraria,* Alfredo Rizzardi, ed., pp. 39-61.

_____. 'Una, due (o nessuna) solitudine.' *Angloamericana,* 2, 7 (Primavera 1981), 5-32.

_____. 'Nova Scotia: Provincia e Microcosmo.' In *Canada: testi e contesti,* Alfredo Rizzardi, ed. Abano Terme: Piovan Editore, 1983, pp. 31-52.

_____. ed., trans. with an introd. *A. M. Klein, Poesie.* Rome: Bulzoni, 1984.

Jannini, Pasquale A. 'Apollinaire, la francofonia e la poesia del Québec.' In *Canadiana: Aspetti della storia et della letteratura canadese,* Luca Codignola, ed., pp. 115-19.

_____. 'Da l'Hexagone a "Possibles": vicende di riviste e poesia nel Québec.' *Angloamericana,* 2, 7 (Primavera 1981), 33-57.

_____. 'La letteratura del Québec nella storiografia francese del Novecento.' In *Canada: l'immaginazione letteraria,* Alfredo Rizzardi, ed., pp. 23-37.

Linguanti, Elsa. 'Le Figure Dell'Adiectio in *Under the Volcano* di M. Lowry: Ridondanza e Significazione.' *Linguistica e Letteratura,* 4 (1979), 369-92.

_____. 'Allo-fanie: i poeti canadesi della West Coast.' *Angloamericana*, 2, 7 (Primavera 1981), 123-53.

_____. 'Il "Paradiso" canadese nell'opera di Malcolm Lowry.' In *Canada: l'immaginazione letteraria*, Alfredo Rizzardi, ed., pp. 139-54.

Marcato Falzoni, Franca. 'Note sul romanzo quebechense della terra.' *Il Lettore di Provincia* (marzo 1978), 76-84.

_____. 'Dal reale al fantastico nell'opera narrativa di Anne Hébert.' In *Canadiana: Aspetti della storia et della letteratura canadese*, Luca Codignola, ed., pp. 97-109.

_____. 'L'enigma nella cripta: una lettura di Hubert Aquin.' In *Canada: l'immaginazione letteraria*, Alfredo Rizzardi, ed., pp. 119-38.

_____. 'Présence de la littérature québécoise en Italie.' In *Lectures européennes de la littérature québécoise*, Jean Cléo Godin et al., eds., pp. 45-63.

Malançon, Joseph. 'L'evoluzione letteraria del Quebec nel dopoguerra.' In *Canada: l'immaginazione letteraria*, Alfredo Rizzardi, ed., pp. 63-73.

Miglior, Giorgio. 'Articolazione sintattica in tre *poems* di Margaret Atwood.' In *Canada: l'immaginazione letteraria*, Alfredo Rizzardi, ed., pp. 107-17.

Morisco, Gabriella. 'Mordecai Richler: dal romanzo realista al romanzo confessionale.' In *Canada: metafora per la letteratura*, Alfredo Rizzardi, ed., pp. 72-89.

Novelli, Novella. 'Studi canadesi francofoni in Italia.' In *Canada: l'immaginazione letteraria*, Alfredo Rizzardi, ed., pp. 257-61.

_____. 'Traductions italiennes de *Maria Chapdelaine*.' In *Lectures européennes de la littérature québécoise*, Jean Cléo Godin et al., eds., pp. 64-74.

Petroni, Liano. *Letteratura francofona del Canada*. Bologna: Editrice CLUEB, 1982.

Prandi, Carlo. '*Maria Chapdelaine*: Linguaggio e senso.' *Francia*, 24 (ottobre-dicembre 1977), 128-38.

Ricciardi, Caterina. 'Irving Layton: On Poetry: A Conversation.' *Angloamericana*, 2, 7 (Primavera 1981), 155-67.

Rizzardi, Alfredo, ed. *Canada: l'immaginazione letteraria*. Abano Terme: Piovan Editore, 1981.

_____. 'Identità e tradizione nella letteratura canadese.' In *Canada: l'immaginazione letteraria*, Alfredo Rizzardi, ed., pp. 9-22.

_____, ed. *Canada: metafora per la letteratura: saggi sul romanzo canadese del 1900*. Abano Terme: Piovan Editore, 1981.

_____. 'L'ultimo Callaghan.' In *Canada: metafora per la letteratura*, Alfredo Rizzardi, ed., pp. 48-61.

_____, ed. *Canada: testi e contesti*. Abano Terme: Piovan Editore, 1983.

Zoppi, Sergio. 'Un premio Goncourt in Acadia: "Pélagie-la-Charrette" di Antonine Maillet.' *Angloamericana*, 2, 7 (Primavera 1981), 59-84.

NORWAY

Hartveit, Lars. 'Alice Munro and the Canadian Imagination.' In *A Sense of Place: Essays in Post-Colonial Literatures*, Britta Olinder, ed.

Göteborg: The English Department, Göteborg University, 1984, pp. 85-90.
Seyersted, Per. 'Canada: A New Literary Continent.' *Norway-America Association Yearbook* (1981), pp. 12-17.
_____. 'Canada: A Fascinating New Field of Study.' *Språk og språkundervisning* (Oslo), 13 4 (1982), 15-21.
_____. 'Canadisk litteratur.' In *Verdens Litteraturhistorie*, vol. 12. Oslo: 1982, pp. 435-48.

POLAND

Kwaterko, Józef. 'Contemporary Prose in Québec.' *Tworczosc,* 6 (1978), 131-36. (In Polish.)
_____. 'Acadia resurrecta.' *Literatura na Swiecie,* 7 (1980), 264-69.
_____. 'L'accueil réservé à la litterature québécoise en Europe de l'Est.' In *Lectures européennes de la littérature québécoise,* Jean Cléo Godin et al., eds., pp. 12-22.

ROMANIA

Teodorescu, Virgil and Petronela Negosanu. *Steaua Marilor Lacuri: 45 Poeti Canadieni Limba Franceza.* Bukarest: Univers, 1981.

SOVIET UNION

Vannikova, N. I. *Canadian Literature in French (1945-1960).* Moscow: École Supérieure, 1969. (In Russian.)
Žekulin, Nicholas G. 'The Russian Translation of *The Clockmaker.*' *Ariel,* 11, 2 (1980), 39-50.

SPAIN

Fernández Sosa, Luis F. 'Northrop Frye y unos poemas anagógicos de Lezama Lima.' *Hispania,* 61 (1978), 877-87.
Jarque Andrés, Francisco. 'La Guerra Civil Española en la litteratura canadiense.' *Mélanges à la mémoire d'André Joucla-Ruan. Études Littéraires,* 2. Aix-en-Provence: Univ. de Provence, 1978, pp. 769-92.

SWEDEN

Olinder, Britta, ed. *A Sense of Place: Essays in Post-Colonial Literatures.* Göteborg: The English Department, Göteborg University, 1984.
Söderlind, Sylvia. 'Identity and Metamorphosis in Canadian Fiction Since the Sixties.' In *A Sense of Place,* Britta Olinder, ed., pp. 78-84.

SWITZERLAND

Bader, Rudolf. 'Frederick Philip Grove and Naturalism Reconsidered.' In *Gaining Ground: European Critics on Canadian Literature*, Robert Kroetsch and Reingard M. Nischik, eds., pp. 222-33.

Péclat, Pierre-Louis. 'La littérature québécoise dans le champ cultural suisse-français.' In *Lectures européennes de la littérature québécoise*, Jean Cléo Godin et al., eds., pp. 78-80.

UNITED KINGDOM

Easingwood, Peter. 'Margaret Laurence, Manawaka and the Edge of the Unknown.' *World Literature Written in English*, 22, 2 (1983), 254-63.

Gurr, Andrew. 'Blue Mountains and Strange Forms.' *Journal of Commonwealth Literature*, 17, 1 (1982), 153-60.

Howells, Coral Ann. 'History from a Different Angle: Narrative Strategies in Rudy Wiebe's *Big Bear.' Journal of Commonwealth Literature*, 17, 1 (1982), 161-71.

——————. ' "If I Had a Reliable Interpreter Who Would Make a Reliable Interpretation": Language, Screams, and Silence in Rudy Wiebe's *Where Is the Voice Coming From?' Recherches Anglaises et Américaines*, 16 (1983), pp. 95-104.

——————. ' "'Tis Sixty Years Since": Timothy Findley's *The Wars* and Roger McDonald's *1915.' World Literature Written in English*, 23, 1 (Winter 1984), 129-36.

——————. 'Re-Visions of Prairie Indian History in Rudy Wiebe's *The Temptations of Big Bear* and *My Lovely Enemy*.' In *Colonisations: Rencontres Australie-Canada*, Xavier Pons and Marcienne Rocard, eds., pp. 145-54.

——————. 'Worlds Alongside: Contradictory Discourses in the Fiction of Alice Munro and Margaret Atwood.' In *Gaining Ground: European Critics on Canadian Literature*, Robert Kroetsch and Reingard M. Nischik, eds., pp. 121-36.

Hunter, Lynette, 'Form and Energy in the Poetry of Michael Ondaatje.' *Bulletin of Canadian Studies*, 5, 1 (April 1981), 33-52.

——————. 'Some Versions of Narrative.' *Bulletin of Canadian Studies*, 5, 1 (April 1981), 68-79.

May, Cedric. 'French Canada's Dissenting Voices.' *Bulletin of Canadian Studies*, 1, 1 (May 1977), 15-26.

——————. 'A Survey of French-Canadian Literary History and Criticism.' *Bulletin of Canadian Studies*, 2, 1 (April 1978), 52-60.

——————. 'Self and Non-Self: The Sense of Otherness in Quebec Poetry.' *Pacific Quarterly* (Moana), 4 (1978), 217-25; rpt. *Bulletin of Canadian Studies*, 2, 2 (December 1978), 52-63.

——————. 'The Flickering Lights of Planet Earth: The Presentation of Manitoba in the Works of Gabrielle Roy.' *Bulletin of Canadian Studies*, 5, 2 (October 1981), 38-47.

——————. *Breaking the Silence: The Literature of Quebec*. Birmingham: Univ. of Birmingham, 1981.

_____. 'La Grande-Bretagne: "la folle entreprise de nommer" et "les courts-circuits du language".' In *Lectures européennes de la littérature québécoise*, Jean Cléo Godin et al., eds., pp. 33-44.

_____. 'Form and Structure in *Les Iles de la nuit* by Alain Grandbois.' In *Gaining Ground: European Critics on Canadian Literature*, Robert Kroetsch and Reingard M. Nischik, eds., pp. 192-204.

Stewart, Malcolm. 'Moore Exiles: Joycean Counterparts in Brian Moore's "Uncle T." ' *Recherches Anglaises et Américaines*, 16 (1983), 131-42.

Thieme, John. 'Scheherazade as Historian: Rudy Wiebe's "Where Is the Voice Coming From?" ' *Journal of Commonwealth Literature*, 17, 1 (1982), 172-81.

Walsh, William, 'The Poetry of Robert Finch.' *Bulletin of Canadian Studies*, 2, 1 (April 1978), 1-15.

NOTES ON CONTRIBUTORS

For the contributors' publications on Canadian literature see the bibliography.

Dr. Rudolph Bader is a research fellow at the English Seminar of the University of Bern, Switzerland. He has a special interest in Australian and Canadian literature. In the summer of 1983 he was visiting professor in the Department of English of the University of Guelph. In the spring term of 1985 he taught the first course in Switzerland on Canadian literature at the University of Bern. Dr. Bader's main interest in Canadian literature is twentieth-century fiction. He is presently working on images of Europe in Canadian fiction.

Dr. Giovanna Capone is Professor of English at the University of Bologna in Bologna, Italy. She is the pioneer in Canadian literature studies in Italy, having become interested in the subject in the early 1970s. In 1976 she organized the first conference with an exclusively Canadian focus in Italy. She was also the first Italian scholar of English to offer a course in Canadian literature. Professor Capone has published widely; she is the author of four books and some twenty-five articles.

Dr. Karla El-Hassan is Assistant Professor *(Oberassistentin)* at the Friedrich-Schiller-University in Jena, GDR. She teaches Canadian and American literature and literary theory. Her special interest is the Anglo-Canadian short story ensemble, which is the area of her postdoctoral thesis. She is also involved in the editing of two anthologies of Anglo-Canadian short stories for East German publishers, and in the writing of a volume meant to introduce Canada to the general reading public in the GDR.

Dr. Michel Fabre has been Professor of American Studies at the University of Paris III (Sorbonne Nouvelle) since 1970. He teaches mainly Afro-American studies and new literatures in English. Dr. Fabre directs the Centre d'études afro-américaines et des nouvelles littératures en anglais (CETANLA), and edits *Afram Newsletter;* he is also president of the Sociéte d'études des pays du Commonwealth. He is currently studying the fiction of Margaret Laurence, Mavis Gallant, and the literature of French-speaking minority groups in Canada.

Dr. Paul Goetsch is Professor of English Literature at the University of Freiburg, West Germany. He did his BA in English Language and Literature at the University of Toronto in 1959, and became one of the first European scholars to publish on Canadian literature. His doctoral thesis on Hugh MacLennan (1961) was one of the first monographs on a Canadian novelist published anywhere. Apart from being a pioneer of Canadian literature studies in Europe, Paul Goetsch has written widely on various genres and periods in English and American literature; he has published four monographs, (co-)edited six volumes, and published some fifty articles and eighty reviews.

Dr. Rosmarin Heidenreich is Assistant Professor of French at the Collège Universitaire de Saint-Boniface, where she teaches French and French-Canadian literature. Dr. Heidenreich—whose parents are of German/Flemish descent and who is married to a German—is a Canadian by birth, but has lived most of her adult life in Europe. She studied at the Universities of Göttingen, West Germany, and Basel, Switzerland, before completing her PhD in Comparative Literature at the University of Toronto. She taught for several years in the English Departments of the Universities of Tübingen and Freiburg, West Germany. She has also worked for German television as editor and moderator for an English language series.

Dr. Coral Ann Howells, born in Queensland, Australia, is a lecturer in the Department of English Language and Literature of the University of Reading, Berkshire, England. She has been Secretary of the British Association for Canadian Studies since 1984. Her main areas of interest in Canadian literature are fiction by contemporary Canadian women writers and the fiction of Rudy Wiebe and Timothy Findley. Her publications include *Love, Mystery and Misery: Feeling in Gothic Fiction* (London: Athlone, 1978), articles on eighteenth century Gothic fiction, and on dreams in George Eliot's novels. She is presently working on a book about Canadian women novelists of the 1970s and 1980s, to be published by Methuen, London.

Dr. Wolfgang Klooss is *Hochschulassistent* (Assistant Professor) at the University of Kiel, West Germany. He teaches English literature and Commonwealth literature, and since 1980 has focused on Canadian literature. He is working on a postdoctoral thesis on Louis Riel and the Métis in nineteenth and twentieth century

Canadian literature; his other special interests are nineteenth century popular literature in Canada and Canadian prairie fiction and drama. Most of Dr. Klooss's publications are in Commonwealth literature, especially African and Canadian literature.

Dr. Eva-Marie Kröller is Assistant Professor in the Department of English of the University of British Columbia in Vancouver, Canada. She specializes in comparative Canadian literature, particularly English-Canadian/Québec literature and Canadian/European literature. Dr. Kröller was born and educated in West Germany. Between 1970 and 1973 she studied at Freiburg University, West Germany, where Professor Paul Goetsch and Rosmarin Heidenreich introduced her to Canadian literature. Her interest in Canadian literature was consolidated by a PhD thesis on 'The Function of Place in the Canadian Literatures,' supervised by E. D. Blodgett of the Department of Comparative Literature at the University of Alberta. She has completed a study of Canadian travellers in London, Paris and Rome (1851-1900), and is co-editing, with Professor Pierre Savard, an anthology of Canadian travel reports about Europe (1800 to the present).

Cedric May is lecturer in the Department of French Language and Literature of the University of Birmingham, England. He teaches French and Québec literature and is the Director of Canadian Studies at the University of Birmingham. Between 1961 and 1963 he taught at MacDonald College, McGill University. He has served as the president of the British Association for Canadian Studies.

Dr. Reingard M. Nischik has been teaching Canadian, American and English literature at the English Seminar of the University of Cologne, West Germany, since 1980. Her interest in Canadian literature goes back to 1978/79, when on a scholarship from the Canada Council she studied for one year at The University of British Columbia. She is especially interested in contemporary Canadian fiction and in narrative theory, narrative technique, and stylistics. She has published on American, English, Irish and Canadian fiction, and is presently working on stylistic elements in selected contemporary short fiction writers in Canada.

Dr. Walter Pache is Professor of English and Comparative Literature at the University of Trier, West Germany. He approaches English literature in the context of other European literatures, but has recently concentrated on Canadian literature in English. Dr. Pache is one of the founding members of the Association for Canadian Studies in the German-Speaking Countries. His involvement with Canadian literature began in 1971/72 when he received a postdoctoral fellowship from The Canada Council and spent a year at the University of Toronto. His main areas of interest in Canadian literature are the late nineteenth century, the work of Frederick Philip Grove, contemporary fiction, and comparative Canadian literature.

Dr. Jürgen Schäfer has been Professor of English (American) Literature at the University of Augsburg since 1974. He teaches English, American and Commonwealth literature. His main interests in the area of Canadian literature are imagology and national consciousness as reflected in literature. He has published widely, mainly on Elizabethan language and literature, on the history of ideas, on American, English and German literature in the twentieth century, and, recently, on Commonwealth literature.

Dr. Pierre Spriet has been Professor of English Literature at the University of Bordeaux III, France, since 1967. Between 1962 and 1967 he taught at Victoria College, University of Toronto. Dr. Spriet is editor of the French interdisciplinary journal *Études Canadiennes/ Canadian Studies,* and one of the founders of the Centre des études canadiennes de Bordeaux. He is author of four books and many articles, mainly on Renaissance literature and English-Canadian literature.

Dr. Franz K. Stanzel is Professor of English at the University of Graz, Austria. He was a founding member and, between 1980-84, Vice-President of the Association for Canadian Studies in the German-Speaking Countries. In June 1984 he organized with Professor Zacharasiewicz of the University of Vienna a four-day symposium on English-Canadian literature in which about sixty scholars from ten countries (including four Eastern European countries) participated. He has written three influential monographs on narrative theory, his latest being *Theorie des Erzählens* (2nd ed., Göttingen: Vandenhoeck & Ruprecht, 1981 [1979], English translation: *A Theory of Narrative,* Cambridge Univ. Press, 1984).

Dr. Simone Vauthier is Professor of English in the English Department of the University of Strasbourg, France. She teaches mainly American and Canadian literature. Professor Vauthier has been editor and co-editor of *Recherches Anglaises et Américaines (RANAM)* for several years. She has been actively involved with Canadian literature since about 1980, although her interest goes further back. Her main area of research is fiction. In May 1983 she organized an international conference on the Canadian short story; the papers presented by scholars from France, England and Germany were published in a special issue of *RANAM*. She is currently working on Canadian short fiction, particularly on stories by Norman Levine, Mavis Gallant, Alistair Macleod, and Margaret Laurence.

Dr. Waldemar Zacharasiewicz is Professor of English and American Literature at the University of Vienna, Austria, where he has taught courses and seminars ranging from Shakespeare and early pastoral poetry to twentieth century fiction. His early interest in environmental theory and national stereotypes has led him to an examination of the rise of Canadian nationalism and its reflection in literary texts. He is presently writing on the evocation of a 'sense of place' in contemporary Canadian short fiction, and on the function of stereotypes in texts published in periods of mass immigration to Canada.